JACKSON SCHOOL PUBLICATIONS

IN INTERNATIONAL STUDIES

Senator Henry M. Jackson was convinced that the study of the history, cultures, political systems, and languages of the world's major regions was an essential prerequisite for wise decision making in international relations. In recognition of his deep commitment to higher education and advanced scholarship, this series of publications has been established through the generous support of the Henry M. Jackson Foundation, in cooperation with the Henry M. Jackson School of International Studies, and the University of Washington Press. A complete listing of the books in the series appears at the end of the book.

HERBERT J. ELLISON

UNIVERSITY OF WASHINGTON PRESS

Seattle & London

BORIS
YELTSIN

AND

RUSSIA'S DEMOCRATIC

TRANSFORMATION

Publication of this book was made possible in part by the Jackson School Publications Fund, established through the generous support of the Henry M. Jackson Foundation and other donors, in cooperation with the Henry M. Jackson School of International Studies and the University of Washington Press.

UNIVERSITY OF WASHINGTON PRESS

P.O. Box 50096, Seattle, WA 98145 U.S.A.

www.washington.edu/uwpress

LIBRARY OF CONGRESS

CATALOGING-IN-PUBLICATION DATA

Ellison, Herbert J.

Boris Yeltsin and Russia's democratic transformation / Herbert J. Ellison.

p. cm.

Includes bibliographical references and index.

ISBN 0-295-98637-9 (hardback : alk. paper)

1. Soviet Union—Politics and government—1985–1991. 2. Russia (Federation)—Politics and government—1991– . 3. Yeltsin, Boris Nikolayevich, 1931–. 4. Presidents—Russia (Federation). I. Title.

DK288.E44 2006

947.086092—dc22

2006015001

[B]

CONTENTS

PREFACE

IN THE LIBERATION OF RUSSIA AND THE OTHER NATIONS OF THE
Soviet Union from communist rule, the crucial leaders were Mikhail
Gorbachev and Boris Yeltsin. The motivation for this book was my conviction that the pivotal role Yeltsin played in that remarkable process—his for-
mulation of the program of revolutionary transformation and his leadership
in its implementation—had not received sufficient analysis and appreciation.

My focus is upon the way Yeltsin developed his program of comprehensive
democratic transformation of the Soviet Union, skillfully acquired the leadership position and the power with which to implement it, and carried it
forward to victory despite enormous obstacles. He was the leader in the
destruction of the communist dictatorship, the liberator of the republics of

the Soviet Union, the architect of a democratic constitutional structure, the founder of a new economic system, and the initiator of a comprehensive transformation of Russia's role in international affairs.

The analysis and judgments I present in this book derive from a long academic career, which has included extensive study and travel in the Soviet Union and its successor states. In recent years I have also had the privilege of working with the distinguished British film producer Daniel Wolf on the production of a four-part series on world communism titled *Messengers from Moscow* (British Broadcasting Service and Public Broadcasting Service, 1993) and a single film on Yeltsin for the Public Broadcasting Service, *Boris Yeltsin: A Legacy of Change* (2000). The many interviews conducted for these films provided extraordinary insights into the situation in the Soviet Union before and after the collapse of communist rule in 1991 and into Yeltsin's impressive role in the transformation of Russia and the other nations of the Soviet Union after that collapse.

As the bibliography for the book indicates, a large body of scholarly and other publications exists for the era with which I am concerned. For understanding Yeltsin as a personality and as a major political leader, I found his three remarkable autobiographical works and the biography by Leon Aron particularly useful. I have also been deeply grateful for the *Current Digest of the Soviet/Post-Soviet Press* (*CDSP-CDPSP*), which provides translated articles from a wide range of publications; indeed, no better such compilation is available anywhere. It was especially significant for this book because the dismantling of the oppressive political constraints on the press during the Gorbachev era continued and grew under Yeltsin, and the Russian press is an amazingly rich source of insight into the dramatic changes of the Yeltsin years and into Yeltsin himself. My use of the *Digest* also serves another purpose. Wherever possible I have endeavored to cite materials in translation— and not only from the Russian press—for the benefit of English-speaking readers and students with limited Russian, to give them easier access to the sources that tell the story of Yeltsin and Russia's democratic transformation.

A few words on usage and transliteration are in order. Where the word *Party* appears capitalized, it is meant to serve as a short, direct reference to "Communist Party of the Soviet Union," reflecting that institution's all-pervasive role in Soviet life—a phenomenon often misunderstood. The transliteration of Russian words is sometimes problematic. I use the Library of Congress system of transliteration, with the following exceptions for given names and surnames, including the names of authors of translated materials: The names of Russian monarchs are anglicized. Soft signs are omitted, and initial *ya, ye, yo,* and *yu* are used, along with the endings *aya, ey, oy,* and *y,* as appropriate. Non-initial occurrences of *ya* and *yu* are used, but non-initial occurrences of *ye* and *yo* are rendered *e.* Also in names, the Russian letter *i kratkoe* is rendered *y.* The spelling of the surname Gaidar departs from this convention. An exception to Library of Congress usage for geographical names is the spelling of Chechnya. Quoted material retains the transliteration used in the source.

ACKNOWLEDGMENTS

I HAVE BEEN EXTRAORDINARILY FORTUNATE IN THE SUPPORT I HAVE received for the writing and production of this book. I should like to thank the Smith Richardson Foundation for its generous financial support, which was arranged with the kind cooperation and understanding of Nadia Schadlow at the Foundation. I am also grateful to George Russell of the Frank Russell Company for invitations to accompany the Russell 20-20 group on trips to Russia, which enabled me to learn a great deal about the political and economic changes under way in the Yeltsin years, as well as to meet and hear Russian officials from whom I learned much about the ongoing process, as I did from the fine reports on the Russian economy that Mr. Russell's company published.

I am also grateful for the kind support I received in the review and acceptance of this volume for publication by the University of Washington Press, and to executive editor Michael Duckworth and his fine colleagues. The reviews and comments from Jack Matlock, Strobe Talbott, and John Keep were immensely helpful in editing the original text, as were those of Oscar Bandelin.

Soviet Union, 1922–1991. Map by Nathaniel Trumbull

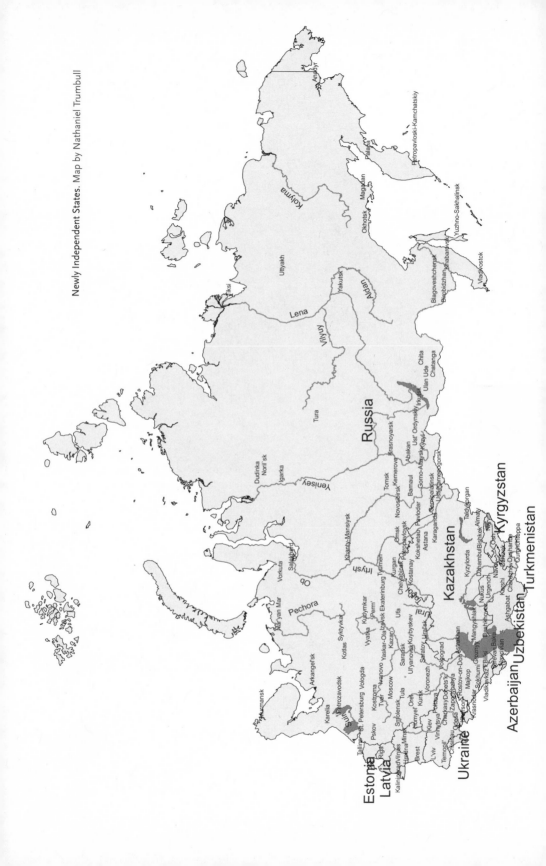

Newly Independent States. Map by Nathaniel Trumbull

BORIS YELTSIN
AND RUSSIA'S
DEMOCRATIC
TRANSFORMATION

INTRODUCTION

BORIS YELTSIN,
RUSSIAN LIBERATOR

THE EXTRAORDINARY CAREER AND LEADERSHIP OF BORIS Yeltsin mark him as the decisive figure in the making and consolidation of Russia's democratic revolution. The first—and failed—effort to build a Russian democracy began with the Revolution of 1905 and the parliamentary and other reforms that followed. They seemed likely to reach a successful completion with the collapse of the Russian monarchy in the February Revolution of 1917. But the democratic provisional government that replaced the tsar was jeopardized from its birth by the heavy burden of Russia's continuing engagement in World War I, and it then fell victim to the revolutionary coup of Vladimir Lenin's Bolsheviks. Lenin quickly replaced it and the popularly elected Constituent Assembly with a dictatorship of his own party, which, under his leadership and that of Iosif Stalin, built a totalitarian socialist system and extended its direct control first over most of the former tsarist empire and then, during and after World War II, over much of eastern and southeastern Europe.

The story of Russia's second democratic revolution, like that of its predecessor, begins with the problems created by imperial expansion and resistance to it from both subject peoples and other powers. The dangers and costs of recurrent resistance to Soviet-imposed or Soviet-supported communist regimes—from Europe to Afghanistan, Africa, and Latin America—and the huge costs of protracted military competition and confrontation with the major powers of Europe, Asia, and North America had created tremendous strains within the Soviet Union.

These strains, deriving from international policies, were compounded by formidable internal problems. One of these was the failure of economic growth and technological modernization in the socialist economy, aggravated by a mammoth military budget and growing criticism of the performance of the regime. Soviet citizens were increasingly conscious not only of the many deficiencies of their system—economic, social, and political—but also of its unfavorable contrast with the spectacular performance of the advanced capitalist states. Domestic criticism of Soviet communism advanced from modest beginnings in the 1950s to major currents of intellectual dissent that were increasingly evading the regime's structures of information and thought control by means of illegal private publications. The most challenging of the dissent movements were those issuing political demands for democracy and the liberation of the nations of the Soviet Union.

The failure of efforts to deal with these problems during the Brezhnev era (1964–82), called by reformist successors "the era of stagnation [zastoi]," convinced the leaders of the Gorbachev period (1985–91) of the need for extensive reforms of both domestic and foreign policy. As has happened often in the historical experience of authoritarian regimes, the reforms unleashed pressures, both in the Soviet Union and in its extended empire, for far greater concessions and changes than the reform leadership was prepared to offer.

Mikhail Gorbachev had brought an impressive group of reformers into his government. One of them, Aleksandr Yakovlev, was the architect of major domestic reforms that included greatly increased openness (glasnost') in public discussion of the country's condition and reform needs. Yakovlev generated plans for reforming the structures and functioning of Party and state institutions, as well as economic policy. In foreign policy the guiding genius was that of Eduard Shevardnadze, who led negotiations on arms control and reduction of regional conflicts generated by Soviet support for Third World revolutions. He also helped to create more permissive policies toward reform in foreign communist parties, most crucially the governing parties of Eastern Europe. This aspect of policy reform contributed much to the liberalization of those regimes and (unintentionally) to the 1988–89 dismantling of communist rule in most of Eastern Europe, a process that had powerful repercussions within the Soviet Union itself.

Boris Yeltsin was yet another example of the reform talent brought into the leadership by Gorbachev. And though toward the end of the Gorbachev era, both Shevardnadze and Yakovlev would leave his service, convinced that he was succumbing to the influence of conservative Party leaders and abandoning the reform mission, Yeltsin broke ranks much earlier. He was discharged from the Politburo and from his role as Moscow Party secretary at the end of 1987, following his harsh attack charging that Gorbachev was failing to sustain the reform effort. He then built an independent power base and reform program that would, during the succeeding four years, greatly expand the reform agenda and its base of support, challenge Gorbachev's leadership, and precipitate an antireform coup attempt by Party conservatives. Although the coup failed, it brought the collapse of communist power, the dismantling of the Soviet Union, and the resignation of Gorbachev, leaving Yeltsin president of a newly independent and substantially reduced Russian state called the Russian Federation.

One of the leading reformers of postcommunist Russia, Anatoly Chubais, compared Boris Yeltsin's importance in Russian history to that of Peter the Great and the reformer-emperor Alexander II. He stressed Yeltsin's role in ending the communist dictatorship and his achievements in building a democracy and a market economy. The high estimate doubtless surprised many of Chubais's auditors.[1]

The image of Russia in the Western media during the Yeltsin era was often one of severe economic, social, and political disorder, including widespread unemployment and poverty, massive corruption in the privatization of the economic holdings of the socialist state, and extensive corruption of government officials. Yeltsin himself was often portrayed by the press and television abroad as an enigmatic, authoritarian former senior communist leader, seriously incapacitated by alcohol and a bad heart, presiding over a failed reform policy.

Yet Chubais's judgment was well informed; he had worked closely with Yeltsin for many years as a central figure in the postcommunist reforms. And despite the conflict and pain of the transition years, there is abundant support for a highly positive view of Yeltsin's achievements in scholarly biographies and specialist studies of his economic, social, and political reforms. Granted, some of the scholarly literature takes a critical view. But this is often due to a failure to distinguish between negative developments caused by Yeltsin's policies and those resulting from the huge legacy of problems inherited from the communist era. Many commentaries give inadequate attention to the enormous strength and persistence of the opposition to reform programs throughout Yeltsin's presidency by powerful reactionary forces, communist and nationalist, which were determined to limit or reverse them. This opposition generated much frustration for the reformers and great pain for the population during the transition.

With proper recognition of the formidable obstacles Yeltsin faced and of the considerable reforms accomplished despite them, it is certainly possible to compare his achievements favorably with those of the major reformers of Russian history. One can acknowledge his pivotal role in the emancipation of the nations of the Soviet Union, the replacement of communist dictatorship by democratic constitutional rule, and the planning and substantial implementation of Russia's shift from a failed communist to a modern market economy. His leadership and his achievements are immensely impressive when contrasted with the failure of democratic leadership following the collapse of tsarist power and the tragic results of the communist policies that followed.

My aim in this book is to provide a comprehensive review and appraisal of Yeltsin's role in Russia's democratic revolution—from his removal from the Gorbachev Politburo in 1987 to his resignation from the Russian presidency at the end of 1999. The first chapter shows how Yeltsin's many contributions to the strengthening and acceleration of the democratic transformation were a major factor in provoking the attempted counter-revolutionary coup of August 1991. I describe how Yeltsin became the central figure both in crushing that coup and in leading the dismantling of communist rule and the Soviet Union that followed. The purpose of the chapter, which begins with Yeltsin's break with Gorbachev, is to tell the remarkable story of how he began as a communist reformer seeking change through democratization of the Communist Party but then lost faith in that possibility and pursued the abolition of the Party's constitutionally guaranteed monopoly of political leadership, before resigning his Party membership. Having become meanwhile the most popular and important leader of the democratic movement, he rose to the leadership of the Russian Republic by espousing a program for replacing state socialism with a market economy and by endorsing a democratic restructuring of the Soviet Union that provided for the sovereignty and right of secession of its constituent republics.

A striking part of Yeltsin's story, in addition to the completeness of his break with the doctrine and Party he had served so prominently and well, is the skill and courage with which he exploited the opportunities provided by Gorbachev's democratizing reforms to acquire a power base for his own far more radical reform program—a program that would bring about the end of communist rule and of its economic and political system and international policy. He won a seat in the new USSR Congress of People's Deputies in March 1989 and then election to the Supreme Soviet. There he became a key member of the executive committee of the Inter-Regional Group, an incipient party of democratic reform, along with the great physicist and democrat Andrey Sakharov and others who shared Sakharov's brilliantly articulated views on democratic reform.

The crucial next step in his progression was to gain election in March 1990 to the Congress of People's Deputies of the Russian Soviet Federated Socialist Republic, a body of which he was elected chairman on May 29 and which declared the national sovereignty of the Russian Republic on June 12. The declaration, over which Yeltsin presided, described the Russian Republic as "a state within a renewed Soviet Union." During the following months he would not only build a firm personal power base in the Russian Republic but also challenge Gorbachev and the Soviet center by resigning from the Communist Party in July, supporting the independence struggles of the three Baltic republics in August, and announcing a program of radical, desocializing economic reform in September. A new phase of his challenge to the Soviet center and to Gorbachev came with his visit to Tallinn in 1991, following an attack on the television center in Vilnius on January 13 by Soviet Ministry of Internal Affairs troops. He joined the presidents of Estonia, Latvia, and Lithuania in a statement denouncing the action and defending the Baltic nationalist claims.

7

The climax of the process by which Yeltsin acquired both immense popularity and a power base rivaling Gorbachev's was his election by popular vote to the new Russian presidency on June 12, 1991. He was also successful in his advocacy of a new union treaty that provided a comprehensive democratization of the federal constitution and granted sovereignty and governmental autonomy to the republics. His expanding influence was a major motivator of an effort by the mostly conservative leaders of the Gorbachev government, first in June and then more aggressively in August, to acquire special powers to contain and reverse his challenges to the traditional communist system of rule. The climax of these dramatic events came with the coup of August 1991, which, but for the decisive opposition organized by Yeltsin, might well have reversed the main reform achievements of the Gorbachev years and would surely have brought severe repression of the democratic movement. The chapter concludes with an analysis of Yeltsin's key role in the ensuing peaceful process of dismantling the rule of the Communist Party and the Soviet Union.

The second chapter, "Politics of Reform," is an overview of the eight years of Yeltsin's presidency of the new, independent Russian state. Having played the decisive role in the final destruction of communist rule and the Soviet Union, Yeltsin's challenge was not only to deal with the inherited crisis of a collapsing socialist economy but also to provide a wholly new economic system, a new structure of government and political leadership, and a new system of international relationships, both with the newly independent states of the former Soviet Union and with the rest of the world. The core task and crucial prerequisite in meeting all these challenges was to build an effective democratic governmental structure and political system for the implementation of his program. Much of the chapter focuses on Yeltsin's determined and eventually successful pursuit of constitutional reform and the introduction of a democratic constitution in 1993, a crucial achievement that was the product of a long and persistent struggle against powerful opposition.

The central apparatus of the Soviet Union and the Soviet Communist Party disintegrated rapidly in the aftermath of the August Coup as the power center surrendered its authority to the republics, with Yeltsin leading the process that brought the formal end of the Soviet Union in December. But the Communist Party's ideological and organizational legacy was still a formidable power in the land, and the new Communist Party of the Russian

Federation, reorganized and greatly strengthened early in 1993, would remain the largest political party throughout the Yeltsin era. Fundamentally opposed to Yeltsin's reform program, and regularly allied with strong nationalist political leaders and parties that also rejected much or all of the Yeltsin reform plan, the communists mounted powerful resistance to virtually every Yeltsin reform initiative and worked continuously throughout his presidency to remove him from the leadership and recapture control of the government. The tacit alliance during the 1990s between communists and ultranationalists led many observers to compare the Russian political situation to that in Weimar Germany, where German communists and Hitler's fascists made up an overwhelming opposition to the democratic leadership of the Weimar Republic, eventually producing the Nazi dictatorship.

Against powerful opposition, and through a series of potentially disastrous economic and political crises and a climactic armed revolt by his political opponents, Yeltsin managed to install a new constitution by popular referendum in December 1993. Under it, before the end of his leadership, three parliamentary elections and a presidential election would be conducted. He carried out extensive restructuring of local and regional government institutions and added an upper house, the Council of the Federation, to the new parliament, the Federal Assembly, in his new constitution. Except in the tragic case of Chechnya, he also made progress toward peacefully integrating both the ethnic republics and the Russian regions into a new democratic federal system of government for the Russian Federation.

A key element of the politics of reform discussed in chapter 2 was the continuing difficulty of achieving constructive cooperation between the executive and legislative branches of the Russian government, both before and after the constitutional change. The new constitution of December 1993 clarified the division of power between the two branches and greatly strengthened the executive, but the continued domination of the communist and nationalist opposition in the ensuing parliamentary elections of 1993 and 1995 extended the government's problem of legislative obstruction of reform to the very eve of Yeltsin's resignation in 1999. Throughout the period, he faced not only legislative obstruction but also repeated efforts by his powerful communist opponents and their allies to block continued reforms and to replace him as president, once by ballot and several times by impeachment. His most formidable opposition was a powerful, ideologically dogmatic Communist Party leadership that remained opposed to his economic reforms, his new constitution, and even to the 1991 agreements granting independence to the republics of the Soviet Union.

Yeltsin's success in introducing and sustaining a democratic constitution despite these challenges was an enormous credit to both his political skill and his democratic commitment. He had demonstrated a willingness to take great personal and political risks in his struggle against the communist dictatorship before August 1991. He retained and exercised the same decisiveness and courage in the years that followed, becoming, in the full sense of the word, the guarantor of Russia's democratic revolution.

Chapter 3 deals with Yeltsin's economic reforms. Just as he urged the introduction of a democracy and affirmed the right of the nations of the Soviet Union to sovereignty and independence, so too he affirmed the necessity of converting from a socialist to a market economy with private enterprise and private property in land. Before the communist collapse he had sought an agreement with Gorbachev on a plan of economic reform for the whole of the Soviet Union, but in vain—Gorbachev remained committed to a socialist economy. Following the Soviet collapse, Yeltsin presented his economic plan for Russia to the Russian Supreme Soviet in October 1991, a plan devised by the distinguished young economist Yegor Gaidar. As deputy prime minister, Gaidar would begin its implementation on January 2, 1992, with price liberalization, followed later by a large-scale program of enterprise privatization and efforts to dismantle the system of collective farming in favor of individual peasant farms with private landownership. The chapter describes how Yeltsin was able to leave a solid framework in economic policy on which his successors could build, despite strong opposition and dangerous political impasses that brought great misery to the Russian population and threatened the entire range of his reform initiatives.

Chapter 4, on the foreign policy of the new Russia, covers the huge changes in Russia's international role in both the Gorbachev and the early Yeltsin eras. Clearly, the major achievement of the Gorbachev years was the end of the Cold War, including the termination of Soviet support for foreign communist parties and revolution and the acceptance or facilitation of the revolutionary overturn of communist power in Eastern Europe.[2] The result was to create a wholly new context for Soviet international relations.

Yeltsin carried the change much farther with the dismantling of the Soviet Union and the granting of independence to its former republics, soon to be known collectively in Russian diplomatic parlance as the "near abroad."

In chapter 4, I review the process and problems of building an entirely new, postcommunist structure of international relationships, beginning with Yeltsin's pursuit of full partnership with the Western democracies. Meanwhile, in foreign as in domestic policy reform, the voices of nationalists and communists were constantly heard, condemning liberal reformers for the vast changes they had wrought in Russia's international role and blaming them for the loss of Russian power and empire and the fate of nearly 25 million ethnic Russians now living in newly established "foreign" states. They proved to be as retrograde in their persistent charges against the "capitalist" (that is, democratic) states as in their contempt for the independence of the former subject nations of the new Commonwealth of Independent States. But Yeltsin remained consistent in both his peaceful cooperation with other former Soviet republics and his pursuit of peaceful and constructive Russian relations more broadly.

Yeltsin's objective of close cooperation with the United States and the other democratic states encountered serious obstacles during his rule, including Russian fears of exclusion and isolation arising from the eastward expansion of NATO to include former Warsaw Pact partners and former Soviet republics. Yet many cases of increased cooperation were achieved as well. Above all, Yeltsin expanded Gorbachev's measures for abandoning the legacy of Soviet-era foreign policy in favor of the policies of what he called "a normal country" in building new relationships with most of Russia's many neighbors in Europe and Asia.

The story of the Yeltsin era ends with his choice in August 1999 of a young prime minister, Vladimir Putin, who would become acting president upon Yeltsin's resignation in December and who would be elected president in the spring of 2000. Putin focused his efforts immediately on the crucial need to form a pro-government parliamentary coalition, a goal that had repeatedly eluded his predecessors. Its achievement was the vital prerequisite for securing legislative backing for the economic and administrative reforms he sought. His coalition-building success gave him the parliamentary majority he needed for functional budgets, taxation, land law reform, and much else. It was doubtless this impressive initial demonstration of political skill that convinced Yeltsin he had found a suitable successor and could proceed with his retirement, which followed soon after the parliamentary elections.

Yeltsin had chosen a successor who he felt shared his commitment to a democracy, a market economy, and a peaceful foreign policy with the special purpose of political and economic integration into the world community of democratic states, their security system, and their increasingly globalized economy. It was also clear that the successor had demonstrated political and diplomatic skills superbly suited to Russia's challenges at the end of the Yeltsin era. And though it was apparent that Putin, like Yeltsin before him, faced major political opposition to his domestic and foreign policy objectives, thanks to his political skills and to the successful installation of the constitution of 1993, the issues could be resolved by parliamentary and presidential elections, an arena in which he showed great talent.

Equally important, Yeltsin had left an institutional legacy strong enough to provide adequate checks and balances in the administrative apparatus. In recent years Putin's critics have raised concern that his policy measures are autocratic. Yeltsin himself has commented from time to time on how his own approach to one issue or another might differ from his successor's; but his remarks so far have clearly demonstrated his confidence in his legacy, and he has not felt it necessary to criticize Putin. In any event, thanks to Yeltsin's accomplishments it would be a good deal more difficult for Putin in 2006 to reestablish authoritarian rule than it would have been for Gennady Zyuganov in 1996 or Ruslan Khasbulatov in 1993. Moreover, Putin is an elected president, and it would require a constitutional amendment for him to serve a third term. In sum, it is up to the Russian people to understand these things and to see to it that the institutions that Yeltsin built for them are preserved and strengthened.

The structure of democratic national and regional governmental institutions in the Russian Federation is doubtless the most important legacy of Boris Yeltsin, one of the greatest reformers of Russian history and one of the most successful and important political leaders of the twentieth century. Along with founding a new market economy, setting a new Russian foreign policy, and marginalizing—within the framework of democratic electoral procedures—the antidemocratic communist and nationalist parties, he preserved, against enormous obstacles and through many perilous passages, the dream of Russian democratic transformation that had been crushed in 1917.

I am now, and always will be,
a believing communist.

—MIKHAIL GORBACHEV, 1990

I hope that we will not be the
only nation to enter the twenty-
first century guided by an obsolete
ideology from the nineteenth.

—BORIS YELTSIN, 1990[1]

CHAPTER 1

REFORM OR
REVOLUTION?

It seems a cruel irony that the two
men who lifted Russia from tyranny
could not lift themselves above
personal enmity. But had they not
collided, Russia might not be free.

—PHILIP TAUBMAN, 1996[2]

YELTSIN AND
GORBACHEV,
1987–1991

T HE REVOLUTION OF 1991 THAT BROUGHT THE COLLAPSE OF COM-
munism and of the Soviet Union was caused by the reactionary
August Coup, which aimed at crushing the Soviet democratic
movement and restoring traditional communist power. Boris Yeltsin was the
pivotal figure in both provoking and defeating the coup, and he led the revolutionary transformation that followed it. Yet without Mikhail Gorbachev's
reforms, Yeltsin could not have acquired the power to turn a potential catas-
trophe into a triumph of Russian democracy. Despite often bitter conflict
between the two men during the four years before the revolution, their separate contributions to Russian reform were essential and complementary.
But the limits of Gorbachev's reform vision, and his efforts to restrain the

Soviet transformation in 1990–91, came dangerously close to handing power to the forces of counterrevolution at the decisive moment in the struggle for Russian democracy.

The essence of the protracted conflict between the two leaders between 1987 and 1991 was ideological. Gorbachev began and ended his leadership career as a communist reformer. Yeltsin began as a communist reformer and ended as a democratic revolutionary. After their sharp break in 1987, Yeltsin's ideological transformation raced far ahead of that of his former mentor. He became the leader of the Russian democratic forces, both within and outside the Party, increasingly setting the agenda and pace of reform and building the base of power that enabled him to replace Gorbachev as leader only four years later.

FROM COLLEAGUES TO RIVALS

During the six years of Gorbachev's rule, he made sweeping changes in the domestic and foreign policies of the Soviet Union. His liberalizing policies radically altered the leadership, role, and power of the Communist Party of the Soviet Union (CPSU) and dismantled major elements of its ideology. He opened the way for contested elections in the Party and state apparatus, greatly increased the state's independence of the Party, and permitted a degree of freedom of public discussion and independent social organization unequaled since the consolidation of the Stalinist system. He transformed the foreign and revolutionary policies of the Soviet Union, negotiating major arms agreements with the Western powers and reducing or ending Soviet support for communist revolutions and regimes in Latin America, Africa, and Asia, a major factor in East-West conflict. His policies also hastened the disintegration of communist rule in the Soviet Union and the collapse of the Soviet "extended empire" in Eastern Europe.

Gorbachev defined his mission as reform, not revolution. Neither at home nor in his dealings with foreign communist leaders did he aim to dismantle communist rule, but rather to change its structure, outlook, and policies to enable it to solve a dangerous accumulation of economic and social problems. Confronted by powerful resistance to change from conservative Party leaders after he came to power in 1985, he responded with sweeping personnel changes and a succession of ambitious reform initiatives that sought to make the Party an effective force for reform.

Doubtless the most important of the early reforms was *glasnost'*—openness—a major reduction of the pervasive ideological controls on filmmakers, writers, editors, journalists, and academics. Facts and opinions on both contemporary and historical issues, the public presentation of which would previously have brought censorship or arrest, were soon being expressed freely. The most sacrosanct policies and leaders (including Lenin) were approached with a critical vigor unprecedented even in the Khrushchev de-Stalinization of the fifties and sixties. *Glasnost'* was essential both for the articulation and popularization of reform proposals and for the development of alternative political programs within and outside the Party. After its introduction, its effects spread rapidly, producing results that sharpened the differences and conflict within the Party leadership. Like other Gorbachev reforms, *glasnost'* had unintended consequences that complicated reform efforts, especially the erosion of support for the Party and its ideology caused by devastating revelations about the hugely costly errors of past policies.

Another key initiative was Gorbachev's effort to democratize the Party organization by changing the system of elections of Party officials—replacing elections that were simply ritual endorsements of single candidates chosen at higher levels with a new and freer system of nominations and multiple candidacies. Delayed for many months, it was finally endorsed by the June 1987 Party plenum. The plenum also approved a draft law for reforming state enterprises, making an initial, though not impressively successful, effort to replace the centralized "command economy" with one that encouraged and rewarded enterprise independence and initiative. It also authorized formation of independent "cooperative" enterprises, mainly in services, and approved cooperation between Soviet and foreign enterprises.

The most important decision of the June plenum was the scheduling of a Party conference for June 1988. Fearing that Gorbachev intended to use the conference (as Stalin had done) as an instrument for purging Party opponents, the plenum required him to deny such an intention before giving its approval. The opposition misunderstood the real danger: that Gorbachev would make the conference an occasion for expression of the views of a broad and varied Party membership and a source of ideas for an expanded reform program.

The Party leaders' anxiety about Gorbachev's reform intentions was rapidly increasing, and the tension between opposing views on reform had reached a crescendo by the time of the September 1987 meeting of the Politburo. It became the scene of a dramatic confrontation between Gorbachev and Yeltsin, his reform-minded first secretary of the Moscow City Party Committee.

GORBACHEV AND YELTSIN

Boris Yeltsin had made his reputation as the first secretary of the Party in Sverdlovsk, one of the most important industrial regions of the country. Born of a peasant family in 1931, he had barely survived the famine induced by Stalin's agricultural collectivization, and his father and uncle would later undergo terms of forced labor on charges of resisting collectivization. The events of his youth revealed a vigorous, intelligent, and very sociable young man with an appetite for adventure (occasionally high risk) and athletics. After graduating from the Urals Polytechnical Institute, he entered the construction industry, where he demonstrated extraordinary energy and managerial skill and advanced rapidly to high-level responsibilities. At the relatively young age of forty-five he was named first secretary of the Sverdlovsk Oblast' Party Committee, a position he would hold for the next nine years. Sverdlovsk contemporaries described him as a strong leader, a demanding and amazingly hard-working boss, and a rare kind of Party secretary who actually moved among the citizenry and gave close personal attention to housing, the food supply, and the transportation and cultural amenities of Sverdlovsk.

Yeltsin's arrival in Moscow in December 1985 to take the leadership of the Moscow City Party Committee and to become (in the following month) a candidate member of the Politburo was a difficult career change. As in Sverdlovsk, he was a "hands-on" administrator, riding the buses and subways to check transportation conditions and investigating firsthand complaints about shortcomings in city administration. Personnel turnover was high, and his disciplinary actions were often stern and occasionally bizarre, as in forcing a retinue of officials to follow him through knee-deep sewage in the basement of an apartment building whose tenants' complaints they had long ignored. His memoir of the period, *Against the Grain,* describes his outrage at the luxurious living of Moscow Party officials and their neglect of the needs of ordinary citizens, revealing a populist streak that Moscow Party leaders found highly offensive.

In less than two years after his arrival in Moscow, Yeltsin's dissatisfaction and impatience had reached the breaking point. A Politburo meeting

called for September 12, 1987, to discuss Gorbachev's speech for the cele-
bration of the seventieth anniversary of the October Revolution would prove
a turning point in his career and in the history of the Gorbachev era. It produced an outburst of angry disagreement with Gorbachev and other colleagues that nearly ended his career.

Yeltsin's relations with Gorbachev and other Politburo members had
greatly deteriorated by the time of the September Politburo meeting, the
occasion when he decided he could no longer continue his current work.
Returning to his office, he wrote a letter of resignation from his positions
as first secretary of the Moscow City Party organization and candidate member of the Politburo, a startling action for a senior Party figure. He felt that
"several members of the Politburo and some secretaries of the Central Committee" had turned against him. He was particularly critical of Yegor Ligachev, head of the Secretariat of the Central Committee, describing his views
and style as a major barrier to the progress of perestroika.

Looking back on the events many months later, Yeltsin acknowledged
that his blunt statements had increased the friction, but he insisted that the
core of the problem was persistent opposition to his reform efforts in Moscow,
especially from Ligachev, "on issues of social justice and the abolition of
elite privileges and perks."[3] Yeltsin took great offense at the elaborate structure of privileges that surrounded Party leaders in Moscow, condemning it
as a betrayal of communist values. His opinion clearly was not widely shared
by his fellow *apparatchiki*.

Receiving no answer to his letter from Gorbachev, he made the aston-
ishing decision to present his case to the plenary session of the Central Committee on the eve of the October Revolution anniversary. Gorbachev's
anniversary speech was a disappointment to the democratic intelligentsia
because it confined itself to criticism of the style rather than the substance
of Stalin's revolution. Yeltsin felt it made extravagant claims for the achievements of perestroika. He listened impatiently through a session dominated
by self-congratulatory speeches and lavish praise for Gorbachev's leadership.
When the chairman made a perfunctory request for questions, he seized
the opportunity to deliver an extemporized speech that would change both
his life and the course of Russian reform.

The only published version of this momentous speech appeared in the
second 1988 issue of the *Bulletin of the Central Committee of the CPSU*, but
Yeltsin included much of it in his own memoir.[4] Even in its edited version,

the speech was unprecedented in the higher circles of Party rule. Yeltsin asserted that perestroika had not thrived, as all preceding speakers had asserted, but had come virtually to a halt, "except for a few changes in the direction of *glasnost'* and democratization." What was needed was a restructuring of "the party as a whole." Noting the failure to reform the style of work of the Secretariat of the Central Committee, he was pointedly critical of its leader, Yegor Ligachev, and of the "adulation of the general secretary [Gorbachev] by certain full members the Politburo," which he described as an incipient "cult of personality" reminiscent of the Stalin era. Omitted from the official transcript were Yeltsin's remarks about the negative influence of Gorbachev's wife, Raisa, which Aleksandr Yakovlev mentioned in a later interview about the meeting.[5]

Having delivered his stinging attack on Gorbachev and his Politburo colleagues, Yeltsin announced that he had submitted his resignation from the Politburo, crediting his ineffectiveness there to his own inexperience but also to "absence of support, especially from Comrade Ligachev," and leaving the question of his continued leadership of the Moscow City Committee of the Party to be decided by the Party Central Committee. The predictable response of his colleagues, when Gorbachev invited them to speak, was a lengthy procession of denunciatory speeches. As it ended, Yeltsin understood that he would soon be removed in disgrace from his post as first secretary of the Moscow City Committee and from the Politburo.

Two days after the event he went into the hospital, following a heart attack, but he was given scant time for recovery. On November 11 Gorbachev telephoned to inform him that he must attend a meeting of the Moscow City Party Committee, despite his indisposition. Yeltsin would later comment, "Perhaps he actually wanted to finish me off physically. I could not understand such cruelty."[6]

A COMRADELY CORRECTION

Yeltsin's painful experience of being forced to leave a hospital intensive care facility, heavily sedated, was followed by a staged serial excoriation by Party colleagues. The official report of the event in *Pravda* described it as a session conducted "in a spirit of Party openness, devotion to principle, and a free exchange of opinions."[7] It bore closer resemblance in style, though not in consequence, to a Stalinist show trial.

Gorbachev set the stage with an enthusiastic review both of the "trail-blazing path of the Soviet people and the Leninist Party" in the "seven post-October decades" and of the great success of his own program of restructuring since the spring of 1985. Describing the unanimous approval of his report on these developments by the Central Committee and the Politburo (as if unanimity were unusual), he then observed, "The statement made by Comrade B. N. Yeltsin had sounded a dissonant note." The statement was not only "politically immature and extremely confused and contradictory" but "essentially demagogic in its content and nature." He was quick to add, "Critical comments addressed to the Politburo, the Secretariat, and individual comrades should not be taken as something extraordinary." The problem with Yeltsin was that he had disrupted the settled agenda and "tried to turn the plenary session's work in another direction by declaring his own special position on a number of questions."

Having condemned Yeltsin's speech without elaborating its "special position," Gorbachev noted that after the speech "it was decided to exchange opinions. . . . Not one speaker [out of twenty-six] supported Comrade Yeltsin." He further observed that "when errors have their origin in personal ambition and the desire to stand out . . . a person has to be corrected," as in the case of "Yeltsin's immoral and irresponsible action." As for Yeltsin's charge that Gorbachev's policies had not been supported by the Central Committee Secretariat, it was "completely absurd."

Gorbachev's speech ended with a harsh assessment of Yeltsin's performance as Moscow City Party secretary. He acknowledged that his "critical approach to shortcomings and his resolute statements urging that accumulated problems be quickly overcome and that negative phenomena in the capital's life be eliminated . . . brought some changes for the better." But in the end Yeltsin had proved an ineffective administrator who "displayed incompetence, a disorderly bustling about, and panicky moods."

Gorbachev then reported that the Central Committee had adopted a resolution recommending that Yeltsin's October speech to the plenary session be declared "politically erroneous" and that the Politburo, the Central Committee, and the Moscow City Party Committee examine the question of relieving him of the leadership of the Moscow Party Committee. The Politburo had concluded, "It is necessary to strengthen the leadership of the Moscow City Party Committee."

The tone of the general secretary's presentation of the "accused" was certain to elicit additional condemnation and the desired votes. For the second time, and now dangerously ill, Yeltsin was obliged to endure serial denunciations (twenty in all) detailing his sins of omission and commission but adding little to the general thrust and tone of Gorbachev's speech. Remarkably, his response was restrained. He confessed arrogant behavior, said that he had "heard a great deal that I had never heard in my entire life," and added that hearing it earlier might have enabled him to avoid his "unpredictable" act, which had precipitated his reprimand and removal. He also affirmed his commitment to the aims of perestroika and insisted that he "had no preconceived intentions and that there was no political thrust to my speech." Rather poignantly, at the end of his brief response, he rejected the charge that he actually disliked Moscow. Despite his apologetic tone, Yeltsin was replaced as first secretary of the Moscow Party Committee the next day, November 12, by L. N. Zaykov, who addressed a citywide meeting of Moscow's Party *aktiv*.

Only a week later, on November 19, Yeltsin was named vice chairman of the USSR State Construction Committee and USSR minister. He later expressed puzzlement—as well he might—that Gorbachev had given him a ministerial position in Moscow rather than assigning him to some remote location. After all, Yeltsin's rude challenge to the conservatives had jeopardized Gorbachev's efforts to push the reform effort forward, and Yeltsin had belittled his achievements and insulted his motives. But Gorbachev chose only to remove Yeltsin from policy discussions in the highest organs of the Party apparatus, where Gorbachev already faced growing criticism from Party conservatives. Imposition of a distant exile on a critic was not his leadership style.

Yeltsin paid a heavy price for his impulsive attack. His memoir describes the terrible physical and emotional suffering of the eighteen months between these events and the remarkable revival of his fortunes in the campaign for a seat in the new Congress of People's Deputies in the spring of 1989. Plagued by chronic headaches, sleepless nights, self-criticism and self-doubt, and a deep sense of betrayal and isolation, he described himself as a "political corpse," whiling away his time in a job he had no enthusiasm for and deprived of the lively human contact and vigorous engagement that had been his joy as Party leader in Sverdlovsk and in the early months of his work in Moscow. But such problems did not prevent his playing a highly

Boris Yeltsin, construction minister, January 1, 1989. © Ted Thai/CORBIS SYGMA

Pro-Yeltsin demonstration in Manezh Square, Moscow, February 24, 1991. One placard reads "Yeltsin Is Our Hope."
© Alain Nogues/CORBIS SYGMA

Mikhail Gorbachev and Boris Yeltsin at the Supreme Soviet of the Russian Federation after the failed August 1991 coup. © Peter Turnley/CORBIS

A defiant Yeltsin, August 22, 1991. During the abortive coup, Yeltsin stood in front of the Russian parliament building and refused to surrender the government to coup leaders. © Peter Turnley/ CORBIS

Aleksandr Rutskoy, Russian vice president, was one of Yeltsin's primary foes in the struggle with the parliament. Gennady Galperin/© Reuters/CORBIS

Yeltsin and the Congress of People's Deputies speaker, Ruslan Khasbulatov, in 1991. The two men would become bitter foes and clash violently in October 1993, after Khasbulatov took over the parliament building and urged citizens to attack the mayor's office and television center. © David Turnley/CORBIS

The Russian White House burns
October 4, 1993, following tank
attacks by troops loyal to Yeltsin.
© Peter Turnley/CORBIS

Ultra-nationalist Vladimir Zhirinovsky, a virulent rival and relentless critic throughout Yeltsin's
tenure as president. © Georges
de Keerle/CORBIS SYGMA

Yeltsin visits Polish president Lech Wałęsa in 1993, signing one of many agreements that helped repair Russian relations with nations that suffered decades of Soviet domination.
© Peter Turnley/ CORBIS

Yeltsin and GDR president Helmut Kohl toast the fiftieth anniversary of the end of World War II in Europe, May 1995. Months earlier, Yeltsin withdrew the last Russian troops from Germany.
© Bernard Bisson/ CORBIS SYGMA

Democratic freedom in action: Protesting the invasion of Chechnya, January 1995. The placard depicts Chechen General Dzhokhar Dudaev, Yeltsin, and Russian Defense Minister Gen. Pavel Grachev. The caption reads: "They have blood on their hands. I spit on them." © Georges de Keerle/ CORBIS SYGMA

Yeltsin gets an earful on an early campaign stop in Yaroslavl, May 3, 1996. © Georges de Keerle/ CORBIS SYGMA

Communist Party leader Gennady Zyuganov voting on election day, June 17, 1996. Yeltsin trailed badly in the polls but rallied with energetic campaigning and dramatic help from oligarchs, the media, and a pivotal endorsement from General Aleksandr Lebed. © Peter Turnley/CORBIS

Yeltsin dances at Rostov-on-Don, June 11, 1996. A few months after the election, an exhausted Yeltsin would undergo major heart bypass surgery. © Yuri Kadobnov/ EPA/epa/CORBIS

Communist protesters call for Yeltsin's resignation and payment of salaries following Russia's financial crisis and devaluation of the ruble, October 7, 1998. © Boris Kudriavov/R.P.G./ CORBIS SYGMA

Yeltsin and his successor, Vladimir Putin, greet Ortho-dox Patriarch Aleksy II fol-lowing Putin's inauguration in May 2000, which marked Russia's first democratic handover of power. © Reuters/CORBIS visible role, only a few months after his humiliation, in the pivotal Nineteenth Party Conference, from June 28 to July 1, 1988.

YELTSIN BUILDS AN OPPOSITION
PROGRAM AND RUSSIAN BASE

In the months leading up to the Moscow conference, conservative Party leaders were busily engaged in efforts to control the delegate selection, as well as in ideological battle with Gorbachev's reforms, particularly *glasnost'*. A letter from a Leningrad Technological Institute chemistry teacher, Nina Andreeva, published by *Sovetskaia Rossiia* in March, defended Stalin's "industrialization, collectivization, and cultural revolution" against his critics, attacked the playwright Mikhail Shatrov (who "kowtows to Trotsky" and "deviates from socialist realism," she said), and affirmed the necessity for young people "to learn the class vision of the world."[8] She characterized the ideological view supporting the current restructuring as "some kind of left-liberal dilettantish socialism . . . preaching . . . the 'democratic' charms of present-day capitalism and fawning over its achievements."

Thought to have been an initiative inspired by Ligachev, the letter was sharply criticized in *Pravda,* along with a vigorous defense of *glasnost'*. The counterattack elicited an acknowledgment by the editors of *Sovetskaia Rossiia* that publication of the article had been an error and that "it would lead all of us away from the revolutionary renewal of society on the basis of democracy and openness."[9] The editors also defended their journal's own highly critical articles on Stalin and his era during preceding months, promising to continue supporting the work of scholars to set the historical record straight. Other journals carried a flood of letters denouncing Andreeva's views and offering moving personal stories of the horrors of life under Stalin. Many of the same issues would come forward in the candid exchanges at the televised Party conference.

The CPSU Central Committee had approved theses for the conference in May.[10] The theses covered the major themes and aims of future reform, especially the internal democratization of the Party and the "restoration" of an independent structure of soviets, from the local to the national level. They reflected a familiar (and historically false) notion characteristic of the Gorbachev era that there had once been a "Leninist" Party in which the con-

cept of "democratic centralism" was authentically democratic and the soviets were democratically governed bodies. The theses also stressed further
expansion of freedom in cultural and intellectual life and the reform of the
structure of relations of the national republics of the Soviet Union.

YELTSIN'S REFORM PROGRAM

The agenda and structure of the televised conference—the freest forum yet
for the discussion of reform—gave Yeltsin and his ideas extraordinary vis-
ibility. The Party *apparat* had worked hard to prevent the election of prominent reformers, and with considerable success. Efforts to prevent Yeltsin's
election, however, had failed. He was denied selection as a conference delegate from Moscow and Sverdlovsk but managed to gain it from Karelia at
the last moment. His access to the press was blocked, as was shown by the
suppression of an interview scheduled for publication in *Ogonek*. Even at
the conference his repeated requests to speak were ignored. He gained the
opportunity to speak only by marching boldly to the front of the hall, rejecting repeated efforts to delay or remove him.[11]

Yeltsin's speech recalled his challenge to Gorbachev the previous October.[12] It endorsed Gorbachev's proposal for sweeping reform of the Party
but complained about the narrow circle of participants in the preparation
of theses for discussion at the conference ("most members of the Central
Committee were not widely involved"). It also offered a radical proposal for
elections of Party officials: "They should be general, direct, and secret from
top to bottom, including elections for the secretaries and the general secretary of the Central Committee." Yeltsin recommended applying the same
practice to the Supreme Soviet, the trade unions, and the Young Communist League and asked for tenure in elected positions to be limited to two
terms. He noted that the current Politburo included members who had served
for as long as twenty years and that this explained the stagnation of policy
and the indifference to corruption at all levels. He also recommended a clean
sweep of the membership of the Politburo and Central Committee upon
the choice of a new general secretary: "then people will not be in a constant
administrative trap. . . . they will not be criticized only after they are dead,
since it will be known that everyone, including the entire elective body, is
answerable to the Party."

Yeltsin offered still more radical proposals. He argued for broad discussion at all levels of the Party and in the country of major resolutions of the Central Committee and for referenda where appropriate. He criticized the current reform effort for its failure to provide serious analysis of the problems that underlay stagnation and for its lack of specific and credible reform programs. He also criticized the lack of openness in the operation of the top organs of the Party, offering the example of the vast sums of money transferred from regional Party organizations to the Central Committee— the funds that financed both "reasonable expenditures" and "luxurious private residences, dachas, and sanitariums." He concluded his speech with a request for his personal rehabilitation, together with the abrogation of the plenary session's judgment of his "erroneous views" in the now famous October session ("the only mistake in my speech was the fact that I spoke at the wrong time—before the 70th anniversary of October"). Noting that it was the custom to rehabilitate people only after fifty years, he asked for "political rehabilitation during my lifetime."

Once the speech had been delivered and vigorously applauded, Gorbachev and his colleagues used the lunch break to prepare an attack against both the speech and Yeltsin's record, with Ligachev leading the pack. That they feared Yeltsin's vigorous return to politics had been evident in their efforts to block his election to the conference, in the suppression of publication of his *Ogonek* interview, and in the attempt to prevent him from speaking at the conference. Now the conference speech would have to be published with the other proceedings in *Pravda* and *Izvestiia*. Given the lack of attention paid to his recommendations in the conference rebuttals, it might appear that Yeltsin's role was insignificant. In fact, it gave him a chance to return to the political limelight, a matter of great importance given the new plan for elections to the Congress of People's Deputies, a body in which he would find a new political career.

Yeltsin's speech had vigorously challenged the governing style and privileges of senior Party officials and called for radical democratization of Party and state structures. It anticipated key criticisms and proposals that came to dominate Soviet reform discussion in subsequent months, not to mention the growing revolutionary ferment in Eastern Europe. It also revealed that Yeltsin's concept of reform was far more radical than Gorbachev's. Yeltsin's stern judgment—"In 70 years, we [communists] have not resolved the main questions—feeding and clothing the people, supplying the service sphere, resolving social questions"—differed stunningly from the assertion in Gorbachev's final conference speech that "the Party's role as political vanguard . . . has the unconditional support of the people."[13] Yeltsin's candid criticism of the Party and its legacy was an important part of his appeal, as his election in the following spring would demonstrate.

Yeltsin decided to stand in the March 1989 election to the restructured Congress of People's Deputies, knowing that the new electoral law gave the Party control of candidate selection through a complex system of candidate proposal and nomination. After passing that barrier, if elected to the 2,250–member Congress of People's Deputies, he would be obliged to resign his ministerial position, and unless he then won election by the Congress to the 542–member Supreme Soviet, he would be neither a government minister nor a full-time legislator. That is, he would be effectively unemployed. It was a daunting prospect, but it soon became clear that he had acquired a national reputation when nearly two hundred constituencies across the country proposed his candidacy. Yeltsin defeated his rival with more than 89 percent of the vote in an election that saw many favored senior Party figures ignominiously defeated.

In one important respect, the new Congress of People's Deputies was a victory for the Party leaders. The rigged electoral system had assured them the support of a majority in the new organization. Still, a worrisome number of government favorites had been defeated, and many deputies were sharply critical of government policy, among them Boris Yeltsin. Gorbachev's effort to co-opt Yeltsin by bringing him into the government was a failure; Yeltsin had other plans. His immediate aim was to gain election to the Supreme Soviet, the permanent standing legislative body, which would now be selected by the Congress. He understood that the Party-supporting majority of that body was unlikely to elect him, and the quick defeat of leading democrats who also sought membership confirmed his pessimism. But a Siberian deputy, Aleksey Kazannik, withdrew in his favor, allowing him to become a member of the Supreme Soviet as well as a committee chairman and an ex officio member of the Presidium.[14]

FORMING AN OPPOSITION PARTY

Yeltsin joined the company of new Supreme Soviet deputies for the opening session on June 10 and quickly joined with other radical reformers on July 29–30 to form the Inter-Regional Group (IRG). Of the 393 deputies who registered for the group's inaugural meeting in Moscow's House of Cinema (they were denied premises in the Kremlin), 269 took out voting credentials to confirm membership in the new organization, and many more confirmed their interest. A bureau of 25 members was formed, led by five co-chairmen: Yeltsin, Yuri Afanasev, Andrey Sakharov, Viktor Palm, and Gavril Popov. They established a contributory fund called the Fund for Deputies' Initiatives and set up a newspaper called *Narodnyi deputat* (People's Deputy). The group was united by a belief that the country was on the brink of an economic crisis and only radical and aggressive reform measures could meet the challenge.

Their platform was very close to that of the Nineteenth Party Conference: restoration of power to the soviets, review of the legal-constitutional status of the republics, provinces, and regions, and direct and equal general elections with a choice of alternative candidates. They stressed political and economic autonomy for regional and local governments, reorganization of the economy to favor the consumer and reduce monopolies, and accountability of public organizations and administrative structures. One of their most important near-term objectives was to assure that the regulations governing elections to the republic and regional legislatures did not duplicate the limits on nomination of candidates and other constraints imposed on the election of delegates to the USSR Congress of People's Deputies.

Gorbachev strongly opposed creation of the Inter-Regional Group. In his speech at the conclusion of the first session of the Congress of People's Deputies he expressed concern that "this kind of artificial demarcation [will] lead to confrontation on specific questions that our Supreme Soviet will have to resolve."[15] His reaction recalls the Leninist tradition of forbidding separate groups and programs within the Party as "factionalism"—a proscribed activity since Lenin forbade it at the Tenth Congress in 1921—though Gorbachev described it as an "artificial" activity, not as a "deviation." There was nothing artificial about an initiative that would soon lead to a demand for the right of citizens to combine freely in social organizations and parties and to a movement for abolishing the power monopoly of the Communist Party guaranteed by Article 6 of the constitution. As Yeltsin noted, the IRG included many of the best minds in the country, closely attuned to changing attitudes in the country at large and now being assiduously applied to the study of ways to accelerate needed reform. The IRG was, in fact, an incipient opposition party, the first in Russia since Lenin destroyed non-Bolshevik political parties and forbade opposition within the Bolshevik Party itself.

When the first session of the Congress of People's Deputies ended in September, Yeltsin made a lightning tour of the United States, with an exhausting two weeks of intensive activity compressed into one when the Central Committee reduced the time allowed for his trip. American reporters savored his ecstatic affirmation of the United States and his contempt for Soviet propaganda images of their country, whereas much of the Russian reportage was critical. Yeltsin's first supermarket visit was "shattering": "When I saw those shelves crammed with hundreds, thousands of cans, cartons, and goods of every possible sort, for the first time I felt quite frankly sick with the despair of the Soviet people."[16]

The months following Yeltsin's return from the United States brought dramatic changes, both in the Soviet Union and in its East European empire. He welcomed the revolutionary changes in Eastern Europe, hoping that the example would encourage more radical reform at home and the realization "that we are practically the only country left on earth which is trying to enter the twenty-first century with an obsolete nineteenth-century ideology." But he worried about rumors of a conspiracy to replace Gorbachev as general secretary of the Party, for although Yeltsin called Gorbachev "my perpetual opponent, the lover of half-measures and half-steps," his replacement by a right-wing bloc would prevent the emergence of more aggressive reform leadership. And he regarded Gorbachev as "the only man who can stop the ultimate collapse of the party."[17]

The statement reveals that Yeltsin still believed in the possibility of reform leadership using the resources of the Party organization to deal with the expanding crisis. He rejected "the immediate adoption of a multiparty system" on the grounds that "the mere existence of several parties does not in itself solve any problems," and "we still need to grow and mature toward a real, civilized multiparty system." For the immediate future, however, he sought a law "guaranteeing that citizens are free to combine in social organizations and parties," together with an end to the Communist Party's power monopoly as guaranteed by Article 6 of the constitution.[18] Events of the spring and summer of 1990 shattered his hopes for the emergence of a vigorous reform leadership from within the Party. Meanwhile, he continued to exploit the Gorbachev political reforms—whatever their limits—to create a greatly expanded base for his own power and program within the

Russian Republic during and after the elections of March 1990. Only a few months after arguing the need to prevent the collapse of the Party, he himself would resign from it.

LEADING THE OPPOSITION

Who would have thought, who would have predicted that this persecuted man, deposed and condemned by a plenary session of the Central Committee, would become the head of the Russian Republic? Despite everything, Yeltsin became a triumph of the democracy in which he had put his faith. He was a victory for the people and he was defended by the people.

—DANIIL GRANIN[19]

The first half of 1990 brought momentous developments for Yeltsin and for Russia. His escalating confrontation with the leadership of the Party was evident in the discussion of the draft platform for the upcoming Twenty-eighth Party Congress, held during a plenary session of the Central Committee in February, at which the most important speeches were those made by Gorbachev and Yeltsin.[20]

Gorbachev's speech began by emphasizing the new forms of preparation for the Party congress—the democratic election of delegates and the broad participation in the discussion of agenda issues. The speech was familiar in both style and themes: the "need for the Party to cleanse itself" of ties to "the authoritarian-bureaucratic system" and its "ideological dogmatism," as well as the reaffirmation of the goal of building "humane, democratic socialism." A central theme was the danger of polarization of the country's leadership between those who claimed that perestroika was "threatening the fundamental principles of the socialist system" and those who argued that "the country's only salvation lies in turning to capitalism." Gorbachev insisted on the continuing leadership of the country by a reformed Party guided by the goal of a reformed socialism: "We remain committed to the choice made in October 1917 to the socialist idea."

The differences between Gorbachev and Yeltsin were striking. Whereas Gorbachev spoke of the "rethinking of the principle of democratic central-ism," Yeltsin said, "We must renounce [it] . . . and replace it with general democratic principles." His brief speech was a forceful statement of a ten-point program that would totally transform the existing system of political power. It called for full democratization of leadership selection at all levels (by equal, secret, and direct vote), acceptance of factions within the Party, openness of governmental processes, including budgets, an end of central control of the Party press, the removal of Article 6 of the constitution, which guaranteed the Communist Party political monopoly, and full toleration of noncommunist political groups. Yet another extremely important reform initiative was his rejection of "the unitary principle of state-building, and accordingly CPSU-building, [in favor of] a voluntary union of peoples and a voluntary union of republic communist parties, including a Russian Communist Party."

Yeltsin had, in effect, declared for a revolutionary transformation of the Communist Party and the Soviet state. Gorbachev's agenda continued to be one of limited and cautious reform, reflecting both a far more positive view of the Soviet legacy and a deep fear that the growing division between traditionalist and radical reform viewpoints held the potential for dangerous conflict and posed a threat to his reform program and leadership. It was clear that the Twenty-eighth Party Congress would be a major event in the Gorbachev reform era. The intervening five months brought frenetic activity on both sides of the deep division in Soviet politics.

At a February 1990 plenary session of the Central Committee, Gorbachev secured approval for the elimination of Article 6 of the constitution, ending the Party's monopoly over political power. For the radical reformers, this was a vital first step, but in taking this action Gorbachev was not responding solely to pressure from Yeltsin and others in the democratic leadership. He was also responding to growing popular pressure for such a change, as was brought home by a march on the Kremlin of 100,000 demonstrators demanding an end to one-party rule. This worrying event was followed by demonstrations on the major political holidays of May 1 and November 7, featuring thousands of Soviet citizens carrying banners denouncing the Party leadership and policies.

March elections in the Soviet republics gave Yeltsin the opportunity to begin building a new power base in the Russian Republic. He was first elected by Sverdlovsk as a deputy to the Russian Congress of People's Deputies and then elected chairman of the Russian Supreme Soviet in May. Gorbachev had been elected president by the USSR Congress of People's Deputies in March and was attempting to expand his power base in the state apparatus. In effect, he was transferring much of the policymaking role of the Party

Politburo to his new fifteen-member presidential cabinet. Meanwhile, it was clear that central control of the "inner empire" was disintegrating, just as it had in the "external empire"—Eastern Europe—during the previous year. Between March and May 1990 the Baltic states declared their independence, and in June the Russian Congress of People's Deputies overwhelmingly supported a declaration of Russian sovereignty, giving its own laws precedence over those of the Soviet Union.[21] The Russian example was followed by Ukraine and Belarus in July.

A RUSSIAN BASE AND A RUSSIAN AGENDA

The election of Boris Yeltsin as chairman of the Russian Republic Supreme Soviet on May 29 was a crucial turning point for his career, for the Russian Republic, and for the Soviet Union. A narrow victory (52.8 percent), it gave him the leadership in the Russian Republic and in the democratic movement that would bring the revolutionary transformation of the Soviet Union to a climax during the ensuing eighteen months. He focused first on Russian sovereignty, offering the most radical proposal on this issue among all those made at the meeting of the Russian Congress of People's Deputies on May 22.

In his statement and in his subsequent exchanges with his first main rival for the Presidium chairmanship, the archconservative I. K. Polozkov (first secretary of the Krasnodar Party Committee), Yeltsin argued for a new constitution for the Russian Republic that would be submitted to a republic-wide referendum for approval. He proposed to give full control over domestic and foreign policy to the Russian Republic and to give the Party's power "to the people and to the soviets." He also supported the freedom of producers to choose their own forms of economic organization, a change to the market and elimination of the administrative-command system in the economy, a professional army, a unified security and internal affairs organization subordinated to the parliament, and full freedom of speech, press, and information.[22] Yeltsin's proposals came directly from the program of the Democratic Russia deputies bloc. They were sharply criticized, not only by his rival Polozkov but also by Gorbachev, who charged Yeltsin with rejecting "the principles that Lenin formulated and that are the basis of the union treaty of 1922, [and of proposing] a renunciation of socialism and Soviet power."[23] Gorbachev expressed support for "full power to the Soviets at all levels," but within a system whereby the newly forming Russian political parties would be joined by a new Russian Communist Party.

Gorbachev's hope for a reform-minded Russian Communist Party that could balance if not block the "radical" reformers in the internal politics of the Russian republic was quickly shattered by the results of the June congress of the new Russian Communist Party. Under the leadership of Polozkov, the congress expressed the views of the most conservative wing of the apparatus—a general hostility toward Gorbachev and a repudiation of perestroika (including *glasnost'*), real soviet power, a market economy, and a democratic press. A major result of the congress was the widespread resignation from the party of individuals and organizations who viewed the new Russian party as a betrayal of all the reform accomplishments of the Gorbachev years.[24]

Meanwhile, Yeltsin was busy developing his own reform program within the Russian Republic, a program that, like his views on republican sovereignty, posed a powerful challenge to Gorbachev. Addressing the founding congress of the USSR Peasants' Union, he countered the socialist positions of fellow speakers Gorbachev and Ligachev with his program for private property in land, free choice of forms of management of farming, and an end to Party intervention. The reporters' account of the event lamented that the other featured speakers and the newly elected head of the Peasants' Union, who continued to support the existing system of collective and state farms, failed utterly to appreciate that "the roots of the problem lie in the essence of all previous agrarian policies—those selfsame policies that deprived the peasant of the right of ownership of the land and other means of production, turning him into a hireling with no stake in the results of his labor, and [that] destroyed the entire rural way of life."[25] The political leadership was united in recognizing that Russian agriculture was in a disastrous condition, but it was sharply divided over the cause of the problem and its solution. There was no doubt where Yeltsin stood.

The two most important issues dividing Yeltsin and Gorbachev were the future structure of the federation and the future structure of the national economy. Underlying both was the question of the future role of the Communist Party. Gorbachev continued to have major differences with the conservatives in the Party because of the scope of his reforms, and the experience of organizing a Russian Communist Party demonstrated the depth of the hostility of that element of the Party toward him. Still, he shared their commitment to the vanguard role of the Party, the socialist structure of the economy, and the Soviet political federation. His differences with Yeltsin were much more fundamental.

As Gorbachev had repeatedly charged, Yeltsin had indeed rejected socialism and the Leninist model of federation. Faced with Yeltsin's demands for Russian sovereignty, private property, and a market economy, Gorbachev reaffirmed his commitment to socialism and to the basic structure of the federal state created by Lenin in 1922. Because Yeltsin felt that Soviet socialism was a catastrophic failure, that the economy was moving rapidly toward complete collapse, and that domination by the old apparatus in the Soviet government continued to block effective reform from that source, he was determined to use his new position both to expand the power of the Russian government and to clear the way for independent Russian economic reform. He began by proposing new constitutional powers and a Russian Republic State Bank.

A contemporary political analyst described these efforts as "a reaction to the sluggishness of the union government and the inconsistency and virtually nonexistent efficacy of its efforts to stabilize the economy and develop the reform."[26] He noted that Yeltsin and his fellow reformers understood "that a full-fledged market economy and a full-fledged State Planning Committee [Gorbachev's euphemism was "regulated market economy"] were simply incompatible."

YELTSIN LEAVES THE PARTY

Yeltsin and other advocates of democratic reform, inside and outside the Party, saw the Twenty-eighth (and final) Congress of the Communist Party of the Soviet Union as a conclusive demonstration that the Party was incapable of providing the reforms the country desperately needed. "It has not been possible to neutralize the effect of the conservative forces in the Party," he said in his first speech at the congress. He observed that the selection of congress delegates had been conservative-controlled: "The Politburo could not bring itself to adopt the only correct procedure for electing delegates under restructuring: democratically, from all platforms and groups, regardless of the party's former structures. If every united group of 6,000 Communists had been allowed to elect its own delegate directly, we wouldn't have wound up with a congress made up as this one is."[27]

The result had been a congress incapable of leading the reform process. Reform leadership had passed to the Soviet Union and republic Congresses of People's Deputies by default. Yeltsin warned the Party leadership that its choice was either to undertake serious restructuring of the Party or to "be ousted from all bodies of legitimate power," ending up neither "in the role of a vanguard [nor] even in the role of a Party with representation in the Soviets."[28]

Yeltsin's notion of "serious restructuring" of the Party and its policy included democratic selection of its leaders and program, divesting itself of state functions, and undertaking the formation of an "alliance of democratic forces" that would include all the newly forming democratic groups. Looking toward reform of the federal government structure, he urged the creation of restructured parties in the republics—genuinely independent and democratic parties, not the dependent annex of the Soviet Communist Party recently created in the Russian Soviet Federated Socialist Republic (RSFSR). He saw this effort as central to the process of building a democratic federation.

Gorbachev's main congress speech offered Yeltsin scant encouragement. It had little connection to the so-called democratic platform that had been drawn up during a January 1990 meeting of 158 candidates for seats in the RSFSR Congress of Peoples Deputies. That platform called for an end to the Party's political monopoly, a new constitution, free speech, restrictions on the KGB, and a market economy. Reflecting the platform of the national movement Democratic Russia, the democratic platform received broad support in the ensuing elections.

Reporting in his speech as chairman on the work of the commission established to draft new Party statutes, Gorbachev displayed anew his penchant for reconciling irreconcilables. Defending the concept of democratic centralism, he argued: "The broadest democratism in Party life should be organically combined with centralism and discipline." Party members would be allowed to join together to support platforms, but only if these were "not at variance with the Party's program goals" and if the groups supporting separate platforms "did not have their own internal discipline." He appeared to have in mind something like nonfactional factions.

The Party's role in the armed forces, to which the "democratic platform" group had objected, was to be settled by the dubious compromise of having the function performed "only by primary Party organizations and elected Party agencies." In general, the new statutes preserved the special role and powers of the Communist Party (its "vanguard" role) and carefully circumscribed its internal democratization. Gorbachev cited a survey indicating that 67 percent of the congress delegates supported "a vanguard-type party" while only 19 percent favored one of the "parliamentary type." Yeltsin, who had already noted the political bias of the delegate selection process, was unlikely to find the poll results surprising or a convincing argument for retaining the Party's special powers.

Yeltsin's response to Gorbachev's speech was the most memorable event of the entire proceedings: he announced his resignation from the Party. He explained that as chairman of the Russian Supreme Soviet he had "an enormous responsibility to the people and to Russia" that obliged him to recognize "society's transition to a multiparty system" and prevented him from carrying out "only the decisions of the CPSU." He must be "prepared to cooperate with all parties and public-political organizations in the republic." His speech and dramatic departure from the chamber were followed by the announcement from the Democratic Platform Group leadership of its intention to form a separate democratic parliamentary party. The Central Committee membership, approved on the following day, further illustrated that methods of selecting the leadership had not changed. The long struggle to achieve authentic democratization of the CPSU was a dismal failure, but as Yeltsin had repeatedly asserted, the Party was being marginalized by a fast-changing society.

REFORMING THE ECONOMY AND THE UNION

Despite his departure from the Party, Yeltsin's leadership of the Russian Republic, his wide popularity, and his recognition as leader of the forces favoring radical democratization and a market economy gave him an increasingly powerful role both in the Russian Republic and in the Soviet Union. He was convinced that the failure of union authorities to provide effective economic reform was the core problem that could bring both a total collapse of the economy and of the Soviet Union itself. Though he endorsed sovereignty for the union republics, his aim was not, as his critics charged, to destroy the federation, but to democratize its political and economic structure.

The Twenty-eighth Party Congress in July 1990 was a turning point for Yeltsin. He had been willing to continue working within the Party if its leadership and program could be effectively reformed. The rejection of democratization of the Party and the continued conservative control of the apparatus convinced him that he must pursue his reform efforts from his base in the Russian Republic, though continuing to seek cooperation with Gorbachev. In the months following the congress he worked on two major tasks: restructuring the union and economic reform. The two were closely connected: agreement of the republics on the principles of a new economic system and policy was essential for the preservation of both the economy and the union. Failure to reach agreement—and quickly—could lead to the collapse of the union as both a political and an economic structure. On the other hand, an effective economic reform program acceptable to the union government and to the governments of the republics was an essential foundation for a new union treaty. During the ensuing year Yeltsin focused on these goals.

He began by negotiating an agreement with Gorbachev to set up a joint Soviet Union–Russian Republic task force of experts charged with preparing a program of economic reform. The task force included an initial thirteen distinguished Russian economic specialists as well as representatives from other republics. Their charge was to design an integrated program of economic measures acceptable to all the republics, in preparation for a union-wide market economy. The starting point was to be the "500–Day Program" already prepared by a distinguished group of specialists headed by the academician S. S. Shatalin and intended to be a program for the entire union. The crisis in the economy, exacerbated by social and ethnic tensions and the often conflicting legislation on economic matters passed by the sovereign republics, posed formidable problems, making the close cooperation of Gorbachev and Yeltsin essential to the reform program's success.

The program the specialists submitted anticipated the rapid introduction of a market economy accompanied by a massive transfer of state property to private ownership in the form of both small private property (apartments and garden plots) and shares of land, privatized large state enterprises, and privatized small enterprises in trade, catering, consumer services, and similar areas. All citizens were to be guaranteed the right to engage in private economic activity. Goods would be exchanged at market prices within a new financial structure that included free exchange of foreign currency and a new banking system designed to serve depositors rather than the state. The planners also proposed to eliminate policies regulating individual incomes and the activities of enterprises while giving the latter responsibility for their own finances and charging interest on credits, eliminating budget subsidies, reducing state capital investments and state purchases, and admitting foreign competition on the domestic market.

In conformity with its commitment to respect the sovereignty of the republics, the plan proposed a "Treaty of Economic Union between Sovereign States" that would recognize their economic sovereignty and provide procedures for concluding agreements on interrepublic deliveries and on deliveries for all-union needs. The spirit of the plan was contained in the notion that economic integration remained a necessity but would be achieved not by dictation from the center but by voluntary bilateral and unionwide agreements among the republics and the union government. The implementation of the reform would be handled in the same fashion. The economic rights of the union government would be those delegated to it by the republics.[29]

Despite the agreement between the union and Russian presidents on creation of a joint drafting group for the new plan, a separate "brain trust" of the union government was meeting simultaneously during August 1990, assuming that it retained the primary responsibility for the final reform plan. One analyst noted that "there is not and will not be an overall, synthetic program that would combine the recent government workups and the program approaches that are being formulated by the working group created under the auspices of M. Gorbachev and B. Yeltsin."[30] The government group had prepared "an option of half-measures and compromises that will not lead to a market but in practice will only create disarray in an already feeble economy."

Despite the discrepancy between the positions of the two groups, the Russian Supreme Soviet voted overwhelmingly on September 11 in favor of the 500–Day Program presented by S. S. Shatalin and G. A. Yavlinsky. The vote was 213 for and 2 against, with 6 abstaining. A proposal was also made to include in the resolution on the program a point on lack of confidence in the USSR Council of Ministers, but it was defeated.[31] Speaking on the Russian Republic's position a few days later, prime minister I. S. Silaev stressed that representatives of all the republics except Estonia had participated in preparing the plan, which was intended to apply unionwide. He acknowledged that it was much more radical than the one prepared by the union government's commission and that all the draft laws being prepared for its implementation would require approval either by the union government or by the other republics.[32] Despite strong endorsement from a conference of Russian Republic enterprise directors and the leaders of the Federation of Independent Trade Unions of Russia (FITUR), Gorbachev rejected the plan.

The rejection revealed the fundamental difference that had developed between the political structures of the Soviet Union and those of the Russian Republic. In the Russian Republic the economic reform decision was arrived at democratically, by vote of the Supreme Soviet. In the union the leadership of the Party made the decision. Speaking to the Central Committee plenum, Gorbachev rejected "a restoration of capitalism" and affirmed once again that "we must move toward a market within the framework of the socialist choice." Whereas the Russian Republic had given full responsibility for reform to the elected Supreme Soviet, Gorbachev continued to insist on "the CPSU's responsibility for the fate of restructuring and the fate of the country."[33] The huge gap between the programs was only one part of the problem; the other was the difference over democratic versus Party rule. Yeltsin had opted for democratic rule; Gorbachev remained committed to the rule of the Party that Yeltsin had abandoned. As the stalemate continued, economic decline accelerated.

In an exchange in the Russian Supreme Soviet in mid-November, Yeltsin was asked about the status of the Shatalin group's 500–Day Program. His response: "There is no '500–Day Program.' You will recall that we confirmed the union program, but the union didn't adopt it." His only encouraging news was that Gorbachev had agreed to form special joint commissions of the Russian and union Councils of Ministers to agree on a "program for stabilizing the economy and changing over to market relations." But he acknowledged the chaotic situation in which "virtually all the republics have different programs of action."[34]

CHALLENGING THE CENTER

The central government was also dangerously slow in responding to the challenge of nationalist leaders in many of the republics. It had still not recognized the declarations of sovereignty by the republics or constitutionally defined a new division of functions between the center and the republics. Gorbachev's draft union treaty of November 1990 had offered no satisfaction, because it retained the traditional powers of the center. Meanwhile, the republics and the center often ignored each other's decrees in what came to be called "a war of laws."

Perestroika had brought an especially powerful upsurge of nationalist and democratic sentiment in the Baltic republics, where forty-five years of subjection to Soviet power had not erased memories of national independence. Nationalist leaders had used *glasnost'* and the new elections and parliaments to build forceful independence movements. By late 1990 and early 1991 it was clear that Lithuania was rushing headlong toward independence, and Soviet forces intervened to seize the nationalist-controlled central television facility on January 13. Local civilian defenders were brutally dispersed, with the loss of fourteen killed and several hundred injured.

Charging that the use of Russian soldiers for this purpose was illegal, Yeltsin gave his full support to the Lithuanian democrats. Fearful that the Lithuanian events were only the beginning of a wider suppression, he once again mounted a vigorous offensive. In his January 22 speech to the Russian Supreme Soviet, he described the action in Vilnius as the opening phase of an effort to replace constitutional bodies with "salvation committees."[35] He argued that the problem could not be solved by repression but only by open and free negotiations and agreements with the republics. The speech elicited many hostile political attacks on Yeltsin in the USSR Supreme Soviet and in the Party press, and Gorbachev soon initiated his own counteroffensive by calling for a nationwide referendum on the Soviet Union. Yeltsin responded by adding to the ballot for the Russian Republic the issue of whether to create an elective Russian presidency—an initiative that would eventually greatly increase his own authority and power and offer a sharp contrast to Gorbachev's avoidance of a Soviet Union presidential election. But the urgent issue of a new union treaty had yet to be settled.

Asked in the referendum whether they favored "a renewed federation of equal Soviet republics," the response of Soviet voters on March 17, 1991, was unsurprisingly positive—76 percent voted yes in the country as a whole, although only a fraction over 50 percent did so in Moscow and Leningrad. The republic authorities in the Baltic states, as well as in Georgia, Armenia and Moldova, refused to support the referendum.[36] Clearly, the purpose of the vaguely worded referendum was to give the appearance of reforming the federal constitution without the substance. Formally receiving the report on the referendum, the USSR Supreme Soviet announced,

"The people's decision . . . in support of a renewed Union of Soviet Socialist Republics . . . is final and has binding force throughout the USSR."[37]
It condemned "the use of slogans of national sovereignty and democracy."
The vote was presented as a popular endorsement of the constitutional status quo.

But the effort to suppress the forces of national sovereignty and democracy was not over. The proposal in the RSFSR to create a popularly elected
presidency received overwhelming support, opening the possibility that
Yeltsin, the most powerful and popular advocate of both sovereignty and
democracy, might greatly increase his power if elected to that office. Party
conservatives had attacked Yeltsin relentlessly after his call for Gorbachev's
resignation over the January action in Vilnius, and the communists in the
Russian Supreme Soviet tried in vain to impeach him in March. Meanwhile,
Yeltsin continued his offensive.

The expanding confrontation reached a climax in late March. On March
26 the USSR government announced the prohibition of rallies and demonstrations in Moscow through April 15, aiming to block a demonstration called
for the twenty-eighth by the Democratic Russia movement, which they knew
would support Yeltsin.[38] The demonstration took place nonetheless, bringing out a crowd estimated at 700,000 that packed the major squares. Its
participants remained peaceful, orderly, good-natured, and undeterred by
the 40,000 police and military assembled to control them.

GORBACHEV RELENTS: A NEW UNION TREATY

Responding to growing popular pressure, Gorbachev shifted his position
on the new form of the federation during the following weeks. On April 23
he reached an agreement with the presidents of the supreme soviets of Russia, Ukraine, Belarus, Uzbekistan, Kazakhstan, Azerbaijan, Tajikistan, Kyrgyzstan, and Turkmenistan to observe existing laws pending the adoption
("in the near future") of a new union treaty, which would be followed within
six months by a new union constitution based on the provisions of the treaty
and then by elections to the new bodies of power. The agreement acknowledged the right of Latvia, Lithuania, Estonia, Moldova, Georgia, and Armenia "to decide for themselves the question of acceding to the union treaty."
It also provided for emergency measures of economic stabilization and a
commitment to opposing all "attempts to achieve political goals through

incitement to civil disobedience and strikes and any calls to overthrow existing, legitimately elected bodies of power."[39]

The agreement was signed only by republics that had participated in the March referendum; it provided that republics that had not signed were free to go their own way, though forfeiting the privileges of membership of "the single economic space" that would be the new federation. Equally important, the agreement provided that the USSR Congress of People's Deputies and the Supreme Soviet would be dissolved and new elections held for a new parliament and a new president. The chairman of the Democratic Party of Russia, Nikolay Travkin, commented wryly on Gorbachev's action, which was Yeltsin's victory as well: "Most likely, it was just as hard for Gorbachev to give up his claims on everything and everyone as it was for Yeltsin to leave the advantageous position of being only an attacker."[40] And while endorsing the wisdom of a policy that gave independence to those republics that sought it, Travkin argued that three of the six—Georgia, Armenia, and Moldova—would "very quickly take steps toward the union."

Only a few days after announcing this daring plan, Gorbachev and Yeltsin had to face difficult and often angry charges from their respective constituencies. Yeltsin was accused of naiveté about the willingness of the Congress of USSR People's Deputies to vote itself out of existence. He was charged with betraying the striking miners who had supported him earlier and whom he now advised to drop their claims and suspend their strikes. His critics also noted the vague language of the agreement, which promised "a fundamental enhancement of the role of the union republics but offered no specifics."[41] Gorbachev's task was the more difficult, for he had abandoned his rejection of the right of republics to claim sovereignty and to secede from the union. Defending his actions at the Party plenum shortly after the agreement, he expressed respect for "our opponents on the other side of the barricade" and argued that differences with them "can now be resolved only within the framework of the democratic process." In words anticipating the motives of the organizers of the antidemocratic coup four months later, he observed that "many people see emergency measures as a means of returning to the political system that existed in our country in the pre-perestroika period. . . . If some people want to return to conditions reminiscent of the time when Article 6 of the constitution [guaranteeing the leading role of the Party] was in effect, that position will not be accepted by society."[42]

CONSPIRING AGAINST THE UNION TREATY
ACT I: THE "PAVLOV COUP"

Gorbachev's conservative opponents, powerful both in his own government and in the USSR Supreme Soviet—despite being only a minority in the latter—would soon try to acquire the power to halt the implementation of a new federal constitution. They recognized that it would almost certainly dismantle the traditional structure of the Soviet Union based on the 1922 union treaty. Their action, undertaken in June, was doubtless precipitated by the fact that the USSR Supreme Soviet endorsed the draft treaty over-whelmingly on May 22. Only three days later the Russian Congress of People's Deputies passed legislation introducing the elective presidency, and on June 12 Boris Yeltsin was elected president by 57 percent of the voters on the first round, though running against three competitors.

Yet another demonstration of Yeltsin's popularity, the election also brought a major increase in his political power, provoking a quick response from his opponents. On June 17, Prime Minister Pavlov, in cooperation with minister of interior Boris Pugo, KGB head Vladimir Kryuchkov, and defense minister Dmitry Yazov, sought Supreme Soviet approval of a trans-fer of the USSR president's emergency powers to the cabinet, arguing that their powers were inadequate to the crisis the country confronted. When the effort provoked strong opposition in the Supreme Soviet, Gorbachev appeared and claimed he had no conflict with his ministers. Pavlov charged the press with misrepresenting his action as an attempted coup, a posi-tion Gorbachev appeared to support by default—that is, by taking no action against his government.

The calmness with which Gorbachev handled the affair inspired press speculation that it had been staged. One prominent political commentator noted that Yeltsin's election on June 12 and the ensuing accelerated work on the draft union treaty had made conservative "Party officials, generals and marshals, and many [Soviet] Union ministers" determined to return to their close cooperation with Gorbachev of the previous autumn, when he had rejected both economic reform and his June 1990 cooperation agree-ment with Yeltsin. Pavlov was perceived as the sort of hard-liner who could help halt the signing of the union treaty and the adoption of desocializing economic reform.[43]

The American ambassador, Jack Matlock, had received a private message from Moscow's Mayor Popov on May 20 urging him to get a message to Yeltsin that a coup was being organized to remove Gorbachev and that the conspirators were Pavlov, Kryuchkov, Yazov, and Anatoly Lukyanov, president of the USSR Supreme Soviet. Directed by President George H. W. Bush to report the information to Gorbachev, Matlock found him in a complacent mood, saying that Pavlov had acknowledged his mistake, the union treaty would soon be signed, and the Soviet Union would enter the world economy at the forthcoming G-7 meeting. He regarded members of the Soiuz group as his main opponents and felt that rumors of a coup had derived from their discussions. On the following day the Supreme Soviet, at Gorbachev's request, voted overwhelmingly to reject Pavlov's request. Matlock found Gorbachev's behavior baffling: "he was acting like a somnambulist, wandering around oblivious to his surroundings. He had dismissed and resented [foreign minister Eduard] Shevardnadze's warnings of December, sacrificed loyal aides like Bakatin, ignored the advice of Alexander Yakovlev and others who had helped him craft perestroika . . . and continued to trust the duplicitous Kryuchkov and an impudent clown like Pavlov."[44]

One puzzling element of Gorbachev's behavior was his response to the pressure for aggressive economic reform to deal with the country's accelerating economic crisis. As in the autumn of 1990, he again rejected a promising reform plan, this one worked out by Grigory Yavlinsky in cooperation with American partners. Yavlinsky was abruptly replaced in a scheduled meeting with President Bush by conservative representatives whose presentation convinced the president that Gorbachev had no effective economic reform plan. Matlock later observed that this action destroyed the possibility of significant American support for the Russian economy at the ensuing G-7 meeting in London and revealed Gorbachev's abandonment of the reformers: "The bureaucrats who had piloted the economy into a tailspin were still sitting in the cockpit."[45]

THE UNION TREATY COMPLETED

The text of the Treaty on the Union of Sovereign States was published on July 23, and Gorbachev announced that it would be "open for signing" on August 20. It embodied the revolutionary concept that the powers of the federal government were delegated to it by a group of sovereign states. The first and most important of the seven "Basic Principles" contained in the treaty made the point: "Each republic that is a party to the Treaty is a sovereign state. The Union of Soviet Sovereign Republics (USSR) is a sovereign democratic state formed as a result of the association of equal republics and exercising state power within the bounds of the powers with which the parties to the Treaty voluntarily endow it."[46]

The treaty guaranteed the right of member states of the new union to establish their own political and administrative systems, but it required that these be democratic systems guaranteeing equal rights to citizens of all national origins, recognizing the UN Declaration of Human Rights, protecting freedom of religion, information, and all economic, social, and personal rights, and providing citizens with support for education, health, science, and culture.

The new union was to be a sovereign state in its own right and the successor of the Soviet Union, but the member states could have their own diplomatic, trade, and commercial relations with foreign states as long as these were consistent with commitments to the union. The government structure of the union was to include a president and vice president and a parliament (Supreme Soviet) consisting of a Council of Republics and a Council of the Union, all elected by universal suffrage.

In sum, the new treaty, replacing the 1922 Treaty on the Formation of the USSR, was intended to establish a democratic federal system providing broad powers for the sovereign member states. Close inspection of the terms of the treaty reveals a serious disjunction between the section on basic principles, which affirmed the sovereignty of all the states of the new union, and that on the structure of the union, which severely limited their powers. Had the constitution been implemented, many issues would have had to be resolved between the republic and union governments. Nonetheless, the affirmation of republic sovereignty and the prospect of fully democratic parliamentary elections at both levels remained, like the decisive move to a market economy, anathema to Party conservatives, and certainly to those who dominated the cabinet and had only recently failed to expand their powers by a peaceful parliamentary coup.

The conservative government leadership and the broader conservative membership of the Party received still more bad news at the July 25 plenary session of the Central Committee. A group of Central Committee members had drafted a Party program that abandoned all the main ideological positions of previous programs. Drawing heavily on Yeltsin's proposals and the reform agenda of Democratic Russia, it endorsed a market economy and called for the extensive sale and leasing of state enterprises and the active incorporation of the Soviet economy into the world economy. It called for the rejection of class struggle and revolution in favor of becoming "a party of democratic reforms, political and economic freedom, social justice and universal human values . . . that fights for general civil concord" in competition with other parties in a democratic polity. It also abandoned the restrictive "canonical texts" of Marxism-Leninism for "the whole wealth of our own and world socialist and democratic thought."

Although Gorbachev was probably not an author of the new program, he clearly agreed with parts of it and was fully prepared to accept the decision of the majority of the Central Committee if it voted in favor of the program. It is no exaggeration to say that in doing so, he was accepting "a revolution in the ideology and views of Party members."[47] He retained his faith in the possibility of renewing the Party, but his long-time colleague Aleksandr Yakovlev had reached a more radical conclusion about the communist ideological legacy: "I am gradually reaching the conclusion that our troubles stem from the dogmas of Marxism. Stalin implemented what is set down in Marxism in a distorted way, but he did implement it."[48] He thought that voting for a new party program was useless: "Votes are cast for any conceivable piece of paper—as long as power remains where it was."

It was precisely the certainty that under the proposed constitution, power would not "remain where it was" that motivated the much more ambitious coup attempt of mid-August.

COUNTERREVOLUTION AND DEMOCRATIC REVOLUTION

Few historical events in the twentieth century surpass in importance or in drama the failed coup of August 17–19, 1991. It was an overwhelming victory for Russian democrats in their long struggle against the power of the Communist Party and the Soviet government—a victory that opened the way to Russian democracy and the peaceful dismantling of the Soviet Union. A final, desperate effort by traditionalist communist leaders to restore the power and authority of the Communist Party and crush the forces of democratic transformation, the coup was aptly called in a contemporary newspaper headline the "Plot of the Doomed."

For Gorbachev, the coup was the cause of deep disappointment and humiliation. He had continued until the end a futile effort to reconcile the aims of conservative Party leaders with those of the democratic and nationalist opposition groups, maintaining Party leadership and a modified socialism. But in the last year before the coup, despite his power to make appointments as general secretary of the Party and president of the Soviet Union, his most important appointees were opponents of organizational and policy reform. The outstanding liberal ministers and advisors in the Party and the government were either marginalized or dropped from the leadership. He had lost the support of the democrats and become dependent upon people who resented the past achievements of his perestroika and sought to reverse course. The coup leaders were the leading officials of his own government, men who had only recently blocked a needed economic reform initiative and whose immediate motive for the coup was their opposition to the new union treaty.

Though the balance of power between Yeltsin and Gorbachev had shifted radically, the years of conflict between them were not over. Yeltsin would lead the opposition to the coup and emerge as the foremost national leader after its failure. An eerie resemblance can be traced between Yeltsin's humiliation by Gorbachev before the Central Committee in 1987 and that of Gorbachev by Yeltsin before the Russian Republic Supreme Soviet after his return from Foros, Ukraine, following the collapse of the coup. Gorbachev was compelled to read "like a naughty schoolboy" a prepared statement condemning the leaders of his government and Party and authorizing government changes dictated by Yeltsin.[49]

But the harshness of Yeltsin's treatment of Gorbachev was understandable. He felt, as did such distinguished former Yeltsin Politburo colleagues as Eduard Shevardnadze and Aleksandr Yakovlev—the main architects of perestroika in foreign and domestic policy, respectively—that Gorbachev had repeatedly capitulated to reactionary forces in the Party since the autumn of 1990. Shevardnadze charged that the weaknesses of Gorbachev's leadership "almost led to a national tragedy." He wrote: "I am completely certain that none other than Gorbachev himself had been spoon-feeding the junta with his indecisiveness, his inclination to back and fill, his fellow-traveling, his poor judgment of people, his indifference towards his true allies, his distrust of the democratic forces, and his disbelief in the bulwark whose name is the people—the very same people who had changed thanks to the perestroika he had begun."[50]

The "junta" Shevardnadze mentioned—Gorbachev's own appointees—was driven by fear and anger in the summer of 1991 to take action to prevent approval of the new union treaty. Its members had worked for many months, with Gorbachev's full cooperation, on new legislation to support the declaration of a state of emergency, which they would use to legitimate their action. Previous experience, particularly in Lithuania, had demonstrated that military force was counterproductive; it provided a cause against which the democratic and nationalist opposition could mobilize mass support. Another method was needed. Prime Minister Pavlov had failed to get parliamentary authorization for emergency powers in June, but in arguing for them he had used the same justification that would be used for the creation of the State Committee for the State of Emergency in August: the rapid decline and disorganization of the economy and the conflicts, especially over revenue, between the union government and the republics.

The conservatives' fear of Yeltsin—the steady growth of his power in Russia and his close ties with other republic leaders seeking to expand their power vis-à-vis the center—was discussed in a confidential Party document: "The tactics of the forces opposing the center and the CPSU have changed significantly. The Supreme Soviet of the RSFSR under B. N. Yeltsin is becoming the seed of consolidation for democratic and national democratic republican movements."[51]

Yeltsin had been the leading force behind the preparation of the union treaty, and he continued to press for radical economic reform. The increase in his power by his election to the new Russian presidency was particularly alarming. For all these reasons he would be a major target of the repressive measures planned as part of the state of emergency, as would the leadership of Democratic Russia, the broad coalition of democratic organizations that had articulated and advanced an increasingly influential program of democratic reforms. The proposed signing of a new union treaty provoked the conservatives' dangerous adventure.

Preparations for a state of emergency accelerated after Gorbachev announced the August 20 date for signing the union treaty and his departure for a Crimean vacation on August 4. Once he left, a storm broke out over the text of the treaty. It became available to his colleagues only after his departure and was immediately denounced as "anticonstitutional" and "antigovernmental" by the president of the USSR Supreme Soviet, Anatoly Lukyanov, and by Prime Minister Pavlov. Both insisted that signing the treaty in its current form was unacceptable. They and their supporters understood that without their proposed changes, the treaty would mean the end of the Soviet Union and of communist power as they had known them, and probably the end of their political careers as well.

They also understood that suspension of the signing would be politically perilous. They remembered the enormous March demonstration in support of Yeltsin, the leading advocate of the treaty, and recognized the great increase in his power since the presidential election. It was therefore urgent to make preparations for the political resistance that would emerge if the treaty signing were obstructed. KGB chairman Vladimir Kryuchkov took charge of preparing for a state of emergency, and the details of the plan were agreed upon on August 17. The report of the parliamentary commission of inquiry into the August Coup that met in 1992 described the plan prepared by the conspirators on August 17:

First isolating the president in his place of vacation and then sending to him . . . a group of persons to demand that he either introduce a state of emergency in the country or resign. In the event that the president refused this demand he would be declared ill and incompetent to perform his functions. The function of the president would be transferred to Vice President Yanaev to form a State Committee for the Emergency, assume full powers, and introduce the emergency regime throughout the country.[52]

In accordance with the plan, a delegation was sent to Foros the next day, August 18, to secure Gorbachev's agreement to the plotters' demands. Its members included V. I. Boldin, Gorbachev's chief of staff, General V. I. Varennikov, commander of ground forces, O. D. Baklanov, a defense industry leader, and O. S. Shenin, a Politburo member and CPSU Central Committee secretary for personnel. Gorbachev rejected their demands, and the delegation returned to Moscow. Just before midnight, Vice President Yanaev formally assumed presidential powers, claiming that Gorbachev was ill and unable to fulfill his duties in a time of national emergency. Early the following morning the coup leaders declared a six-month state of emergency, to be administered by a State Committee for the State of Emergency

(SCSE), a group whose opponents soon christened it "the Gang of Eight."[53] Central TV and Radio broadcast their statements, along with a statement from Anatoly Lukyanov intended to give the impression that the USSR Supreme Soviet supported the SCSE, although there had been no supporting vote.

The "gang" announced that its purpose was to overcome "the chaos and anarchy that are threatening the lives and security of the citizens and the security of the Soviet Union." The special powers of the emergency authority, the SCSE, included the right to suspend the authority of noncompliant government bodies at all levels, to invalidate laws considered in contradiction to those of the union, to suspend activities of political parties, public organizations, and mass movements, to assume the functions of the USSR Security Council, to confiscate all armaments in the possession of individuals, institutions, and organizations, to control all news media, to prohibit rallies, street processions, and strikes, and to undertake "a decisive struggle against the shadow economy." The unannounced plans included a roundup of the leadership of the republics and of the entire Russian democratic movement, beginning with the Russian president.[54] The coup leaders also promised to take measures to improve the lives of citizens in many ways, from food and consumer goods to services, housing, and even garden plots.[55] Meanwhile, the "extremist forces" (read democrats) were charged with having embarked upon "a course aimed at liquidation of the Soviet Union," "an ungoverned slide toward a market," and the "destruction of the unified national-economic mechanism."[56]

Supreme Soviet chairman Lukyanov led the attack on the draft union treaty, charging that it had not incorporated the changes recommended by the USSR Supreme Soviet. He also announced an extraordinary session of the USSR Supreme Soviet for August 26 to ratify the decision on establishing a state of emergency—a week after its introduction without the constitutionally required Supreme Soviet vote.

Boris Yeltsin received news of the coup by television at his dacha on August 19. After preparing a statement of response, he quickly left for Moscow and the Russian White House, which housed both the presidential offices and the chambers of the parliament, the Russian Supreme Soviet. Inexplicably, an armed guard deployed nearby by the coup planners did not stop him from entering the building. His official statement, joined by Prime Minister Silaev and Ruslan Khasbulatov, acting chairman of the Russian Supreme Soviet, urged national resistance to the "right-wing, reactionary, unconstitutional coup" and defended the union treaty. Noting that the current coup attempt was the latest of a series of efforts against democratic changes, he declared the committee and its acts illegal and unconstitutional and appealed for non-cooperation by the military, "a general strike of unlimited duration," an opportunity for Gorbachev to speak to the nation, and an immediate convening of an Extraordinary Congress of USSR People's Deputies.[57] On the same day he issued a special presidential decree describing the coup as a crime against the state and declaring all its actions illegal and invalid on the territory of the RSFSR. He warned officials of the republic that implementing the orders of the SCSE would bring prosecution under the RSFSR criminal code.[58]

The coup organizers had brought military forces to intimidate the president and the parliament, who were now besieged inside the White House. Nevertheless, Yeltsin and parliament members were able to appear outside on occasion, and on that first day Yeltsin made a dramatic speech from atop a tank in front of the White House. In the afternoon he prepared measures for taking over the functions of the USSR government organizations on the territory of the Russian Republic and appealed to military personnel not to cooperate with the SCSE. In the course of the day a battalion of the Taman Division went over to the side of the Russian government, and ten tanks arrived to defend the parliament. Further support from the military came late in the evening when eight armored scout vehicles arrived at the request of the commander of airborne forces, General P. S. Grachev, "to protect the legal Russian authorities." Volunteers were building barricades of rocks and metal bars around the White House, and people were arriving in droves to demonstrate their support. On many of the walls copies of the newspaper *Kuranty* had been posted, displaying the banner headline "Plot of the Doomed."

During the night of August 19–20 the crowd outside the White House continued to grow. As the radio station set up in the White House broadcast news and appeals for support, the crowd reached an estimated 200,000 by noon on August 20, listening to speeches from Russian government leaders and supporters. As evening came the White House was surrounded by barricades and was protected by a mixed force of about a thousand, including volunteers, armed professionals, and Afghan war veterans, while a crowd of seventy thousand lined the Krasnaia Presnia Embankment. The six armored columns maneuvering around the building during the night did not dare attack through the thirty-five to forty rings of civilians, holding hands and providing a human shield, though loudspeakers from the building warned them not to stand in the way of the tanks. By eight in the morning on August 21 the armored columns had departed. It was soon announced that the troops were leaving Moscow at the decision of the Collegium of the Ministry of Defense and that the curfew in Moscow had been lifted. During the day the USSR Supreme Soviet declared the removal of Gorbachev illegal, and at ten in the evening Yeltsin announced the end of the coup.

AFTER THE COUP

Despite all the difficulties and very grave trials that the people of Russia are experiencing, the democratic process in the country is assuming ever deeper dimensions and is becoming irreversible. The peoples of Russia are becoming the masters of their fate.

—BORIS YELTSIN, AUGUST 19, 1991

From the very beginning of the coup, the firm and uncompromising position of Boris Yeltsin, the Russian Republic parliament and government, and their well-thought-out measures, supported by the masses, were the main obstacles against which the conspirators' actions were dashed.

—ANATOLY BUTENKO, SEPTEMBER 18, 1991

The organizers of the coup had totally miscalculated their chances of success. Their claim to be the saviors of an imperiled country had little credibility from the start. Then, on the morning of the first day, their acknowledged nemesis, Boris Yeltsin, whom they had failed to detain, seized the initiative with his familiar energy and determination. He sped to the White House, made it the headquarters of the resistance, and gave powerful expression to the opposition cause. His words and example galvanized the capital in mass opposition to the coup, confronting the military with the horrifying prospect of driving tanks into civilian crowds.

The conspirators intended to deny a voice to their opponents by seizing control of the press, radio, and television, but the effort failed. The most dramatic act of press defiance took place in the composition room of *Izvestiia* on the first day of the coup, when production workers refused to produce the evening edition without including Yeltsin's appeal, "To the Citizens of

Russia." Despite threats of loss of their apartments and salaries, they stood firm, publishing the issue the next morning with an abridged but effective version of the speech. They had earlier printed the full text manually, providing copies for eager Muscovites and the soldiers on the tanks in Pushkin Square.[59] The only person to lose his job was the editor, who had the dubious distinction of being pegged as reliable by the SCSE and was removed by his staff.

On August 20 the staff of *Literaturnaia gazeta* initiated a meeting of the Democratic Press Front to resist measures aimed at muzzling the press. The group declared its refusal to meet SCSE requirements of reregistration of their publications. It was soon apparent that even the publications whose editors the coup leaders had counted on for compliance were unwilling or unable to control their subordinates. One of the most important elements of the irreversible democratization mentioned by Yeltsin was stoutly defended.

The military leadership was seriously divided by the coup. The Collegium of the Ministry of Defense had not been informed of Yazov's inclusion in the SCSE. Air Force general Y. I. Shaposhnikov, who reacted negatively to the announcement of the emergency, met with Yazov on the twentieth and suggested the immediate return of all forces to bases, the dispersal of the SCSE, and the handing of power to the Supreme Soviet. He then struck an agreement with General Grachev, commander of airborne troops, to notify the Russian parliament that they would take no action against it. Finally, on the morning of August 21, the Defense Ministry Collegium ordered all forces to return to their bases. General Shaposhnikov, named by Gorbachev on his return to replace Yazov as defense minister, commented to a reporter after the events that

on the whole, the armed forces are no longer what they were five years ago. Since 1985 our life has become more democratic, like small streams coming together into a big river. And now democratic life is a great flow. That group of individuals found themselves on a small island in that flow and thought they could make the island into a dam. It didn't work. And it won't work. Life is moving forward. People have changed. The armed forces refused to follow the extremists.[60]

The pathetic weakness of the coup planning, the determination, courage, and numbers of the Russian democrats, the leadership of Yeltsin and his colleagues, and the inability of the coup organizers to control the communications media or secure the effective support of the military together explain the short life and ignominious collapse of the August Coup. The conspirators clearly had not reckoned with the power and popularity of an independent Russian Republic and its leaders or with the transformation of the outlook of the general population. Nor had they learned to deal with a new political world in which laws and constitutions had acquired real meaning. Acting without meeting the legal requirement of Supreme Soviet approval of the declaration of emergency rule, they were repudiated by that body, as they had been after the failed coup attempt in June, after Yeltsin's election.

Despite the failures of leadership and organization, however, the Russian democratic movement was gravely imperiled during the fateful days in August. There was no exaggeration in Shevardnadze's assertion that the coup "almost led to national tragedy." Yeltsin's crucial leadership in the resistance to the coup was the product of both the comprehensive transformation of his personal political views and his courageous political leadership role in the Russian democratic movement. He had emerged from humiliation and isolation in late 1987 to exploit the expanding resources for independent political action—the independent press and political organizations and the new institutions of elective government at the USSR and republic levels. He had steadily broadened his own understanding of the scope of necessary reform—arguing for replacement of Party dictatorship by fully democratic elections and multiparty democracy and seeking recognition of the sovereignty of the republics and a comprehensive democratic restructuring of the federal system, including the right of secession and abandonment of the Soviet socialist economy. Unable to achieve a democratized Communist Party that would accept the equal claims of other parties in a democratic system, he resigned his membership. Unlike almost all other leaders of the Russian democratic movement, he had extensive experience in the exercise of political power. And unlike most of his former colleagues among the communist hierarchy, he was prepared to make a clean break— ideologically and politically—with the old order.

Yeltsin was, in brief, precisely the kind of leader that was tragically missing from the democratic leadership of Russia following the February Revolution of 1917. Another contrast with the February Revolution was the context in which this one occurred—not in the midst of major war at a time of huge military losses and devastating retreat, but in the aftermath of a peaceful emancipation of the subject states of Eastern Europe, the abdication of leadership of the world communist movement, and a negotiated conclusion to nearly half a century of cold war.

Whatever his failings in adapting to the necessities of domestic change before and following the August collapse, Gorbachev and his reform collaborators deserve enormous credit for these crucial advantages, which combined with the defeat of the August Coup attempt to give Yeltsin and the Russian democrats a unique opening. One can readily join Philip Taubman, quoted at the opening of this chapter, both in regretting the enmity between the two remarkable protagonists in this decisive period of Russian history and in affirming that "had they not collided, Russia might not be free." Yeltsin's views on the issues over which they collided were key both to his subsequent successes in peacefully dismantling the Soviet Union and in initiating the transition to a market economy and democracy. Of the two men, he was much the better prepared for the opportunities and challenges of the era that followed the August Coup.

THE SECOND RUSSIAN REVOLUTION

The result of the coup was precisely the opposite of its leaders' intention: not the reversal of the democratic and nationalist transformation of the Soviet Union but the destruction of the power of the Communist Party and the dismantling of the Soviet Union.

Gorbachev returned to Moscow on August 21 and on the following day issued a decree revoking all the decisions of the SCSE and removing its members from office. As he resumed his leadership, the Central Committee and Secretariat of the Party moved quickly to distance themselves from the coup and its leaders and to reaffirm what Gorbachev called "the all-around renewal of Soviet society, which the CPSU began in April 1985 . . . and is in the highest interests of the Soviet people."[61] He met on August 23 with the leaders of the nine republics that had previously endorsed the union treaty, discussing measures for handling the country's acute economic problems and winning unanimous endorsement of the earliest possible signing of the union treaty, a commitment that soon proved meaningless.

Gorbachev's meeting with the Russian Republic Supreme Soviet revealed major problems for his effort to regain his presidential role and powers. His replacement appointments for dismissed coup leaders had already offended most deputies, who saw them as people whose tacit consent had supported the coup. And his defense of the Communist Party against charges of complicity in the coup was unconvincing, especially when its central organs and most of its regional committees had supported the actions of the SCSE.[62] Even after being pressed by Yeltsin to read aloud to the chamber a section of the meeting minutes detailing the discussions of the SCSE conspirators, Gorbachev continued his defense of the Party and of Leninist socialism. When Yeltsin closed down the Russian Communist Party and its publications, Gorbachev protested, but on August 24 he was compelled simultaneously to suspend the activities of the CPSU and resign as general secretary. Meanwhile, Yeltsin dominated the selection of new heads of key USSR ministries.

The Soviet Union began to disintegrate rapidly in the aftermath of the coup that was intended to preserve it. Not only had the authority of the CPSU been shattered, but also that of the executive and legislative branches of the USSR government. The exchanges in the packed hall at an extraordinary session of the Supreme Soviet on August 26 were symptomatic. Gorbachev's speech acknowledged his own errors of leadership, including his failure to eliminate the Party's monopoly on power, but he claimed to have "come back a different person" who would tolerate no delays in carrying out reforms. He offered a specific program: resumption of the process of signing the union treaty; creating temporary governing bodies for the period of transition to a new constitution; reforming the USSR Supreme Soviet; measures to assure control of the armed forces and security and police agencies; and an early changeover to a market economy. Once the union treaty was signed he wanted immediate elections for the legislative bodies and for the presidency. In sum, he talked as if there was still a Soviet Union to be reformed, a mistaken view still shared by the USSR Supreme Soviet.

During several days of debate the Supreme Soviet supported many of these program proposals, suspended the Communist Party, removed Anatoly Lukyanov as chairman of the Supreme Soviet and authorized his arrest, and set up a commission to investigate the coup. But even as the members planned a reformed Soviet Union, they were interrupted for the report of a delegation led by Anatoly Sobchak, newly returned from consultations with the Ukrainian Supreme Soviet, that "the former Soviet Union is gone for good."[63] A parliamentary reporter observed that the adjective "former" was used here for the first time.

Events in Ukraine had moved with great speed following the collapse of the coup, bringing many surprises. At the opening of the emergency session of the Ukraine Supreme Soviet on August 24 a huge crowd had demanded independence and "departification," an end to the permeating power of the Communist Party in state and society. A vote of 321 to 20 endorsed a resolution on Ukrainian independence, with the issue to be finally decided in a December 1 popular vote that would also select a Ukrainian president. The parliament adopted an act of independence giving itself control of all local military forces and total legislative control, and it removed Communist Party organizations from police and intelligence structures. Leonid Kravchuk, chairman of the Ukrainian Supreme Soviet, received powers amounting to those of president. Preparations were also made for prosecuting the leaders of the Ukrainian Party who had supported the coup attempt in Moscow. Looking toward the future, Ivan Drach, the head of Rukh, the Ukrainian nationalist coalition, rejected restoration of political union with Russia. The European Union inspired his vision for the future of Ukrainian institutions.

The Belarusian Supreme Soviet convened on the same day as the Ukrainian, though under pressure from the democratic opposition rather than from its overwhelmingly communist membership, mostly representatives of the Party and state apparatus who had sat quietly during the coup. As it opened, a crowd of fifty thousand demanded the resignation of its chairman, Nikolay Dementey, and of the Supreme Soviet Presidium, accusing both of supporting the coup. A spokesman for the demonstrators appeared before the Supreme Soviet, demanding disbandment of the Belarusian Communist Party and television airtime for the opposition.

In the heated debates that followed, the Supreme Soviet secured Dementey's resignation, the independence of the police and security agencies and of industrial enterprises from Party control, and partial nationalization of Communist Party property and other resources. Though the Belarusian communists preferred to remain in the union, this would have meant accepting Gorbachev's decree suspending activity of the CPSU. They therefore joined the opposition in a nearly unanimous vote on sovereignty and independence that also transferred all USSR property to republic ownership. They saw this as the best way to preserve communist power under the leadership of a national party.[64]

The coup also brought a rapid acceleration of the independence movement in the Republic of Moldova. Parliament chairman Aleksandru Moshanu opened an extraordinary session of the parliament on August 27 by announcing, "The Republic of Moldova must become free, declaring its independence." His view was widely shared in the parliament. During the coup, all political movements in the republic except the communists had come together in opposition to the state of emergency—hence the decision of President Mircea Snegur to disband the Communist Party and nationalize its property. Snegur rejected the union treaty and called for talks to end the "illegal occupation" and withdraw Soviet troops.[65]

The Baltic republics were quick to affirm their national independence in the wake of the coup. On August 20, as Soviet tanks advanced on Tallinn, the Estonian Supreme Soviet affirmed the country's independence, which the Russian Federation (the new name for the Russian Soviet Federated Socialist Republic) recognized the next day. Because support for the coup had been widespread among highly placed Russians in Estonia, the dismissals and arrests of such supporters were numerous as the government consolidated its position.

The Latvian leadership had responded quickly to the state of emergency, denying that its representatives had any legal authority in the republic on the first day of the coup. Supporters of the Moscow coup attempted a power seizure in Riga, using military forces from the Baltic Military District under the command of Colonel General Fedor Kuzmin, who announced his intention to take control of Estonia, Latvia, and Lithuania in the name of the SCSE. Latvian Communist Party first secretary Alfred Rubiks announced his intention to create a committee similar to the one in Moscow and to ban all political parties except the Communist. The parliament then proclaimed national independence on August 21, on the basis of the 1922 constitution, just as news of the failure of the coup in Moscow was received. On August 23 the Russian Federation government recognized Latvian independence; the Soviet government offered recognition on September 6. Two days later the parliament declared the activity of the Latvian Communist Party unconstitutional and seized all its property. It also initiated criminal proceedings against officials of the Party charged with cooperating in the coup, beginning with Rubiks.

Lithuania, the first of the Soviet republics to declare its independence (in March 1990), had been repeatedly harassed since that event, and upon declaration of the emergency in Moscow it was faced with Soviet troops occupying the Kaunas television and radio center. President Landsbergis appealed to the population to surround the parliament building as a protection, but the speedy end of the Moscow coup opened the way for quick action by the Lithuanian leadership. It demanded the removal of Soviet armed forces, confiscated the property of the Lithuanian Communist Party, and carried out a purge of pro-Soviet officials in key positions. As in the other Baltic republics, Lithuanian independence was recognized immediately by the Russian government, and by the USSR on September 6.

Events in the Transcaucasus showed the same rush for independence. The Armenian leadership had long been alienated from Moscow by its handling of the conflict between Armenia and Azerbaijan over Nagorno-Karabakh, and in January 1991 the Armenian parliament voted to boycott the all-union referendum on preservation of the USSR. In March the parliament voted to hold a September referendum, under the terms of the constitutional Law on Secession, on whether Armenia would remain a part of the union. During the coup a delegation of Soviet generals arrived in Yerevan, unsuccessfully seeking a meeting with Levon Ter-Petrosyan to plan a local state of emergency. Ter-Petrosyan later revealed that the republic's Defense Committee had resolved to take the armed forces underground for guerrilla resistance if the state of emergency were indeed imposed.[66] In the September vote, 94 percent of the electorate supported independence, and one month later Ter-Petrosyan was elected Armenian president. Though an ardent admirer of Yeltsin, whose leadership in the Russian Federation had saved both Russia and the other republics of the former USSR from the reimposition of communist power, Ter-Petrosyan was not eager to cooperate with Gorbachev. He noted, "The coup's organizers were his diligent pupils."

The coup leaders had also sent Colonel General Valery Patrikheev to Georgia during the coup, aiming to establish subordination to the SCSE, but the effort was in vain. Though his agents took control of the airport and train stations, he found the parliament rejecting his plans and supporting Yeltsin. His only support came from the Central Committee of the Communist Party and from separatist leaders in Abkhazia and South Ossetia. The Georgian president, Zviad Gamsakhurdia, a popular leader since his election in May, indicated his willingness to cooperate with the SCSE, a decision he later justified as a means of avoiding Soviet military intervention. It later cost him his presidency. Meanwhile, the parliament supported full independence and on September 6 voted to sever ties with the USSR.

The powerful nationalist movements in other non-Russian republics of the Soviet Union had no real counterparts in Central Asia. In discussions of restructuring the union preceding the coup, local leaders affirmed republic sovereignty as the foundation of discussions but defended the concept of union as a federation or confederation with a unified economy. Uzbekistan alone had a history of statehood, but no organized independence movement. As elsewhere in the Soviet Union, the coup radically changed the political environment. Three of the five Central Asian republics declared their independence immediately after the coup.

In Uzbekistan, President Islam Karimov asked the parliament for a declaration of independence, arguing that it was time to establish independent diplomatic representation internationally and assume full responsibility for Uzbekistan's internal affairs. Both the communist establishment and the small group of democrats received his proposals eagerly. Much of the Party establishment had been alienated by Moscow's aggressive earlier campaign against pervasive corruption in local management of Uzbekistan's lucrative cotton production. The members of Birlik, a popular front of reformers, resented Moscow's enforcement of an environmentally and socially destructive cotton monoculture. Once it was clear that the coup was failing, Karimov resigned from the Politburo and, only a few days later, urged the Uzbek Party Central Committee to break ties with the Soviet Party. Though left unchanged in structure, the party was renamed the Popular Democratic Party. At the end of the year Karimov was elected president by direct vote, running against a weak pro forma opposition candidate.

The reaction of President Nursultan Nazarbaev of Kazakhstan to the coup was similar to that of Karimov. Once the coup had failed, he condemned the organizers and lauded Yeltsin and the Russian resistance. He also resigned from the Politburo and Central Committee, on the grounds that they had supported the coup. He then resigned from the Communist Party of Kazakhstan and secured from its Central Committee a full suspension of activity on August 28, though it was allowed to reconstitute itself under the name Socialist Party in September with the former *nomenklatura* still in control of the government. Nazarbaev signed Kazakhstan's formal declaration of independence on December 16. Throughout the transition, the Kazakh leadership was concerned about the reaction of the 40 percent of the population that was Russian, fearing a possible movement for annexation of the heavily Russian northern region to the Russian Federation. There was no sign of any such movement.

Kyrgyzstan was a unique case both before and after the coup. Its president since October 1990, the physicist Askar Akaev, had undertaken extensive democratization, earning the hostility of communist hard-liners. At the time of the Moscow coup, the local KGB head, supported by the leaders of the Kyrgyz Communist Party, attempted to remove him from office. Akaev quickly dismissed the KGB head and took measures to secure control of key government buildings and communications facilities. At the opening of the Moscow coup he broadcast Yeltsin's appeal against the state of emergency and mounted a counterattack on the Communist Party that included the banning of Party activities and the seizure of its assets. Though subsequently criticized by democratic leaders for a self-serving law on presidential elections and for his ethnic policies, Akaev had accomplished a speedy victory over the Communist Party. Kyrgyzstan declared its independence on September 18.

For Tajikistan the August Coup marked the opening of a painful and costly struggle between the communist leadership and an anticommunist opposition. The struggle had begun eighteen months earlier, in February 1990, with demonstrations in Dushanbe that demanded the resignation of the communist leadership of the republic. Communist Party head Kakhar Makhkamov placed restrictions on noncommunist groups, aiming particularly at the Islamic Renaissance Party, a potentially serious threat to communist power. The same fear motivated his decision to endorse the Moscow coup. Though he reversed himself quickly after the coup's failure, the main opposition groups organized a demonstration at the end of August demanding the resignation of the republic's government leadership and the dissolution of the Supreme Soviet. Even Makhkamov's resignation as president at the end of August failed to bring the situation under control. Democratic, nationalist, and Islamic opposition groups remained dissatisfied even after the parliamentary declaration on national independence on September 9. They had failed both to gain control of the presidency in the subsequent election and to secure a permanent ban on the Communist Party. The stage was set for the continuing conflict that resulted in civil war in 1992.

REPLACING THE UNION

Instead of a gradual transition from the unitarian Soviet Union to a softer, freer confederation, we had a complete vacuum at the political center. The center—in

the person of Gorbachev—was totally demoralized. The emerging national states
had lost faith in him. Something had to be done.

—BORIS YELTSIN[67]

Within only a few weeks of the collapse of the August Coup it was clear that
Gorbachev's goal of returning to the unsigned union treaty was futile. The
coup had threatened a dictatorship of the center rather than the democratized federation envisaged in the treaty, and Gorbachev, the leading propo-
nent of the treaty's revival, had appointed the coup conspirators. For most
of the political leaders of the non-Russian republics the coup's failure marked
the end of Russia's will and capacity to determine their national destinies.
They were now free to choose either full independence or some form of
confederation with Russia and other republics. If the latter, then Yeltsin was
the most credible Russian negotiating partner. He had been a consistent
supporter of democratization and national sovereignty and the chief architect of the union treaty whose signing the coup had blocked. He had led
the opposition to the coup and had set an example, both before and after it,
of an independent and anticommunist national policy, both as Russian president and in his relations with other republics.

Once again, as in the long struggle over the union treaty that preceded
the coup, the leadership in redefining and restructuring relations between
the center and the former Soviet republics—now rapidly becoming new independent states—fell to Yeltsin. Several states would initially reject any affiliation, and others would welcome it, but none would support the concept
of the union as a central governmental structure and a sovereign state as
envisaged in the union treaty. That possibility was destroyed by the coup,
not by Yeltsin, as his communist and nationalist detractors of later years
would repeatedly charge.

The most important relationship of the center was that with the RSFSR,
soon to be renamed the Russian Federation. The balance of power between
their respective leaders, Gorbachev and Yeltsin, had been totally transformed
by the coup. In the popular view, and in that of republican leaders, the coup
was the result of Gorbachev's incompetent (or sinister) leadership. The entire
country and Gorbachev himself had been saved from disaster by the courageous leadership of Yeltsin. Moreover, Yeltsin had been perceived for more
than two years as the foremost advocate of the power of the republics vis-

à-vis the center. After the coup he had forced the dismantling of the Communist Party and its control of the military, police, and other organizations that sustained its power.

In early September Yeltsin presented his proposals for the relationship between the center and the republics to the USSR Congress of People's Deputies.[68] Noting the "cold war" that had been going on between the two up until the August Coup, he argued that its cause was a failure to understand that the republics' pursuit of sovereignty "was not intrigues by democrats but an objective trend of our times." He remained optimistic about the relationship among the republics: "The coup thwarted the signing of the union treaty, but it could not destroy the republics' desire to build a new union." He proposed four major elements for the new federation: an economic union, a political union permitting various degrees of integration into the federation (or confederation), union armed forces with union control of the common nuclear arsenal, and full protections for human rights and noninterference in the internal affairs of other partners in the union.

Movement toward implementation of these proposals was slow, but on November 14 six of the republics—Russia, Belarus, Kazakhstan, Kyrgyzstan, Turkmenistan, and Tajikistan—met in Russia at Novo-Ogarevo. They agreed to form a confederal state to be called the Union of Sovereign States (USS) that would perform functions delegated to it by the parties to the treaty and would have a president, a government and parliament, and a single currency system. Much remained to be done to provide a full structure for the new political system. The absence of a Ukrainian representative—the Ukrainian Supreme Soviet had asked for participation by Ukrainian representatives to be delayed until the December 1 referendum on Ukrainian independence—greatly weakened confidence in the future of the USS. The fact that the acronym formed by the Russian initials for the proposed union, SNG, sounded like the Russian word for snow, *sneg*, gave rise to the witticism that the new union, too, would melt like snow.

The Ukrainian referendum provided heat for a fast melt. With a turnout of 83.7 percent of the electorate, 80 percent approved the Act on the Independence of Ukraine passed by the republic's Supreme Soviet after the failure of the Moscow coup. Leonid Kravchuk, the head of parliament, won the presidency with a vote of 60 percent. Asked what would happen to the union treaty proposed by Gorbachev, Kravchuk replied simply, "Ukraine will not sign it." He also expressed confidence that "the democrats of Russia—and

Boris Nikolayevich [Yeltsin] with them—will recognize Ukraine as an independent state in the near future."[69] Kravchuk insisted that there was no need for a renewed union government; bilateral treaties between independent states would be sufficient to manage relations among the successor states of the Soviet Union.

Only a few days later, on December 7–8, the leaders of Russia, Belarus, and Ukraine met at Belovezhskaia pushcha, a hunting lodge near Brest in Belarus, where they approved an agreement on forming a new relationship between their three states. The opening paragraph of the agreement announced that "the USSR as a subject of international law and geopolitical reality is terminating its existence," and the first article proclaimed the founding of "a Commonwealth of Independent States" (CIS).[70] In an interview following the signing, Kravchuk said, "We have done everything we could so that there will never again be a center in our lives, so that no center will again be in charge of our states."[71] This was assured by Article 11, according to which "the norms of third states, including the former USSR, may not be applied on the territory of the states signing the Agreement," and by Article 14: "The activity of agencies of the former USSR on the territory of the member-states of the commonwealth is terminated."

The agreement envisaged extensive cooperation in political, economic, social, and cultural affairs, for which later agreements would provide specifics. Other articles spoke broadly of "a common military-strategic space under a joint command, including unified control over nuclear weapons," "a common economic space," the inviolability of the signatories' borders, and the protection of the rights of national minorities (crucial for millions of Russians now suddenly living in foreign states). The final articles (13 and 14) provided that the agreement was "open for accession by all member-states of the former USSR, as well as for other states that share the goals and principles of this Agreement." Minsk, Belarus, was named the capital of the new commonwealth.

Gorbachev reacted negatively to the initiative of the three Slavic states. He rejected the constitutional validity of the termination of the USSR by the three presidents without a vote of the Supreme Soviets of their republics, even as the USS proposal prepared by the USSR State Council was still before those bodies.[72] A similar response came from President Nazarbaev of Kazakhstan, though he was prepared to have the Supreme Soviets of the republics discuss both proposals and found either one acceptable.[73] Stanislav Shushkevich of Belarus stood firmly with Kravchuk and Yeltsin. The leaders of the three Slavic republics, he said, had concluded that the USSR was moving toward a chaotic and dangerous disintegration, and the State Council meetings were occasions when "we only sit and listen to what the president says, but he barely listens to what we say." As for convening a USSR Congress of People's Deputies, "the deputies from Ukraine and Belarus wouldn't go . . . and some deputies from Russia wouldn't go either." Shushkevich explained the choice of Minsk for the CIS capital by saying that "in Moscow, the unnecessary structures that were eliminated are reborn right away under various new signboards. We were afraid that these structures would crush us."[74]

The three states also completed important agreements on economic cooperation in their statement "On the Coordination of Economic Policy." The agreements replaced and surpassed those forthcoming from the work of the USSR Interstate Economic Committee, begun two months earlier. They included preservation of the ruble as the common monetary unit, coordinated limitation of budget deficits, and limitation of the monetary supply. The states also agreed to free up prices together on January 1, 1992, and to submit to their parliaments a 28 percent value-added tax. Russian deputy prime minister Yegor Gaidar explained the urgency of these actions and the fact that the new tripartite treaty, with its base in Minsk, was the only way of gaining crucial Ukrainian participation.[75]

The distinguished journalist and economist Otto Latsis offered thoughtful insights into the way in which the "bulldozer" operation of the leaders of the three republics had transformed the search for a new union structure. He believed it was immensely important that "a way of acting jointly with Ukraine has been found," though he regretted that the three republics had "demonstrated disregard for the other partners, after countless speeches about the equality of all the sovereign states." But to those who accused the three leaders of the new initiative of destroying the union he responded that "what is occurring is not the destruction of the union—it was destroyed long ago and was dealt a final blow by the August putsch. . . . we are being offered an opportunity to choose a new version of the union treaty."[76]

Conservative members of the USSR Congress of People's Deputies undertook a last-ditch effort to halt the implementation of the Minsk agreement—which would put an end to the USSR Supreme Soviet—by convening an extraordinary congress session. The effort ended following a December 10 meeting of congress parliamentarians addressed by prime minister Gennady Burbulis and state counselor Sergey Shakhray, who reminded them that the previous congress had abolished all subsequent congresses and that the Russian Supreme Soviet was prepared to ratify the CIS agreement. The speakers also stressed the failure of the union government to make any progress with its plans for a union treaty and the urgent necessity of action by the leaders of the three republics, an action of which Gorbachev had been informed by Yeltsin before the Belovezhskaia pushcha meeting. To make the change more palatable, the Russian delegates were invited to work with the RSFSR Supreme Soviet and other Russian governing bodies.[77]

The last hope of opponents of the CIS agreement was the December 12 meeting of the USSR Supreme Soviet, called to discuss the ratification of the CIS by the Russian parliament the previous day and its plan to recall the Russian deputies from the USSR Supreme Soviet. The meeting proved a disappointment to opponents of the CIS. According to the *Izvestiia* parliamentary reporter, "Most of the speakers urged their colleagues to accept existing reality and to try to find a fitting way of withdrawing from the political stage."[78] Such was the feeble "defense" of the old structure of union government. It was clearly doomed; it remained only to determine which of the other republics would join the founding three in the new CIS.

Ratifications by the parliaments of the three organizing republics were speedy and strong. Yeltsin delivered a compelling argument for ratification to the Russian Supreme Soviet. He stressed the need finally to eliminate "the self-reproduction of the center's command structures," the danger of "goods blockades, closed borders, and economic wars" between the republics, and the menacing "calls to restore control over the entire territory of the former Soviet Union by any means." The deputies were encouraged by the news that the Central Asian republics would also join. The resolution ratifying the Minsk agreement was passed by an overwhelming majority vote.

Ukraine's decision was less straightforward. Although a solid majority passed approval of the agreement, the parliament included a number of recommendations for change that involved limitations on movement of citizens across republic borders, national rather than commonwealth military forces, and modifications of the concept of a single currency. The recommendations, if enforced, would amount to significant revisions of the original agreement.[79] In Belarus the news of Ukrainian ratification—despite the recommendations—added greatly to the case of the supporters of ratification. By a vote of 263 for, 1 against, and 2 abstentions, the Supreme

Soviet ratified the treaty and terminated Belarusian commitment to the 1922 union treaty. The only controversial issue concerned the disposition of the property of the Belarusian Communist Party, which, it was decided, should pass to the republic.[80]

Attention now turned to Ashkhabad, Turkmenistan, where President Saparmurad Niyazov was hosting the leaders of the Central Asian republics, at his initiative, for action on the Minsk agreement. The result was the signing of a joint statement and the completion of a draft agreement indicating the willingness of Kazakhstan, Kyrgyzstan, Tajikistan, Turkmenistan, and Uzbekistan to join the CIS. According to the draft agreement, all five republics were to be given the rights of founding members, equal to the Minsk three. The meeting for formal signing was scheduled for December 21 in Alma-Ata (Almaty), Kazakhstan, with approval by the republican parliaments to follow, bringing the agreement into force.[81] Having now become a strong supporter of the CIS—a significant change of attitude over the previous month—President Nazarbaev announced: "It's time that Gorbachev stopped intimidating the peoples by talking about inevitable war, famine, and territorial claims."[82]

The eleven republics participating in the Alma-Ata conference arrived at major agreements on the principles and structure of the new commonwealth. The principles included democracy and human rights, full sovereignty and equality of member states, and the preservation of peace and accord among nationalities. The commonwealth would be "neither a state nor a supra-state formation," and its members would share equally in its governance.

The members agreed to joint command of military-strategic forces and unified control over nuclear weapons, as well as the right of member states to opt for a nuclear-weapons-free status or that of neutral states. They also agreed that the commonwealth was open, with the members' consent, to accession by other former member states of the USSR and to other states sharing the "goals and principles of the commonwealth." Finally, they were committed to the formation of a "common economic space and of all-European and-Eurasian markets."

Such were the basic conditions of the commonwealth agreement signed on December 21. Four additional agreements were signed on December 23. One was a protocol of the conference that entrusted Marshal Yevgeny Shaposhnikov with the command of the armed forces until the completion of an armed forces reform plan, for which proposals would be reviewed by the heads of state.

The coordinating institutions of the Commonwealth of Independent States would consist of the Council of Heads of State and the Council of Heads of Government. It was agreed that Russia would be the successor to the USSR's UN and Security Council positions and that Russia would join Ukraine and Belarus in assisting other states of the commonwealth in securing UN membership. The commonwealth assumed responsibility for fulfilling the terms of all treaties and agreements of the former USSR.[83]

The completion of the meetings and agreements at Alma-Ata marked the end of the troubled and dangerous transition that followed the August Coup, and with it, the formal end of the Soviet Union. The new commonwealth included all but four of the fifteen republics of the former Soviet Union—Estonia, Latvia, Lithuania, and Georgia—although Georgia would join in 1993.

EPILOGUE

Due to the situation that has taken shape as a result of the formation of the Commonwealth of Independent States, I am ceasing my activity in the post of president of the USSR. . . . I have firmly advocated the independence of peoples and the sovereignty of republics. But at the same time I have favored the preservation of the union state and the integrity of the country. . . . A policy line aimed at dismembering the country and disuniting the state has prevailed, something that I cannot agree with.

—MIKHAIL GORBACHEV, SPEECH OF RESIGNATION AS PRESIDENT, DECEMBER 25, 1991[84]

Mikhail Gorbachev's retirement from the Soviet presidency elicited extensive commentary on his career in the Russian press, much of it justifiably complimentary and appreciative.[85] But the lines just quoted from his valedictory statement reveal his failure either to understand the role of nationalism in the demise of the Soviet Union or to appreciate the political skill with which Yeltsin had circumvented the bitter nationalist resentment inspired by the August Coup. Yeltsin had achieved peaceful transformation of the federal system before the formal termination of the USSR in December.

Gorbachev has repeatedly commented that the coup greatly complicated the task of saving the union treaty, which is obvious. What he has not acknowledged is that the coup was substantially the result of his own government appointments and policies and that it shattered any confidence the republican leaders might have retained that it was possible to build an authentic democratic federalism in cooperation with him and with the union center. The eagerness of the leaders of the national republics to quit the union after the coup was the consequence both of Gorbachev's foot-dragging approach to the restructuring of the union that preceded it and his appointment of officials who sought to crush the independence of the republics. His record rendered him incapable of leading the way to a new union treaty, leaving Yeltsin the formidable task of avoiding total political and economic collapse and rescuing the remnant of a federal system that was still achievable.

Gorbachev's assertion that he had "firmly advocated the independence of peoples and the sovereignty of republics" is extraordinary. His policies and his agents had consistently fought the nationalist movements and demands that emerged so powerfully in the closing years of his power. Although it is true that his policies of *glasnost'* and partial democratization in the republics had been crucial to the powerful upsurge of nationalist movements and their political demands, it is equally true that he either ignored or suppressed them. It was Yeltsin who recognized and worked with the nationalist leaders and whose leadership and credibility created the Commonwealth of Independent States out of the chaos that followed the collapse of communist power and the Soviet Union. Now that he had added the peaceful emancipation of the nations of a vast multinational empire to his defense of the Russian democratic movement in its moment of greatest peril, Yeltsin could turn his attention to the urgent needs of the newly independent Russian state.

This raises again the question posed by the quotation from Philip Taubman that opened this chapter, which suggests that the Yeltsin-Gorbachev conflict might have brought the overthrow of communist rule in 1991.

It is clear that the abortive August Coup precipitated the collapse of communist power. It is also clear that Yeltsin was a major target of the coup organizers, who perceived him as the central figure in a movement that would put an end to the power of the Party and the Soviet system if they did not acquire the special powers with which to suppress it. Gorbachev's own continual conflict with Yeltsin took place in a context in which he was attempting to prevent precisely the kind of decisive conflict between conservative communist and democratic forces that erupted in August. The conflict he most feared came after he accepted Yeltsin's plan for a new union treaty. Defenders of the traditional system rightly recognized that introducing a thoroughly democratic federal system would end the communists' monopoly rule and the Soviet Union. Hence, in this case it was Gorbachev's concession, rather than his resistance, that precipitated the denouement—though he had resisted the new treaty until the last moment and conceded only when confronted with a formidable demonstration of the power of the democratic movement supporting Yeltsin. Many previous statements indicating his disagreement with Yeltsin's plans to discard Lenin's 1922 union treaty, the socialist economy, and Party rule suggested that Gorbachev shared many of the views of Yeltsin's conservative opponents. Moreover, he had already broken with key members of his own impressive reform team—notably Aleksandr Yakovlev and Eduard Shevardnadze—whose ideas and leadership had been crucial to his previous reforms.

What mattered most in the prospects for continuing democratic reform following the failed coup was the independent organizational power and popular support that Yeltsin had built skillfully and courageously during the years following his initial conflict with Gorbachev. He had become the most powerful and influential reform leader in the country, and his strong base as popularly elected president of the Russian Republic enabled him both to lead the crucial movement for a new constitution and to thwart the coup attempt that it precipitated. His remarkable leadership skills, applied first to securing approval of the treaty by Gorbachev and the republics and then to blocking the coup, were subsequently applied to dismantling the Soviet central government and the ruling power of the Soviet Communist Party and to freeing the republics. He was able to accomplish these feats both because of the independent power and influence he had acquired before and since his departure from the Communist Party and because of his firm commitment to democracy and the sovereign right of self-determination of the nations of the Soviet Union. As president of a newly independent Russian state that had shed a vast empire, he would now face an eight-year test of his leadership skills and his vision of Russian transformation. His struggle to build a new Russia despite the legacy of seventy-four years of communist rule had just begun.

CHAPTER 2

THE POLITICS
OF REFORM,
1991–1999

FOLLOWING THE END OF THE SOVIET UNION AND THE FOUND-
ing of the new Commonwealth of Independent States, Yeltsin
and his colleagues turned their attention to the challenges of political and economic reconstruction within Russia. The tasks they set for
themselves—the building of democracy and a market economy—would have
been daunting under the most favorable circumstances, and the Russian situation was scarcely that. With the economy near collapse and the structures
of national and local administration in disarray, a sense of pending chaos
prevailed. The country's inherited constitution, with its weak executive powers and cumbersome legislative structure, was poorly suited to the demands
of radical reform, and in any case the political leadership lacked a basic con-

sensus on what those reforms should be and how to attain them. The building of a system of political parties had barely begun. Yeltsin faced much resistance to his plans for political and economic reform and widespread hostility over his role in dismantling communist power and the Soviet Union.

The eight years of Yeltsin's presidency of the new Russia would be dominated by a sustained and powerful effort to block the implementation of the plan he and his reform team offered for achieving a transformation to democracy and a market economy. The opposition, chiefly communist and nationalist, remained powerful until near the end of his leadership, succeeding in either blocking or crippling the major reform programs. Yeltsin's opponents even attempted a counterrevolutionary coup in 1993 and, in 1999, tried to impeach him and cancel the 1991 agreements granting independence to the republics of the Soviet Union. Yeltsin's successes in restructuring the economy and the political system despite such relentless and powerful opposition offer compelling evidence of the same skills and courage he had displayed as a political strategist and tactician in the democratic struggle before the communist collapse. Equally impressive was his tenacious and successful pursuit of constitutional reform and his willingness to confine the protracted and perilous struggle for Russia's democratic future to a constitutional framework providing for democratic parliamentary elections and an elective presidency.

FACING COMMUNIST OPPOSITION

From the beginning Yeltsin rightly anticipated strong communist resistance to his reform program and took steps—ultimately futile—to try to weaken the remnant party. He suspended the Russian Communist Party (RCP) on August 23, 1991, following with measures to close its buildings and force the dissolution of its local organizations. On November 6 he ordered the party banned.[1] But the decision was reviewed by the Constitutional Court under Valery Zorkin, and the court's decision of November 30, although it did not restore the property owned by the former Soviet Communist Party, did restore the local party organizations and legalize the party. Meanwhile, the leaders of the RCP, notably its head, Valentin Kuptsov, and its capable ideological secretary, Gennady Zyuganov, were busily engaged in rebuilding the party organization and seeking to return to the fold the several splinter groups that had formed in the pre-coup period and afterward.

Their efforts eventually produced a successful outcome at the Second Congress of the Communist Party of the Russian Federation (CPRF), as the RCP was now called, in February 1993. The party was organized to allow inclusion of the splinter communist parties, and its ideological positions were sufficiently broadly formulated to allow for an ideologically diverse but united party, now under the leadership of Zyuganov, working closely with Kuptsov. Zyuganov had rejected the positions of the more radical communists and temporarily limited their effect. At the other end of the spectrum, he had also excluded from the CPRF's options that of moving from traditional communism to social democracy on the model of communist parties in Eastern Europe.

The unification strategy had succeeded, bringing together the majority of Russian communists, roughly 450,000 in number, to form the strongest party in the Russian Federation. The future would bring frequent and serious conflicts with the leadership of the radical splinter groups, but the CPRF was now the center of power in Russian communism. Zyuganov had also made a broad appeal to nationalists, seeking their alliance with the CPRF membership both within and outside the Supreme Soviet. Communist-nationalist collaboration would soon be the major force in the powerful opposition to the Yeltsin reform program.

Thus began the tumultuous eight years of Boris Yeltsin's leadership of post-Soviet Russia, a period of building, with a deeply divided political leadership, a new state structure, a new political and administrative system, a new economy, and a new foreign policy. It would be a period of frequent and often fierce political conflict, one in which the Yeltsin government confronted recurrent political and economic crises, some with the potential for full-scale counterrevolution, generated both by problems with the reforms and by communist and nationalist resistance to their implementation and to Yeltsin's leadership. Remarkably, the period also brought the installation of a successful new constitution under which the country held three parliamentary elections and a presidential election. It then saw the voluntary early resignation of the president, followed by a second presidential election and a peaceful transition of power.

The crisis points would include an attempted coup by opposition parliamentary leaders in September-October 1993, a constitutional referendum and parliamentary elections in December 1993, the double challenge of resurgent communist power in the parliamentary elections in 1995 and the serious possibility of a communist victory in the presidential election of 1996, and a disastrous financial collapse in August 1998. All the parliamentary elections through 1995 produced an opposition majority, but the new presidential constitution introduced by Yeltsin in 1993—the constitution of the "second republic"—gave him the executive power needed to contain many of the opposition initiatives and continue the reform process. And despite unfavorable parliamentary election results in December 1995 and discouraging early poll results in the following months, Yeltsin was elected to an additional term of office against his communist opponent in July 1996. Just as he had been the key figure in the democratic leadership of the late Gorbachev era and in the months following the August Coup and the Soviet collapse, Yeltsin would continue to play the key decision-making role in Russia's postcommunist transition. Proving once again the firmness of his democratic commitment, he chose the course of early resignation in December 1999, confident that a promising successor and the parliamentary elections of that month, which produced a pro-government majority, held solid promise for the stability and extension of his reform achievements.

Throughout his crucial years of power, Yeltsin showed himself to be a sturdy advocate of democratic institutions and practices, even though he confronted recurrent opposition-dominated legislatures and, in the presidential election of 1996, the serious possibility of being replaced as president by a communist leader who intended to reverse his major reforms. His achievement has been widely underestimated, even though his tenacious pursuit of constitutional reform and commitment to democratic practice eventually produced a stable constitutional order despite the chaotic conditions of post-Soviet Russia. How this remarkable feat was accomplished is the special focus of this chapter.

BUILDUP TO AN INSURRECTION

None of the political crises of the Yeltsin era presented a greater challenge to the authority of the president and to his reform plans than the parliamentary rebellion of October 1993, an armed occupation of the Russian White House and attempted overturn of the president and his government mounted by radical communist and nationalist opponents. The action was the climax of eighteen months of conflict between Yeltsin and the leadership of the parliamentary bodies, the Russian Congress of People's Deputies and the

Supreme Soviet, that had begun early in his reform program and erupted in violence following his dissolution of both bodies on September 21, 1993.

Yeltsin's action followed many months of failed attempts at peaceful constitutional reform, by which he sought to build a foundation for an effective executive power and arrange elections for a new parliament. His aim was to escape a protracted and dangerous political impasse that not only blocked further progress of his reform program but also threatened a major reversal of it. His September 1993 decree dissolving the parliament and calling for a referendum on a new constitution and elections for a new parliament was a desperate effort to build a new political system that could provide stability, facilitate further reform, and enable the supporters of democracy and market economy to achieve their goals.

The response to the decree was a counterthrust by the parliamentary leadership, which sought to mobilize popular and military support to depose the president and seize political leadership. Neither popular nor military support for the insurrection was forthcoming, and Yeltsin defeated it as he had the 1991 August Coup. He then moved forward in December with a referendum on a new constitution and parliamentary elections that the leaders of the insurrection had rejected.

The events leading up to the October insurrection replicated many features of the period between the collapse of the autocracy and the Bolshevik Revolution in 1917. The ideological conflict and dual power of the president and the soviet organizations resembled the confrontation between the Provisional Government and soviets from March to November 1917. The armed rising against the Yeltsin government by parliamentary leaders recalled the Bolshevik October insurrection against the Provisional Government. It replicated as well the events of August 1991, when impending approval of a new union treaty, a constitutional reform of which Yeltsin had also been the architect and chief advocate, precipitated a coup attempt by conservative communist leaders. The October 1993 insurgents were determined both to end Yeltsin's reform program, which they had already used their legislative power to delay and weaken, and to seize control of executive power. Many of them spoke openly of their determination to "restore the Soviet Union." Their immediate goal was to block Yeltsin's plan for constitutional reform and new elections and to end his presidency.

The attempted coup was as dangerous to the cause of Russian democracy as the 1991 August Coup. Despite Yeltsin's sustained efforts at orderly and peaceful constitutional reform, his opponents had consistently blocked his efforts, portraying themselves meanwhile as defenders of constitutional order against despotism. The leader of the opposition to the Yeltsin government's policies—and later the key political figure in the October insurrection—was, together with Yeltsin's own vice president, Aleksandr Rutskoy, the chairman of the Russian Supreme Soviet, Ruslan Khasbulatov, who had been supported for that position by Yeltsin himself in October 1991.

A Chechen born in Groznyi (the son of parents exiled by Stalin to Kazakhstan during World War II), Khasbulatov had received a doctorate in economics from Moscow State University and later a professorship and Academy of Sciences candidate membership. He not only coveted the role taken by Yegor Gaidar, the prime minister, in leading Yeltsin's economic reform program but also rejected Gaidar's plan for rapid introduction of a market economy. His opposition to Gaidar's economic policy was intensified by his envy of the man who had received the ministerial role he coveted. He soon became the main opponent of both Gaidar and Yeltsin. Gaidar acknowledged him to be a formidable challenger: "For a long time my skepticism regarding Khasbulatov as an economist obscured the fact that here was a considerable political talent, one of the greatest to come out of the turbulent perestroika years. . . . Khasbulatov had some inner feel for the Stalinist methodology of power."[2]

CONFLICT OVER ECONOMIC POLICY

Much of the opposition to the government's reforms in the Congress of People's Deputies and Supreme Soviet between 1991 and 1993 came from deputies who opposed the wholesale dismantling of the socialist economic system. Both their opposition and their popular support were greatly magnified by Russia's economic dislocation at the time, particularly the severe inflation that accompanied the reforms, though the inflation was chiefly the result not of government actions but of those of the Supreme Soviet and the Central Bank. These actions included the giving of huge subsidies to state-owned enterprises, which created inflationary budget deficits, and the refusal to provide legislation on private property in land, effective taxation, and other institutions and policies required by a market economy. The economic problems of the transition derived less from flaws in the reform measures, as the opposition claimed, than from the burdensome legacy of the communist era and the disruptive actions of the Supreme Soviet and the head of the Central Bank, Viktor Gerashchenko.

In addition to Yeltsin himself, a major target of the parliamentary opposition, skillfully orchestrated by Khasbulatov with the assistance of Vice President Rutskoy, was Gaidar, the chief designer of the economic reform program. Yeltsin had boldly assumed responsibility for the reform policies by retaining leadership of the government through the initial stage of economic reform, but Gaidar became prime minister in June 1992, an office he held, under increasingly severe parliamentary attack, until he was replaced by a senior figure in the Russian energy industry, Viktor Chernomyrdin, in December. From April to December 1992 the parliamentary offensive against the president and his government steadily increased in severity and bitterness. Not only were major elements of the government's reform policy negated by new legislation, but Khasbulatov and the parliament sought increased power over ministerial appointments, and Khasbulatov's armed parliamentary guard was used to take control of the offices of *Izvestiia,* an independent newspaper supporting reform, in an attempt to make it an organ of the antireform parliamentary leadership. Speedy action from Yeltsin restored the newspaper's independence and disarmed the guard.

Yeltsin desperately sought compromise and cooperation with the Seventh Congress of People's Deputies, which convened on December 1, 1992, near the end of the first year of the reform program. He acknowledged the problems that had accompanied the reforms, promising financial support and tariff protection for troubled enterprises as well as reduction of inflation and a stable ruble. But he also affirmed the need for further reform measures, particularly privatization of land and of large enterprises. His effort to keep Gaidar in place by sacrificing two ministers and giving the parliament control of four key ministries proved a failure. He lost Gaidar despite his concessions and was obliged to replace him with Chernomyrdin, the senior manager in the gas production industry (Gazprom), who supported a far more conservative economic policy.

In the bargaining that preceded Gaidar's removal, the parliament approved continuation of the emergency powers with which Yeltsin had governed for the previous year and promised an April 1993 referendum on a new constitution, to be prepared by the legislature. The referendum commitment was soon repudiated, however, with the assertion that the extensive amendments to the 1978 constitution (amendments that required only a simple majority vote and already numbered several hundred) provided adequate constitutional reform. Yeltsin rejected this claim because the amendments had complicated rather than solved the constitutional crisis.

CONFLICTS OVER POLICY
AND CONSTITUTIONAL STRUCTURE

The Eighth Congress of People's Deputies, opening on March 10, 1993, annulled the Congress's December agreements with Yeltsin. Yeltsin then pressed in vain for agreement on constitutional reform. The ideological differences between him and the Congress of People's Deputies remained irreconcilable, and only the temporary special powers it had previously granted him had allowed him to continue reform. While the Congress argued, correctly, that the language of the 1978 RSFSR constitution (but not the Soviet-era reality that gave full power to the Party) made it the supreme power of the land, Yeltsin pressed for major constitutional change. He planned an April 25 referendum on four questions: whether Russia should be a presidential republic; whether the Congress of People's Deputies should be replaced by a much smaller, permanent, bicameral legislature; whether a Constituent Assembly rather than the Congress of People's Deputies would approve a new constitution; and whether Russian citizens would acquire the right to buy and sell land. The Constitutional Court promptly declared Yeltsin's decree on the referendum illegal, and a vote on the president's impeachment was scheduled for March 28 before an extraordinary congress.

When the Congress failed by 72 votes to secure the requisite two-thirds majority for impeachment, its leaders agreed to a referendum, but on its own set of questions: Do you trust the president of the Russian Federation? Do you approve of the policies carried out by the president and the government since 1992? Do you deem it necessary to hold early presidential elections? Do you deem it necessary to hold early parliamentary elections? They would soon regret their decision, for the April referendum results were favorable to Yeltsin. The vote of 49.5 percent for early presidential elections was positive for him (a majority vote in favor would have indicated that the electorate wanted to replace him) and stood in contrast to the 67.2 percent vote for early elections of people's deputies. The 53.3 percent endorsement of Yeltsin's social and economic policies was also encouraging, given the difficulties imposed on much of the population by the reform process, and it contradicted the opposition's claim of wholly negative public attitudes to the reform policies. One of the most encouraging signs of support for Yeltsin was the fact that in only fourteen of the eighty-nine members of the Russian Federation (the regional administrative divisions) was the idea of early elections for president more popular than that of early elections for deputies.[3]

Many of Yeltsin's supporters thought he should act quickly on parliamentary elections, arguing that the referendum had endorsed him and his policies. He chose instead to focus on the task of constitutional reform, because hard experience had convinced him that there was scant hope of effective government within the framework of the existing constitution. He would later write, "The Congress conceived by Gorbachev was . . . not even a parliament with all the attributes of such a legislative body." It was "filled with the former bosses of the Communist system," and "when you have fifteen hundred people in a hall, that's not a parliament or a senate but a popular assembly."[4] The Gorbachev-era electoral system had bequeathed continued domination by communists—the core of a problem that was compounded by the unmanageable size of the assembly and an ineffectual definition and division of executive and legislative powers in the constitution.

Much of the problem Yeltsin and his liberal reformers confronted indeed lay in the membership of the Congress of People's Deputies and the Supreme Soviet. Coming mainly from the *nomenklatura* at the time of their election to the Congress and the Supreme Soviet in March 1990, about 80 percent were communists, and most of these retained managerial posts. The 268 members of the Supreme Soviet (which made the basic decisions on economic and constitutional questions in its twice-yearly meetings), elected by the Congress, had responsibility for current political and legislative matters.

The membership of both bodies included substantial numbers of opponents of the aggressive economic reform program of Yeltsin's government, but this opposition was greatly magnified by the attitudes and policies of Supreme Soviet chairman Khasbulatov. As Richard Sakwa has observed, "The democracy that Khasbulatov defended in society at large appeared lacking in the operation of parliament itself." Leading democrats charged Khasbulatov with "authoritarian methods of rule and of issuing regulations that violated existing Russian legislation." The leaders of the reform coalition in the parliament, seeking Khasbulatov's resignation, criticized his "tendency to usurp the functions of the government" and noted that one of his leading associates, General Vladislav Achalov, had been implicated in the 1991 August Coup.[5] Yeltsin and Khasbulatov were both elected to top posts in the Russian parliament in May 1990, and they had worked together on many issues. Khasbulatov's break with Yeltsin was based on his firm opposition to the radical economic reform, and he played a key role in replacing Gaidar with the more conservative Chernomyrdin in December 1992. During the ensuing year his focus was on the struggle with Yeltsin over the introduction of a new constitution for the Russian Federation.

YELTSIN'S LONG EXPERIENCE IN CONSTITUTIONAL REFORM

To understand Yeltsin's choice of the course that led to protracted constitutional struggle and the political crisis of September-October 1993, it is helpful to recall his Soviet-era experience with constitutional reform at both the union and the republic levels. From the beginning of his presidency of the RSFSR in the spring of 1990 he had sponsored the proclamation of Russian sovereignty and had begun to organize a program of radical political and economic reform. By the following November he had mounted a major campaign for a new treaty for the federal system of the Soviet Union, a campaign that finally secured a new union treaty in July 1991—the destruction of which was the central purpose of the organizers of the August Coup.

Yeltsin's struggle for a new constitution for what would become the Commonwealth of Independent States aimed to give Russia and the other USSR republics effective control over their domestic affairs. A reporter's summary of his speech to the RSFSR Supreme Soviet on November 13, 1990, at the beginning of his campaign for a new union treaty, described his sense of Russia's problem: "The separation of functions between the center and Russia has not been officially recognized. There is constant *diktat* from the center, as in the case of the economic program and reform. Everything goes through the center, and the republic Supreme Soviet and government have virtually no real power."[6]

Yeltsin's campaign for a new union treaty continued for many months. The treaty reached the initial approval stage in April, and it was formally announced that it was complete and would be "open for signing" on July 23, 1991. It was during this process that he added a Russian Republic referendum on an elective presidency to Gorbachev's referendum on a reformed federal system. When the referendum on the presidency succeeded, Yeltsin arranged the implementing legislation, which was passed by the RSFSR Supreme Soviet in April and the RSFSR Congress of People's Deputies on May 22. The election that followed on June 12 gave 57 percent of the vote to Yeltsin in the first round against three competitors.

Before the vote on the Law on the Presidency in the Congress of People's Deputies, unsuccessful efforts were made to delay it, with the intention of blocking its passage. The character of the opposition to the law was indicative of the opposition to Yeltsin as president of the RSFSR and, later, the Russian Federation. The *Izvestiia* correspondent noted the strong opposition to the new presidency and to Yeltsin. Deputy S. N. Baburin, co-chairman of the reactionary Union of Salvation, called it "a betrayal of the constitution," and deputy O. Kazarov, chairman of the Ulyanovsk Province Soviet Executive Committee, argued that "a vote for a presidency in Russia and for B. Yeltsin . . . would be tantamount to voting for capitalism."[7]

Yeltsin's huge popularity, both in the results of the referendum and in the subsequent presidential election, revealed his wide public approval. But many prominent leaders in the Congress of People's Deputies and Supreme Soviet regarded him as a dangerous enemy, as did the organizers of the August Coup. For his part, Yeltsin advised the Congress that "the introduction of a presidency in Russia is not an end in itself but a means of implementing highly important reform-oriented decisions."[8] In sum, long before independent Russian statehood, the president had learned much, both about the strength of the opposition to his plans to transform the economic and political system and about the need for an effective presidential power to overcome it. Two years after the achievement of independence and the launching of his reforms, the evidence was vastly more compelling that new elections alone would not solve the problem. A new constitutional structure was essential.

Following the referendum, and encouraged by an outcome that indicated popular support for his reform program, Yeltsin returned to the struggle for a new constitution. The six months of that struggle were fraught with risk of severe conflict or even civil war. His management of the conflict was an impressive demonstration of his political acumen, tenacity, and courage. The main tasks were to achieve an effective relationship between the executive and legislative institutions at the national level and to integrate into the constitutional system a new structure of relations between the regional governments and the center, a task reminiscent of Yeltsin's earlier efforts on a new union treaty for the Soviet Union.

FOR AND AGAINST A PRESIDENTIAL CONSTITUTION

Yeltsin's original questions for the April referendum, rejected by the Congress of People's Deputies, had aimed to secure popular support for the structural principles of a new constitution. He recognized that without replacing the existing constitution with one that provided a functional parliament, a strong executive, and a clear definition of their respective powers, there was little hope of completing his ambitious economic reform program or of building an effective Russian democracy.

For the previous fifteen months the Congress of People's Deputies, and the Supreme Soviet that it chose, comprised a strong opposition majority whose leaders used all available means, including impeachment proceedings, to thwart and challenge Yeltsin's reform efforts at every step. His notion of a "presidential constitution" was one that combined a strong executive power with a democratically and directly elected parliament of manageable size. Both notions were clearly unacceptable to his opponents, who regarded the inherited Soviet constitution as providing for the political primacy of the Supreme Soviet, with the president as its executive agent. Their concept of the constitution ignored the change made by popular referendum in the spring of 1991, which had provided for Yeltsin's presidential election by popular vote rather than by the Supreme Soviet. Their aim was to assure parliamentary political domination over the executive branch, in order to strengthen their campaign against Yeltsin's reforms. This attitude was clear in Khasbulatov's statements and behavior in his parliamentary leadership role, though in his writing he claimed to support a relationship between executive and legislative power on the model of that of European democratic states.[9]

Yeltsin pursued his objective vigorously, issuing a decree on May 20 convening a Constitutional Conference, with its opening plenary session scheduled for June 5. Its membership included four representatives from every republic and region of the Russian Federation (two each from the executive and legislative branches of government), as well as representatives from labor and professional organizations and from political parties and movements. The conference membership totaled 762 delegates, and Yeltsin assumed its chairmanship.

The delegates were to focus their work on the president's draft constitution, reviewing it critically and proposing amendments. They were divided into five working groups: representatives of federal bodies of state power; representatives of bodies of state power within the Russian Federation (territories, provinces, autonomous regions, and the cities of Moscow and St. Petersburg); representatives of local self-government; representatives of political parties, trade unions, public organizations, mass movements, and religious denominations; and representatives of goods producers and entrepreneurs. The coordinators of these groups were to make up the working commission responsible for revising the draft constitution into final form by June 16. They were expected to examine, analyze, and vote on proposals and critical comments, with the aim of submitting five or six basic amendments to the plenary meeting that would conclude the conference's work, presenting to the president the finished draft of a presidential constitution, and suggesting procedures for its adoption.[10]

Even before the opening session it was evident that major conflicts would take place over the substance of the new constitution and the procedure for its approval. One pressing issue was the rights of the autonomous regions of the former RSFSR. Their leaders, noting that Yeltsin had given the Russian administrative regions the same representation in the working group as themselves, insisted on a higher status than that of the "Russian provinces." At a conference of soviets organized by Khasbulatov, the Bashkir deputy Damir Valeev, speaking for the delegates from Bashkortostan, Tatarstan, Yakutia, and Adygeia, argued that neither the parliamentary nor the presidential draft constitutions recognized their special rights.[11]

The demands of the ethnic republics elicited similar demands from Russian regions. Meanwhile, the ethnic republics' demands grew. Valeev also insisted that the ethnic republics should have their own tax and financial systems, as well as "the right of self-determination up to and including the formation of their own states."[12] Before long even Russian administrative units such as Vologda and Chita were talking of becoming republics. The challenges and perils ahead in the building of a stable and integrated Russian Federation were formidable. They would increase enormously when it became clear that Yeltsin intended to dismantle the hierarchy of soviets in the governmental structure and replace it with a new system of elective local government.

The opponents of Yeltsin's constitutional plans were busily organizing before the opening session of his Constitutional Conference, convening their own meeting on June 3, two days before the opening of the conference convened by the president.[13] At that meeting the Russian Communist Workers' Party and the Working Russia movement had their own draft constitution, prepared by people's deputy Yury Slobodkin. They had collected 1.09 million signatures for it. The Communists of Russia offered an independent but similar draft that upheld the soviet principle of governmental organization and abolished the institution of the presidency. Meanwhile, Vladimir Zhirinovsky and his Liberal Democratic Party proposed a strong presidency, the abolition of the existing federal system, and the replacement of the national territorial divisions (ethnic republics) by a structure of *gubernii* (provinces) for the entire country. They argued that acceptance of ethnic units in the federation would bring the disintegration of Russia.

The composition and attitudes of the opposition to Yeltsin's constitutional initiative at this alternative conference amply justified his decision to proceed independently in organizing and leading a presidential conference. Among its eighty-nine participating political parties and movements, the largest delegation (350 people) was from the extreme reactionary National Salvation Front. As a Russian reporter observed, such a group "didn't have to argue over adopting a decision on 'the criminal nature of the actions of the president of Russia, who is trying to push through his own version of the Basic Law by unconstitutional means,' or on reaffirmation of the soviet structure of government."[14] The advocates of such views would play a powerfully disruptive role in the months between the meeting of the president's Constitutional Conference and the attempted coup in October.

THE CONSTITUTIONAL CONFERENCE

Yeltsin's opening speech at the Constitutional Conference included a description of the historical context and aims of his constitutional reform plan.[15] He recalled, "A republic was proclaimed in our country on September 1, 1917, by a decree of the Provisional Government," but "the process of its formation was cut short by the October Revolution, which proclaimed a Republic of Soviets. Now a new republic is being born—a federal democratic state of the peoples of Russia." Noting the tradition of "free Novgorod and the reforms of Peter the Great and Alexander II [the *zemstva* and the judicial reform]," he argued that "a democratic state system is not contraindicated by Russia's traditions . . . [but] Russia has never had authorities that were bound by the law."

He also observed that "democratic law" had begun to emerge after August 1991, but the pace of democratic transformation had since slowed. He then made a statement guaranteed to alarm the vast army of beneficiaries of the political structure inherited from the Soviet era: "It eventually became obvious that the Soviet type of power does not lend itself to reform. Soviets and democracy are incompatible. The new constitution must clearly outline a fundamentally different method of organizing power. On this basis, and in the shortest possible time, this method must be implemented through elections at the federal level."

He assured his listeners that he did not intend "to take the route of forcibly overcoming the totalitarian legacy" but sought rather to deal with the "two dangers" that beset the country: the current political stalemate, with hostile confrontation between the legislative and executive branches, which would persist, and the "danger of drastic revolutionary actions." The ensuing analysis argued that the two-tiered legislative structure—the Congress of People's Deputies and the Supreme Soviet—maximized both dangers. A constitutional reform was imperative.

Yeltsin's arguments for convening the Constitutional Conference revealed a clear understanding of the nature and causes of the political crisis of the new Russian state and the need for a new constitution. He noted, "The operation of the two-tiered legislative structure, including the huge Congress and the smaller Supreme Soviet, nullifies the separation of powers and, at the same time, the idea of local self-government." He also observed that though it had been nearly three years since the Constitutional Commission of the RSFSR had published its draft of a new constitution (1990), and almost a year since the Sixth Congress of People's Deputies had approved its basic provisions, the leadership of the Supreme Soviet wanted no discussion of a new constitution and had rejected the president's proposal for a referendum on the Constitutional Commission's draft. Because the Supreme Soviet "had . . . rejected the draft of a new constitution that they themselves had approved," the president of the Russian Federation "was obliged to take the initiative in resuming the process of constitutional reforms." In effect, the new draft contained the essential provisions of the one that had been abandoned.

Immediately after the conclusion of Yeltsin's opening speech, parlia-

mentary speaker Ruslan Khasbulatov, interrupting the agreed-upon schedule of speakers, rushed toward the rostrum, demanding the right to respond.
He was given the floor, but his effort to speak was drowned out by clapping—
a technique often used in the Congress of People's Deputies to silence opponents. When Yeltsin tried unsuccessfully to stop the disruption, Khasbulatov
marched out of the hall, followed by seventy conference participants. He
delivered his speech denouncing the president and his Constitutional Conference on a staircase to a group of journalists.[16] The Supreme Soviet vice
chairman, Nikolay Ryabov, observed that "he should have been allowed to
speak so that people could have gained an understanding of the intrinsi-
cally confrontational and provocative nature of the Khasbulatov line."[17] Khasbulatov spelled out his thoughts in a speech to the Supreme Soviet a few
days later, attacking Yeltsin for his call for a new structure of representative
government to replace the soviets. He described the soviets as "the sole agents
who have the right to approve or disapprove drafts of the Constitution."[18]
Simply put, he was insisting that only the Congress of People's Deputies
had the authority to approve a new constitution, either independently or by
submitting its choice to a referendum.

Despite Khasbulatov's attitude and responses, Yeltsin sought both to secure
the return to the Constitutional Conference of delegates who had departed
the chamber with him and to work with Vice Chairman Ryabov to gain
effective cooperation with the Supreme Soviet in reconciling differences
between its constitutional draft and the president's. For this purpose he
convened a special plenary session of the Constitutional Conference on June
10. He also met with members of the Presidium of the Supreme Soviet,
including Ryabov and chairmen of parliamentary committees, in a session
that Ryabov described as aiming "to remove the suspicion and confrontational attitude that had come about between the president and some of the
deputies and soviets at the local level."[19] The announcement indicated that
the floor would be given first to Khasbulatov (Yeltsin reported that he had
ordered an investigation into the problems at the opening session a few days
earlier), and then other members of the Supreme Soviet would be given
opportunities to speak. The *Izvestiia* reporter acknowledged that Yeltsin had
taken "another step aimed at reaching a compromise that would ensure the
representative nature of the Constitutional Conference and the possibility
of arriving at a single draft of a new constitution."[20]

Khasbulatov did not attend the plenary session, and its attendees had time only to highlight unresolved issues confronting the remaining sessions of the conference. Yeltsin explained his earlier strictures on the soviet form of local government, arguing that the soviets "have combined within themselves normative monitoring and executive-administrative functions." This explained "their desire to supplant the executive bodies of power and their rejection of the separation of powers."[21] Other discussion focused on alternative models of relations between the central government and the governments of the federal units. Speaking as the representative of the Supreme Soviet, Ryabov stressed the need to develop a single draft and to agree upon a procedure for its adoption based on a consensus worked out with the participation of the members of the Russian Federation, the president, and representatives of the Supreme Soviet. Others argued that it would be better to follow the "Polish path" and concentrate on democratic election of a new parliament that would then be charged with preparing a new constitution in a more leisurely manner.

The distinguished Sergey Stankevich—historian, government advisor, and people's deputy—eloquently presented the latter option. He suggested, "The constitution that we can adopt now will most likely be a document . . . that will allow us to get through the bulk of the transitional period . . . in an organized fashion."[22] He noted several positive achievements in moving toward such a document: a promising dialogue between the regions and the republics, with the president serving as mediator and conciliator; the fact that "the idea of a strong presidency has been accepted in principle," though with limitations on the right to dismiss the parliament; and a general understanding of the need for an orderly transition to a new constitution.

There were, meanwhile, encouraging indications in mid-June of growing support for the Constitutional Conference and of dissatisfaction with Khasbulatov's negative line. A statement signed by a group of Russian Federation people's deputies announced their "support [for] the initiative of the president of the Russian Confederation in convening the Constitutional Conference . . . [and asserted that] the making of constitutional decisions cannot be the exclusive right of the Congress of People's Deputies." The statement took a clear position on the appropriate procedure for completing the constitution:

The work of adopting the draft constitution cannot be allowed to reach a deadlock in the Congress. We think that the draft constitution that is put into final form at the Constitutional Conference can be submitted to an extraordinary Congress of People's Deputies only by the president of Russia, who is the chairman of the Russian Federation's Constitutional Commission. As a preliminary step, the draft must be initialed by a majority of members of the Russian Federation. The Congress has no right to make any changes in the draft that have not been cleared with the president and the members of the Russian Federation.

The published statement was reported to have been signed by 315 deputies, though one of them reported that no more than 150 supported the final two sentences of the statement, which called for boycotting the Congress and having it dissolve itself.[23]

By mid-June it was evident that the inclusion of a substantial number of Supreme Soviet deputies from the regions of the Russian Federation had not only given them a voice in the deliberations of the Constitutional Conference but also encouraged them to support the president's efforts to achieve a new constitution. Writing about the representatives of the Federation and the prospects for their acceptance of the constitution, a journalist noted: "It is clear that the members of the Federation will support the person whose policy is stronger and who really possesses the initiative. Today the initiative is in the hands of the president."[24]

The inclusion of a sizable number of deputies and a large number of members of the Supreme Soviet was also an important element in validating the work of the conference. The presentation of the draft constitution for approval at a plenary session in the Kremlin Grand Palace on July 12 marked an important stage in the long effort to complete a new constitution. The president announced that five thousand amendments had been made to the draft presented on June 5 and that many experts, such as members of the European Commission for Democracy through Law, had given it a positive assessment. He argued that the extensive participation of deputies in the Constitutional Conference refuted the claims of some that it was a "presidential constitution." He was concerned about achieving agreement on a method of approval of the constitution and deeply worried about a major substantive issue that remained unresolved:

The only question that it has not yet been possible to resolve within the framework of the constitutional process is the status of the members of the Federation. Economic advantage is impelling territories and provinces to proclaim themselves republics. The task now is not to succumb to the temptation to republicanize the regions but to eliminate inequality, above all in the sphere of taxation and subventions. . . . overnight changes in state formations . . . could explode the still fragile framework of the Russian Federation.[25]

Yeltsin clearly hoped to eliminate pressure to "republicanize" (that is, acquire the special privileges of republics) in the provinces and territories by eliminating the discrepancies between them and the republics, especially in financial matters.

He faced as well the need for a law on elections to the new parliament. His preference was for action by the Supreme Soviet, but failing that he proposed to ask the members of the Federation to submit a proposal on a procedure for elections. He also proposed that the Constitutional Conference be made a standing body available for consultation on future constitutional issues—what a journalist called "an institution of a civil society . . . a public chamber."[26] At the end of the plenary session the president called for an immediate vote on the draft constitution prepared by the Constitutional Conference. Of the 585 delegates present, 433 (74 percent) voted yes, 62 (10.6 percent) voted no, and the remaining 90 (15.4 percent) did not participate.

The vote was encouraging except that the majority of the members of the conference from the republics had voted against approval. Despite this response, the presidential chief of staff, Sergey Filatov, expressed hope that within two months it would be possible to arrive at a draft acceptable to two-thirds of the members of the Federation, and that with their approval "the Congress's opinion would no longer be the basic factor."[27] Other optimists foresaw the possibility of converting the Constitutional Conference into a full-fledged Constituent Assembly, but the prevalent opinion was pessimistic both on approval by the republics and regions and on the feasibility of bypassing a Congress vote. The tax system and issues of separation of powers between the center and the republics were the major barriers to agreement with the members of the federation.

BLOCKING CONSTITUTIONAL REFORM

Even as Yeltsin and his colleagues reviewed their options, Khasbulatov, continuing his effort to block the president's constitutional reform initiative, convened in his office a meeting of seventy of the eighty-nine heads of the territory, province, and republic soviets, securing an agreement that the draft of the new constitution would have to be ratified by the soviets of all the members of the federation. With summer vacation already under way for many, it was clear that the requisite meetings could not be convened before October. And the probability of approval had been drastically reduced by "the territories' and provinces' race for the privileges of the former autonomous entities," which had now moved to the local level. The widespread resentment toward the special status of the republics was stated pithily by the chairman of the Irkutsk Province Soviet: "We are willing to leave them the attributes of statehood: a state language, citizenship, an emblem, a flag, and an anthem. But everyone must have equal powers."[28]

Aleksandr Kotenkov, director of the State Legal Affairs Administration, suggested a possible way out of the stalemate over constitutional approval. Following a compelling defense of the soundness of the draft constitution's treatment of federal-regional relations, he offered a plan for accelerating the approval process: "A Congress of People's Deputies must be convened without delay. True, it cannot be ruled out that attempts will be made to 'wreck' things through an article-by-article discussion of the draft. Then the next step would be a referendum on the basis of the president's right of legislative initiative and a demand by one-fifth of the deputies."[29]

Meanwhile, the Supreme Soviet pursued its own policy on the constitution. On July 16 it approved, on first reading, a Law on a Procedure for Adopting a New Constitution, which eliminated two of the methods still under consideration by the government (passage by a new parliament or by a constituent assembly) and allowed only two—acceptance by the Congress or by referendum. The referendum method was made more rigorous by requiring acceptance by 50 percent of all registered voters and two-thirds of the members of the Federation. From the government's viewpoint, an encouraging aspect of the session was the widespread disapproval of Speaker Khasbulatov's negative approach toward cooperation with the government and his disparagement of the Constitutional Conference's work. But the new law imposed serious constraints on the conference's future actions for securing approval of its constitutional plan. Khasbulatov was taking every possible measure to block approval of a constitutional proposal from the Constitutional Conference.

Equally discouraging for the conference and the president was the parliament's proposal to its Constitutional Commission that it continue work on its own draft constitution but consider "one more draft"—the draft approved by the Constitutional Conference on July 12. At the same time, opposition leader Vladimir Isakov detailed the parliament's priorities for constitutional reform—a procedure for adopting a new constitution and a mechanism for implementing the treaty that had created the Russian Federation—which matched those of the Constitutional Commission. It was proposed that Isakov join Oleg Rumyantsev and Nikolay Ryabov to serve with a joint working group of the parliament's Constitutional Commission and the president's Constitutional Conference. Throughout the discussions it was clear that Khasbulatov wanted no reconciliation with the government on the constitutional question. He repeated: "We must not give in. We have two drafts—a bad one and a very bad one."[30]

Khasbulatov's attitude and the planned system of review in the parliament virtually precluded parliamentary passage of the constitution submitted by the Constitutional Conference. The parliamentary resolution of July 20 was key. It provided that the parliamentary review would be prepared by the Constitutional Commission, chaired by Oleg Rumyantsev. The commission's draft constitution had received parliamentary approval in the spring of 1992. But though the Kremlin contended that its Constitutional Conference had incorporated the appropriate elements of that constitution in its own proposal, the parliament's position was the reverse: that the 1992 draft by the parliamentary Constitutional Commission was the foundation document. As one observer noted: "It is perfectly obvious that the fruits of the two months of debates in the Kremlin, collected in a folder called the 'agreed-upon' presidential draft, will be assessed by the parliament as a package of amendments to the official Rumyantsev draft, along with all the other amendments subject to 'consideration and generalization.'"[31]

This approach brought strong condemnation from deputy prime minister Yury Yarov, who described it as treating the president's Constitutional Conference draft as "some sort of raw material for processing."[32] To make matters worse, Khasbulatov had changed the review process in the parliament by creating a new Joint Committee on Constitutional Reform, headed by Isakov, one of the leaders of the reactionary National Salvation Front. The Joint Committee was given equal powers with Rumyantsev's Constitutional Commission. Khasbulatov aimed to seize control of the constitutional restructuring process from the president in order either to block the expansion of presidential power or—his long-time priority—to reduce it.

Yarov observed that the government might, in the end, choose to conduct a referendum on three alternative methods for securing a new constitution: approval by the existing parliament, by a new parliament, or by an elected constituent assembly. At the time, however, the only relevant events scheduled were the next plenary session of the Constitutional Conference in late August or September and an autumn session of the Congress of People's Deputies somewhat later.

Clearly, the conflict between the legislative and executive branches was moving toward a major confrontation over the pivotal constitutional issue. Unfortunately, Khasbulatov silenced parliamentary advocates of cooperation and compromise with the government. Vice chairman of the Supreme Soviet Ryabov commented in June on Khasbulatov's arbitrary removal of independent-minded committee chairmen, asserting that he had "cast off once and for all the mask of a democrat, which he has constantly been trying to pass himself off as, and essentially embarked on the path of establishing a dictatorship of personal power."[33]

As chairman of the Supreme Soviet, Khasbulatov had been a determined opponent of Yeltsin's major reform initiatives and had made a persistent effort both to reduce Yeltsin's presidential powers and to remove him from office. Threatened now with constitutional reform that would substantially increase the president's power, he was implacable.

YELTSIN RESPONDS TO THE CHALLENGE

The president was more than equal to the new challenge. Speaking to a group of media executives on August 12, he accused "a segment of the Supreme Soviet" of organizing a plan for "carrying out the directives of the second congress of the National Salvation Front aimed at abolishing the post of president, taming the legislators, and breaking up the reforms."[34] He stressed the attack on privatization and "the hyper-deficit budget adopted by the Supreme Soviet [which] would mean the collapse of the monetary system, the destruction of the ruble, and the undermining of Russia's entire state system." He emphasized as well the repression by "the parliament's bosses" of "dissidents throughout the system of soviets." He concluded with a stern warning: "Elections to a new parliament must be held this autumn, without fail. If the parliament itself doesn't make this decision, the president will make the decision for it."[35]

Meanwhile, Yeltsin continued his quest for a new constitutional structure, seeking to enlist the support of regional leaders. Speaking on August 13 to a meeting of the Council of Heads of Republics in Petrozavodsk, he called for formation of a new body of power—a Council of the Federation. The Council would consist of 178 members, two representatives (one from the executive and one from the legislative branch) from each of the Federation's eighty-nine members. He supported the idea of a joint meeting of the Constitutional Conference and the Constitutional Commission in September, because it might arrive at agreement on a transition-period constitutional law. "If we had such a law, we could hold new elections and resolve the situation of dual power that is tormenting the country."[36]

The proposal met a broadly favorable reception, and the participation by all the republics except Chechnya was evidence of the support for the president's initiative. Some of the heads of the republics expressed reservations, particularly about introducing the new body by presidential decree. They preferred the creation of a consultative body chaired by the president but possessing a broad mandate for dealing with problems of constitutional reform and the implementation of the federal treaty. The majority of delegates clearly welcomed the opportunity, as a reporter noted, "to become an alternative to the present parliament or at least to exert a strong influence on its activity." He also observed that "in Petrozavodsk the president succeeded once again in seizing the initiative from parliament, and his main task now is not to lose this initiative."[37] That the views of republican leaders on his constitutional plan were mixed was evident from the assertion of President Mintimer Shaymiev of Tatarstan that Yeltsin's constitutional plan was "unitary in content . . . [and] federal only in form." But Shaymiev represented the pinnacle of "autonomist" aspiration among the ethnic republics, and the later settlement with Tatarstan would require a unique bilateral treaty with Moscow.

Khasbulatov moved quickly to challenge Yeltsin's initiative at Petrozavodsk, convening the chairmen of the republic, territory, and province soviets in his own conference. Though he intended to keep the proceedings confidential and excluded the press, one of his dissident deputies described his aim as being "to neutralize and destroy all the positive results of the conference in Petrozavodsk."[38] His effort failed, largely because Yeltsin's plan for the Council of the Federation was widely accepted, especially because it included not just the heads of republics but also territory and province administrators and the heads of the soviets. At least one reporter was convinced that "the president has won the months-long struggle for the votes of the 'members.'" He argued that the federal treaty had created a treaty-based federation and that the members of that federation required a body representing their interests.[39] The question remained, however, how that body would fit into the constitutional structure and what its powers would be. The first clue was a proposal presented by deputy prime minister Vladimir Shumeyko, following Khasbulatov's failed conference, that the Council of the Federation be transformed into the upper house of a new parliament.

As the constitutional debate continued, the president repeated his plea for the Supreme Soviet to agree to new parliamentary elections, arguing that this was the only peaceful way to end a political stalemate that "is having a ruinous effect on the Russian state and is limiting the possibilities for constructive reformist activity."[40] As before, Khasbulatov offered no response to Yeltsin's appeal, though his vice chairman, Ryabov, suggested that the congress scheduled for November 17 could both adopt a new constitution and schedule elections for February or March 1994. Khasbulatov concentrated instead on the struggle against Yeltsin's constitutional reform plans, using a "Conference in Defense of the Constitutional System" dominated by opponents of the president to charge that Yeltsin intended to create "the very worst form of dictatorship" and was "acting like one of the early Bolsheviks."[41]

A key element in the background to the growing constitutional crisis, and in the president's eventual decision to take drastic action to get new parliamentary elections, was the protracted and extremely perilous crisis created by parliamentary opposition to the efforts of the minister of finance, Boris Fedorov, to secure passage of a financially responsible budget for 1993. The parliament's budget implied a 50 percent budget deficit, which Fedorov called "an almost unique phenomenon in world experience" that "threatened an economic collapse under the burden of hyperinflation."[42] In a press interview on August 23 Fedorov delivered a comprehensive critique of the parliament's handling of the current budget and its freewheeling expenditures on agricultural and industrial subsidies without legal procedures for repayment. He addressed the national crisis in nonpayment of debts, noting parliament's failure to support bankruptcy measures or measures to secure debt repayment. He also stressed the dangerous consequences of financial policies within the CIS ruble zone—the CIS states that retained the Russian ruble as their currency. He described it as "a zone in which one country indiscriminately provides facilitative credits to a dozen other states, in which $17 billion a year is pumped out of Russia, and in which our population pays for 'friendship' with a 25 percent jump in inflation."[43]

Concluding a brilliant review of the country's financial plight, Fedorov lamented that on the several occasions on which he had addressed the deputies he had found them "totally deaf to everything said by a representative of the government. . . . they are predisposed to reject everything completely. . . . The only way to resolve this conflict is to hold elections very soon."[44] Like the president, the finance minister had concluded that the country's deepening crisis was irresolvable without early parliamentary elections.

Meanwhile, Yeltsin continued his efforts to complete the combining of the constitutional proposals of the Constitutional Conference and the Supreme Soviet. On July 12 an agreement had been reached that all members of the Federation would have their soviets consider the draft constitution prepared by the conference. But only one of the forty soviet sessions planned for August had been held, partly because of the conflict with the vacation period but also because the Supreme Soviet immediately distributed to the soviets the draft constitution prepared by its Constitutional Commission, countering Yeltsin's plan to distribute a consolidated version of the two drafts.

ON THE EVE

Despite challenges and threats from Khasbulatov aiming either to compel his obedience or remove him, Nikolay Ryabov pressed ahead with the working group Yeltsin had created, which included representatives of the Supreme Soviet Constitutional Commission and the Constitutional Conference and was charged with combining the two draft constitutions.[45]

The work seemed to go well, and the group found positive elements in both drafts. They preferred the "Federal Structure" section of the "president's draft" but thought the "Civil Society" and "Citizens' Rights" sections of the Supreme Soviet draft, prepared under Oleg Rumyantsev, superior. They also decided to rewrite the "System of State Power" section "in order to find a compromise between a purely presidential and a purely parliamentary form of government."[46] Ryabov was hopeful of completing the work of the joint group by October 5, in order to present recommendations for discussion by the Constitutional Conference and the Constitutional Commission shortly afterward. Despite Rumyantsev's resignation from the group (attributed by one member to his "Jefferson syndrome"), prospects appeared favorable for a successful completion of the report.

During the final week before his September 19 dissolution of the parliament, Yeltsin's schedule included several events that were bound to influence his decision on resolving the constitutional conflict with the parliament. At his September 14 meeting with the Presidential Council, at which he presented his plan for "decisive actions," he was given full support for the position that "it is impossible to resolve the constitutional crisis by working with the present leadership of the Supreme Soviet."[47] The next day he met with a group of writers he had invited to the Kremlin. Among several eloquent appeals for action by the president, the words of A. Nuykin were representative: "We urge you, Boris Nikolaevich, not to become obsessed solely with constitutional matters in the search for a legitimate solution. After all, your opponents are past masters at bogging down any problems in endless coordination-and-agreement meetings. . . . It seems that the very idea of giving top priority to legitimacy has been skillfully imposed on us by those who themselves spit on it."[48]

Two days later the Supreme Soviet adopted a resolution "on the emergency situation in the national economy," calling for submission of the issue to the Congress of People's Deputies. It also discussed legislation dealing with the "criminal liability of executive branch officials for failure to carry out the parliament's decisions." As the *Segodnia* report noted, "instead of holding debates on the country's constitutional system, the Congress apparently will engage in replacing the government and limiting the president's opportunities to influence the country's domestic policy."[49]

Both Khasbulatov and Rutskoy carried the attack further at a September 18 meeting of chairmen of local soviets in the Parliamentary Center. Announcing that "there can be no compromise, no search for accord with the executive branch," Rutskoy asserted that "the president has never governed the country, and the leadership has been exercised by people directly subordinate to the [American] CIA." The head of the St. Petersburg City Soviet noted that the excitement of the speakers and the audience was because they "don't know what to do about Saturday's de facto founding of the Council of the Federation and Yeltsin's statement on agreeing to a presidential election."[50] Doubtless many members of the enthusiastic audience were inspired by Rutskoy's invitation to "re-create the Soviet Union."

Khasbulatov's speech accused Yeltsin of acting regularly under the influence of alcohol. He ignored Yeltsin's recent concessions, especially his willingness to discuss an early presidential election. Spreading alarm, he urged the soviet leaders to take up positions of armed defense throughout the country, charging that the president was preparing to introduce emergency rule. A reporter who covered the meeting noted that Khasbulatov had used unprecedented language in publicly insulting the president, for which "all the responsibility for the consequences will rest with him."[51]

Such was the immediate background to Yeltsin's decision to dissolve the Congress of People's Deputies and the Supreme Soviet and to hold, soon afterward, a referendum on a new constitution and simultaneous elections to the new parliament for which it provided. The action was one of the boldest and most important of his political career. That he was condemned and fought by the members and leaders of both bodies, and that they would have recourse to armed opposition, is scarcely surprising, though the criticism from Gorbachev and from liberal leaders such as Rumyantsev and Grigory Yavlinsky, as well as from many foreign journalists and scholars, did Yeltsin a great injustice. By September he had patiently and vainly tested every conceivable means of achieving a peaceful compromise with the parliament that would provide the executive power he needed just to defend his reform accomplishments, not to mention expanding them.

He had conducted a long and exhausting struggle for economic and political reform, against persistent parliamentary opposition and obstruction. Equally important, and often ignored by his critics, is that the Supreme Soviet—which he called "the parliament from another country" (the Soviet Union)—was headed by a relentlessly ambitious and authoritarian leader who had systematically silenced or removed opponents of his obstructionist policies within the parliament while espousing the view that the parliament was constitutionally the sovereign power, making the president merely the executive agent of that body's all-powerful chairman. Khasbulatov had made it clear that he would block all movement toward a functional constitution and that he would continue to sabotage the government's economic and other reform efforts. His clear aim was a personal monopoly of both legislative and executive power and total obstruction of Yeltsin's program of political and economic reform.

It was becoming increasingly clear how crucial Yeltsin's introduction of the elective presidency in 1991 had been. Without that change he would have been unable to take the vigorous initiatives that precipitated the 1991 August Coup and that enabled him to lead the ensuing peaceful dismantling of the power of both the Soviet Communist Party and the Soviet Union. But his experience with the Russian Supreme Soviet under Khasbulatov after Russian independence demonstrated that only a new constitution and new elections could provide the Russian president with the powers and the support to defend his reforms and move ahead with the large tasks remaining in building a Russian democracy and a functioning market economy.

To his great credit, Yeltsin sought constitutional change in cooperation with the Supreme Soviet for many months, with patience, imagination, and democratic commitment. By late summer 1993 it was apparent that his efforts were in vain. Khasbulatov was totally obstructionist and dedicated wholly to the expansion of his own power and drastic reduction of that of the president. The only constitutional change Khasbulatov would accept was one that gave the chairman of the Supreme Soviet the central executive power. He was engaged in a struggle with Yeltsin stunningly similar to that of Lenin with the Provisional Government under Prime Minister Kerensky in 1917, except that his was the role of counterrevolutionary, seeking a communist restoration, whereas Yeltsin, like Kerensky, sought to defend and extend a democratic revolution.

REFORM AND REBELLION

In the past few months, Russia has been going through a profound crisis of statehood. Literally all state institutions and political figures have been drawn into a fruitless and pointless struggle headed for destruction.

—BORIS YELTSIN[52]

Such were Yeltsin's words introducing his Decree No. 1400 of September 21, 1993, dissolving the Supreme Soviet and scheduling elections for a new bicameral legislature for December 11–12 of that year.[53] The elections were to be accompanied by a referendum on a draft constitution based on the work of the Constitutional Commission and the Constitutional Conference. The new parliament, the Federal Assembly, would consist of two houses—the State Duma and the Council of the Federation.

Part 3 of the decree provided for interim arrangements until the scheduled December elections and adoption of the new constitution. Regulation of the federal bodies of power was to be based on the statute "On Federal Bodies of Power during the Transitional Period," derived from the draft Russian Federation constitution approved by the Constitutional Conference on July 12, 1993. The Council of the Federation was invested with the functions of a chamber of the Russian Federation Federal Assembly, its powers to become effective after the December elections. Elections to the lower house of the new parliament, the State Duma, were to be based on the statute worked out by the Russian Federation people's deputies and the Constitutional Conference, with elections in December. The question of election for president of the Russian Federation was deferred to the meeting of the Federal Assembly.

Though the powers of the representative bodies of the members of the Russian Federation were preserved, the decree provided that no meetings of the Russian Federation Congress of People's Deputies were to be convened and that the powers of that body were terminated. The Constitutional Court was instructed "to convene no meetings pending the beginning of work by the Russian Federation Federal Assembly." The Central Bank of the Russian Federation was to be guided by presidential decrees and government resolutions and accountable to the Russian Federation government "pending the beginning of work by the Russian Federation Federal Assembly."

The concern with assuring foreign governments of the democratic purposes of the decree was evident in the statement that "the holding of elections to the State Duma of the Russian Federation Federal Assembly is dictated by a desire to preserve democratic transformations and economic reforms . . . in keeping with the principles of the Russian Federation's constitutional system, above all the principles of people's rule, the separation of powers and federalism, and is grounded in the will of the Russian Federation's people as expressed in the referendum of April 25, 1993."[54]

Yeltsin delivered his speech on national television from the Kremlin. At the time, most of the parliamentary leaders and fifty to sixty deputies were present in the White House. The vice chairman, Yury Voronin, announced that a coup had occurred. Aleksandr Rutskoy announced that he was assuming the duties of the president, who had forfeited his office by an unconstitutional action, and that he would make a public announcement on TV, though that proved impossible when it was learned that the communications equipment in the building had been switched off.[55] Ruslan Khasbulatov made his first formal announcement at a press conference soon afterward: "An outright coup d'état has been staged. The initiator and perpetrator of this coup was Russia's former president, Boris Nikolaevich Yeltsin."[56]

He appealed to soviets across the country to meet and review the events in Moscow and to support the Supreme Soviet "in the struggle against the putschists," and he urged servicemen and members of the police and security agencies to ignore orders based on the president's decree. He also announced that Yeltsin was bringing troops to Moscow and that the Supreme Soviet was planning its defense. His final appeal was for all Russian Federation deputies to come immediately to Moscow for an extraordinary congress. Khasbulatov announced the appointment of General Achalov as commander of the White House defense. The head of the Constitutional Court, Valery Zorkin, appeared at the press conference to announce that the court was beginning discussion of Yeltsin's action.

An extraordinary session of the Supreme Soviet was convened shortly after midnight on the morning of the twenty-second. Its first action was to pass a resolution terminating the powers of President Yeltsin, after which Rutskoy took the oath of office as president and then read a decree declaring Yeltsin's September 21 decree invalid. Shortly afterward, Valery Zorkin presented the decision of the Constitutional Court that Yeltsin's decree and his television address contradicted the constitution. The Supreme Soviet also approved new leaders for the "power ministries"—Defense (General Achalov), Security (Viktor Barannikov), and Internal Affairs (Andrey Dunaev in an acting capacity).

The reaction of the military leadership to the new appointments was quick and firm. A few hours after the announcement, General Grachev conferred with the deputy ministers of defense and the commanders of arms and branches of the service. He also met with the commanders of the military districts, fleets, and individual arms. All confirmed their loyalty to Grachev and the president. Grachev's characterization of his proposed replacement was to the point: "Colonel General Achalov is an extremist who is taking up arms without thinking. He is guilty of bloodshed in Vilnius, Tbilisi, and Central Asia, and he tried to unleash a civil war in Moscow in August 1991."[57]

The parliamentary leadership's attempt to gain control of Central Bank policy also failed. The bank's chairman rejected the Supreme Soviet decree of September 22, which claimed control over financial operations of the bank and ordered it to suspend the financing of executive bodies of power on the grounds that the bank reported to the Ministry of Finance and its chairman was a member of the Council of Ministers. The chairman's support of the government suggested the wisdom of Chernomyrdin's rejection of Yeltsin's proposal to replace him.[58]

As the confrontation between president and parliament intensified, Valery Zorkin presented a significant proposal for compromise. He began by noting that although the president's decree "does not conform to the Russian Federation Constitution . . . I share the assessment of the situation in the country and in the top echelons of state power that were given in the decree's preamble, as well as the goals that the president is setting for himself." He proposed a procedure for escaping the confrontation between the executive and legislative branches of government by agreeing to early, simultaneous presidential and parliamentary elections and establishing an arrangement for the transition using the existing cabinet and president as the executive and the Supreme Soviet as "the guarantor of observance of legality during elections." He proposed using the Constitutional Court as the "guarantor of the agreements that are reached [between president and parliament]."[59]

By the time Zorkin made his proposal, on September 22, there was scant hope of such negotiations between the parties to the conflict. Moreover, Yeltsin had previously objected to simultaneous presidential and parliamentary elections, fearing the danger of a political vacuum without continuity of executive power during the constitutional transition.

REACTIONS OF "OUTSIDE OBSERVERS"

Among political party leaders, the president's decree was divisive, and it received support only from democratic parties and movements such as the Party of Economic Freedom and the council of the Democratic Russia movement. Even among democrats, support was not unanimous, and members of the Republican Party and the Social Democrats criticized the decree. Parliament leaders seized upon the dissent in the democratic camp, seeking endorsement of a condemnation of the president's actions by public groups and political organizations and managing to bring together such unlikely bedfellows as the Russian Social Democratic Center, the National Salvation Front, and the Federation of Independent Trade Unions. Traveling in Italy,

Mikhail Gorbachev gave an interview condemning the unconstitutionality of the decree and insisting that Yeltsin was seeking a "pocket parliament" when instead he should schedule simultaneous parliamentary and presidential elections.[60] Meanwhile, one of the most respected of Russian democratic leaders, Grigory Yavlinsky, while acknowledging the illegality of the president's decree, also condemned the parliament for "trying to develop dual power no longer in the form of political rhetoric but in real actions." He warned, though, that the new constitutional structure "could be a continuation of Russia's permanent crisis."[61]

The regional political response within the Russian Federation to events in Moscow reflected two main factors. One of these—negative for the president—was the recognition that the abolition of the power of the national soviet bodies would be duplicated in the regions. Only those province and territory soviets seeking the status of the national formations— and counting on Yeltsin's support—endorsed this policy.[62]

On the other hand, Yeltsin could take much satisfaction from the positive reaction that came from the "near abroad"—the CIS. Only three days after the publication of Decree 1400, he hosted a long-scheduled meeting of the leaders of the CIS states in the Grand Palace of the Kremlin, a meeting he regarded as highly congenial and unusually productive. During it he received the consistent endorsement of his policy from fellow heads of state, though "their assessments of the former Supreme Soviet were hardly expressed in diplomatic terms."[63] They had not forgotten Yeltsin's role in their achievement of independence or missed the statements by his political opponents about restoring the Soviet Union.

THE PARLIAMENTARY REBELLION

As Yeltsin acknowledged in his memoir, he was utterly unprepared to deal with the armed rebellion organized in the White House within a few days of the dissolution decree. Having failed to prevent occupation of the White House by many of the deputies, he was soon confronted with both the pretensions of an alternative government and an effort to mount an armed coup d'état. His reckoning had been that Khasbulatov and Rutskoy were deluded by the belief "that all they had to do was give one push and everyone in the country would dash after the Communist Bolshevik parliament as it retreated into the past."[64] Certainly he was right about the lack of response to parliamentary appeals to the military, to workers, and to other groups, but he soon confronted a militant White House leadership, heavily armed and determined to launch attacks on key buildings and institutions in Moscow in a manner consciously modeled on the Bolshevik coup of October 1917, whose organizers had tried their first armed takeover of a government building on September 23. Hoping to avoid violence, he had arranged for police carrying only truncheons to surround the White House, confident that the problem would soon disappear. The White House leaders were given a deadline of October 4 to surrender their arms, and negotiations for a settlement were held at the Danilov Monastery with the cooperation of Patriarch Aleksy II.

The events of Sunday, October 3, would shatter the complacency of Yeltsin and his government. In his morning meeting with the Council of Ministers he had reviewed the political situation in Moscow, but with no discussion of the possible use of force in the event that the arms in the White House were not surrendered. Yeltsin's hope was that the deputies would soon recognize that their action was futile and that they were meanwhile missing opportunities to prepare for the forthcoming parliamentary elections. His hope was shattered only a few hours after the meeting when he received a call at home informing him of breakthroughs on the police cordons around the White House, the storming of the mayor's offices, and a large-scale attack on the Ostankino Television Center. It would soon become clear that the anti-Yeltsin element in the parliament had won support in the military, including that of two generals who helped organize armed resistance to Yeltsin's changes both outside and inside the White House.

Yeltsin returned by helicopter to the Kremlin for urgent discussions with his colleagues. Minister of Internal Affairs Viktor Yerin informed him about the collapse of police control around the occupied White House and elsewhere, but Defense Minister Grachev assured him that troops would soon arrive in Moscow, both to support the police and to conduct other emergency operations. From Ostankino came reports of rebel gunmen equipped with grenade launchers and armored personnel carriers breaking into the building, gaining control of studios, and cutting off TV channels. In addition to dealing with the immediate crises, Yeltsin took measures to introduce a state of emergency in Moscow, including special powers for the police. But the interior police forces were inadequate, and there was still no sign of the troops Grachev had promised. The situation had become very dangerous.

Such were the developments that inspired a plan for an attack on the White House and its occupants. The bold plan was suggested to Yeltsin by an assistant to one of his colleagues, and he later expressed gratitude for it, feeling that it had been the only effective option for dealing with an armed insurrection. The plan called for using ten tanks to deliver a decisive blow to the armed defenders. The Collegium of the Defense Ministry reported full support for the president from the troops. By late evening on the third, military control had been restored around Ostankino, and a crowd of several thousand had assembled at the Moscow City Soviet in response to Yegor Gaidar's televised appeal for support of "the president, the government, and democracy."

The attack on the White House early the following morning, October 4, with tanks firing on the building, was the centerpiece of the Yeltsin government's offensive. At noon the defenders requested a cease-fire but would not agree to surrender their weapons in advance. Soon the top floors of the building were burning and large numbers of wounded were being evacuated. By early evening the last of the defenders had surrendered and been sent on buses to Lefortovo Prison. The first bus carried Khasbulatov and Rutskoy; the second, short-term ministers and the commander of the White House defense, Albert Makashov, who had earlier promised harsh revenge against deputies who refused to join the attempted coup.

A PERSPECTIVE ON OCTOBER 1993

In the years since the October events, they have been much discussed by Russian politicians and by Russian and foreign journalists and scholars. Even in the last year of Yeltsin's presidency, his parliamentary opponents included "shelling the White House in 1993" in the list of impeachment charges on which votes were conducted. Predictably, the Communist and Agrarian Parties voted unanimously in favor of the charge, as they did on the other four charges, but the impeachment effort failed.[65] Nearly six years after the events of October 1993, the communists were seeking again to remove Yeltsin and replace him with their "own" presidential choice, this time prime minister Yevgeny Primakov. As in the 1996 presidential election challenge by Gennady Zyuganov, they failed. The episode demonstrated both Yeltsin's political skill and the solidity of the political system he had put in place after crushing the parliamentary insurgency of 1993.

Another way of viewing the clash with the parliament is to compare it with the events of the 1991 August Coup, but not in the way in which Yeltsin's parliamentary opponents of 1993 did, equating his actions and intentions with those of the reactionary coup leaders of 1991. The 1991 August Coup and the October insurrection were efforts to halt and reverse the government's reform policies. In both cases Yeltsin had the central role in the reform process, and the immediate issue precipitating the conflict was that of a constitutional reform he had initiated. In 1991 the constitutional reform issue was the new union treaty, of which Yeltsin had been the chief advocate. Recognizing that its passage would vastly reduce the power of the union government and replace subservient republics with sovereign, democratically ruled members of an authentic federation, the conservative communist opposition decided to strike.

Similarly, in 1993 the attack on the government was precipitated by Yeltsin's decree dissolving the existing parliament and announcing plans for a new constitution and democratic elections to break a protracted and dangerous stalemate in the reform effort. This action inspired the effort of Khasbulatov and Rutskoy to remove the president and maintain the existing constitutional order—an effort that included armed resistance and an appeal for mutiny in the army. As in 1991, Yeltsin was the leading advocate of constitutional reform and new elections and had already been engaged in many months of persistent and patient efforts to achieve them by peaceful cooperation with his implacable opponents. Another similarity between the two events was that Yeltsin was the key defender of the reform process against an effort at counterrevolution.

In October 1993 the public did not experience the joyous feeling of victory that had prevailed in 1991, but many polls indicated strong public support for Yeltsin's action. One such poll, asking whether the president or the Supreme Soviet had been wholly or mainly responsible (two categories) for the bloodshed in Moscow on October 3–4 found 53.5 percent blaming the Supreme Soviet and 3.5 percent blaming Yeltsin. (None of the parliamentary deputies had been killed, but as many as 178 other people had died and about a thousand had been injured.) Equally significant was the response on the transition to market reform, which gained a 63 percent endorsement, as opposed to a mere 6 percent who favored the previous system of economic management.[66]

Another similarity between the two situations was that once the crisis passed, Yeltsin followed through with major reform initiatives—the peaceful dismantling of the Soviet Union and communist rule in 1991 and the completion of a new constitution and scheduling of a constitutional referendum and parliamentary elections in 1993. By any serious measure the "first republic" (1991–93) had failed as a political structure by the autumn of 1993, and Yeltsin's bold move to replace the Soviet-era Congress of People's Deputies and Supreme Soviet was badly needed. Public opinion polls agreed. The ensuing ten weeks would be dominated by efforts to complete a final draft of the new constitution, form the new structure of political parties, and prepare for the December elections. It was a period of intense activity and major decisions rivaling in importance the events of the autumn of 1991.

As in the aftermath of the August Coup in 1991, Yeltsin lost no time in implementing his plans for Russia's future. Simultaneous voting on a new constitution and elections for the new parliament were scheduled for December 12. The presidential decree of October 15 announced that the new constitution would be the one approved by the Constitutional Conference and that it would take effect with the announcement of the results of the vote.[67] While Russia's political leaders rushed to prepare for the December elections, the government worked intensely at defining the regulations for electoral participation of parties and individuals and at refining the constitution that would be presented in the December referendum. Yeltsin's diligent efforts on constitutional reform would bring abundant benefits, demonstrating once again the importance of his understanding of the crucial role of the constitutional question in Russia's future.

THE NEW CONSTITUTIONAL ORDER

In a television address on November 9 the president offered his view of the importance of his proposed constitution: "Today it is clear that if a new constitution had been adopted in time we would have been able to protect democracy without resorting to extreme measures. We have had to pay a high price for the lack of a democratic constitution. With its adoption we will gain a powerful tool for solving the most crucial problems in the state and society."[68] Yeltsin's decisions on the content of the new constitution and the method of its ratification would have a great effect on both the short-term political transition and the long-term political achievements and stability of the second republic. It is instructive to review his motives for those decisions.

The method of ratification he chose—popular referendum—was criticized by both democratic and nondemocratic politicians. The suggested alternative was to hold elections for the new parliament and give that body responsibility for approving the new constitution. Yeltsin obviously shared the view of a member of the Constitutional Commission that there was no guarantee that "the new parliament will not repeat the unfortunate experience of its predecessor, dragging out the adoption of the basic law for a prolonged period . . . the shortest path to a repetition of tragedy."[69]

The results of the December parliamentary elections would amply confirm Yeltsin's misgivings about the constituent assembly proposal. The communists and their Agrarian Party allies had great strength in the newly elected State Duma and remained fierce opponents of the new constitution. During the constitutional referendum the communists would even manipulate polling regulations to weaken its chances of approval in rural areas, later claiming falsely that the government was guilty of fraudulent practices in the referendum polling. They also sought to organize a parliamentary vote to convert the newly elected parliament into a constituent assembly to revise the newly approved constitution, arguing that it was imperative to "put the executive branch under the control of the legislative branch."[70] Yeltsin responded by pointing to the distinguished and broadly representative membership and intensive work of the Constitutional Commission. When he announced the date for the referendum on the new constitution, he explained that the version submitted to nationwide vote would be "the draft constitution of the Russian Federation that was approved by the Constitutional Conference."

Yeltsin continued to stress the importance of a clear separation of executive, legislative, and judicial powers, and the constitution was thorough and effective on this issue. Critics insisted that he had given the president supremacy over the legislature. The evidence offered for this charge began with the procedure for appointment of the chairman of the government (the prime minister). The president was required to submit his nomination to the State Duma, and if three nominations were rejected he could dissolve the Duma and schedule new elections (Article 111). The president also possessed the right to dismiss the government or to refuse a proffered resignation. The Duma could vote no confidence in the government by majority vote, and the president could choose either to dismiss the government or not. In the event of a second vote of no confidence within three months, the president could either dismiss the government or dissolve the Duma. The president was also given the right to request a vote of confidence from the Duma, and if the vote was negative either to dismiss the government or dissolve the Duma and schedule new elections within seven days (Article 117).

Clearly Yeltsin was determined to avoid the repetition of two of his major problems during the first republic: the parliament's insistence on cabinet changes under threat of withdrawal of all legislative cooperation and the parliamentary leadership's efforts to usurp control of government personnel and policy. These problems had created the crisis of dual power that blocked or severely constrained the government's reform policy initiatives. Yeltsin was well aware of the continuing sharp divisions between the various factions of the Russian political leadership and the widespread opposition that remained to his efforts to build a market economy and democracy. He was also convinced that the membership and policy of the executive branch must be separate from those of the legislative branch, an arrangement that only a presidential constitution could provide.

Later events would more than justify his choice. On several crucial occasions the opposition's fear of his using the constitutional prerogative of dissolving the Duma and calling a new election would serve him well. The results of the December elections would also confirm the wisdom of his choice of a presidential as opposed to a parliamentary constitution. Given the irreconcilable differences still separating the main groups of the Russian political leadership at that stage of the postcommunist transition, an opposition-dominated parliament whose majority controlled the government might well have created an even worse situation than the one that produced the October 1993 crisis.

THE REGIONS AGAIN

The draft constitution also sought to settle the complex issues connected with the claims of the republics of the federation for special status, claims that had already engendered competitive pursuit of special status by some Russian regions. Article 5 listed the categories of members—republics, territories, federal cities, an autonomous province, and autonomous regions—and then described them as "equal members of the Russian Federation." It was noted that the republics had constitutions whereas all other members had charters, but "in relations with the federal bodies of state power, all members of the Russian Federation are equal among themselves." The absence of any mention of the 1992 federal treaty in the draft constitution and of acknowledgment of the special status of the ethnic republics was sharply criticized by republican leaders.

In an early November meeting with the heads of republics and regions, Yeltsin explained his choices. The federal treaty would continue to exist as a legislative document alongside the constitution. He rejected the demand for recognition of republic sovereignty, explaining that this would mean a confederation, not a federation, adding, "I support the right of nations to self-determination, but I rule out secession from Russia."[71] Yeltsin later accepted a proposal from the Karelian leader, Viktor Stepanov, that all members of the federation be described as sovereign, but with full recognition of the sovereignty of the federation. Another concession provided for election of the members of the upper chamber of the first Federal Assembly, with the regional power structures acquiring the right to form their own delegations subsequently.

Throughout the troubled transition of 1993 Yeltsin had demonstrated political skill in controlling extravagant demands by the ethnic republics and some of the Russian regional leaders and simultaneously winning their support in his struggle with the parliamentary opposition. He now faced a challenge to the formation of an effective federalism within the new constitutional structure—granting sufficient authority to the regions to maintain their support without jeopardizing the integrity of the federation.

In exchange for his concessions, Yeltsin gained acceptance of the right of ministers who got into parliament to retain their ministerial positions. A reporting journalist noted that Yeltsin's compromises "do not call in question the possibility of attaining the set goal—conducting a decisive reform in the country while preserving, or more precisely, restoring sufficient legitimacy for the authorities."[72]

The chief administrator of Sverdlovsk Province, Eduard Rossell, who published the "Constitution of the Urals Republic" in the local newspaper and followed it with the proclamation of the republic on October 3, presented another challenge to the new constitution. The climax of a process begun the preceding April, the project received nearly unanimous endorsement by the Sverdlovsk Province Soviet on October 27. Presidential advisor Sergey Stankevich rejected the move. While accepting that it was "reasonable to retain elements of the state attributes of the republics, which have their own traditional character," he described the appearance of the Sverdlovsk Republic as "the last act in a parade of sovereignties that in fact covered up the redistribution of property and power by regional elites to their own benefit at a time when a weakened federal center was caught up in a prolonged and self-destructive conflict with a pseudo parliament."

One of the leaders of the Party of Russian Unity and Accord, which strongly endorsed federalism as the essential foundation of the postcommunist Russian state, Stankevich was prepared to consider the introduction of something like the German *Länder* in the form of groupings of Russian provinces at some future time. But "both they and the republics must accept a ban on secession, the priority of federal over local legislation, and guarantees against unilateral revision of powers assigned to the lands and republics by mutual agreement."[73]

THE NEW PRESIDENCY AND PARLIAMENT

Clearly Yeltsin had remained firmly committed to the concept of a presidential constitution, and the draft constitution submitted for approval in December was precisely that. Elected for a four-year term, the president would act through a cabinet he named, albeit with the Duma retaining the right of approval (with the constraints indicated earlier) of his choice of prime minister. He would also have a presidential administration to conduct his daily business, its head occupying a position comparable to that of the US president's chief of staff. He would have the right of legislative initiative and the power to issue rules and decrees consistent with the constitution and laws of the federation. He would have the right of appointment of the vice chairman of the government and the heads of the federal ministries (on the advice of the prime minister) and would present to the Council of the Federation candidates for the Constitutional Court, the

Supreme Court, the Higher Court of Arbitration, and the position of prosecutor general. He would appoint judges of other federal courts, diplomatic representatives of the country, and the supreme commander of the federal armed forces.

The president could be removed from office (Article 93) for "high treason or the commission of another grave crime." The action would have to be initiated by at least one-third of the deputies to the State Duma, on the basis of a finding by a special commission formed by that body. It would also require a finding by the Russian Federation Supreme Court on the elements of a crime in the president's actions and a finding by the Constitutional Court that constitutional procedures were observed, as well as a two-thirds supporting vote in both houses of the legislature. The entire process following the bringing of the accusation would be limited to three months, after which time the accusation would be considered to have been dropped. Impeachment initiatives against President Yeltsin were attempted, but always unsuccessfully. The charges, most notably in the final impeachment attempt in May 1999, were more a reflection of political differences and aims than a meaningful application of the sorts of charges implied in the language of the constitution.

The president was to be elected for a four-year term, with a limit of two terms. There was no vice president, the provision being that the prime minister would substitute for the president when he was temporarily indisposed and that the prime minister would replace him in the event of death or full incapacity, scheduling an election for a new president within three months.

Yeltsin initially yielded to pressure to accept a new presidential election in June 1994, but he repudiated that agreement in early November, opting to serve out his term, which would end in June 1996.[74] For his supporters, deeply fearful that the executive branch might fall to communist control, the decision brought great relief. When the proposal for simultaneous parliamentary and presidential elections was first made the previous September, one supporter expressed their view: "President Boris Yeltsin is a transitional figure; when any real danger of a return to communism disappears in Russia, he will no longer be needed as president. Then the post-Yeltsin era will begin. The president has proved that he is a guarantor against the restoration of communism. Today, he is the only guarantor."[75]

The proposed changes in the structure and membership of the legislature and in the legislative procedures of the new constitution were equally significant. The introduction of a bicameral legislature was a major structural change, providing additional review of legislation and representing the perspectives and interests of the numerous and greatly varied members of the federation. The lower house, or State Duma, was to be a body of 450 elected members. The upper house, the Council of the Federation, was to be elected in the first round of elections, after which the system would change to one in which each of the eighty-nine regional governments would name a delegate from its legislative and executive branches, providing a membership of 178 delegates in that body. Each house would elect its own chairman and vice chairman.

In mid-October Yeltsin issued a decree (no. 1661) titled "On Certain Measures to Ensure State and Public Security during the 1993 Election Campaign."[76] Its aim was to deny participation in the forthcoming elections to public associations that had "provoked and organized the armed rebellion in the city of Moscow on October 3–4, 1993." It denied electoral participation as associations or parties to organizations such as the National Salvation Front, the Russian Communist Workers' Party, the Russian Young Communist League, and Russian National Unity. It also excluded persons charged in connection with the October 3–4 rebellion and the earlier armed attacks on military facilities from participation as candidates for deputy in either chamber of the Federal Assembly and from election to bodies of power in the members of the Russian Federation.

The Communist Party of the Russian Federation was allowed full electoral participation by the minister of justice and the chairman of the Central Electoral Commission on the grounds that the party had come out against "political extremism" and in support of "early elections as a peaceful way out of the crisis that has developed in the country."[77] For the CPRF, as for other parties involved in the last-minute expansion of the number of authorized parties from 92 to 126, the time pressure on preparation for the elections was great.

For Yeltsin, the key political party was Russia's Choice, led by Yegor Gaidar. Though it was not formally a government party—Yeltsin rejected formal identification with any party—he could count on it for full support of the new constitution and his economic reform program. At the opposite pole were the CPRF and the nationalist parties, most importantly Vladimir Zhirinovsky's Liberal Democratic Party of Russia (LDPR)—soon to prove immensely powerful at the polls—which were Yeltsin's most resolute opposition. Between the two poles were parties that either called for a faster (and less corrupt) reform program (Grigory Yavlinsky's Yabloko) or preferred a more cautious pace (the industrialists of Civic Union). Thirteen parties received the approval of the Central Election Commission and were able to compete for a portion of the Duma places elected by proportional representation. For these the seats were given to parties in numbers proportionate to their vote tally, and they prepared candidate lists in advance. Aspiring deputies could also compete for seats in direct competition with other candidates in single-member constituencies that elected half the membership of the Duma.

PARLIAMENTARY AND PRESIDENTIAL ELECTIONS

The December 1993 election results were a serious reversal for Yeltsin and his reform program, giving the victory to the communist and ultranationalist opposition. But because the new constitution was approved in the simultaneous referendum, the election results confirmed the wisdom of Yeltsin's struggle for the new constitutional structure. It gave the president effective control over the executive branch—something missing in the communist-era constitution—so that opposition dominance in the legislative branch could be better controlled.

Nevertheless, the nationalist Liberal Democratic Party of Russia received the largest party list vote (23 percent) for the Duma. An effective campaign orator, Zhirinovsky had emphasized Russia's loss of empire (which he proposed to restore and even expand) and great-power status and the economic and political disorder of the country. The CPRF received 12.4 percent, but because it was allied with the Agrarian Party, which received 8 percent, it followed closely behind the LDPR. The position of Russia's Choice (15.5 percent) was therefore weaker than that of either the communist-agrarian partnership or the LDPR.

Of the 444 deputies elected to the Duma, the group that could be described as firm supporters of the Yeltsin-Gaidar reforms numbered approximately 92 (71 members of Russia's Choice and 21 "sympathizers"). Adding the members of democratic factions—the Yavlinsky bloc (Yabloko), with 20, and Sergey Shakhray's Party of Russian Unity and Accord, with 25—gave a total of 137.

The opposition to the government and the reforms won substantially more seats than its supporters: 50 communists, 36 agrarians, 15 representatives of Nikolay Travkin's Democratic Party of Russia, 23 Women of Russia, and 30 independent candidates known to oppose the ruling reformers, for a total of 154. Another important factor in the new Duma was Zhirinovsky's LDPR (64 seats), a maverick political force that could shift the balance on important votes. Because Russia's Choice had already identified Zhirinovsky as a fascist, cooperation on that side was foreclosed.

Missing in these figures were 90 independents elected to the Duma, believed to divide roughly in half between the government and opposition factions. It was clear that the pro-government parties had no possibility of delivering a majority vote against the united opposition groups, whereas the opposition would likely have little difficulty forming a majority on issues on which they accepted cooperation.

The newly approved constitution did, however, offer some protection against antireform decisions emanating from the Duma—the right of legislative veto by the upper house, the Council of the Federation. A total of 178 people was chosen for that body, two deputies from each member of the Russian Federation, with each Federation member constituting a single election district regardless of its size or population. Candidates were required to acquire signatures equal in number to 1 percent of the population of the administrative unit. The elected deputies included 21 firm opponents of reform, including communists and members of the Russian National Assembly, and 35 more moderate critics of the government. The political commitment of 67 of the members was uncertain, and only 50 were members of Russia's Choice. The situation was more favorable to the government than that in the Duma, but certainly less favorable than had been hoped.

Reviewing the election results, one Russian commentator predicted that "the executive branch will have far more problems with the Federal Assembly than it did with the Supreme Soviet. . . . we can expect another round of internecine struggle in the leadership."[78] Certainly the opposition was significant in both houses, and particularly in the Duma. Moreover, the behavior of democratic leaders, both during the elections and in the new parliament, indicated a worrisome lack of understanding of the importance of solidarity in their ranks in the face of powerful continuing opposition from the communists and the great strength of Zhirinovsky's new party.

But the writer dealt only with the election results and ignored the fundamental constitutional change Yeltsin had wrought. That change brought a new order to Russian politics, with clearly defined powers of the branches of government, especially the executive and legislative branches. The president now had the constitutional power to end an impasse in relations with the Duma by exercising his right to dissolve that body and call new elections under such circumstances. He had avoided the danger that the introduction of the new constitution might be postponed and had defeated proposals for a parliamentary, rather than presidential, constitution, which, as the election results indicated, would have been a political disaster. He had also wisely rejected simultaneous parliamentary and presidential elections (the latter would be held in 1996) and scheduled an early second round of parliamentary elections for 1995.

The aftermath of the December 1993 parliamentary elections was difficult for Yeltsin and for key reformers in his entourage. Both Yegor Gaidar and Boris Fedorov resigned, and the new parliamentary majority was hardly favorable to the reform program. But Yeltsin reaffirmed the reform course in his key policy speech to the Federal Assembly in February.[79] On the question of whether his reform course had been the correct choice, he responded: "I was convinced then and I am convinced now that there is no other way." He noted the depth of the ideological chasm that continued to separate the reformers from the opposition but insisted that the new constitution, adopted by a nationwide vote, "is a basis for accord in Russia today." He expressed concern about "the rapid social stratification in society" (though rejecting "a return to universal egalitarianism in a state of poverty") but asserted that the core problem, key to the solution of others, was the weakness of the state: "A strong, effective state is a highly important condition for continuing the transformation of our country. Without it no healthy, civilized market will be established, democracy will not show its true merits. . . . The state in its present form is not performing its most important functions. This refers above all to safeguarding order and the rights and security of its citizens. The country is being engulfed by crime."

Yeltsin also outlined a series of basic reforms: a new civil code, the de-monopolizing of Russian production, measures to attract foreign investment, the reform of taxes, and many others. He returned, as he had often done in the past, to the need for support of agriculture and "above all, the right of private ownership of land." In his comments on foreign policy he emphasized, as before, the need to expand cooperative relations with the states of East and West, and he gave special emphasis to closer relations and cooperation with the former Soviet republics within the CIS.

Certainly one of the most important features of the speech was Yeltsin's emphasis on the importance of the new constitution as the instrument for defending and expanding his reform program. Events of the first six years under the new constitution, the final years of Yeltsin's presidency, would justify his confidence. The profoundly conflictive ideological divisions within Russian political life, along with the huge parliamentary power of the communist and ultranationalist parties that continued to delay (and threaten to reverse) the progressive transformation of the Russian political and economic system, remained the country's basic problem. That problem could not be removed merely by introducing a new constitution and democratic elections. It would require a major change of outlook among both the general population and the political leadership. But the new constitution provided a stable and predictable political environment in which that process could proceed, as the record of the second republic demonstrates. Nonetheless, the December 1995 parliamentary elections and his uncertainty about the outcome of the June 1996 presidential election challenged Yeltsin's hopes and confidence severely.

THE 1995 PARLIAMENTARY ELECTIONS

Despite worrisome poll indications in previous months, the 1995 Duma elections came as a considerable shock to the Russian democratic political leadership. The results were an ominous indicator of future conflict between the president and the Duma and a bad omen for the presidential elections six months ahead.

Voter turnout was 64.4 percent of the 107.5 million registered voters, or just over 69 million. Of the forty-three parties competing, only four received the minimum of 5 percent of the votes required for party slate seats in the Duma: the Communist Party of the Russian Federation (22.3 percent), the Liberal Democratic Party of Russia (11.18 percent), Our Home Is Russia (10.13 percent), and Yabloko (6.89 percent). The tally of party deputies, indicated

TABLE 2.1

Results of the 1995 Russian Parliamentary Elections

PARTY	Slate NO. SEATS	%	Constituency NO. SEATS	%	Total NO. SEATS	%
Communist Party of the Russian Federation	99	44.0	58	25.7	157	34.8
Liberal Democratic Party	50	22.2	1	0.4	51	11.3
Our Home Is Russia	45	20.0	10	4.4	55	12.2
Apple (Yabloko)	31	13.8	14	6.2	45	10.0

Note: Percentages in the "Slate" and "Constituency" columns are shares of the 225 seats in each category. Percentages in the "Total" column are shares of the 450 seats in the two categories together. The percentages in the last two columns do not total 100 because the majority of the constituency seats went to candidates unaffiliated with any of the four major parties.

as "slate" (the party slates from which seats would be awarded in proportion to the party vote) and "constituency" (single-seat constituency) is shown in table 2.1.[80]

The communists' triumph was spectacular, their vote rising by a percentage roughly equal to the drop in the vote for Zhirinovsky's party, which had beaten them badly in 1993. They took more seats than the other three parties combined. The new "party of power," Our Home Is Russia, offering a more conservative program, had replaced Russia's Democratic Choice, the party formed from the "Russia's Choice" bloc in June 1994, and ranked between the Liberal Democrats and Yabloko in its total. Coming only half a year before the presidential election, the results would contribute greatly to the status and influence of CPRF leader Zyuganov, making him Yeltsin's main competitor for the presidency. Far better organized and led than Zhirinovsky's Liberal Democrats, the previous Duma's front-runner, the communists were a more serious challenge to the government.

As in the 1993 election, the liberal parties (even though this time they did not have the same time pressure) had failed to join forces, with the result that only one party, Yavlinsky's Yabloko, passed the 5 percent minimum and emerged as a major party in the new Duma, with a strength ranking close to that of Our Home Is Russia. Yegor Gaidar had attempted unsuccessfully to convert Russia's Democratic Choice into a larger coalition of democrats called Russia's Choice/United Democrats, but he found little cooperation. Russia's Democratic Choice failed even to reach the 5 percent cutoff in the elections, so the former "party of power" simply faded from the political scene. An important indicator of the reform forces' failure to cooperate was that they entered the 1993 elections with four parties and the 1995 race with thirteen. With the system of party lists, this divisiveness greatly reduced the number of democratic deputies and gave their opponents more seats.

From the standpoint of the government's relations with the new parliament, the central fact was that the opposition parties held a commanding majority. The communists, with nearly 35 percent of the membership of the Duma, would be capable of forming a majority coalition on individual questions.

The membership of the new parliament, like that of its predecessor, would seriously test the new constitutional system. Yeltsin could be thankful that he had rejected a parliamentary constitution, under which the new electoral results would have enabled the communists to form a coalition government and possibly name a prime minister from their party. His presidential constitution gave him not only presidential control over governmental appointments and policy but also the right to issue decrees. Moreover, it gave him the right to dissolve the parliament and call new elections in the event of a no-confidence vote or the rejection of ministerial appointees. These provisions continued, in the newly elected Sixth Duma as in its predecessor, to prevent dangerous confrontations between president and parliament as under the old constitution.

There remained, however, an opposition majority in the legislature until the elections of December 1999, at the end of the Yeltsin era. This situation brought frequent protracted delays in approval of budgets and of much of the legislation crucial to the transition to a functioning market economy. This was particularly apparent in matters affecting the conversion of the socialist economy (such as opposition to private ownership of both rural and urban land), in the reform of the tax system, in the expansion and regulation of private enterprise, and in measures to attract and facilitate foreign private investment—such as foreign rights of enterprise ownership, the banking system, and financial policy. The lack of Duma cooperation, most importantly that of the Duma communists, would play the major role in the government's failure to control the nearly disastrous August 1998 financial crisis. The main immediate concern, however, was the relationship of these electoral results to the forthcoming presidential election. The obvious danger was the possibility that the resurgent communist power would produce a communist president.

JANUARY TO JUNE 1996: HOW YELTSIN WON

The 1996 Russian presidential election was one of the most important events in the process of building the Russian democracy, both because of its outcome and for its further confirmation of the new constitutional order. But only three months before Yeltsin's victory a serious possibility existed that the election might be postponed, mainly because polls indicated that it was likely to produce a communist president, Gennady Zyuganov. His party's performance since its parliamentary victory in December 1995 had often been threatening and irresponsible. In March 1996 the communists, supported by Zhirinovsky, secured a 250–98 vote in the Duma calling for repeal of the agreement reached between Russia, Belarus, and Ukraine in December 1991, creating the CIS, and for restoration of the Soviet Union. (Zhirinovsky concluded his speech in favor of the measure with his familiar tasteless drama, waving manacles for the signers of the Belovezh agreement.) Their action elicited anger and alarm from other CIS members.[81] Irate responses came, too, from many respected Russian journalists and political leaders. One of several such responses presented in a single article captured the essence of the communist action and its challenge to complacency about the possibility of a Zyuganov presidency:

By asserting that the 1922 union treaty is still in effect, the red Duma is declaring its neighbors in the near abroad to be not internationally recognized sovereign states but rebellious enclaves whose status is unclear.

We are told that there is nothing to fear in Zyuganov's coming to power, but though not even in power yet, he has pushed through a parliamentary act that denies the existence of Russia's neighbors as independent states and is likely to provoke conflicts that will make the Chechen campaign look like a Young Pioneers' game.[82]

The months following the communist victory in the December 1995 parliamentary elections were deeply worrying for Yeltsin. The power and policy of the CPRF and its allies in the Duma had been troubling, but he now confronted a serious possibility that the democratic elections for which he had provided in the new constitution might add opposition dominance of the executive branch to that of the legislative, threatening all the major changes his leadership had accomplished since 1991. Opinion polls in early 1996 were returning results highly favorable to Zyuganov. Yeltsin's responses to these challenges in the opening months of 1996 were increasingly fearful, leading in March to his considering a dangerous course of action.

The departure of Gaidar and Fedorov from his administration following the setback in the elections of 1993 was an early indication of Yeltsin's retreat from the reform course, even though he reaffirmed that course in his February 1994 "state of the nation" speech to the parliament. Another marker was his appointment of men who were fierce critics of the reformers as the two most important presidential advisors—Oleg Soskovets as the first deputy premier and the reactionary Aleksandr Korzhakov as head of the presidential security service. They urged a retreat from the reform course of the past and accommodation to the mood of the country as indicated by the spectacular vote for the CPRF in the recent elections.

The conservative shift in Yeltsin's views, as well as his strategy in appointing people whom he felt would strengthen his position, was a response to the communist performance and its indication of the diminishing popularity of the democratic leadership. The election results made him receptive to the advice of conservative colleagues who urged him to move away from his democratic and market reform program in the forthcoming presidential campaign. His change of course brought a reduction in his support of reformers, evident in his removal from the cabinet of foreign minister Andrey Kozyrev, first deputy prime minister Anatoly Chubais, and chief of staff Sergey Filatov. These changes were followed by a major rightward shift in Yeltsin's advisory group. His new chief of staff, Nikolay Yegorov, was a nationalist who had been a strong advocate of the invasion of Chechnya. The new foreign minister, Yevgeny Primakov, brought a marked shift away from Kozyrev's liberal, pro-Western orientation, a change welcomed by the communists and Zhirinovsky. An ominous indicator of the significance of these changes was the appointment of Soskovets as head of the election campaign, with Yegorov and Korzhakov as his partners. The effect of these choices on Yeltsin's views and policy choices was soon apparent.

In his memoir about the final phase of his presidency, Yeltsin described candidly and regretfully his consideration of postponing the presidential election of 1996. He acknowledged that on March 23, following a discouraging evaluation of the political situation from Korzhakov, who recommended against going forward with the election, he asked for preparation of decrees that would ban the Communist Party, dissolve the Duma, and postpone the presidential election. When he presented his plan at a meeting of government ministers and members of the Security Council, it was sharply criticized by minister of the interior Anatoly Kulikov, who argued that the course would not have military backing, and by Prime Minister Chernomyrdin. Despite the critical reception of the plan, Yeltsin concluded the meeting with the comment that he had a majority at least for postponement of the election and announced his intention to "think it over by myself."[83]

Shortly after the meeting, Yeltsin's daughter Tatyana Dyachenko arrived with Anatoly Chubais for a meeting with Yeltsin, and in a heated exchange the two argued compellingly against banning the Communist Party and postponing the election. In his memoir Yeltsin expressed deep gratitude for their guidance and support, and shame about the course he had thought to take. He also repeated admiringly the powerful arguments presented by Chubais, who would soon displace Soskovets in managing the campaign, offer a vigorous reaffirmation of the reform course, and devise a wholly new election strategy that would bring a decisive victory. He could well be grateful that he had been dissuaded from a decision that would almost certainly have brought a major political crisis and could have done irreparable damage to the constitution and the development of Russian democracy.

Once convinced to change course and mount a campaign reaffirming the reform program, Yeltsin added new people to the existing advisory council, including Viktor Chernomyrdin, Moscow's mayor Yury Luzhkov, deputy prime ministers Yury Yarov and Sergey Shakhray, and his daughter Tatyana. He also created a strategy group chaired by Chubais, intending to use his links with the business community, those of Sergey Shakhray with regional leaders, and the skills of outstanding specialists in TV advertising (Igor Malashenko) and opinion polling (Aleksandr Oslon).

The new program was launched speedily in early April.[84] A national coordinating structure, the All-Russian Movement for Social Support for the President (ODOP), was established to link a broad range of social, political, and civic groups to support Yeltsin. Chubais worked closely with this organization to build a national campaign that made lavish use of anticommunist documentaries, special TV programs, and even rock concerts to appeal to young people. These activities, combined with strong support from major journals, distributed a powerful campaign message: forward to freedom and prosperity with Yeltsin or back to repression and penury with the communists. A slenderer, steadier, and more vigorous Yeltsin maintained a grueling schedule of travel and appearances, projecting an image of confidence in his own strength and his message that added greatly to public confidence in both.

Yeltsin's team also pressed for action to remove sources of dissatisfaction with his leadership, especially the seemingly unending and painful problem of unpaid wages and the war in Chechnya. At the beginning of April he announced both the full payment of the wages and the beginning of withdrawal of Russian troops from Chechnya. The latter action brought support from members of Russia's Democratic Choice and Yabloko, for whom the war had been an obstacle to cooperation in the election.

Yeltsin also undertook alliance initiatives with the other two democratic candidates. The polls indicated increasingly close competition between Yeltsin and Zyuganov and the virtual certainty of a runoff election between them. It was clearly important to seek advance commitment to second-round support from Yavlinsky and the popular General Aleksandr Lebed in the expectation that their numerous supporters could be convinced to vote for Yeltsin once their first-choice candidate was out of the race. Lebed responded positively to the promise of financial support for his candidacy and a position in the government, whereas Yavlinsky set stringent conditions for such a commitment that quickly ended negotiations. The deal with Lebed would later prove to be a decisive factor in the final Yeltsin victory.

The June 16 first-round election produced a highly favorable result for Yeltsin, who received 26.7 million votes (35.28 percent) to 24.3 million (32.03 percent) for Zyuganov. The result was especially encouraging in view of the substantial third place for Lebed, with 11 million votes. The result more than confirmed the wisdom of the pre-election agreement with Lebed, who was appointed head of the Security Council two days after the election. On the day after the appointment, two of Chubais's aides were arrested on a charge of carrying $500,000 in cash that was probably money for the Yeltsin election campaign. The affair was regarded as a plot by presidential security service head Korzhakov, intended to eliminate his rival Chubais, whose favor with Yeltsin he clearly resented. Yeltsin dismissed Aleksandr Korzhakov, Mikhail Barsukov, and Oleg Soskovets, convinced that they could not be trusted. He later described in his memoir the discovery, after suffering a heart attack on June 26 (which was kept secret), only seven days before the second round of elections, that Korzhakov had concealed from him a much earlier report by several doctors concerning the dangerous condition of his heart.

Yeltsin learned the news of his election victory in the second round on July 3 in a hospital bed. He had received 40.2 million votes (53.83 percent) to 30.1 million (40.31 percent) for Zyuganov. The victory reflected his popular support and a highly successful campaign strategy, but it was also aided by his virtual monopoly over national television and his ability to distribute large financial and other favors to key segments of the population and important regions of the country. To a considerable degree it was also facilitated by procedural differences between presidential and parliamentary elections.

WHY ZYUGANOV LOST

The organizational unity of the CPRF gave it, within the context of the party list system, a considerable expansion of its parliamentary representation that was not translatable into actual votes in the presidential competition. Moreover, the presidential campaign, chiefly a confrontation between Yeltsin and Zyuganov, made possible a sharp polarization of positions that was exploited extremely effectively by Yeltsin's team, who offered the stark choice between moving forward with reform and returning to the negatives of the communist past. In the end, a communist victory would have required the support of a large segment of voters who were firmly committed neither to the government nor to the CPRF.[85]

Zyuganov's strategy for broadening his support base was to use the appeal of nationalism, an extension of the "national front" theme that he had used for some time. He presented himself as the leader of the "national patriotic bloc" and made continual references to "the fatherland" and to its moral and spiritual traditions rather than to communist ideological principles.

Not surprisingly, he abandoned his appeal for abolishing the presidency, which he had made frequently after the communist victory in the 1995 Duma elections, in favor of supporting a strong presidency under legislative control. The appeal of the existing presidential constitution, with a communist president and communist legislative dominance, was obvious. Other communist party positions were familiar, such as the need to rebuild Russian military power, restore the union of republics, and return to "popular power" (code for government by the former Soviet structure). Otherwise, the emphasis was on issues with broad appeal, such as wages and pensions. There was no discussion of re-nationalizing the economy, but rather acceptance of a mixed economy, though with strong government control at the top, including public ownership of land. Zyuganov sought to assure the new private owners of their security and to assure all parties that the new freedoms and political pluralism and the reform process would continue. He extended his reassurances even to foreign business and financial leaders during a visit to the World Economic Forum at Davos, Switzerland, where he promised to welcome and protect their investments in Russia and insisted that he had no plan for radical change.

The particulars of Zyuganov's attack on Yeltsin at home were long familiar: that Yeltsin had destroyed the Soviet Union and imposed a genocidal policy in Chechnya, that he had turned over power in the country to greedy oligarchs and a criminal mafia, and that he had worked with Western advisors who had severely damaged Russian interests, as had his autocratic style of rule.

Zyuganov's main calculation, based on the experience of the recent parliamentary elections, was that the country was undergoing a leftward trend. He believed he could secure a substantial segment of the opposition voters by appealing to their dissatisfaction with Yeltsin's rule and the country's many internal problems and by using a strongly nationalist theme in his speeches and party publications. It would soon become clear that he had not reckoned with the anticommunist sentiment of much of the electorate, including many of his proposed nationalist allies. Equally important, his strategy failed to take into account the crucial body of centrist voters who could be won over only by convincing evidence that the Russian communist leadership had made an ideological and organizational shift to social democracy, as parties in the newly independent Central and East European states had done. But for Zyuganov and his colleagues, European social democracy was democratic but not socialist and therefore unacceptable, a position that prevented them from making an effective appeal to centrist voters.

Given this constraint, Zyuganov proved a weak campaigner. His answers to direct questions about property, fiscal management, and other such issues tended to be evasive, and though he occasionally spoke positively of the social democrats, he was quick to reaffirm his loyalty to the communist tradition. Widespread doubts about the scope and sincerity of the communist break with the past greatly weakened Zyuganov's effort to broaden his voter base by forming a "Bloc of National-Patriotic Forces of Russia." Moreover, measures taken to win the support of the radical communists—such as the March Duma vote Zyuganov had sponsored repudiating the Belovezh agreements—belied his claims about a new communism. Meanwhile, the regional leaders whom Yeltsin wooed effectively were anxious not only about their possible replacement after a Zyuganov victory but also about the threat to their regions' control of local economic power and resources under a communist leadership committed to nationalization and centralization.

Such were the reasons the communists gained fewer centrist voters in the presidential election than they had in the parliamentary elections of 1995. A belated effort to broaden their support by announcing an appealing list of members of a "government of national trust" failed when several of the nominees rejected the plan. Zyuganov's campaign was plagued by the ideological and structural legacy of the Communist Party. Even its strong organization, which had been useful in rebuilding its base in the post-Soviet era, became a serious constraint on the leadership's efforts at program reform to meet the demands of the presidential race. Moreover, Yeltsin's formidable campaign and campaign resources, particularly those for television and the press, enabled him to present the competition as one between the new Russia and its communist past. He had made the election a referendum on communism, and the ambiguity of the positions of the communist leaders, reinforced by the voices of Stalinists and revanchists among the radical splinter communist parties, confirmed the sense of centrist voters that the positive gains of the postcommunist era would be lost with a communist presidential victory.

THE FINAL PHASE OF YELTSIN'S LEADERSHIP: ECONOMIC AND POLITICAL CRISIS

The last stage of the Yeltsin era, from 1996 to 1999, was marked again by challenge and crisis. His supporters' joy over his victory in the presidential election was much reduced by the parlous state of the president's health. His severe heart condition was soon complicated by pneumonia, and not until November 1996 did he undergo the heart surgery that would substantially restore his strength. Moreover, Yeltsin's victory did not alter the fact that the communists retained the power in the Duma they had acquired in the December 1995 elections, and they would do so until near the end of his presidency. From that position they continued to obstruct and harass Yeltsin and his colleagues, employing their voting strength, as before, to block reform measures, obstruct budgets, and seek Yeltsin's impeachment. Even when Russia confronted a nearly disastrous financial collapse in the summer of 1998, an extended effect of the East Asian financial crisis, they denied him the voting support he desperately needed to qualify for International Monetary Fund (IMF) emergency credits. They used the collapse that followed to extend their influence over his government and attempt constitutional changes and his impeachment.

But despite recurrent crises and powerful communist opposition, Yeltsin, in his final years of power, not only managed and survived but also undertook new reform initiatives with leaders of the younger generation. The last of these was Vladimir Putin, organizer of the campaign for the highly successful parliamentary elections of December 1999—and Yeltsin's successor as president.

Yeltsin spoke with feeling during the presidential election campaign about the inadequacy of the reforms so far and about Russia's widespread poverty. He promised a vigorous renewal of the reform initiative and of efforts to deal with unpaid wages and pensions. Regrettably, his health problems postponed such initiatives for many months. As in the past, he turned to a young reformer, Boris Nemtsov, a thirty-seven-year-old physicist and mathematician who had served in the Russian parliament since 1990, to renew the reform program. Nemtsov had been appointed Yeltsin's representative in the Nizhnii Novgorod region in 1990 and soon gained election as governor of the region by the regional council. He was elected governor by popular ballot in December 1995, with 60 percent of the vote, even as the communists and nationalists gained a solid majority in the elections to the State Duma. By this time Nemtsov had become a very visible regional governor and reformer.

Arriving in Moscow, Nemtsov quickly increased his national prominence and popularity, rising in the opinion polls above both the president and the prime minister, under whom he served. Appointed first deputy prime minister, he was given broad governmental responsibilities in a wide range of difficult and sensitive areas, such as railways, housing and construction, energy, control of monopolies, and social programs. He demonstrated the kind of energy and determination that had made his region a model of independent reform among the Russian regions, but he soon found himself in conflict with vested interests in the partial privatization of Sviazinvest, a government-owned communications conglomerate. The aim was to set a new standard of open bidding to replace the clandestine deals of the past, in which the "oligarchs," who had gained enormous wealth and power from previous privatizations, bought government properties at bargain prices. When the bidding was completed, one of the oligarchs, the banker Vladimir Gusinsky, began a harsh attack on Nemtsov via his NTV Television and his newspaper, *Segodnia*, charging Nemtsov with corruption. Renowned for his honesty and forthrightness, Nemtsov responded bluntly: "The government has gone from word to deed in declaring that the rule of seven bankers will no longer exist."[86]

The conflict over the Sviazinvest privatization was only part of the attack on Nemtsov in the early months of his new role in Moscow. Given responsibility for anticorruption action and for reducing government expenditures on housing and the bureaucracy, he was certain to make enemies. Like other liberal reformers, he was attacked by both the communists and the nationalists in the Duma and by the oligarchs—previously staunch supporters of Yeltsin in the presidential election. The communists opposed him (using scurrilous charges as patently false as Gusinsky's), as they had long opposed Anatoly Chubais, because of his commitment to privatization and the government's fiscal responsibility, whereas the oligarchs were defending their profits from the privatization of state-owned properties. Meanwhile, Nemtsov's efforts to reduce government expenditures threatened the financial interests of millions. Such was the continuing predicament of the government reformer.

Despite his unpopularity among such powerful forces in Russian politics, Nemtsov continued his reform efforts, though some of his responsibilities were reduced during the late summer and autumn. From the government's point of view, the main cost of the privatization squabble was twofold: it challenged the credibility of the privatization program as a whole, and it thwarted the effort to gain desperately needed revenues from the sale of state properties. As events of the following year—profoundly influenced by the East Asian monetary crisis—would demonstrate, such revenues could make the difference between fiscal stability and fiscal collapse.

RUSSIA AND THE EAST ASIAN ECONOMIC CRISIS

When the East Asian economic crisis began in July 1997 with the devaluation of the Thai baht, the first repercussions were felt in Malaysia, the Philippines, Indonesia, and the Czech Republic. By October the effects had reached Hong Kong, Brazil, and Russia.

Russia's economic situation bore scant resemblance to that of the East Asian countries. While they had enjoyed a growth boom, with a massive influx of foreign investment, the Russian economy had suffered a steady decline and a desperate shortage of investment, domestic or foreign. Russia was thus an incidental victim of the East Asian crisis, struck simultaneously by the sharp decline of oil prices that it brought and by the withdrawal of global investors from "emerging markets." Nearly 60 percent of Russia's foreign earnings and 25 percent of government revenue came from energy exports. The 50 percent decline in oil prices struck hard, aggravating the already severe problems of meeting current expenditures and paying interest on debt. Meanwhile, the rapid rise in interest rates greatly increased the burden of Russia's large short-term debt, creating a vicious circle in which growing concern about the government's capacity to pay raised the risk premium on interest rates. Thus did the East Asian economic crisis shatter the rising hopes in 1997 for Russian economic recovery.

After declining 43 percent between 1989 and 1996, Russia's GDP had experienced its first modest growth in 1997, and the stock market soared, rising 285 percent that year alone.[87] Thanks mainly to exports of oil, gas, and metals, Russia enjoyed a 1997 merchandise trade surplus of $18 billion. By June, interest rates on the bonds that the government used to finance much of its deficit were down 200 percent, to 19 percent. Banks were beginning to shift funds from government bonds to business loans, though the much lower rate on bank deposits (7.4 percent) and concerns about the security of deposits continued to discourage the expansion of ruble savings as a source of loan capital. Another positive sign in 1997 was a steady rise in federal revenues as a share of GDP—up to 13.1 percent in April 1996 from 8.8 percent a year earlier. These developments, combined with hopes of

Duma passage of a tax law that would significantly increase government revenues, reduce borrowing, and lower interest rates, encouraged the belief that Russia was poised for economic recovery and growth. Beginning in November 1997, however, all the positive trends were rapidly reversed. Interest rates soared, the stock market declined, and private investors were again unable to borrow at economic rates.

The government's revenue shortfall aggravated the already serious and socially dangerous problem of arrears in payment of wages and pensions. The overdue amount had been much reduced in late 1997 but began to rise again in 1998, reaching a total of 608 billion rubles ($99 billion) by the end of April, 8 billion of which was attributable to the state sector, the rest to the private. There were also reports of delays in pension payments in March, and by the end of that month 88 billion rubles were owed to the state pension fund. Chronic failure to get control of these arrears was one of the main factors in Yeltsin's dismissal of the Chernomyrdin government.

The two most urgent problems confronting the government in March and April 1998 were the renewed rise in wage and pension arrears and continuing shortfalls in tax collection. The consideration of a new tax law, which was needed to improve revenue, was postponed by the Duma until early 1999, leaving the government facing an enormous shortage of funds for wages and pensions, declining revenues, and pressure for expanded government borrowing, with its negative effects on interest rates and investment.

One possible short-term solution to these problems was the profitable sale of state-owned shares in key enterprises and the enhancement of revenues from those that were to be retained (especially the main electricity supplier, United Energy Systems). But erstwhile Yeltsin supporters such as prominent businessmen Boris Berezovsky and Mikhail Khodorkovsky opposed open and competitive privatization of the kind introduced by Nemtsov in the spring of 1997, while entrenched bureaucrats blocked the management reform of enterprises still owned by the state. Meanwhile, the Duma opposition blocked tax reform, land privatization, and other reforms needed to complete the transformation of the Russian economy and restore growth.

Yeltsin was greatly concerned about the effects of economic deterioration on the 1999 parliamentary elections and the presidential election in 2000. He had little time left to improve government performance by increasing revenues to meet the backlog of wages and pensions and to reduce the indebtedness that blocked investment and growth. Moreover, he needed an instrument of his policies—a prime minister who was an effective administrator, who had no hint of private interest or corruption on his record, and who could head a reinvigorated reform program.

A NEW GOVERNMENT FACES FINANCIAL COLLAPSE

As he had done in the past, Yeltsin moved aggressively to break up the logjam in the stream of reform. On March 23, 1998, he dismissed his entire cabinet, which enabled him to get rid of obstructionists and build a reform team under new leadership. He lost Chubais as deputy prime minister, but Chubais had become a visible symbol of negative features of earlier privatizations. And he could be useful on the board of United Energy Systems. The task was to find a prime minister who could replace the cautious Chernomyrdin, reinvigorate the government's reform initiatives, and possibly develop into a future presidential candidate. The Duma strongly opposed Yeltsin's young and little-known choice, Sergey Kirienko, and approved him only when confronted with the possibility of dissolution on the crucial third vote.

Kirienko's career had begun with conventional engineering training and Communist Youth League activism in Gor'kii (now again Nizhnii Novgorod). Military service and a stint as a shipyard foreman were followed, at the opening of the postcommunist era, by training in finance in Moscow and then a bank chairmanship and presidency of the large Norsi oil refinery. After Nizhnii Novgorod mayor Boris Nemtsov moved to Moscow to become minister of fuel and energy in March 1997, Kirienko followed to become deputy minister of fuel and energy in May and then minister in November. It was from this position that he was asked to become Yeltsin's nominee for prime minister in March. Successful in business and government, he had acquired a reputation for honesty and independence.

Kirienko stressed his commitment to the fundamental economic policies of the government but also noted the government's need for broader public support. From the beginning he stressed the importance of rebuilding Russian industry, of combating poverty, and of putting an end to delays in payments of pensions and public sector wages. Commenting on recent economic policy, he stressed the success in achieving a stable ruble and controlling inflation, as well as the huge expansion of the private sector and the halting of the slump in output. On the negative side, he talked about unrealistic budgets, the underestimation of growing state debt, weak government control of state monopolies, and the slowness of tax reform.

At an early stage Kirienko won the confidence of trade union leaders and began to work with the heads of state committees, who were not cabinet members but played a major role in matters such as management of state monopolies, support of small business, management of bankruptcies, and relations between federal and regional agencies. He also proved appealing to regional political leaders, who were gaining great importance in Russian politics. In short, he defined a practical and important work agenda and showed signs of being an effective manager.

Following the Duma's approval of his appointment on April 25, Kirienko formed the strongest reform cabinet of the postcommunist era. Particularly notable was the Government Council—the core of a much downsized cabinet whose members, like Kirienko himself, had extensive experience in private business, government, or both.

Within a few weeks of assuming power in late April, the Kirienko government was confronted by a deepening fiscal crisis. Its opening coincided with the renewal of strife in Indonesia and the fall of the Suharto government on May 21. Combined with the downgrading of Korean banks and rumors of American and German interest rate increases, developments in Russia raised investor concern about the country's stability and the security of Russian investments.

In May the ruble came under greater pressure than at any time since a precipitous fall in value on a day known as Black Tuesday in October 1994.[88] Since the government had established a "currency corridor"—a range of variation in currency value that was regarded as acceptable—in 1995, the ruble had been the symbolic anchor of the economy, discouraging inflationary expectations and encouraging foreign investors to lend to the Russian government, companies, and banks. By committing to the corridor and taking action to prevent fluctuations above or below the predetermined range, the government constrained the printing of money by the Central Bank and assumed responsibility for financing deficits by borrowing on the domestic and international financial markets. It was by this means that inflation was reduced from 200 percent at the beginning of 1995 to 7.5 percent in mid-1997.

Although the system was a good one, it was used excessively during the two years after its introduction, causing Russia's short-term debt to rise from 3.5 percent of GDP at the end of 1995 to 13.5 percent two years later, a huge debt with an average maturity of less than a year. The Kirienko government's vigorous efforts to lower government spending greatly reduced the need for new financing, but the accumulated debt imposed the necessity of raising an average of 8 billion rubles ($1.2 billion) each week as existing debt matured. When investors were less willing to hold ruble-denominated bonds, the government was obliged to raise interest rates, which simultaneously increased its debt burden and doubts among investors about its ability to pay.

As the Russian stock market plummeted (off 17 percent for the week ending May 20, 1998, and 40 percent from January 1, 1998), the Central Bank raised the refinancing rate for bonds held by private banks to 150 percent and spent $1 billion in two days to defend the ruble. During the same week the fact that representatives of the IMF visited Moscow without announcing plans for a resumption of payments on its $9.5 billion loan to Russia was taken as a negative sign by investors. During the following week the interest on short-term bonds passed the 50 percent mark, and on Wednesday, May 27, the government failed to sell enough to pay upcoming obligations. Stocks dropped 11 percent in a single day, and only a dramatic (and temporary) increase of interest rates to 150 percent restored the market.

The crisis had arrived in earnest, with the serious threat of a run on the ruble. Devaluation was not an option, both because inflation and other consequences would shake the confidence of the population and because it would do severe injury to Russian banks heavily burdened with short-term foreign currency debt. Because the Central Bank had already spent heavily to prop up the ruble, and because greater dependence on short-term debt would only increase the concern of foreign investors, the government's options had narrowed dangerously. At the same time, the huge rise in interest rates had further reduced hopes of economic recovery.

It was clear that only major debt restructuring—the conversion of short-term debt to long-term—and drastic measures to reduce expenses and increase revenue could prevent further deterioration of the financial situation. Plans were quickly prepared for aggressive reduction of state expenditures—an effort that proposed to pare expenses by an amount equal to the revenue deficit. Another important initiative was the appointment of the brilliant financier Boris Fedorov to head the tax service. Fedorov, a former World Bank representative and finance minister and the successful manager of Russia's 1993 inflation crisis, was given a mandate to use firm measures to deal with tax evasion, rebuild the collection system, and push for the long-delayed tax law. This was doubtless the most reassuring initiative for the IMF and World Bank, which had long pressed for the matter of tax collection to be made the first priority of government fiscal reform.

Restructuring the state debt presented a formidable challenge in the crisis environment of mid-1998. The total debt was $200 billion, or 45 percent of GDP, a moderate figure by international standards. Of that total, $130 billion was inherited from the Soviet era and had already been restructured, with annual interest payments of $7.2 billion, only 1.2 percent of current GDP. The immediate problem was the short-term debt. Of the total of $70 billion, $45 billion was held by state banks, which would continue to hold it, leaving $25 billion held by Russian private banks and foreign investors.

Both the seriousness of the situation and the deep frustration of the leadership were evident in Yeltsin's June 23 speech announcing the government's "anticrisis program," which was designed to restore confidence in Russia's financial markets. Presented to a cabinet session to which many parliamentary deputies and business leaders were invited, the program's central feature was a series of previously announced measures to reduce the expenditures of the federal government by 42 billion rubles ($6.8 billion). The plan included heavy cuts in government employment and reduction of subsidies to industry, agriculture, and transportation. The program also proposed to bring off-budget funds, including the pension fund, into the federal budget and to introduce revenue increases totaling $20 billion per year. New revenue was to be obtained by increasing the powers of the tax authorities, raising the land tax, and increasing penalties for illegal production of alcohol (which challenged the state monopoly and reduced revenue significantly).

The plan was obviously designed to make it absolutely clear to the financial markets and the IMF that the Russian government was determined to reduce expenditures and increase revenue in order to restore confidence in Russian markets and protect the ruble. Yeltsin underlined his commitment by a veiled threat to use the power of presidential decree if the Duma failed to pass the enabling legislation before the summer recess. The response from Zyuganov was to press forward his efforts to impeach the president.

In previous weeks Zyuganov had stressed not only the impeachment plan but also the end of cooperation with the government and support for strikes and other popular actions aimed to isolate and weaken the government. He balked only at the proposal of the communist chairman of the Duma Security Council on June 20 to use any means, "including illegal ones," to remove the Yeltsin leadership.

Russian leaders stressed the need for a $10–15 billion loan under the IMF's Supplemental Reserve Facility Program to stabilize the financial markets and to facilitate the reduction of government bond rates. Without this change, they noted, it would be impossible to reduce interest payments, encourage foreign and domestic investors and domestic saving, and reduce the huge gap between ruble- and foreign-denominated lending rates.

A FINAL EFFORT

The protracted negotiations with the IMF delegation in Moscow were accelerated by the growing sense of crisis in early July. The Central Bank's hard currency reserves were being consumed at an increasing rate as short-term interest rates passed 100 percent. Fear of a massive devaluation of the ruble and collapse of the banking system, followed by renewed inflation and spreading social unrest, created a growing urgency. Certainly Western leaders had grown accustomed to financial crises elsewhere in the world over the previous year, but the strategic importance of Russia and concern about the economic and political fallout from its financial collapse gave rise to a special sense of emergency. The precipitating event was the collapse of the Russian bond market on Wednesday, July 8, when even a 120 percent interest rate failed to secure adequate sales, a signal of impending financial collapse. Under pressure from the US Treasury, the IMF moved quickly to negotiate a vast package of financial support that was announced on July 13, surpassing even the earlier Russian request.[89]

Under the new program, Russia was promised a total of $22.6 billion in loans from the IMF, the World Bank, and Japan during 1998–99, $14.8 billion of it in 1998 and $7.8 billion in 1999. Of the total, $15.1 billion came from the IMF, $6 billion from the World Bank, and $1.5 billion from Japan. The United States agreed to loan the IMF $2.1 billion, and the remainder of the money came from Japan, Germany, France, and Saudi Arabia. Anatoly Chubais, the Russian negotiator responsible for the loan, acknowledged both the length and arduousness of the negotiations but proudly proclaimed the outcome a sign of "restoration of faith in Russia's ability to overcome its difficulties."[90] The outcome was also the result of vigorous American support for IMF action, which included a recommendation to double the financial package and a commitment of American funds.

After the success with the IMF, there remained the crucial question of the Duma's willingness to approve the legislation required to implement the government's austerity program—the measures for reducing expenditures and increasing taxation. The extraordinary two-day session that began just two days after the IMF announcement proved immensely encouraging, bringing rapid approval of a new tax code and a reduced corporate tax rate aimed at improving tax compliance. At the end of the first day of the session, foreign financial specialists appeared confident that a combination of new legislation and, as necessary, presidential decrees would meet the requirements of the IMF Board meeting scheduled for July 20. The second day brought further progress, with the passage of a large number of laws suggested by the government's anticrisis program and further concessions to the government's position on sales and income taxes. Meanwhile, the dramatic rise of the Russian stock market (up nearly 20 percent in the five days following the IMF announcement) and the decline of bond interest rates indicated the positive view of events among Russian and foreign investors.

But the period of good news ended rapidly. By early August the news was alarming again. The continuing spread of the effects of the East Asian crisis to emerging markets, especially those in Latin America, exacerbated Russia's financial problems, raising interest rates on the government's short-term debt and sending the stock market once again into a nose-dive. By mid-August the crisis had arrived in earnest, and the government appealed in desperation for further assistance from the international financial community, warning that lack of support would bring a financial collapse. The climax of the crisis came on August 17. Unable to borrow funds at feasible rates as both domestic and foreign investors fled from Russian short-term bonds, the government simultaneously reduced its support for the ruble and announced a forced restructuring of its debt—in effect defaulting on it. The result was a rapid collapse of the ruble, of Russia's poorly capitalized banks, and of Russian credibility on international financial markets.

AFTER THE COLLAPSE

Even the communist opposition do not speak of revolution; they speak of new elections.

—ANDREY KOZYREV, FORMER RUSSIAN FOREIGN MINISTER,
AFTER AUGUST 1998

Liberal reforms in Russia are dead and will not spring back to life at least until the 2004 presidential elections.

—ALEKSANDR LIVSHITS, FORMER RUSSIAN FINANCE MINISTER,
AFTER AUGUST 1998

The financial collapse of August 1998 was a major turning point in the history of postcommunist Russia. President Yeltsin's adversaries in the Duma seized the opportunity created by financial collapse and leadership weakness to encroach on the president's right to appoint the government—the key power that had enabled him to maintain the momentum of his reforms against powerful parliamentary opposition since the introduction of the 1993 constitution. Yeltsin's situation was now so weak that he did not want to risk the political collapse that might be precipitated by a confrontation with the Duma over his new government, particularly the prime minister. The conservatives in the Duma wanted the highly respected and accomplished Yevgeny Primakov to fill that office, and Yeltsin complied.

Yeltsin's previous governments had been center-right in membership, and the communists, because of their categorical rejection of his reform program, had been consistently excluded. Reformist, market-oriented democrats set the policy direction, although conservatives, notably the long-serving prime minister Viktor Chernomyrdin, had significantly moderated or slowed the implementation of the reform agenda. The numbers of democratic reformers varied in the several cabinets from 1992 to 1998, but they were almost always influential, and key figures such as Yegor Gaidar, Anatoly Chubais, Boris Fedorov, and Boris Nemtsov had played the dominant role in the main phases of reform.

The government of prime minister Yevgeny Primakov was the first to have a center-left membership and to bring communists into key positions, most importantly into responsibility for economic policy. The background of the new prime minister was unlike that of any of his predecessors in the Yeltsin era. His post-Soviet career—as head of the Foreign Intelligence Service (1991–96) and then as foreign minister (1996–98)—coincided closely with his career in the Soviet years. Trained as an Arabist at the Institute of Oriental Studies, he had a career as journalist in the 1950s and 1960s and then served successively as director of the Institute of Oriental Studies and the Institute of World Economy and International Relations. Even before replacing Kozyrev at the Foreign Ministry he had been a major foreign policy advisor for Yeltsin, influencing policy on international issues.[91]

His career offered much evidence of the expanding influence of the intelligence services on Russian policy. His appointment as foreign minister and then prime minister demonstrated his growing influence. As foreign minister he defined the main purposes of Russian policy as countering the "unipolar" (that is, hegemonic) designs of the United States and forming strategic alliances with other powers whose interests he perceived as conflicting with those of the United States. He had little to say about economic and political reform, but once he was in power it was apparent that he intended to modify important economic reforms, strengthen state power, and reduce the new democratic rights of regional and local governments.

If the opposition leaders imagined that removing the Kirienko government, naming their own new prime minister, and taking leading positions in the cabinet would solve Russia's economic problems, they were badly deceived. They had forced out the leading reformers, and their obstruction of the government's efforts to secure the needed Duma approval of the July IMF bailout had been a major factor in the August financial collapse. But the background and views of their chosen prime minister offered no evidence of his promise as manager in a time of economic crisis.

Primakov faced a formidable task in forming a new government. Some of the most distinguished centrists—Grigory Yavlinsky (who had proposed Primakov's appointment), for example—refused to serve in his cabinet. The decision to retain finance minister Mikhail Zadornov from the previous cabinet brought bitter attacks from the communists, who wanted no participation by any of the hated "marketeers." Primakov recognized that Russia would need extensive international economic assistance in the form of grants and debt restructuring and that credibility with the IMF and with foreign governments and banks would depend not only on the crisis management program but also on the membership of the cabinet. The appointment of the communist Yury Maslyukov as economics minister clearly contradicted that purpose and revealed the new power of the communists. Maslyukov was recommended by Primakov and approved by Yeltsin because of the need for communist support.

Primakov's conundrum was how to reconcile the views of the communists with the requirements of dealing with international financial institutions. The communists had sought entry to the government not to serve as pliant assistants in restoring the policies of the previous government but to replace them and to achieve constitutional changes that would greatly expand their power. The negative effects of their attitudes and their new power would soon hamper negotiations with international lenders on Russian foreign debt.

As the new alignment of political forces proceeded, the economic situation deteriorated rapidly. Inflation, which had been 0.2 percent per month in August, rose to 38 percent in September. Average wages declined to $70 per month, and unemployment increased rapidly in the large cities, where financial and trading firms shed employees by the tens of thousands. Government figures indicated that 44 million people were living below the poverty line (552 rubles, or $32, per month), 25 percent more than one year earlier. Already in September imports were down by 65 percent, and consumers, fearing rising prices and goods shortages, cleared shops of goods. The food situation became more difficult because importers lacked cash to pay for foreign purchases and because the country experienced its worst grain harvest since 1967—down almost 50 percent below average.

The massive bank collapse that came with the fall of the ruble took with it depositors' savings, and firms were unable to offer credit to buyers, shifting to cash-only operations and adding further to economic decline. The banks' plight required immediate attention, leading the government to develop a plan for eliminating nearly a fifth of the country's fifteen hundred banks and taking sizable stakes in the larger banks deemed most crucial to the financial system. The banks were estimated to need $2.2 billion just to resume functioning. With unpaid debts of $6 billion to foreign banks, they had no prospect of borrowing abroad and hoped to resume operation by selling equity stakes, though the only prospective purchaser appeared to be the Russian government.

The financial plight of the government was equally grim. Its draft budget, prepared for discussions with the IMF on October 20, showed expected revenues at 65–75 billion rubles and expenditures of 130 billion ($7.68 billion). If it was to hold back inflation it could afford to print no more than 20 billion rubles, leaving a minimum budget deficit of 35 billion. With private borrowing foreclosed by the financial collapse, the only hope was IMF assistance, which director Michel Camdessus indicated would require major changes of fiscal policy. Meanwhile, government revenues had declined, the current account balance had been reduced by 80 to 90 percent, and the regional governments were withholding revenues from the center as their own situations deteriorated. The Russian Central Bank announced that it had no idea whether it would receive sufficient revenue for the fourth quarter and that it was unable to borrow either from domestic or international capital markets. The government was pleading with foreign governments and international agencies not just for financial support but also for humanitarian aid, especially medical and food supplies.

In September the Russian GDP was down 9.9 percent over the previous year's level, and industrial production was down 14.5 percent. Primakov talked of government subsidies for industry but clearly had no money available to provide them. And because industry needs low inflation to flourish, a government effort to bolster industry with inflation-producing subsidies would only have added to the problem.

In sum, the Russian economic predicament was dire. After several weeks of discussion and several leaked "draft" budgets, the IMF delegation, which had said it would not release new funds until it received a feasible crisis plan, ended talks in Moscow without a new agreement and with no new date set for resumption. A foreign financial specialist in Moscow commented that "muddling through has become official government policy, and I am getting the feeling that they believe the law of gravity is optional."

COMMUNIST CHALLENGE RENEWED

While some observers argued that the appointment of Yevgeny Primakov as prime minister with communist support opened the way to better cooperation between the executive and legislative branches of government, the experience of the early months of his administration contradicted that view. The central purpose of the communist leadership was to limit the president's power by changes to the constitution. One proposed change was to eliminate the president's power to dissolve the Duma if it rejected his appointment for prime minister. Another was to replace popular election of the president with election by the parliament. The aim was to subordinate the president to the Duma, in which the communists were the largest party, with 35 percent of the seats (42 percent with the votes of allied parties). In sum, the purpose was to return to something like the constitutional structure before the constitution of December 1993. With such arrangements the communists could control the selection of the prime minister and dominate both the executive and legislative branches of government.

In effect, the elimination of leading reformers from the government and the admission of communists had led not to greater cooperation in implementing the program of the president and the prime minister but to the communists' use of their expanded power to pursue their own program. With most of the reformers now removed from the government and with their own representatives in it, the communist leaders increased their pressure for Yeltsin's impeachment and for constitutional change. With Yury Maslyukov controlling economic policy, they could block efforts to restore the Russian financial system by cooperating with the IMF, the World Bank, and the governments and private bankers that held Russia's large foreign debt. As the weeks passed, with Maslyukov and Zyuganov denouncing the IMF for its insistence on fiscal prudence as a precondition for lending, many Western bankers effectively wrote off Russian debt, and prospects for the desperately needed cooperation of the IMF faded rapidly. Observing Maslyukov's hostile approach to the IMF, former prime minister Chernomyrdin asked, "How can we make threats when we need loans?"[92]

It was clear that the communist presence in the government, especially in the management of economic policy, prevented the prime minister from solving his most pressing problem, the Russian foreign debt. That Primakov retained Maslyukov in the government in spite of this was explained by a Russian television commentator quite simply: it was because of "the red majority in the parliament."[93] An effort to remove Maslyukov would bring a repetition of the confrontation of the previous August. Primakov attempted to reach an accord with the Duma by which the president would refrain from dissolving it in exchange for its agreement to drop the impeachment effort and avoid a vote of no confidence in the government. The Duma's communist leadership rejected the proposal. Meanwhile, the lack of an effective economic program and increasing communist control of government policy brought further negative developments.

The most obvious of these was continuing economic decline, greatly aggravated by the government's lack of an effective policy. Already in December wages were down nearly 40 percent in comparison with the previous year, almost all of the decline since September. The government was facing increasing difficulty meeting the cost of the welfare system, which the Duma continued to expand. A new law in preparation proposed to give assistance to all households with incomes below the official subsistence level, just at a time when a 40 to 50 percent increase in the number of qualified recipients was forecast. If passed, the law would drastically reduce funding for health, education, and other underfunded services.

Nor was much success achieved in rebuilding the financial system. Restructuring and recapitalization of the banking system was bogged down in differences with the Duma over management of the reform process through the new Agency for Restructuring Credit Organizations (ARCO). And meanwhile, at the point when loan negotiations with the IMF were failing, the Duma passed a budget based on the assumption of $7 billion in foreign aid. The government had almost no hope of meeting its 1999 debt obligations, had virtually cut itself off from new foreign lending, and was unable to market its bonds even domestically. The ruble was down 46 percent in real terms since the previous July.[94]

Thus, in the first months of 1999, Russia—its government seemingly immobilized—confronted its most dangerous economic and political crisis since the early nineties. Neither the prime minister nor the parliament appeared capable of dealing with the crisis, and the president offered little leadership.

YELTSIN SEEKS A SUCCESSOR

As on many past occasions, just at the point when he seemed to have abdicated leadership, Yeltsin reemerged with a roar, dismissing Prime Minister Primakov on May 12, 1999, and replacing him with Sergey Stepashin, the former manager of the Chechen war and a veteran of the security services. Surprising many, Yeltsin triumphed in the ensuing confrontation with the Duma, whose opposition leaders failed to secure the impeachment spearheaded by the communists and had to accept his new prime minister or face dissolution. The new government focused on the debt crisis, securing confirmation of the $4.5 billion IMF loan already negotiated by Primakov, and on the increasing problems in Chechnya and Dagestan, where armed violence was mounting alarmingly.

Only three months later, the cycle of changes in governmental leadership repeated itself. Yeltsin was chiefly preoccupied with the December 1999 parliamentary elections and, even more, with prospects for the presidential election in June 2000. The Russian scene was alive with talk of candidates and coalitions, and the trends were not favorable to the president. Most worrying was the formation of a powerful center-right coalition movement, Otechestvo (Fatherland), which brought together against Yeltsin former allies such as the powerful Moscow mayor Yury Luzhkov and prominent regional executives and centrist political leaders. On August 9 Yeltsin struck again, dismissing the Stepashin government and appointing a new prime minister, Vladimir Putin, a former KGB officer and long-time presidential aide, and announcing that Putin was his favored candidate for the presidency. For the moment, however, Putin's first priority had to be the mounting crisis in the Caucasus, which had expanded just as he became prime minister with Dagestan's declaration of independence from Russia, an act supported by the very Chechen warlords who had humiliated Russia in the Chechen war.

Amid much confusion, one point at least was clear: the ten months remaining before the June 2000 presidential election would find Yeltsin engaged in a struggle to determine the future of the presidency and of Russian policy, a struggle at least as dramatic and crucial as the one that preceded the 1996 election. Meanwhile, the continuing problems of the economy—the unsolved government debt problem, the continued decline of GDP, the failure to secure new investment, and the growing proportion (30 percent) of the population living below the subsistence level—were further complicated by a crisis in the Caucasus potentially as dangerous as the one that had brought the costly Chechen secessionist war of 1994–96.

PUTIN AND YELTSIN

The Russian reform leader Anatoly Chubais once described Boris Yeltsin as one of the three greatest leaders of Russian history, ranking him with Peter the Great and Emperor Alexander II.[95] Yeltsin destroyed the communist dictatorship, freed the national republics of the Soviet Union, launched a vast program to create a market economy, and then, in 1993, replaced a nonfunctional communist constitution with one modeled on that of a Western democracy. Three parliamentary and two presidential elections at the national level and a vast decentralization of power to elected regional and local governments followed these events. And although one cannot ignore the many shortcomings of the reform process—particularly in the economy— his successor, Vladimir Putin, would have had scant hope of realizing his own program for Russia without the Yeltsin legacy.

Putin's early career had been with the KGB in East Germany.[96] He returned to his native St. Petersburg in 1991, soon becoming a member of the reform team of his former law professor, Anatoly Sobchak, the liberal mayor of that city. He became deputy mayor in 1994. His performance in that role brought him to Moscow in 1997 as deputy head of the presidential administration, on the recommendation of Chubais, and in 1998 he was appointed head of the Federal Security Service. This extraordinary rise of a hitherto obscure political figure reached a spectacular climax in 1999 when Putin became, in rapid succession, secretary of the Security Council (March), prime minister (August), and acting president (December), following Yeltsin's resignation.

During his KGB career Putin had mastered German and acquired considerable firsthand knowledge of Europe before serving for six years in St. Petersburg, managing foreign economic relations for Sobchak, a position in which he had close contact with foreign businessmen. He also ran the local branch of the government party of Prime Minister Chernomyrdin. The oft-heard statement that he became prime minister with no previous political experience was clearly wrong. Once appointed in August 1999, he quickly demonstrated brilliant political skill in organizing a coalition and program that broke the parliamentary dominance of the communists and their allies in the elections only four months later.

This stunning political victory, soon to be followed by Putin's victory in the presidential election the following March, achieved a transformation of the relationship between president and parliament, opening the way for major new political initiatives. Yeltsin had succeeded in building a strong presidential power in the 1993 constitution, but the parliamentary elections of 1993 and 1995 (especially the latter) gave the communists and their parliamentary allies a veto over legislation needed in vital areas such as landownership, privatization of state-owned enterprises, banking and foreign investment, taxation, and budgetary control. Such opposition, which continued until the final days of Yeltsin's presidency, greatly reduced the effectiveness and scope of his reforms, as well as the power and fiscal resources of the central government.

Despite this obstacle, Yeltsin had repeatedly renewed his reform efforts, placing power in the hands of young reformers such as Gaidar, Fedorov, Chubais, Nemtsov, and Kirienko, both before and after gaining increased power under the constitution of 1993. But much essential legislation was postponed for years, and even Yeltsin's presidential power was occasionally imperiled, as in the 1996 presidential contest with communist Zyuganov, in the political crisis that followed the August 1998 financial collapse, and in the impeachment efforts of his parliamentary opponents. The most dangerous and distressing consequence of the extended confrontation was the reduction of Russia's GDP and the decline of the living standard of the population during much of the 1990s, largely a consequence of the government's failure to complete essential economic reforms.

The year immediately preceding Putin's appointment was a low point in the Yeltsin presidency, initiated by the currency collapse and the massive banking and government debt default and followed by the extension of communist influence and presence in the government for the first time in the Yeltsin years. But once again Yeltsin seized the initiative, appointing first Stepashin and then Putin as prime minister and preparing for a new course.

THE STRUGGLE FOR THE PARLIAMENT

Putin became prime minister in August 1999. Often a crisis month in Russia, that August was no exception. He assumed leadership of a country whose economy was showing signs of recovery, but he faced a dangerous situation in Chechnya, which had never stabilized after the 1994–96 war and where warlords, as well as radical religious, nationalist, and other anti-Russian elements, dominated. He was now confronted with renewed military conflict in Chechnya in the wake of Chechen-supported efforts to separate Dagestan from Russia and Chechen terrorist bombings in Russian cities. In contrast to the 1994–96 Chechen war, this one was strongly supported by Russians angered by the bombings. And the second military campaign appeared, in its early stage, to be better managed than the previous one. Putin gained rather than lost popularity in the early course of the war.

In the approaching parliamentary elections Yeltsin hoped to reduce the powerful position of the communists and their allies in the Duma, where they controlled 47 percent of the votes and remained a barrier to his reform plans. He also faced a growing challenge from Moscow mayor Yury Luzhkov, who expanded his new party, Otechestvo, into a powerful, popular, center-right coalition called Otechestevo/Vsia Rossiia (Fatherland/All Russia, OVR) by joining with former prime minister Primakov and an influential group of regional leaders. Luzhkov's economic plan differed markedly from that of Yeltsin's economic reformers, advocating heavy protection of domestic industries and government funding of large development projects.

Putin developed an imaginative and highly successful political strategy to meet these challenges, using the powerful resources of the presidency and the new government. The key elements were the formation of a new government party, Edinstvo (Unity), and close cooperation with other parties to form a broad pro-government electoral alliance. The media supporting the government and the president mounted a powerful attack on Luzhkov, whose coalition ended up in the December elections with less than half the party-list Duma seats forecast by polls in September. The effort was aided by the formation of another coalition, Soiuz pravykh sil (the Union of Rightist Forces, URF), led by former prime minister Sergey Kirienko, and by Putin's drawing together the majority of the leadership and parties of Russian liberalism in cooperation with Unity. It was precisely the kind of democratic coalition that had failed to form in the 1993 and 1995 parliamentary elections, and Putin's negotiating skills played a vital role in its success.

The December 19, 1999, election results gave eloquent testimony to the success of the strategy. The communists and their allies were reduced from 47 percent to 26 percent of the Duma membership, while Unity and the URF, neither of which had existed in 1995, captured 22 percent of the vote together. They could count on substantial support from Zhirinovsky's party and Yavlinsky's Yabloko, for a total of 31 percent. Moreover, Luzhkov's Otechestevo/Vsia Rossiia achieved less than half the vote anticipated in the party-list election results, and soon after the elections his coalition began to lose members to Unity.

Another advantage of the new political situation following the December elections was the addition of a large number of deputies with a pragmatic rather than an ideological approach to legislation, who were likely to work well with a reformist government. The simultaneous removal of reactionary elements (communists and their allies) and the electoral success of the reformist right liberals of Kirienko's URF offered a great improvement in the prospects for both political and economic reform.

In sum, a major political transformation had been accomplished, for which Putin deserved most of the credit. He had initiated the formation of a strong pro-government party, which proved vastly more effective at the polls than Chernomyrdin's now defunct Our Home Is Russia. He also showed himself a gifted political organizer and coalition builder, negotiating cooperation among national and regional political leaders of the center and right who were supportive of the new constitutional and economic order and of his plans for reform. The reduction of communist parliamentary power and the increased strength of the reform leaders, united for the first time in the postcommunist era, explains the rapid improvement of Russian debt and equity markets following the elections and the striking economic growth of the years of the first Putin presidency.

PUTIN'S REFORM PROGRAM

Much of the commentary in the Western press on Putin's political success stressed the popularity of the second Chechen war, at least in its early phase, and implied that a reversal of fortune in that war would cause his support to weaken significantly. Although there is little doubt that a badly mismanaged war would have had a negative political effect, the notion that the war alone explained Putin's popularity and his success was misleading. In addition, his party-building and interparty coalition-building efforts were highly successful. He presented well the kind of political program needed to build a strong government party and a broad coalition, and he accomplished a major shift of legislative power in the government's favor in the December elections. Meanwhile, there was evidence that the communists' support was declining. Their supporters—heavily older generation—were declining in numbers. A new generation of leaders, both in Moscow and St. Petersburg and in the regions, like Putin himself, felt no nostalgia for the old Soviet order and had a strong preference for consolidating and reforming the new one.

Putin did an impressive job of presenting his political program, which he described with intelligence, skill, and brevity in a document titled "Russia at the Turn of the Millennium" posted on the Russian government's website at the end of 1999. He began by identifying the characteristics of the economic and social system that had been built in the leading states in the last part of the twentieth century, characteristics that defined the so-called postindustrial society with its new products developed by advanced science and technology, its new information and communication systems, and much else. He noted that the rapid changes had also brought serious environmental and social problems but argued that the achievements of the leaders represented the future and that the challenge for the majority of states left behind was to strive for the level of the leaders and innovators.

Putin was candid about Russia's current predicament: a nearly 50 percent decline in its GNP during the 1990s to a level now one-tenth that of the United States, and a per capita GDP one-fifth of the G-7 average. He also stressed low productivity, the desperate need for replacement of obsolete production machinery, the low level of foreign investment, the shortage of investment capital, and the uninterrupted decline of the real incomes of the population.

This description of the problems of the Russian economy was something on which almost all Russian political leaders could agree. What separated them were their assessments of the causes of Russia's predicament—whether they placed the main blame for the shortcomings on the marketizing, privatizing reforms of the 1990s or stressed the enormous burden of the Soviet legacy, affirmed the direction of the Yeltsin-era reforms, and offered credible proposals for dealing with a still-incomplete transition. Putin's words placed him firmly in the second group. Thus his explanation of the reform disappointments of the 1990s:

We had to install market elements into a system based on completely different standards, with a bulky and distorted structure.

We had to pay for the excessive focus of the Soviet economy on the development of the raw materials sector and defense industries, which negatively affected the development of consumer production and services.

We are paying for the Soviet neglect of such key sectors as information science, electronics, and communications [and] for the absence of competition between producers and industries, which hindered scientific and technological progress.

Putin then described Russia's current position as a "transition stage": "Despite problems and mistakes, it has entered the highway by which the whole of humanity is traveling. Only this way offers the possibility of dynamic economic growth and higher living standards, as the world experience convincingly shows."

Putin described his program as "combining the universal principles of a market economy and democracy with Russian values." He rightly observed that the central problem of the 1990s was the fundamental split in basic values and ideological positions among Russia's political leaders. But he also believed that period had given the people the opportunity "to use a diversity of forms of ownership, free enterprise, and market relations" and that they "have accepted values such as freedom of expression, freedom to travel abroad, and other fundamental political rights and human liberties." The task of the present leadership was to build on the new political possibilities evident in the December parliamentary elections and to offer a program of governmental and economic reform.

He argued the need for building a strong state—not a totalitarian state, but one that was a "democratic, law-based, workable federal state." He stressed the need for a responsible and honest civil service, a strong civil society, a larger role and authority for a reformed judiciary, reform of relations between regions and the center, especially in budget and finance, and an offensive against crime. It is significant that Putin also argued for firm control of the executive branch of government, noting that the main threat to human rights and democracy generally came from abuses of executive power.

On economic policy, he began with the general proposition that Russia would need a larger role for state direction of the economy—especially through the period of its transformation and recovery—than was familiar in the United States or Britain. It must vigorously support the expansion of investment, domestic and foreign (noting the dangerous decline of domestic investment and the failure to attract significant foreign investment). Putin called for government support of targeted industries—those that provided goods to the domestic market, fuel and energy, and raw materials. These needed support with loans and special tax arrangements. He proposed to encourage all forms of economic organization, large and small. And he stressed the need for a functional financial system with tax reform, an end to nonpayment and barter, low inflation and a stable ruble, protection of the stock market investor, reform of the banks, and a drastic reduction of the role of the shadow economy. Extensive domestic economic reform and integration into the global economy were his main themes.

Putin also noted the sad neglect of agricultural reform and urged the introduction of market reforms and individual ownership of farmland, along with support for technical modernization. Finally, a central feature of his proposed reform program was to focus government resources on the support of science, education, culture, and health and on dealing with the catastrophic decline of incomes—down from 60 percent to 30 percent of GDP in the new era.

Putin's road ahead promised to be a difficult one, given the imposing scale of economic and social problems inherited both from the Soviet era and from the difficult transition of the previous decade. Even leaving aside the tremendous problem of the renewed conflict in Chechnya—a huge distraction and cost at a most unfortunate time—there remained the persistent problem of the competing and conflicting programs of the major political parties. On the positive side, a new generation of political leaders had emerged, committed to a clearly articulated and immensely promising program of social, economic, and political reform. And unlike either Yeltsin or previous prime ministers, Putin could count on a parliamentary majority for much of his program. For his appointment, for his forthcoming presidential election, and for the constitutional structure within which he could proceed with his leadership and his program, he had good reason to be grateful for the solid achievements of the turbulent Yeltsin years. To those advantages he would soon add a spectacular performance in the presidential election.

FROM ACTING TO ELECTED PRESIDENT

Campaign staffs for Vladimir Putin remind one of Soviet-era advertising: "Fly Aeroflot!" Well, of course we will. What other airline is there? Judging from all the public opinion polls and many other indicators, the acting president isn't in need of any special support.

—SERGEY SERGIEVSKY[97]

The progress of Putin's political career from his appointment as prime minister in August 1999 and his assumption of the acting presidency following Yeltsin's resignation on December 31 to the presidential election on March 26, 2000, was remarkable. The reporter just quoted, writing nine days before the presidential election, had no doubt about the outcome. In a field of eleven candidates, Putin received 52.94 percent of the vote (39,740,434 votes), winning the presidency on the first round. CPRF chairman Zyuganov received 29.21 percent (21,928,471 votes), and Yabloko candidate Yavlinsky got 5.8 percent (4,353,452 votes). The totals for Putin and Zyuganov were remarkably close to the final results in 1996, though the gap between them, in comparison with that between Yeltsin and Zyuganov in 1996, had increased by 10.1 million to an impressively larger 17.8 million.[98] The downward trend in Zyuganov's presidential vote matched the trend in the communist parliamentary performance over virtually the same period. The newly elected president, only the second since Russian independence, began his presidency with political advantages that far exceeded the best Yeltsin had ever enjoyed. He would soon demonstrate his intention and ability to use those advantages vigorously.

CHAPTER 3

BUILDING A
NEW ECONOMY

ONCE IN CONTROL OF INDEPENDENT RUSSIA, YELTSIN AND his reform team made the bold decision to launch their radical program to transform the collapsing socialist command economy into a market economy. The sheer scale and complexity of the changes they undertook are stunning: the conversion of a huge economy based on comprehensive state ownership, with all aspects of planning and operation directed by the Party and state bureaucracy, into one based on private property, private enterprise, and a free market. This daunting task was undertaken simultaneously with the building of a new governmental and legal system, a new Russian state, and a new foreign and security policy.

Moreover, the reformers faced bitter opposition from much of the country's political leadership on the aims, methods, and substance of their policies—opposition that would block or distort much of their reform program, greatly increase the pain of the transition for the population, and exacerbate the dangerous political crises of the ensuing decade.

The lack of effective legislative support for the reform program until the end of the Yeltsin era was an enormous handicap in every aspect of restructuring the economy, from the necessary structural and legal changes to supportive policies of fiscal and monetary management. Both the Communist Party of the Russian Federation (CPRF) and its close ally in the countryside, the Agrarian Party, were powerful opponents of the reform program, and working with other parties and individuals they were able to deny the government crucial support. This disadvantage was partially offset by the president's power to issue decrees and to dissolve the Duma (to be followed by new elections), introduced in the 1993 constitution. But opposition administrators dominated much of the governmental and economic apparatus and could easily obstruct the implementation of decrees. Moreover, the president could only initiate reforms by decree. They required parliamentary action for implementation, and the political opposition continued to dominate the parliament after the introduction of the new constitution. Hence, a full decade was required to accomplish one of the most fundamental changes required by a market economy—the establishment of private property in land—not to mention a host of other vital economic reforms.

Yeltsin obtained an early one-year expansion of executive power that provided a crucial counterweight to opposition control of the Congress of Peoples Deputies and the Supreme Soviet. In October 1991 the Congress granted him special powers for the legislative regulation of economic reform and the postponement of all elections for one year.[1] By the end of 1992, however, the reaction of the Congress and Supreme Soviet against his economic reforms had created an obstinate opposition that compelled him to remove his reform leader, Yegor Gaidar, and replace him with a conservative energy industry executive, Viktor Chernomyrdin. With the opposition becoming more aggressive and dangerous during the following year, Yeltsin recognized that his only hope for a sustained and effective economic reform program lay in the introduction of a new constitution that would expand the executive power.

THE LEGACY OF GORBACHEV'S ECONOMIC REFORMS

Some transfer of ownership or control of state property had already begun under Mikhail Gorbachev. The sale of state-owned apartments was introduced in December 1988, and in April 1989 workers were allowed to lease state-owned enterprises. A government-commissioned report by the economist Leonid Abalkin called for much broader reform—freeing of prices, economic competition, currency convertibility, and a stock exchange. But Gorbachev aimed to reform the Soviet economic system, not to replace it. His reservations allowed Yeltsin to seize the economic reform leadership following his election to the leadership of the Russian Supreme Soviet in May 1990. Yeltsin then named two talented young economists to develop Russia's own economic reform program. Grigory Yavlinsky became deputy prime minister, and Boris Fedorov, minister of finance.

At first Yeltsin and Gorbachev cooperated, convening in August 1990 a group of economists under Stanislav Shatalin that prepared an ambitious "500–Day Program" of economic reform in the autumn of that year. Supported by Yeltsin, the program was approved overwhelmingly by the Russian Supreme Soviet, but Gorbachev rejected it as too radical. From that point forward, the conflict between the two leaders over the pace and scope of economic reform increased rapidly. In November, as Yeltsin's government adopted many of the ideas in the Shatalin proposal, Gorbachev warned him that the Russian government could not pursue an independent reform program. Ignoring the "advice," Yeltsin proceeded with planning for land reform and private enterprise.

As Yeltsin increased his authority—gaining special powers from the Supreme Soviet in April and election to the Russian Republic presidency by popular ballot in June 1991—he pressed economic reform further, introducing new legislation on housing privatization and on the privatization of state and municipal enterprises. The weakness of Gorbachev and the Soviet center after the collapse of the August Coup enabled him to pursue his reform program more aggressively within Russia. He announced a three-part program of price liberalization, privatization, and tight monetary and fiscal policies to the Russian Congress of People's Deputies in October 1991, and the Congress granted him decree powers to implement it. During November and December he assembled his team of reform advisors and was prepared to move forward at full speed with the advent of Russian independence in late December.

Yeltsin's choice of the distinguished young economist Yegor Gaidar as chief planner of the Russian economic reform program was one of the most important decisions of the postcommunist transition. In the debates over restructuring the Soviet socialist economy that were a central feature of the late Gorbachev era, Gaidar represented the radical wing. He planned a program that would begin with price liberalization, a stringent government fiscal policy retaining a minimum budget deficit, and an early move to a program for privatizing both the urban and rural economies.

Gaidar's view was that genuine market prices and the obligation of enterprise managers to compete on the market without government subsidies were prerequisites for a functioning market economy. Enterprises would become more efficient if their managers were disciplined by the possibility of bankruptcy rather than sheltered by lavish subsidies, which also generated large, inflationary budget deficits. Gaidar's initiatives were based on a bold and realistic assessment of the Russian economy and its needs, but they faced strong political, practical, and theoretical opposition that would greatly erode the efficacy of his reform program.

Gaidar's most prominent opponents occupied powerful positions. The chairman of the Russian Central Bank, Viktor Gerashchenko, argued that the only solution to the rapid price rises that would follow the removal of price controls was to match price inflation with an increased issue of currency. The chairman of the Supreme Soviet, Ruslan Khasbulatov, who shared this view, would spare no effort to assure budget deficits by securing parliamentary authorization for large expenditures. Vice president Aleksandr Rutskoy took essentially the same position.

Managers from the state managerial bureaucracy, whose functions were to be eliminated under Gaidar's plan, augmented the high-level opposition to his initiatives. These managers were comfortably situated in the state-owned enterprises. They had already gained new administrative autonomy from the Gorbachev reforms, and their independence had increased with the subsequent dismantling or erosion of Party power and police surveillance. They viewed the radical economic program as a threat to their growing organizational powers and personal revenue. Organized as the Russian Union of Industrialists and Entrepreneurs and as the Russian Association of Banks, they could provide a determined organizational resistance to the radical reform program. They and others, including farm managers and traders in agricultural products, became the main practical opponents of the reforms.

On the matter of privatization, the managers' attitude largely depended on the advantages it would bring them. In agriculture the choice was clear: the managers of state and collective farms organized effectively to obstruct transfer of ownership of the farms to the peasant cultivators and to retain administrative and financial control over the land that brought them profit. Managers of urban enterprises often saw a personal advantage in securing greater control and even ownership.

Energy and metals producers were the strongest opponents of Gaidar's proposed price liberalization. The existing official prices of these resources were very low—far below world market levels. Their managers, who were heavily involved in export, planned sales abroad on their own account that offered them immense profits so long as Russian prices stayed below foreign prices.

Thus the manufacturing, agricultural, and natural resources firms circumvented the radical reformers' efforts to avoid industrial subsidies as a threat to fiscal stability. They received generous government subsidies— ostensibly to help them in the economic transition and to support employment in social programs for workers but also for their own financial advantage. Industrial and agricultural firms also sought and received cheap credits as a form of subsidy.

Finally, proponents of alternative theories and programs of economic transition, who generally rejected rapid price liberalization, broad privatization, and strict control of government budget deficits, lent broad intellectual support to the pragmatic opposition to Gaidar's program. Many of these people advocated a vision of reformed socialism and, like Gorbachev, remained committed to an essentially socialist economic system. Adherents of this position were numerous among the economic specialists in the Russian Academy of Sciences. Some took a favorable view of Chinese economic reform, seeing it as a possible model. Ironically, the views of such people provided substantial support for Gaidar's opponents among the emerging class of private entrepreneurs.

Gorbachev's long delay of serious economic reform had left an economy nearing general collapse, greatly complicating the reform task.[2] Production had declined by nearly 13 percent in 1991, and the budget deficit was a spectacular 30 percent of gross domestic product. The republics were withholding funds from the center, jeopardizing the funding of social benefits, and price subsidies rose. Facing huge military expenditures, declining production, and a reduced capacity to meet the deficit with exports of oil, gas, and gold, Gorbachev turned to massive foreign borrowing. Meanwhile, the shops emptied as inflation caused panic buying and production of food and consumer goods declined.

The perilous condition of the economy demanded quick action from the reformers. They were concerned to preempt the process of *"nomenklatura* privatization,"* in which large numbers of enterprise managers, freed from effective control by Gorbachev's reforms, had begun to treat their enterprises as their own property. They were selling assets and products illegally and pocketing the proceeds, an activity that was particularly profitable in the energy and metals industries. Already in October 1991 Yeltsin had noted, "The party-state elites have actively engaged in their personal privatization."[3] He argued for abandoning debate about whether private ownership was desirable and turning to the task of orderly privatization.

The increased power and independence of the managers of state enterprises were among the major legacies of the Gorbachev-era economic reforms. Gorbachev had sought to strengthen the economy by giving them greater autonomy and responsibility, as he did in the 1987 Law on State Enterprises. But as party power and control declined in the final phase of his rule, these "red directors" increasingly used their expanded control of publicly owned enterprises and natural resources for private profit. Such activity was greatly facilitated when Gorbachev granted them privileged and profitable positions in domestic and international trade, as well as huge cash transfers from the state treasury in the form of enterprise subsidies and cheap credits. The many thousands of enterprises granted foreign trade privileges as a part of the reforms were especially favored by their access to oil and metals, which they sold abroad at world prices after buying them at a fraction of their market value.

Gorbachev's 1988 Law on Cooperatives had also created a means for managers of state enterprises to transfer profits to private enterprises they created under the provisions of the new law. Commercial banks were among the most important of such enterprises. Many of the new "oligarchs" of the Yeltsin era acquired their wealth in commercial banking, exploiting the opportunities created by the turbulent financial conditions of the late Gorbachev and early Yeltsin years to build huge fortunes. They gained spectacular profits from cheap state credits and by purchasing valuable state industrial and resource holdings at a fraction of their value. Oil, for example, could be purchased in Russia for less than half of 1 percent of its value on the export market, and cheap government credits were enormously lucrative in a time of soaring inflation. The names of new entrepreneurial figures such as Potanin, Berezovsky, and Gusinsky would become famous both in Russia and abroad for the men's enormous wealth and political influence. They used their influence to protect their own interests by blocking formation of a profit-oriented rather than a rent-seeking market economy. They became formidable opponents of the policies of the reformers appointed by Yeltsin.

THE POLITICS AND ECONOMICS OF THE YELTSIN REFORMS

The program initiated by the young reformers in early 1992 challenged the privileges and ambitions of this new group of entrepreneurs by seeking to eliminate fixed commodity and export prices. It also challenged the military-industrial complex, reducing military acquisitions by 70 percent. The powerful energy lobby, headed by Viktor Chernomyrdin, not only blocked the freeing of oil prices but secured the appointment of Chernomyrdin himself as energy minister in May 1992 and as prime minister six months later, enabling him to limit the reform process. As the reform government sought desperately to control inflation and balance the budget, the state companies producing oil and metals secured profits equaling nearly a third of GDP in 1992, enriching managers, politicians, and traders who stashed their bounty abroad, beginning the process of "capital flight" (transferring financial gains abroad for safekeeping).

The reformers faced still more formidable problems because of basic structural features of the inherited Soviet economy. These included the monopolistic structure of all basic industries, the widespread dependence of state enterprises on state credits and on the bureaucratic managerial apparatus that regulated the economy, the extraordinarily large proportion of industry dedicated to military production and dependent almost entirely on state purchases, and the rigidly bureaucratized and centralized structure of industrial management both at the enterprise level and in the managing Party-state apparatus. The abrupt shift to the reform policy removed much or most of the previous guaranteed market for the products of existing industries, as well as the directing bureaucracy that had managed the relations between them, their suppliers of raw materials, and intermediate manufacturers and that had provided needed credits.

The problems created by these changes were further complicated by the termination of state control of prices and foreign trade. The freeing of prices quickly refilled the empty shelves in the shops, but it was accompanied by a rising wave of price inflation. Meanwhile, the freeing of prices and the ending of the state monopoly over foreign trade allowed an emergent group of independent entrepreneurs to build large trading operations and independent financial institutions—the first private banks. Their opportunities for trade gains were vastly expanded because the liberalization of prices of consumer commodities did not apply to most industrial commodities. Commodities such as oil, metals, and timber, acquired at low domestic prices, brought huge profits in foreign sales and facilitated the use of bribes and other criminal methods to bypass already inadequate customs services and border regulation. Such were the conditions and opportunities that facilitated the acquisition of great private wealth during the first stage of reform.

Meanwhile, the economic condition of the general population deteriorated rapidly as rampant inflation consumed savings along with confidence in the ruble, encouraging capital flight and general economic decline. The government's effort to control inflation during the first half of 1992 by limiting the money supply brought a cash crisis rather than control of prices. Responding to parliamentary pressure to increase the cash supply in mid-1992, it precipitated even worse inflation and was forced to undertake greater external borrowing to secure sufficient budget funds.

Such was the environment in which the government launched its program for privatizing state property. Called "voucher privatization"—a reference to the certificate received by each citizen that provided an equal share of state property—it was launched late in 1992, achieving the privatization of a few of the mid-size and large firms and nearly fifty thousand small shops.

The removal of Gaidar as prime minister in December 1992 marked the end of the first phase of economic reform. The main achievement of the period was to extend the political revolution of late 1991, which had dismantled communist rule, into an economic revolution that would transform the structure and functioning of the national economy. The inherited economic structure had been severely shaken, but replacement by the intended new model had only begun. Meanwhile, the problems of inflation, wage arrears, accumulations of nonpayments in inter-enterprise transactions, and huge shortages of state revenue had created formidable opposition to the government, forcing Gaidar's removal.

The new prime minister, Chernomyrdin, was accepted by the parliament in the expectation that he would abandon his predecessor's reform policies. Chernomyrdin's decision to bring Gaidar back into the government, where he would soon become first deputy prime minister, together with his continued privatization, his heavy reductions of government expenditures, and generally discouraging economic trends, served to increase the parliament's hostility toward the executive leadership and intensify the political struggle, which reached a violent climax in October 1993.

Throughout the year the government experienced great frustration as it sought to maintain a balanced budget. Increased printing of currency to expand Central Bank credits aggravated already dangerous levels of inflation, limiting that option for generating government revenue. And after the dismantling of the former system of channeling revenue to the central treasury from state-owned enterprises, efforts to use conventional tax collection proved discouraging. The voluntary assumption of tax obligations by newly independent enterprises was greatly diminished by their dire financial condition at a time of declining industrial and agricultural production. Faced with an overwhelming burden of federal and local taxes, they devoted much of their energy and ingenuity to tax evasion, as in turning to the "shadow economy"—unregulated economic operations immune to taxation. The reality was that the government was urgently pressed to provide more support for failing enterprises and had scant hope of increased revenues from them. Meanwhile, new private enterprises, making up the largest segment of economic expansion, were often wholly inaccessible to tax authorities.

There was also little hope of foreign borrowing as a source of desperately needed credits. With increased currency emission from Central Bank credits already generating inflation, the government was compelled to turn to internal borrowing. In May 1993, at the point when the federal budget deficit had reached its highest level since Russian independence, the government announced creation of a new program of issuing short-term notes (GKOs) to provide government revenue. The subsequent expansion of internal borrowing became a major focus of efforts to reduce the budget deficit in succeeding years. The huge rise of inflation (940 percent in 1993) made short-term bonds an attractive alternative to expanded currency issue, especially because it was clear from the relentless growth of inter-enterprise debt that further reduction of state credits to industry was unacceptable.

Another obstacle to the reformers' program was the policy of the Central Bank, a body over which the government had no effective control. While the energy and other lobbies deprived the state of crucial revenues, the Central Bank issued highly subsidized credits to enterprises, equal to 32 percent of GDP, a particular boon to Russian private bankers. To the huge cost of these credits was added the burden of Russian subsidies for exports to other CIS countries, even as the retention of the ruble zone until the spring of 1993 denied the Russian government the power to control monetary emission and encouraged greater printing of money in former republics seeking to increase their share of the total holdings of the ruble zone. A final blow to the reform plan was the huge outlay of government funds for import subsidies—largely for food—that were paid to the state agricultural monopolies and traders.

The cumulative effect of these setbacks on the reformers' efforts to achieve macroeconomic stability and to maintain public support for their broader reform program was devastating. The federal budget for 1992 showed a deficit of 11.1 percent of GDP, and the same year saw a huge inflation in consumer prices of 2,650 percent. Predictably, the blame for the deficit was assigned to the economic reform team rather than to the special interests whose political power and massive profiteering had imposed deprivation and liquidation of savings on much of the population.

Yeltsin's decree providing freedom of trade in January 1992 was met with the same determined opposition as his attempt to free commodity prices. Although the January decree brought a huge upsurge of small private trading across the country, the opposition of the established traders, in cooperation with local political officials, quickly suppressed much of the activity and replaced the permissive decree with strict licensing regulations in the spring of 1993.

Despite the negative results of the first year of the reform effort and the creation of large fortunes by bankers and industrialists supported by a substantial group in the parliament, the reformers made impressive gains in 1993. By the end of the year the former ruble zone was replaced by national currencies, and subsidized credits and import subsidies had been abolished. The achievement of these important objectives was greatly aided by the support of the International Monetary Fund, whose lending requirements the reformers used to gain acceptance of their own programs. By the end of the year they had also achieved unified exchange rates. But the strong performance of the reformers' nationalist and communist opponents in the December 1993 parliamentary elections brought a major reduction of the role of reformers in the government. Deputy prime ministers Yegor Gaidar and Boris Fedorov were replaced, and only Anatoly Chubais, the architect and administrator of the privatization program, remained.

With the reformers now weakened, Prime Minister Chernomyrdin and first deputy prime minister Oleg Soskovets quickly pressed for tax exemptions for the natural gas giant Gazprom, the metallurgical industry, and the alcohol- and tobacco-importing National Sports Foundation, exemptions cumulatively equal to roughly 6 percent of GDP. And though the reformers had liberalized commodity prices in 1993, lobbyists kept them low by securing export limits. Even after yielding to IMF pressures to remove such limits, the energy managers used their control of pipelines to constrain exports and keep domestic prices down. The result was a significant rise in the government budget deficit, which brought a 27 percent drop in the ruble exchange rate on Black Tuesday—October 11, 1994. This calamity enabled Yeltsin to dismiss some of the leading economic policy makers and appoint Anatoly Chubais first deputy prime minister with responsibility for macroeconomic policy.

Chubais and the reform group in the Duma had considerable success during 1995. They reduced the government budget deficit by 50 percent, sharply cutting enterprise subsidies, regional transfers, and tax exemptions, and they achieved a major reduction of the inflation rate. Russia received its first IMF standby loan, and for the first time government economic policy received close cooperation from the Russian Central Bank and improved support from the Duma, where Gaidar's Russia's Democratic Choice party was now the largest faction. Meanwhile, important progress was made in privatizing state enterprises.

PRIVATIZATION

The first phase of the program of privatization, voucher privatization, was concluded in July 1994. At that time the privatization total included 16,500 enterprises with 21.8 million workers, accounting for 62 percent of GDP.[4] The remaining state-owned enterprises included some of the most profitable ones—especially those in minerals, energy, and telecommunications—for which a second stage of privatization was planned. A notable feature of the privatization up to this time was that about three-quarters of the enterprises had been privatized under Option 2 of the law of July 1991, which allowed employee ownership. This arrangement usually meant continuation of management by the state-appointed directors, little or no change of management style or effectiveness, and continuing pressure for large government subsidies. The arrangement had been a prerequisite for securing the support of the Supreme Soviet for the privatization legislation, because the red directors had powerful influence in that body, and the Option 2 procedures enabled them to consolidate their enterprise control. Otherwise negative on the privatizing policies of the young reform leaders, they understood the advantages of legal ownership over the "expanded management prerogatives" they had invented previously.

The new stage of privatization in 1995 focused much more heavily on securing a financial return to relieve the large government budget deficit. The effort to stabilize the financial system with reduced spending and a large ($6.25 billion) standby loan from the IMF in April 1995 had brought a major decline in inflation and a significant reduction of the state budget deficit (to 2.9 percent of GDP), but at the cost of increased wage arrears and tax evasion.[5] Desperately seeking additional revenue, the government looked to privatization sales. It had managed greatly to reduce (by nearly 70 percent) dependence on the inflationary policy of printing money to cover budget deficits by turning to both external and internal borrowing, which together provided 93 percent of its funding. The hope was that profitable privatization would further ease its budgetary problems and inflationary pressures. The previous privatization had been disappointing in this regard, producing only $22.3 million—a mere 2.5 percent of the expected return—forcing growing reliance on the restructuring of Western debt and much-expanded internal borrowing (through the GKOs and Federal Bond Notes, or OFZs).

The new privatization initiative came initially not from the government but from a group of the wealthiest entrepreneurs of the new Russia, men who had profited greatly from the opportunities of the Yeltsin era. Like the other oligarchs, the initiator of the plan, Vladimir Potanin, had built a considerable fortune in banking (Bank Menatep), seizing the opportunity provided by the collapse of the Soviet banking system and the ensuing opportunities for private bankers to gain handsome profits for their banks in the process of transmitting state credits to enterprises. They had also bought many enterprises being sold cheaply by the state in the first phase of privatization. Now they sought to exploit the government's financial weakness to acquire large shares of the country's most valuable industries.

Potanin developed his scheme, called "loans for shares," in late 1994. His objective was to acquire ownership of a hugely valuable enterprise called Norilsk Nickel, a client of his bank. The plan was to offer the cash-strapped Russian government a large loan in exchange for the right to manage the company, using his holding company, Interros, as the management agent. Although Yeltsin approved the scheme, it was clear that its implementation would require allies, and Potanin soon formed a group that included Mikhail Khodorkovsky of Oneksimbank and the heads of four other major banks. Early discussions assigned Norilsk Nickel to Potanin, the huge Siberian oil company Yukos to Khodorkovsky, and other enterprises to about a dozen future oligarchs.

The group now had the task of selling the scheme to the government, and the response of Anatoly Chubais, the architect of Russian privatization, was crucial. Chubais's initial reaction was negative, because the plan was clearly insider privatization, lacking openness and competitive bidding. He was won over, however, chiefly because of the government's desperate need for non-inflationary funding and because he saw the sponsoring group of dynamic young entrepreneurs as offering precisely the kind of managerial talent that Russia needed to replace the incompetent red directors.[6] When the scheme was presented to the cabinet in late March 1995, the sponsors offered the government a loan of up to 9.1 trillion rubles ($1.8 billion) in exchange for the transfer of management responsibility for four giant firms: Norilsk Nickel, Yukos, United Energy Systems, and Russian Telecommunications (Rostelekom). When the proposal was accepted (minus the last two companies), the sponsors continued to push their plan.

In reality, the government did not control the companies it was agreeing to sell. The future oligarchs received, in effect, a government mandate to wrest control of them from the red directors who had protected their control against the earlier privatization program. They set about this task energetically but in some cases were blocked by the current company heads, as in the cases of the oil companies Lukoil and Surgutneftegaz. They emerged from their long struggle with just twelve companies and still needed to gain the support of the newly appointed head of the State Property Committee (GKI), Alfred Kokh. Aware of the treacherous political challenges of coming months and of the cost of failure to achieve the privatization income the government desperately needed, they presented the Potanin loans scheme to the cabinet in August. Meanwhile, the *apparatchiki* had been won over and the laws written. On August 31, 1995, Yeltsin signed the requisite decree. The government would auction off the right to manage the state's shares in major companies—ostensibly in open auctions but in fact in transactions dominated by insider deals and excluding foreigners from bidding on the major companies sought by the future oligarchs.

The terms of the loans to the government provided that the creditors would receive a low rate of interest for three months and that the loans would terminate in September 1996. At that time the government could either repay the loans and reclaim its shares or sell off the shares used as collateral, paying the lender 30 percent of the difference between the sale price and the initial loan. The lenders were in charge of the auctions and could exclude competitive bids, assuring their future ownership. But the fact that the transfer of ownership was postponed until late 1996 or 1997 bound the lenders to the Yeltsin government in the 1996 presidential election, because the communists, however effectively the presentation of "loans for shares" might have obscured the intended outcome, were certain to block the full ownership transfer if they won the presidency.

In the loans-for-shares auctions the future oligarchs, especially Potanin and Khodorkovsky, proved exceedingly skillful in neutralizing or winning the acquiescence or support of the red directors of the firms they sought and in blocking competitive bids. They also emerged with control of the companies they sought (Norilsk Nickel for Potanin and Yukos for Khodorkovsky), as did other members of the organizing consortium. A small group of oligarchs emerged with control of most of the vast energy, metal, and timber resources of Russia, at prices that represented a pathetically small fraction of their true value.

The success of the procedure by which the banks gave loans for shares and then took over enterprises was testimony to its effective design. Oneksimbank had won a loan-based auction for 78 percent of the shares of Yukos. Only two weeks after the investment it secured an unscheduled meeting of the company's shareholders and took control of the company without opposition from the directors, who had been well prepared in advance. The takeover of Norilsk Nickel by Menatep, which won a collateral-based (loans for shares) auction for 38 percent of the company's shares for $170.1 million, was more difficult. The firm's board rejected the request to convene a special shareholders' meeting for changes in the charter and the board's membership. However, GKI head Alfred Kokh affirmed that the bank was now a de facto stockholder with many of the rights of an actual shareholder. Thus the bank acquired control of a concern made up of six enterprises, possessing a capital of 31 billion rubles, and producing 99.8 percent of Russia's platinum (40 percent of world output), 96 percent of its cobalt, 90 percent of its nickel, and more than 50 percent of its copper. A journalist commenting on the sense of urgency that motivated the organizers of these changes noted that "the political situation in our country is such that one can expect absolutely anything, even nationalization."[7]

The concern of the lending banks over the future of the new privatizing procedure was fully understandable. Like the Yeltsin government, they were worried about the outcome of the presidential election. They had just witnessed the formidable Communist Party performance in the parliamentary elections, an event that was followed by the resignation of first deputy prime minister Anatoly Chubais, the "father of privatization." Though the Chubais economic team remained in place, those familiar with Chubais's role appreciated the seriousness of the loss. As one knowledgeable commentator put it:

Chubais was the focal point of key government functions: the reform strategy, implementation of the budget, financial stabilization, the restructuring of the economy, the privatization of property, the securities market, interaction with the West in the area of support for the government's economic course. . . . Chubais is not just a name but a whole technology of reforms . . . [providing] the swiftest possible translation into reality of Boris Yeltsin's most important economic reforms.[8]

Fearing the effects of the widespread unpopularity of Chubais, a man unjustly blamed for most of the complications and shortcomings of the reform years, Yeltsin had pressed for his removal, despite the resistance of Prime Minister Chernomyrdin. Adding insult to injury, Yeltsin would soon appoint Chubais's opponent Oleg Soskovets to head his presidential election campaign. Ironically, the ever loyal and efficient Chubais would soon play the crucial role both in presenting the reality of Communist Party intentions to Western government and business leaders and in rescuing the presidential campaign from Soskovets's hopelessly incompetent management and organizing an electoral victory.

Deeply concerned about the efforts of the CPRF's Gennady Zyuganov to convince Western governments and business leaders that he would not reverse the Yeltsin-era economic reforms, Chubais attended the World Economic Forum in Davos, Switzerland, in early February 1996, which included a special session on "Russia's Future." He had noted an article by Zyuganov on the op-ed page of the *New York Times* on February 1, the eve of the conference, stating that his party now accepted the irreversibility of the Russian economic transformation and sought something like social democracy on the West European model, which would include security for both Russian and foreign private investment in the Russian economy. He stressed his party's complete break, ideologically and organizationally, with the Soviet Communist Party.

A distinguished Russian reporter, Mikhail Berger, observed that in a debate featuring Zyuganov and a second presidential candidate, Grigory Yavlinsky, the latter was a more vigorous critic of Yeltsin's "party of power" than of Zyuganov.[9] Berger then provided his own criticism of Zyuganov, noting his repeated claim that he favored the market but his insistence that it must be a "regulated market"; Berger asked whether this meant a "State Planning Committee." Referring to Zyuganov's statement that the communists sought a balance of public and private property, Berger opined that although Zyuganov had not specified the proportions, they would probably be something like 90:10.

Berger greatly appreciated the performance in the debate of "Zyuganov's main and perhaps only serious opponent, Anatoly Chubais." He wrote that "Chubais contrasted Zyuganov's statement in Switzerland with what the CPRF platform says on the same points and with what the CPRF leader himself says about them when he is in Russia." The party platform advocated return to public ownership of property that had been privatized "against the public interest" (as defined by the CPRF), and it portrayed the period of a mixed economy as one that would be followed by a "stage . . . dominated by public forms of ownership." Chubais also remarked on the contrast between Zyuganov's friendly approach to the IMF at Davos and an article published in Russia in which he had said that "foreign emissaries from the IMF and other world financial centers were behaving like gauleiters in Russia . . . [and] that dollars . . . had dealt a harder blow to the Russian economy than fascist tanks and planes had." In short, Chubais challenged illusions that Zyuganov had sought to purvey about communist intentions.

Only a few days after the Davos meetings, the communists and their allies in the Duma confirmed the truth of Chubais's charges about communist plans for reversing privatization. On February 9, 1996, the Duma set up a commission to investigate privatization. As plans for the commission developed, it became clear that its proponents intended to bypass the usual role of Duma committees in such inquiries and conduct the review in the full Duma, where the leftist majority could sidestep the most relevant committee—the Committee on Property and Privatization. They also changed the name of the proposed investigative body to "Commission to Analyze the Results of Privatization in 1992–96 and to Establish the Responsibility of Officials for Its Negative Results."[10] The name of the commission was in clear conflict with Zyuganov's reassurance to foreign business leaders at Davos about his acceptance of privatization, but it was consistent with his efforts to discredit the Yeltsin government.

PARLIAMENTARY AND PRESIDENTIAL ELECTIONS

The problems of economic reform, and particularly the problem of funding government operations, were at the core of the political crisis Yeltsin confronted at the beginning of 1996. The Russian population had endured remarkably stoically the enormous dislocation and deprivation that accompanied the transition to a new economic system, but its dissatisfaction had already been evident in the parliamentary elections of December 1993, which had caused Yeltsin to reduce his economic reform efforts. The democratic parties had gained 30 percent of the seats in the Duma in those elections, but they were outnumbered by the combination of 19 percent going to the communists and their allies and 15 percent to the misnamed Liberal Democratic Party of Zhirinovsky—both consistently opposed to the democrats and their economic reforms. The situation worsened during 1994 and 1995 as the smaller parties and independents tended increasingly to vote with the communists and nationalists.

The December 1995 elections had showed a decided shift against the parties of democracy and market reform. Seats in the Duma held by the democratic parties declined from 30 percent to 24 percent of the total. And although seats held by the Liberal Democrats fell from 14 percent to 11 percent, those held by the communists and their close allies, the agrarians, rose dramatically, from 18 percent to 44 percent, so they were now able to block legislation and government budgets. The CPRF had risen from the wreckage of the RSFSR and Soviet Parties to become the most powerful political party in Russia. The Russian democrats had meanwhile experienced a further decline of popular support.

With such parliamentary election results, and with January 1996 polls showing Yeltsin's popularity at 6 percent, there was a serious possibility that the communist leader Gennady Zyuganov might win the presidency in June and reverse the marketization and privatization of the economy. The development of a new Yeltsin campaign strategy in March, the infusion of massive financial and media support from people fearful of a communist victory, and the ideological and organizational rigidity of the communists combined to produce a miraculous 54 percent vote for Yeltsin in July. The wealthy and powerful new entrepreneurs, especially the oligarchs Boris Berezovsky and Vladimir Gusinsky, were particularly valuable to Yeltsin for the financial and media support they gave his campaign. Some gained appointments in the government formed after the election, which included none of the earlier reform leaders.

During the election campaign Yeltsin promised the removal of wage arrears, expanded support for social programs, and generous state credits for troubled business and agricultural enterprises. In the aftermath of the election such promises were impossible to fulfill, because budgetary reserves were low and opportunities for acquiring new credit were limited. The government was obliged to reduce expenses and to repudiate many commitments, including the promise to pay back wages. Credits to industry and agriculture were also reduced, bringing a return of rising inter-enterprise debt.

Meanwhile, as tax collections became more difficult there were warnings of a future financial collapse, and the use of internal borrowing instruments (GKOs and OFZs) more than doubled in the second half of 1996. In the same period the government's dependence on the bankers behind the loans-for-shares scheme increased with the appointment in August of Vladimir Potanin as first deputy prime minister. The continuing decline of tax collection increased the sense of a growing fiscal emergency and the attractiveness of privatization deals with the new capitalists seeking privatization of state assets in mining, oil, and energy.

In the aftermath of the presidential election the government's financial management displayed some of the most negative features of earlier years.

Though Yeltsin spoke frequently during the electoral campaign about the shortcomings of his own reforms and of the need to address the widespread poverty of the population, his health problems left him with little energy for a vigorous renewal of the reform initiative. During the campaign he had generously spent public funds to encourage support of his candidacy, substantially increasing the budget deficit for 1996. Meanwhile, the treasury bills used to finance the government deficit—and provide hefty revenues for the privileged Russian banks holding them—had reached 150 percent in interest, imposing a budget cost equal to 4 percent of GDP.

RENEWED REFORM AND FINANCIAL CRISIS

In December 1996 Yeltsin turned once again to Anatoly Chubais for support in a growing crisis, naming him head of the Administration of the Russian President. In March 1997 Chubais and the reforming governor of Nizhnii Novgorod, Boris Nemtsov, were named deputy prime ministers. The policy aim was to stabilize a dangerous fiscal situation by spending reductions, internal and external borrowing, and sales of state property. But the burden of credits to industry and agriculture, the heavy costs for the military, and the huge arrears in wages presented formidable obstacles. Efforts to increase tax income also continued to disappoint. Pressure on the large companies to increase tax payments had little effect when the most promising tax prospects, the large energy companies, were themselves receiving meager payment from their customers for gas and electricity.

The government's fiscal situation was somewhat relieved by pressing large companies to take loans to make tax payments.[11] But neither this measure nor the sale of additional shares in lucrative companies such as Yukos, the national telecom company Sviazinvest, and Norilsk Nickel provided sufficient revenue, especially because the uncompetitive bidding procedures brought minimal returns. The massive loss of potential government revenue through corrupt privatization is illustrated by the purchase of a majority of Yukos shares by Khodorkovsky and his five partners. The process, begun in the autumn of 1995, gained them a 78 percent share in Yukos for $309 million. By the time the deal was finalized in the summer of 1997, the company had a market capital of $6 billion, and six years later that figure had grown to $24 billion.[12]

During the spring and summer of 1997 the combination of modestly increased tax payments from large companies and installment payments on an IMF loan (a response to Russian fiscal stabilization) relieved budget pressures slightly, but funding shortages soon forced large sales of state bonds on foreign markets, and the interest rate on domestic credit instruments rose to 150 percent. The government came under increasing pressure not only financially but also politically as reaction developed to the corrupt privatization deals. The scandal surrounding the privatizations forced the resignation of Alfred Kokh as deputy prime minister for privatization and the November resignations of Chubais as finance minister and Nemtsov as fuel and energy minister. Ironically, all of them had tried in vain to achieve authentically competitive privatizations during the summer of 1997, and their opponents were recent beneficiaries of the loans-for-shares privatizations.

The year 1998 brought the collapse of the Russian financial system—state and private—in a catastrophic collision with the East Asian economic crisis. Despite the reformers' tenacious efforts over six years, basic structural reform of the government's financial system was still woefully inadequate, leaving the leaders searching desperately for revenues from taxation, borrowing, and privatization sales of state-owned assets.

From the beginning the economic reforms had created broad opportunities for traders, enterprise managers, and bankers to acquire private wealth. These opportunities reached a climax in the loans-for-shares privatizations, which transferred for a pittance a major share of the country's economic resources to a handful of so-called oligarchs. Having gained great wealth by illicit means, some of them used their newly acquired wealth and power, including control of the press, to block and discredit the efforts of Boris Nemtsov and others to reform subsequent privatization auctions. Their aim was to exclude domestic and foreign competition in privatizations, thus increasing their own gain. The consequence—as in their opposition to effective tax measures—was to aggravate the persistent and dangerous government financial crisis. Such behavior compounded the problem of the huge share of economic activity in oil and gas, timber, fishing, banking, and retail and foreign trade that went unreported and untaxed.[13]

Meanwhile, the IMF's decision to grant Russia a standby credit encouraged an increase in foreign portfolio investment by nearly five times (from $8.9 billion in 1996 to $45.6 billion in 1997), and direct foreign investment increased by 2.5 times in a single year (1996–97). The huge increase of the dependence of the Russian financial system on foreign funds was evident in the fact that they accounted for 30 percent of the holdings on the Russian stock market in 1997 and 38 percent of the holdings in government treasury bills. Adding the figures on foreign investment in the bonds of enterprises and of regional and local governments, and loans of $20 billion from international financial institutions, it is clear why the Russian financial system was highly vulnerable to the kind of international financial crisis that appeared in East Asia in 1997 and brought financial collapse to Russia in the summer of 1998.

The government's heavy dependence on short-term financing with treasury bills was especially risky, as their soaring interest rates soon demonstrated. Meanwhile, the government had failed to cut subsidies and collect taxes effectively, and massive tax avoidance was facilitated by the widespread practice of handling inter-enterprise payments by barter (half of the total) and other noncash payments. The use of such practices was strongly supported by large enterprises, especially those owned by the oligarchs who had funded Yeltsin's election campaign and sought government financial favors in return. The two leading supporters, Berezovsky and Gusinsky, also opposed the government reformers' efforts to establish open bidding in sales of state enterprises in the summer of 1997, and they joined Chernomyrdin and the Duma communists in supporting increased budget deficits, which reformers wished to control and reduce. Yeltsin had indicated an intention to strengthen the efforts of the reformers by adding Nemtsov to the government in the spring of 1997, but his support of the reformers' efforts proved inadequate. Late in the year, however, he showed increasing dissatisfaction with economic conditions in the country, particularly the huge arrears in wages and pensions that had brought widespread suffering to workers and pensioners.

Yeltsin removed Chernomyrdin as prime minister in March 1998, replacing him with the young reformer Sergey Kirienko. By that time the budget deficit had finally been brought under control, but the interest on government short-term debt had reached 100 percent. That huge and unsustainable debt combined with cumbersome bureaucratic regulation and high taxation to discourage both domestic and foreign investment. The effects of the Asian financial crisis continued to spread, and international investors, recognizing Russia's financial weakness, chose both to sell stocks (bringing a summer stock market crash) and to avoid renewal of short-term treasury bills, forcing the government to pay ever higher interest rates.

The problems this growing crisis posed for the Kirienko government were greatly complicated by the responses of domestic interest groups. The oil interests, including Berezovsky, favored currency devaluation as the best means of avoiding a spontaneous collapse of the ruble, though it would bankrupt the Russian commercial banks with their large hard currency obligations. Regional governors opposed transfer of a larger share of their revenues (collectively 50 percent larger than those of the federal government) to the center, because they provided huge, politically useful resources for subsidies. And there was scant prospect of economizing by reducing the state bureaucracy, which had added over a million workers since the early nineties. Unsurprisingly, the Duma, too, refused to come to the government's aid in the crisis. It rejected tax revisions that would have allowed taxation of barter transactions, and it rejected a proposal for legislation supporting transfer of more regional revenue to the center.

International events in the late spring rapidly increased the threat to the Russian financial system. Foreign investors became increasingly concerned about Russian financial stability as problems increased in Asia with the fall of the Indonesian government, the weakening of Korean banks, and discussion of German and American interest rate rises. In May the pressure on the ruble was greater than at any time since October 1994: Russia had entered a period of severe financial crisis.

Following the establishment of the currency corridor in 1995, which limited currency emissions and committed the government to meeting budget deficits by borrowing on the domestic and international financial markets, the ruble had remained stable. Inflation had dropped from 200 percent in early 1995 to 7.5 percent in mid-1997. Although the system was sensible, inadequate budgetary control allowed short-term treasury bill debt to rise to 13.5 percent of GDP by 1997 and required that 8 billion rubles ($1.2 billion) be raised each week to refinance existing debt. As investors became more reluctant to hold ruble-denominated bonds, interest rates were rapidly raised, adding both to the debt burden and to investors' doubts about the government's financial stability. When the government was denied resumption of IMF payments on its $9.5 billion loan, the interest rate on treasury bills had to be raised to 150 percent to restore the market.

Fearing the consequences of currency devaluation—loss of popular confidence and a massive collapse of Russian banks burdened with foreign currency debt—the government felt it had no alternative but to seek support for conversion of its heavy short-term debt load to long-term debt, reduce expenses by $6.8 billion, and increase revenue to eliminate the budget deficit. Both required the support of the Duma, where Yeltsin was initially met with Zyuganov's demand for his impeachment and the refusal of any cooperation on proposed budget cuts and tax measures. The other challenge, to refinance the $25 billion held by Russian private banks and foreign investors, required an appeal to the IMF. The Russian leaders sought a $10–15 billion loan under the IMF Supplemental Reserve Facility Program to stabilize financial markets. Protracted negotiations were suddenly accelerated following the July 8 collapse of the Russian bond market, and US pressure encouraged the IMF to move quickly on a $22.6 billion support package backed by the United States, Japan, Germany, France, and Saudi Arabia, as well as the World Bank.

Following the announcement of IMF support, an extraordinary session of the Duma gave speedy approval to a new tax code and corporate tax rate, along with other components of the government's "anticrisis program." These actions, combined with a decline in bond interest rates and a recovery of the stock market, gave misleading assurance that the crisis had passed. But the continued spread of the East Asian crisis—now to Latin America—brought a new rise in interest rates on government bonds and another stock market crash. Further appeals for international support went unanswered, forcing the government on August 17 to reduce its support for the ruble and announce a unilateral restructuring of its debt—in effect a default. The announcement brought the collapse of the ruble, of the Russian private banks, and of Russian credibility on international financial markets. It also brought the resignation of Kirienko and his replacement by Yevgeny Primakov, a choice of prime minister dictated for the first time by the Duma, marking a significant turn in the political leadership and in the power relationship between the Duma and the president.

The economic consequences of the August financial collapse were many. As predicted, the fall of the ruble brought a massive bank collapse that not only claimed the savings of depositors but also forced a shift from credit and barter to cash transactions, contributing to a serious economic decline. Inflation rose from 0.2 percent per month in August to 38 percent in September. A serious decline in wages and a large rise in unemployment brought rapid deterioration of living standards for much of the population. The proportion of the population living below the poverty line ($32 per month) rose quickly to 25 percent higher than the level of a year earlier. Within a month of the financial collapse, imports had dropped by 65 percent as the ruble's exchange rate with hard currencies plummeted and imported food and consumer goods were priced out of the market. The loss of imported food was significant, because the 1998 grain harvest was nearly 50 percent below the average of recent years.

Some results of the financial collapse, however, would serve the cause of economic reform. The large reduction in the costs to the budget of foreign financing and inflated rates on treasury bills was a major benefit, saving the equivalent of 10 percent of GDP. And the sharp decline of imports improved the trade balance at the same time it encouraged domestic production that had been hampered by the competition of cheap imports. The question at this point was what the political outcome of the financial crash would be, for that would influence the choice of future economic policy.

TESTING PRESIDENTIAL POWER

For opponents of the market reform the events of August 1998 were final proof that the reforms initiated in 1992 had been a total failure. Having obstructed efforts by the Kirienko government to stave off financial collapse, they now sought both to increase their power and to apply their own program. The final sixteen months of Yeltsin's presidency thus brought a new and crucial phase in the struggle for Russia's future. The focus of all parties was on the parliamentary elections scheduled for 1999 and the presidential election of 2000.

Following the financial collapse, Yeltsin faced an opposition majority in the parliament determined to have its way in appointing a new prime minister. Under their pressure he was eventually forced to appoint his foreign minister, Yevgeny Primakov, the only candidate acceptable both to him and to the opposition. The significance of this appointment was twofold. It was the first time Yeltsin had compromised the presidential prerogative of appointment of ministers, and Primakov had long championed a policy of cooperation with the communists. He proceeded to appoint the first center-left government of the Yeltsin era, turning the crucial portfolio for economic policy over to a communist, Yuri Maslyukov, a former Politburo member and chairman of the State Planning Committee, Gosplan. The communists had not only succeeded in expelling the leading reformers from the government but also gained a prime minister more sympathetic to their views on economic policy. They now began to press for constitutional changes to reduce the president's powers and increase those of the parliament they dominated.

Primakov had acknowledged Russia's need for international economic assistance, but his appointment of Maslyukov greatly reduced his credibility with international financial institutions. His challenge was to reconcile communist-inspired economic policies, which emphasized heavy government expenditures for subsidies and social benefits, with the requirements of fiscal stability set by international lenders. Russian banks were desperately in need of international investment or government support to resume operations, but foreign investors were uninterested and the government lacked the resources. The government budget presented to the IMF in late October showed revenues at roughly half the level of expenditures, and after extended negotiations and repeated and ineffective budget revisions the IMF delegation left Moscow with no agreement. The result was a stalemate in efforts to restore and strengthen the Russian financial system.

During subsequent months the Duma continued to block plans for restructuring the banking system, denying the newly created Agency for Restructuring Credit Organizations the right to seize bank shares and interfere in the operations of banks for restructuring purposes. Meanwhile, the Russian Central Bank continued giving credits to troubled banks, and several banks received subsidized agricultural loans.[14] Despite such discouraging developments, however, there were important indications that the financial collapse had prepared the way for significant economic improvement. The year 1999 brought economic growth of 3.2 percent, the first solid sign of growth in a decade of economic transition.

In effect, beginning with the negotiations for a new prime minister in September and continuing through the impeachment vote in the spring of 1999, little was accomplished in restoring Russia's international financial credibility, though shortly before his dismissal in May Primakov seemed to be making some progress with the IMF. The communists, meanwhile, although giving the government no effective support in its efforts to restore the financial system, continued to demand political concessions from the president. Yeltsin has described a January 1999 meeting in which Primakov reintroduced the question of the president's surrendering his constitutional right to dissolve the Duma, a proposal first made in the midst of the September-October government crisis. In his memoir on the period he described this proposal as an effort to weaken the presidential power: "The incident made me think about how easily the foundation of the constitution could be undermined and how quietly the government could be transformed from a presidential republic to a parliamentary republic."[15]

He also described the way in which Primakov "had rallied the antimarket, antiliberal forces around him and was trampling on the freedom of the press," and he commented on the proliferation of questionable legal actions against businessmen in the spring of 1999: "Virtually the entire Russian business community was driven to despair about their own futures. The situation threatened to create a real split in the country over the central issue of the economic reforms."[16]

Yeltsin had concluded that Primakov "had too much red in his palette" and that it was time to appoint a new prime minister. As the communists pressed forward with their plans for a vote to impeach him, Yeltsin devised his own counterplan to catch them off guard by dismissing Primakov and replacing him with the power minister, Sergey Stepashin. The communists continued to prepare for the impeachment vote, scheduled for May 17. Their charges against Yeltsin included the "genocide of the Russian people," the destruction of the Russian army, the dispersal of the parliament in 1993, and the war in Chechnya. Unable to convince Yeltsin, with Primakov's mediation, to surrender the key constitutional power of naming his own prime minister, they tried impeachment. Their intention was to protect Primakov against dismissal and pave his way to the presidency, first by a successful impeachment vote on May 17 and then with a vote in support of Primakov (of which they were confident) in the Council of the Federation to install him as acting president. This would lead to a new presidential election, which the constitution required be held within three months of a president's stepping down.

Anticipating this plan, Yeltsin appointed Stepashin deputy prime minister, making him eligible to succeed the prime minister. He then dismissed Primakov on May 12, completing the maneuver. Yeltsin's memoir reveals that his intention even at the time he appointed Stepashin was to make Vladimir Putin prime minister, but "it was simply too early."[17] He would wait three more months to make that appointment. Meanwhile, the opposition lost both Primakov and the impeachment vote. Yeltsin had successfully defended the presidential constitution and his economic reforms. He had now to prepare for the December parliamentary elections and the presidential election of 2000, both crucial to the lasting success of his revolution. After nine months of personal and political peril he seemed once again to have control of events, aided by highly favorable political and economic developments. He had countered a powerful attack on both his economic reforms and the presidential constitution and was now undertaking measures to strengthen the power of the government.

THE LONG STRUGGLE FOR AGRICULTURAL REFORM

The agrarian sector is the least amenable to social reorganization, and from this standpoint Stalin's collectivization is the only plan of radical agrarian restructuring that has been implemented since the medieval 'enclosure.'

—MIKHAIL LEONTEV[18]

In no sector of the Soviet economy were the Communist Party's economic and social models more ill conceived, or the results more pathetic, than in agriculture. Committed to the dogma of agrarian socialism, the Bolsheviks destroyed the greatly reformed system of peasant farming created between the emancipation of the Russian serfs in 1861 and World War I. That system, especially with the Stolypin reforms begun in 1906, had brought unprecedented progress and prosperity to the villages. It was based on private landholding, improved farming methods, a rapidly expanding cooperative movement for credit, purchase of equipment, and sale of farm production, and growing commercialization of farming with access to urban and foreign markets. The new system was rapidly changing peasant life, creating a new rural society of increasingly prosperous peasant landowners and making Russia the world's largest grain exporter.

After gaining power, the Bolsheviks first nationalized the land and then, from 1929 onward, imposed a system of large-scale socialist farms. The independent peasant farmers were forcibly converted, at the cost of millions of lives, from landowners and independent farmers to agricultural laborers, and 25 million small farms were reduced to a quarter-million large farms by the mid-1930s. Subsequent decades brought many fewer and much larger farms, along with huge investments in electrification, mechanization, fertilizing, and other measures of modernization. Combined with the socialist form of labor organization, modeled on the urban factory, the change was intended to provide a model of efficient socialist agriculture for the world.

Throughout its existence, the system continued to disappoint. In the late Soviet period, at its highest level of development, it used 40 percent more land, nine times more labor, and vastly more machinery and fertilizer to achieve roughly 12 percent of the labor productivity of American agriculture. Meanwhile, the Soviet Union had become the world's largest grain importer, spending many billions of dollars on grain imports. In its final years the farming system consumed about a quarter of all new capital investment but continued to produce meager results. Making the situation worse, an inefficient storage and transportation system caused losses of food of up to 60 percent en route to markets. The sole redeeming feature of the new agrarian order—and one resented by communist ideologues—was the large private production by the peasants on their modest household garden plots, a tiny fraction of the arable land (about 3 percent) that produced astonishingly large proportions of available dairy products, meat, fruit, and vegetables.

The food supply problem became genuinely urgent in the last phase of Gorbachev's rule, leading him to appeal to Western leaders for emergency food deliveries. His discussion of agricultural problems, however, featured the familiar Soviet emphasis on state control of distribution and made no mention of structural changes, and he consistently resisted proposals for creating private farming. His last major legislative action on agriculture was described as "the development of all forms of land use on an equal footing."[19] A Russian legal scholar noted that the law left the existing land system intact, giving "the collective farm, state farm, cooperative member, leaseholder and private farmer . . . only fictitious land rights." He emphasized that "the redistribution of land in favor of peasant farming is purely a formality; in fact, they are defenseless against the high-handedness of the bureaucratic apparatus of collective farms and state farms."[20]

The political representatives of that apparatus, the agrarian deputies in the USSR Supreme Soviet, rejected efforts at radical change in the land system, reaffirming the permanence of the principle of collective land possession— exactly as the tsarist government had done before the reforming prime minister Petr Stolypin introduced full property rights and independent farming for the peasants in 1906 and afterward.

Boris Yeltsin inherited formidable challenges in agriculture: a failed system of socialist farms, severe problems in food production and distribution, and powerful resistance to reform from vested interests in the existing system of agricultural management and marketing. Agricultural producers confronted a serious problem in the enormous inflation of prices for industrial products, which had increased from 15– to 70–fold while prices for agricultural products had risen 4– to 6–fold. Monopolist industrial producers were imposing inflated prices on products for the countryside.[21]

Russian agricultural production suffered a setback from the economic changes introduced by the reforms, which aimed to privatize both production and landownership. By 1995–96 some 270,000 private farms had been created, but they accounted for only 3.1 percent of agricultural production. The large farms (collective and state) continued to dominate the agricultural economy but suffered a sharp decline in production—nearly 65 percent between 1990 and 1998. These farms confronted three major negative changes in their economic situation: the loss of the large state financial support that had been their mainstay under the former system; the great increase in the prices of industrial products their operations required; and competition from agricultural imports, which reduced their income from sales. The inevitable result was a steep drop in agricultural output, with declines in the production of grain (60 percent), meat (46 percent), and milk (40 percent) between 1990 and 1998. The agricultural production deficit was partially offset by an increase of more than 50 percent in production from private garden plots in the countryside, but these produced mainly potatoes and vegetables.

The minister of agriculture in the early phase of Russian independence (1991–92) was Viktor Khlystun, a strong advocate of peasant farms who had worked with the Association of Peasant Farms and Agricultural Cooperatives (AKKOR). He supported agricultural laws favorable to peasant farming. His unlikely neighbor in the Ministry of Agriculture building, responsible for managing grain deliveries to the state, was Vasily Starodubtsev, a prominent figure in the 1991 August Coup and head of the Agrarian Union, the organization of farm chairmen strongly opposed to the breakup of socialist farms.

The government soon found itself captive to the interests and programs of four monopoly organizations: the Agrarian Union, a body controlled by the managers of collective and state farms; Roskhlebprodukt, the joint-stock company managing grain collections; Exportkhleb, which managed agricultural imports; and Rosselkhozbank, which handled agricultural banking operations. Roskhlebpodukt's operations generated inflated procurement prices for grain that enriched its private owners and imposed heavy costs on the government budget, while Eksportkhleb used a government-subsidized exchange rate and the low prices provided by Western exporters (who received subsidies from their own governments) to provide handsome returns to grain traders. The combination of private profiteering and huge government expenditures led to government efforts in 1993–94 to reduce grain imports. The effort was threatened by the passage of the May 1993 Law on Grain, which provided for price supports combined with government payment of one-third of producers' costs, raising already high returns on grain production and imposing a burden of 500 billion rubles on the state budget. The program also threatened forfeiture of a World Bank grant for Russian agricultural restructuring equal to the cost of the new subsidies.[22]

The dissolution of the parliament in September 1993 brought the removal of Oleg Lobov as first deputy prime minister and the entry into the government of Gaidar and Fedorov, a change quickly followed by the ending of all subsidized credits and state grain procurement and the introduction of liberalized grain and other food prices. In public interviews before the government changes, Fedorov warned of the extreme danger of the collapse of the budget under the huge burden of agricultural subsidies, industrial subsidies, and financial support for former republics in Central Asia. At the same time, Lobov urged larger monetary emissions.[23] Progress in reducing these dangers, including the revocation of the Law on Grain in December, was promising, but it was soon threatened by the shift of political power favoring the CPRF and Agrarian Parties in December 1993.

Meanwhile, although free trade in grain was expanding and thereby lowering market prices, the government's procurement price exceeded the market price by 40 percent. Roskhlebprodukt, supported by key government figures, continued to press for huge increases in subsidized credits to purchase more grain, despite the absence of a grain shortage. The result for 1993 was a 180-percent profit margin for grain production, despite which, in 1994, the Ministry of Agriculture and Food recommended government grain acquisition prices of more than double the current market level.[24] The

fact that Roskhlebprodukt favored an acquisition price at the top of the pre-
vailing market level suggested that the existence of a grain market outside
official procurement was acting as a constraint on government procurement
prices.

The Duma action on the 1995 federal budget displayed again a commitment to large agricultural subsidies. The 9.4 trillion rubles originally
allocated (later reduced by 0.4 trillion) made up 3.8 percent of the total budget;
it was higher than the allocation for education and double that for health
care.[25] And that was only the beginning of public expenditures in support
of agriculture. Local budgets provided 14 trillion rubles, 20 trillion were provided in tax breaks, 7.6 trillion in goods provided on credit, and 21.6 trillion in canceled debt, for a total subsidy figure of 72.2 trillion rubles—in
support of an agricultural economy whose total output for the year was 53
trillion rubles. The subsidy level of 119.2 percent of output was more than
double the highest level among Western countries. It was clear that government subsidies had "turned out to be not a tool helping the transition
to a market economy but a reincarnation of Soviet economic practices."[26]

The massive low-interest lending (8–10 percent) was also responsible
for criminalization of the agricultural economy. Low-interest credits were
resold at full commercial rates of interest on the secondary market, the
profits pocketed by the farm managers. Moreover, state guarantees of lending to farms by petroleum companies and equipment suppliers were used
to increase prices and "service" charges. Loans were made without concern
for the credit reliability of the agricultural enterprise, because the state guaranteed payment. In 1995–96, lease subsidies valued at 4.15 trillion rubles
were given to a private firm, Rosagrosnab (Russian Agricultural Supply Company), with no competitive bidding. Its special charges for "service" and insur-
ance greatly increased the costs to agricultural enterprises and encouraged
inefficient suppliers to raise prices (an average of 20 percent), while the state
paid the bill.[27]

PRIVATE LANDOWNERSHIP

In contrast to Gorbachev's policies, Yeltsin's economic reform planning in
the RSFSR had long emphasized the need for private farming based on private landed property. After the proclamation of Russian sovereignty, the
RSFSR Congress of People's Deputies discussed the need for agrarian reform.

In December 1990 an extraordinary congress passed a resolution providing for private ownership of farmland by peasants withdrawing from collective farms. It qualified this provision, however, by imposing a ten-year moratorium on sales of such land. Moreover, the heads of Party committees, who still dominated at the local level in most regions of the country, remained opposed to the results of the congress vote and obstructed people's withdrawal from the collective farms. During the final year of the existence of the Soviet Union, exercise of the withdrawal right was effectively applied in the RSFSR in only a handful of cases.

In December 1991, as the Soviet Union came to an end, Yeltsin renewed the land reform initiative in the Russian Republic, issuing two decrees: "On the Acceleration of Privatization" and "On Urgent Measures for the Realization of Land Reform in the RSFSR." All farms were to be reorganized beginning on January 1, 1992, choosing one of three alternative plans: to disband and divide up the common land and agricultural equipment, to reorganize as joint-stock companies, or to remain cooperatives. A survey of fourteen provinces in various regions by the Ministry of Agriculture, reported in February, revealed that commissions for the reorganization of collective and state farms had been set up as required and that 40 percent of the collective farms had held meetings on the form of their future farming system. Of these, 40 percent had opted to become associations of peasant farms, 32 percent to become joint-stock companies, and 21 percent to become cooperative enterprises with ownership in the form of shares. A mere 7 percent decided to keep the established form of collective farm. The survey reported much conflict in the proceedings, especially over defining the shares of collective land for individuals. The report noted that farms that sought to remain collectives encountered serious opposition from local government bodies.[28]

At first glance, the fact that 93 percent of the farms had been reorganized might appear to indicate a reform success. The language of the decree, however, gave the leadership of the supervisory commissions to the collective farm chairmen and state farm directors. As a Russian commentator observed: "It puts the agrarian revolution in the hands of the farm managers. The only intact structure of pure Stalinism (after the collapse of the KGB, ideological fortresses, district Party committees, the CPSU, etc.) is thus invested with the powers of local reformers."[29]

The traditional power brokers in the countryside were reconfirmed. The power to manage the restructuring of the farms enabled them to dominate the formation of the new system of control of land and other property in the countryside and block essential reforms. They firmly opposed full private property in land, with the right of sale, because that would allow outside investors and innovators to enter the system and challenge their control, which was now greater than in the past. Their central purpose was to prevent the introduction of the full rights of peasant property in land and to maintain the massive agricultural subsidies without which the hopelessly inefficient agricultural economy they dominated could not survive. Hence, the story of Russian agriculture in the Yeltsin era revolves around two reform issues: private property in land and government agricultural subsidies.

SEEKING PRIVATE PROPERTY IN LAND

Throughout the Yeltsin era the government made repeated attempts to establish private property in agricultural land, complete with the right of sale, exchange, and mortgage. An early effort in the Congress of People's Deputies in April 1992 came close. A proposal to amend the constitution to permit unrestricted buying and selling of land was defeated by a vote of 428 to 419. Its opponents, mobilized by the collective farm and state farm lobby, raised the familiar objection that free sale of land would open the way to speculators, but a press commentator rightly noted that "they are defending not the land but themselves."[30]

The agrarian faction of the Congress, supported by the Supreme Soviet's Agrarian Committee, had demonstrated its power. At the same time, it had come into conflict with vice president Aleksandr Rutskoy, who was responsible for agricultural policy. Rutskoy had previously been regarded as a supporter of the collective farm chairmen and an opponent of radical reform, but now he favored conversion of the farms into private property by the issuance of certificates of ownership, either by free grant (to those already on the land) or by sale.[31] His position appeared to confirm the charge of the agrarian faction that the government supported a breakup of the collective and state farms. Their leaders had commented at the congress on the deal negotiated by the Association of Peasant Farms and Agricultural Cooperatives of Russia, which promised delivery of 25 percent of members' output at market prices in exchange for subsidies, machinery, credit, and priority claim in privatization and conversion actions.

In fact, although the government was giving the peasants a choice of forms of farm organization, its policy actually denied property ownership rights to independent farmers.[32] During his year-long responsibility for agricultural policy, Rutskoy—despite his initial clash with the agrarians—came increasingly under the influence of Agrarian Union head Mikhail Lapshin. Before his dismissal from that responsibility in April 1993, the Federal Center for Agrarian Reform, which he headed, encouraged "an unprecedented war against the private farmer" by state farms and agro-industrial complexes and by bureaucrats in the Ministry of Agriculture.[33] The purpose of its program was to protect state farms against privatization.

In September 1993, after the dissolution of the Supreme Soviet and the suppression of the ensuing insurrection, Yeltsin attempted to move land reform forward by presidential decree.[34] His Decree No. 1767 gave owners of land the right to sell it, bequeath it, mortgage it, exchange it, or contribute it "to the authorized capital of joint-stock companies, associations, and cooperatives, including those that have foreign investments." The decree entitled peasants holding land by lifelong possession or bequest or by right of permanent use to be granted ownership. The owners of shares of land were also given the "right, without the consent of other co-owners, to separate out physically a plot of land for the operation of a peasant (private) farm."[35]

Supporters welcomed the introduction of the right of private ownership, which had been suspended by the ten-year moratorium imposed in 1991 on buying and selling land and by other restrictions. One commentator noted that "the free buying and selling of land is the beginning of a normal agrarian transformation," and "the freer the land market becomes, the more rational will be the structure of Russia's future agricultural production." As for the current condition of agriculture: "We are now in a situation in which it is not the farmers who are feeding the country but the entire country that is feeding the farmers and their skinny cows on the skimpy rations of constantly increasing subsidies."[36]

Prior to the decree, the intrigues of collective and state farm chairmen had been a formidable block to peasants' efforts to obtain independent farms, and they continued to be an obstruction afterward. Farm chairmen used votes by general meetings of the farm membership to validate decisions, denying individual petitions for withdrawal of land from the collective. In effect, the farm chairmen were challenging the authority of the central government by using a voting process that had no legal foundation to deny farm members their right to separate their landholdings. Yegor Gaidar stressed that the government "failed to see to it that this right [of individual withdrawal] was not merely on paper."[37] But it was not a problem of inattention; rather, the land policy proclaimed in Yeltsin's autumn decree required parliamentary support in the form of enabling legislation, and the outcome of the December 1993 Duma elections produced a majority in opposition to the reform plan. The pro-reform parties, with 116 seats, were outnumbered in the Duma by 145 seats for the left (Communist and Agrarian) and nationalist (mainly the Liberal Democratic) parties.[38] The minority position of the reformers was reflected in the fate of efforts to secure a new land code during 1994.

The 1993 constitution guaranteed the right of private landownership (Articles 9 and 36), but efforts to gain parliamentary approval for the civil code affirming this right and other legal foundations for a market economy faced powerful opposition. Even though the code contained the restriction that the provisions on private landownership would "enter into force only after adoption of the land code," the Council of the Federation initially rejected it. In the debate, Vasily Starodubtsev appealed to his fellow state farm chairmen to "reign in obscurantists like Chubais and Gaidar who are trying to make it possible to sell land."[39]

The conflict over the land code and the sharply opposed visions of Russia's future economic system, rural and urban, that it reflected were central features of the remainder of Yeltsin's presidency. Like the now diminished reform group in the Duma, Yeltsin was convinced that a free land market, with full rights of property legally guaranteed, was the essential foundation for Russia's future growth and prosperity. The obstacles to achieving the goal were enormous: the powerful combination of residual socialist ideology, the still dominant structure of land relations of the communist era, and the political power of the state and collective farm chairmen and their supporters in the Agrarian and Communist Parties. Well aware of these obstacles, Yeltsin featured "the grave crisis in agriculture" in his State of the Nation address in February 1995, insisting that "the drafting and adoption of a land code have obviously been dragged out too long."[40]

In March 1996 he renewed the struggle for peasant landownership rights with his decree "On the Exercise of Citizens' Constitutional Rights to Land." The decree instructed government bodies to complete the issuing of landownership certificates authorized under earlier law but not yet provided to 8 million of the 12 million rural property owners in agricultural cooperatives, associations, and joint-stock companies who had been granted shares of collective farmland. The owner would be entitled to claim the land or to leave it in the common tract and receive a contract for payment of dividends on its production, as well as to lease additional land for private farming. Owners could also freely transfer ownership or sell their land shares. The aim was to encourage private farming and a land market, but the decree's prospects were weak, both because of the Agrarian Party's continuing opposition in the Duma and the evident lack of interest on the part of former state and collective farm members in forming independent farms. During the year preceding the decree, one in five private farms (about sixty thousand) had collapsed, with the owners giving up their land. One commentator wrote:

It is clear that farmers will pool their brand new deeds, conclude contracts with the chairman, and work just as they did before. And their "dividends," at best, will be a ton of grain, a sack of potatoes, or a truckload of firewood. It is naïve to expect anything else, for the time being, since price disparities, draconian interest rates, and the absence of markets (currently filled with imported goods) have resulted in a situation in which the overwhelming majority of Russian agricultural enterprises incur only losses from their production.[41]

In December 1995 the results of parliamentary elections were once again unfavorable to the reform cause. The communist representation in the Duma rose 130 percent, to 157 seats. And although the agrarians dropped by nearly 40 percent (from 33 to 20 seats), and the nationalists by 12 percent, the reform parties' decline of 45 percent (116 to 64 seats) greatly weakened their influence. From Yeltsin's point of view, however, the decline of the agrarians and the 45 seats gained by the new government party, Our Home Is Russia, seemed to offer new opportunity.

In March 1996 he issued two new decrees—one that legalized mortgage lending and another titled "On the Exercise of Citizens' Constitutional Rights to Land." The purpose of the mortgage law was to facilitate exchange of land to get holdings of economic size into the hands of effective farmers and to give those who wished to leave the land the possibility of gaining market value for their holdings. The second decree supported the right of withdrawal of the land from the community, whether for sale, bequeathal, or the conduct of independent farming.

Since 1991 some 40 million Russian citizens had acquired ownership of plots of land, and 12 million residents of rural areas held land allotments in the newly formed agricultural-industrial associations and joint-stock companies. The State Statistical Committee (Goskomstat) claimed that 71 percent of all people engaged in agriculture were now in the private sector. As already noted, however, the nonstate ownership was largely pro forma, because rural producers were fettered by a system of communal landownership. The peasants had claim to permanent usage of their land but not effective ownership of it. Purchase and sale of land required approval of the other members of the farming group, and decisions continued to be dominated by the same leadership, whatever organizational changes had occurred. The same was true for the control of farm equipment, animals, and buildings.

In many ways the situation of the peasants, regardless of the form of reorganization they opted for under the new legislation, was worse than it had been in the Soviet era, when the authorities planned farm production, bought the grain and other produce, provided the tractors and combines, and provided extensive subsidies. Now all this support apparatus had disappeared, and the peasant's lot had become much harder.

The argument used by defenders of the existing system was that with the introduction of private property, the land would quickly be bought up by enterprising Russians and foreigners, and most of the peasants would end up as landless laborers. In fact, under the existing system, the peasants had at best a certificate issued by the Russian State Committee on Land Resources and Land Management confirming their land allotments. Effective control of the allotments lay with the farm managers, who dictated the use of the common property just as they had done under the old system, paying the new owners neither rent nor dividends but modest payments in kind. Meanwhile, the debate among the political leadership continued to be occupied with the seemingly irresolvable issue of incorporating full property rights into the land code. That issue remained unsettled at the end of the Yeltsin era, and throughout the second half of the 1990s the number of private peasant farms remained small and declining, accounting for only about 6 percent of total agricultural land.

OBSTACLES TO PRIVATE FARMING

Critics of the government's agrarian policy frequently noted that the overwhelming majority of the peasants showed little interest in embarking on independent farming operations. This was true, but not for the reasons the communists and agrarians offered—a residual loyalty to socialist agriculture. There is much evidence that farm managers orchestrated the use of controlled voting and group pressure on individuals to prevent or discourage them from acting on their ownership rights. Beyond that problem, it is clear that the attractions of operating independently were far outweighed by the disadvantages—the lack of access to farm equipment, fertilizer, common land, water, market connections and access, and much else. Another important factor was the legacy of demographic decline of the Russian villages during the final decades of communism, when young, energetic men had fled the dead-end village economies in droves for the opportunities of the cities, so that the remaining village population was disproportionately composed of women, children, and the elderly.

Adding to these problems was the persistent Duma opposition to private farms. The Draft Law on Peasant Farming worked out in early 1998 placed virtually prohibitive restrictions on the exercise of the right of private farming. During the Yeltsin years, as I have noted, the number of private farms slowly declined, despite the fact that at least technically, 49 percent of the land used for agriculture had been divided up among shareholders. Moreover, almost one-third of all agriculture enterprises still had not been privatized at that late date, meaning that a large proportion of the peasants had no legal basis for withdrawing land from the collectives.[42]

The cumulative effects of a badly failed agricultural policy were clearly evident in agricultural output during the reform years. By 1995 gross grain output had dropped from 116.7 million metric tons (mmt) in 1990 to 66 mmt, a decline of 43.4 percent. The decline continued through 1999 to 54.7 mmt, though the latter figure was partly a result of the severe drought of 1998–99.[43] The grain production of the former collective and state farms had dropped by more than half during the 1990s. The decline of feed grains brought a reduction in livestock herds. By 1999 meat and milk supplies were 37 percent and 55 percent, respectively, of the appropriate level for the population. Meanwhile, with wages and pensions low and real incomes declining, scarce domestic supplies and the higher cost of imports brought an increasing gap between food prices and incomes.

At the end of the Yeltsin era Russia desperately needed new initiatives in agricultural policy. During the 1990s more than 17 million hectares of land had been taken out of cultivation, and the decline in field crops brought with it a decline in all other sectors of the agricultural economy. The insolvency of most of the farms meant that they were unable to buy sufficient supplies and machinery to expand production. Use of fertilizer had dropped catastrophically, and purchases of tractors, trucks, and grain-harvesting combines in 1999 were, respectively, 4 percent, 7 percent, and 8 percent of the numbers purchased by Russian farms in 1990.

But the failure of the former state and collective farms to succeed as market-based farms is only part of the story of postcommunist Russian agriculture. The distinguished economic journalist Otto Latsis noted in 1995 that whereas output was declining on the large enterprises, the output of small-scale personal farming (garden plots) and, even more so, that of private farms showed steady increases, particularly in livestock and milk production. Latsis observed: "State statistics attest to the fact that collective-type farms, even after the conversion of many of them from collective and state farms to new types of organizations, continue to lose the competition with family plots and private farms."[44]

Still, how could one use the term *collective farm* years after collective farms—at least in name—had been abolished? Latsis's answer: "A collective farm is a way of life. At least three generations of Soviet people lived in it, and most of today's rural population still does."

Although fewer than 14 percent of Russia's agricultural enterprises in 2000 were officially collective farms, "all the rest of the open-type joint-stock companies, limited-liability partnerships, closed-type joint-stock companies, agricultural cooperatives, associations and silent partnerships are actually collective farms," wrote a journalist that year.[45] As late as 2000, collectives had defeated the effort to replace them with privately owned farms, though they lagged behind private plots in production. Their 46.1 percent of total agricultural production in 2000 put the 2.1 percent of the private farms in the shade, but private plots were still ahead with 51.3 percent. In the wake of the 1998 financial crisis, when real wages dropped by a third and only 18 percent of the population was being paid regularly, 44 percent of surveyed Russians reported to pollsters that they survived thanks to household gardens on farms or dachas.[46]

A major element in the declining production of the collective farms was the pervasive official corruption that deprived peasants of the intended benefits of the massive agricultural subsidies received from Moscow, which were skimmed off by administrators from the level of the regional capital to that of the farm manager. Such practices, combined with the inadequate prices paid for obligatory grain deliveries, perpetuated the peasant predicament of the Soviet era in a greatly exacerbated form. Local administrators and their cronies, from the farm chairmen and district officers to the governors' offices, were profiteering from misallocation of federal subsidies and credits and by taking control of local grain trading. These abuses reached a new level during the harvest season of 1999, the second year of drought, when provincial governors sought not only to block the "export" of grain crops from their territories but also to exploit the inflation of grain prices by reducing the price paid to farms and accumulating large reserves for their own disposition.[47] The net grain exporting regions had established barriers to shipment of grain to other parts of the country: "Twelve growing regions have brought the entire country to its knees."[48]

Two of the most egregious examples were Aleksandr Rutskoy, governor of Kursk (and former Russian vice president and leader of the parliamentary rising against Yeltsin in 1993), and Tula governor Vasily Starodubtsev. The actions of both men constituted arbitrary requisitioning of local grain production. The profits available from such actions were substantial, but in Kursk the arbitrary grain requisitions were not accepted passively: "In a collective appeal to the governor and the deputies to the province Duma, farm directors and private farmers are demanding an explanation of why they have to buy farm machinery and fuel at market prices but then hand over the harvest at fixed prices, for almost nothing."[49]

Apparently Rutskoy had failed in an earlier attempt to get police to stop trucks carrying grain to neighboring provinces, but he succeeded in 1999 by sharing the profits from sales of such grain with the police. Of Starodubtsev a reporter noted that "under the guise of fighting for the province's 'food independence,' the Tula governor is returning to the Bolshevik-tested form of work with farmers known as forced requisitioning of grain."[50]

YELTSIN AND STOLYPIN

In assessing the results of Yeltsin's efforts at agrarian reform, it is useful to compare them with Stolypin's reforms in the late tsarist era. In both periods the reformers faced the challenge of converting communal landholding into private landholding and creating a new social class of independent farmers, and both confronted heavy opposition. Stolypin broke the socialist opposition to the introduction of private property by a change in the electoral law that created the legislative support he needed—something Yeltsin lacked. Stolypin faced no equivalent of the powerful agricultural bureaucratic apparatus that opposed Yeltsin; he could count on the implementation of his program by an óbedient bureaucracy. Moreover, the Stolypin reform process was greatly aided by the legacy of agrarian reforms since the emancipation of the serfs, most notably the self-government organizations (*zemstva*), which had become a major reform force in rural life.

With these advantages, Stolypin was able to introduce a comprehensive set of measures to facilitate the transition to independent farming. The process began with the survey and reallocation of communal land, permitting the peasants to choose their own form of individual landholding (various plots or compact farms), followed by title registry of the newly surveyed land, which carried full property rights. The restructuring of landholding was also accompanied by support from the government-funded Peasants' Land Bank and by a fast-growing, government-supported cooperative movement (Russia's was the world's largest by 1914) that provided cooperative credit, equipment purchase, crop sales, and other support services. Finally, the government provided support for the migration of peasants from overpopulated regions to underpopulated parts of the empire, where they were given land and settlement assistance. The point of this comparison is not just the scope but, more important, the considerable advantages of the reform implementation process in the Stolypin years. When blocked by the left in the Duma, Stolypin was able not just to issue decrees but also to count on their implementation by the local bureaucracy.

SIGNS OF CHANGE

The last phase of the Yeltsin era was marked by two important new developments that offered hope of a breakout from the stalemate in postcommunist Russian agriculture. The first of these was the appearance of a new generation of agricultural entrepreneurs who brought to the countryside an impressive combination of talents in organization, finance, and production that enabled them to amass sizable landholdings by purchase or lease. An *Izvestiia* article in early 1998 described an example, under the surprising title, "Why Dmitry Rybak Needs 100,000 Hectares of Land."[51] Its opening line explained the surprise: "While politicians argue about the fate of the land code, the collective farmers of Dzerzhinsky District, Kaluga Province, are busily selling their land to the Ugra joint-stock company—or, to be more precise, to the Moscow-based entrepreneur Dmitry Rybak, who holds the controlling block of shares in the agricultural firm."

Rybak had already acquired 25,000 hectares of land, aimed for 100,000, and had a swarm of eager sellers awaiting him. The purchases were made possible by Yeltsin's 1996 decree "On the Exercise of Citizens' Constitutional Rights to Land," which allowed owners of land shares to sell them without the consent of others with whom they held land shares in common. Rybak's Ugra Agrofirm included a model hog-raising facility using advanced Swedish machines and computers, a sausage factory, a hotel, and employee housing. A forty-eight-year-old engineering institute and Moscow State University graduate, he was inspired by readings in Russian agricultural history to learn that "in the last century the Russian countryside, without any subsidies, fed not only our country but half of Europe as well . . . [and] agriculture can be profitable today too."

Similar enterprises were reported in the rich "black earth" region near Volgograd, where an agrobusiness called ZAO Heliopax had taken over a failed collective farm, paid off its heavy debts, and invested $2.6 million. Whereas opponents of peasant land sales had envisaged impoverished landless peasants as the result of such sales, the inhabitants of the collective, who had previously earned a pittance, if anything, from their land and labor, found that they, too, benefited from the prosperous new commercial farming operations—both from land sales and from promising employment opportunities at nearly double their previous (often unpaid) wages. For the country as a whole, the new enterprises promised to bring again into cultivation some of the 17.8 million hectares of farmland—an area half the size of Germany—no longer cultivated.[52]

Another challenge to the failure of the Duma to pass a law supporting private property in agricultural land came from progressive regional governments, such as those of Samara and Saratov Provinces. During the summer of 1998 both provinces approved laws providing for private property in land with the right to buy and sell. When the prosecutor general challenged the Saratov law in the provincial court, Saratov governor Dmitry Ayatskov responded by threatening to go to court against the Duma's current draft land law, which prohibited the purchase and sale of land.[53] He noted that the Saratov law was in fact based on Chapter 25 of the Russian

Civil Code, which granted citizens and juristic persons the right to own land. Governor Konstantin Titov of Samara stressed the importance of the provincial law both for agriculture and for the encouragement of foreign investment.[54]

As the Yeltsin era drew to a close without Duma passage of legislation supporting the purchase, sale, and mortgaging of land, it was encouraging at least that over the course of eight years, much headway had been made in dismantling the old system. And although parliamentary opposition to needed legislation, together with the vested interests and obstruction of the old farm administrative apparatus, had greatly weakened the implementation of key presidential reform decrees, those decrees had provided incentive and support for local initiatives and innovations that suggested at least the beginnings of promising new models for the restructuring of Russian agriculture.

Meanwhile, however, the overwhelming majority of peasants had experienced a serious decline in their standard of living, including the deterioration of health, educational, and other public services and a reduction in net income of nearly two-thirds. They were again heavily dependent on the products of their private garden plots. The effects of these conditions were apparent in the decline of the birth rate and the rise of the death rate in rural areas and in a consequent population decline. It was painfully clear that an effective partnership between a reforming president and the parliament would be needed to remove the barriers to effective and desperately needed agricultural reform.

YELTSIN'S ACHIEVEMENT IN ECONOMIC REFORM

In an October 2003 interview Yeltsin paid high tribute to the two chief designers and implementers of his economic reform program, Yegor Gaidar and Anatoly Chubais. He described his great admiration for their intelligence and courage and acknowledged the tremendous personal strain they had experienced and the political risk they had taken in leading the reform program. He noted: "The command economy had to be replaced by a market one. . . . the transition would not be painless . . . [and he needed] a kamikaze crew that would step into the line of fire and forge ahead, however strong the discontent might be."[55] Certainly the central point to be made about the

Yeltsin economic reform effort is that it made solid progress in dismantling the socialist command economy and building the main framework for a market economy. Having dismantled Communist Party rule and the Soviet Union, Yeltsin chose the leadership team that set the reform course, and he sought to provide the political support that the reform program required.

The scale of the Yeltsin team's achievement in privatizing both the urban and rural economies is impressive, and the reversal of the Communist Party's fortunes in both the 1996 presidential and the 1999 parliamentary elections (continuing in those of 2003) offered assurance of the irreversibility of the change. But Yeltsin left much of the job unfinished, and the remaining problems of the new economic system were serious. Government revenue was still a problem, though taxes were high and often duplicative. Much of the revenue was wasted even as the serious social needs of much of the population were neglected. The parliament's failure to pass a functional tax code was one part of the problem. Another was the persistent competition for revenue between the federal center and the regions.

Russia still had far to go in developing the basic legal and institutional structure of a market economy. One major deficiency was the lack of effective legislation providing for private property in land for urban and rural areas. Another was the continuing weakness of the financial situation, in which heavy capital flight continued, domestic investment was low, and foreign investment had been greatly discouraged following the financial collapse of 1998. Meanwhile, the lack of legislation on private property in land and of supportive legislation on mortgages was a constraint on the development of private enterprise in both the urban and rural economies. These problems, combined with the heavy burden of bureaucratic regulation and taxation, explain the large proportion of business enterprises in the "unofficial" economy and the still small proportion of officially licensed enterprises in Russia in comparison with the economies of Poland and Hungary, not to mention those of Western Europe.

Vladimir Putin's description of his views on future economic policy suggested that he was committed to continuing the building of a market economy, that he understood the huge problems Yeltsin's economic reformers had inherited from the Soviet period, and that he had a good sense of both the achievements of the Yeltsin years and the problems remaining to be solved. In these matters he appeared to be representative of the young reformer generation to which Yeltsin had long been committed. Also encouraging was his skillful leadership in the preparations for the December 1999 parliamentary elections, which brought the government, for the first time, a parliamentary majority with which it would be able to secure supportive legislation for its programs and undertake major new reform initiatives.

CHAPTER 4

THE NEW
RUSSIA AND
THE WORLD

THE CHALLENGE OF DEVELOPING A NEW FOREIGN AND SECU-
rity policy for Russia after the collapse of the Soviet Union was
met with plans and policies that departed as radically as those in
domestic policy from the legacy of the Soviet past. The scope of policy change
greatly surpassed even that of the Gorbachev years, both because of the vast
transformation of the structure and power of the new Russian state and its
international situation after the events of August 1991 and because of the
radical changes in foreign policy introduced by the new democratic leadership. Although Gorbachev had made enormous strides in reducing the Soviet
Union's confrontation with the Western powers, particularly by negotiating
arms controls and emancipating the states of the Warsaw Pact, the changes

made by Yeltsin and his colleagues went much further. They advocated full self-determination for all the republics of the Soviet Union and envisioned a new Russian state modeled politically and economically on the Western democracies—a state that would become, in the words of Yeltsin's address to the US Congress in June 1992, "a partner in the building of global democracy." Aiming to build a democracy and a market economy, the new leaders envisaged Russia as a full partner of the democratic states in international relations.

Such a radical shift in foreign policy, a definitive departure from communist tradition, was bound to generate powerful opposition from much of the membership of the inherited legislature, the Russian Supreme Soviet. Though that body was dissolved in September 1993 and replaced through new elections in December, parliamentary opposition to the government's foreign policy, like that to domestic reforms, continued to be a major problem until the parliamentary elections of December 1999 created a pro-government parliamentary majority. The commitment of democratic leaders such as foreign minister Andrey Kozyrev and prime minister Yegor Gaidar to close alliance with the Western powers was heavily criticized, as was Yeltsin's role in granting independence to the Soviet republics. Both communists and nationalists denounced the repudiation of Lenin's union treaty of 1922. Their attitude on this key issue combined with their parliamentary political power to generate fears of a revival of Russian imperialism in the non-Russian former republics, in the newly liberated states of Eastern Europe, and in Western capitals, complicating the Yeltsin government's efforts to achieve the new international relationships it sought.

The new policy leadership also had to reckon with enormous changes in Russia's power and international role. The end of the Soviet Union and the collapse of communist rule had abruptly transformed Russia from a unique and dominant multinational Eurasian imperial power with a population of nearly 300 million to a much smaller Russian national state with half its previous population. Its economic and military power was greatly reduced, and it was engaged in a protracted and dangerous internal political struggle to build a new structure of governmental and economic institutions to replace those inherited from the communist era.

The new leaders faced the task of rebuilding relations with the NATO powers, the former Warsaw Pact states of Eastern Europe, the former republics of the Soviet Union, and powerful neighbors in East Asia. These challenges were further complicated by the separatist aspirations of ethnic groups in the Russian Federation and in other former Soviet republics that sought either independent statehood or a substantial expansion of their rights of self-government within the newly independent states. These struggles would greatly complicate the transition throughout the Yeltsin era and beyond. Unlike the pressure for independence of the republics of the Soviet Union, that of minority national groups within those republics, seeking either national independence or attachment of their territory to a neighboring state sharing their ethnicity, proved immensely difficult to settle, not least because the heads of the former Soviet republics, under Yeltsin's leadership, had affirmed the permanence of the republic borders inherited from the Soviet Union in 1991. They feared that compromising that principle would bring a flood of demands for further territorial changes.

Russia's new leaders confronted their foreign and security policy problems with greatly reduced military power. Gorbachev had at first continued the established Soviet policy of large increases in defense expenditures, though he changed course when he became aware of the weakness of the Soviet economy and the pressing need to reduce arms competition and defense expenditures. The limits on Russia's economic capacity, combined with the powerful competitive advantages of the United States both economically and technologically, indicated a pressing need to seek accommodation and compromise rather than endless and increasingly unsustainable confrontation. After the collapse of communist power in 1991, both the remaining motive and the capacity for military competition quickly disappeared, replaced by a desperate effort to rebuild the economy and to maintain adequate military production and defense capacity for national security.

RUSSIA AND THE WEST

No aspect of the search for a new foreign and security policy was more difficult or confusing for both sides than Russia's relationship with the United States and its Western allies of the Cold War era. It involved not only a transformation of bilateral and multilateral diplomatic and security agreements and relationships but also an equally difficult transformation of mutual perceptions and expectations developed over half a century of political and ideological confrontation.

Yeltsin inherited an important advantage in US-Russian relations from the successful conclusion of the Cold War in the Gorbachev era.[1] Gorbachev was well aware that the Cold War confrontation remained a powerful argument for Party conservatives against his domestic reform measures and that the massive Soviet military budgets precluded funding for essential domestic improvements. He welcomed the opportunity to reduce the Cold War tensions, and he did so through his impressive domestic reforms, his pursuit of arms reduction, and his reduction of Soviet support for foreign revolutionary activities—all of which contributed greatly to the negotiation of major arms reduction agreements with US president Ronald Reagan, which supported an acceleration of his reform program during 1989.

Gorbachev's speech at the United Nations in December 1988 was remarkable evidence of a major ideological transformation—abandonment of the communist concept of global class struggle. The ensuing year brought Soviet withdrawal from Afghanistan and Soviet acquiescence, rather than repression, in the face of the revolutions that overturned communist regimes in Central and Eastern Europe. A meeting with US president George H. W. Bush, Reagan's successor, on Malta in December 1989 brought resumption of active Soviet-American cooperation in such important matters as the reunification of Germany and its continued NATO membership.

During the following year Gorbachev continued his reform program, which included the immensely important step of creating the office of president for himself. This change eliminated the constitutional political monopoly of the Communist Party and gave the president a new independence from the Communist Party Politburo. The effects of this change on Soviet-American relations in the Bush era were dramatically illustrated by the support given Gorbachev by President Bush during a speech in Kiev on August 1, 1991, urging the non-Russian Soviet republics to support the new union treaty scheduled for a vote later that month. That plan for a democratic federal constitution, initiated by Yeltsin—and the climax of Gorbachev's long pursuit of Russian reform—precipitated the coup that would soon bring the collapse of his government and the Soviet Union.

Russian-American relations following the formation of the new Russian state in 1991 can be divided into three phases. The first two—both during the Yeltsin era—were separated by a sharp shift from the optimistic pursuit of a partnership of democratic states under the foreign policy leadership of Yeltsin and Kozyrev, to the disillusionment and alienation caused by the West's lack of support for Russia's difficult economic transition and by Russia's exclusion from America's postcommunist security systems in Europe and East Asia. By the end of 1995, Kozyrev's policy seemed a failure, and the feeling that the failure had contributed to the great increase in nationalist and communist strength in the Duma elections led Yeltsin to replace him.

Kozyrev's removal in 1996 was followed by the third phase, during which his successor, Yevgeny Primakov, crafted a policy founded on a perception of the United States not as Russia's partner but as the sole superpower, pursuing global hegemony in a "unipolar" world. Abandoning the search for partnership with the United States, Primakov sought a "strategic partnership" with China and cooperation with other states to build a separate "pole" of power to balance that of the United States. The pursuit of cooperation with NATO was not wholly abandoned, but NATO extension into the former Warsaw Pact states and the new CIS states was viewed as a threat to Russian security.

At the opening of the Yeltsin era both Russian and American spokesmen talked confidently of replacing rivalry and conflict with a constructive partnership of democratic states. But the early euphoria inspired by this vision was later replaced by serious conflicts over issues of arms, alliances, and regional policy. Some of these—over NATO expansion, Yugoslavia, nuclear proliferation, and missile defense, for example—resembled the confrontations of the Cold War. Yet tremendous achievements beyond the peaceful dismantling of the Soviet Union also were made—the denuclearization of all but one of the former Soviet republics and a huge reduction of both Russian and American arsenals of weapons of mass destruction.

The greatest disappointment for the Russian democrats who led in the early phase of policymaking was the failure to achieve a partnership role in the Eurasian security structures of the states they regarded as models for their transformation and the appropriate international partners and supporters for building a new Russian political and economic system. Foreign Minister Primakov shifted Russia's foreign policy focus from Europe and the United States to the other former Soviet republics (now called the "near abroad") and to East Asia. Russia began to seek cooperation with other powers in Europe and Asia as a counterbalance to American power and ambitions. The outlook of the second phase of Yeltsin-era foreign policy was reinforced by Primakov's appointment as foreign minister in 1996 and prime minister in 1998.

The new phase brought major changes of both policy and policy leadership, including a fundamentally negative view of the American global role and a foreign minister whose evaluation of US motives and definition of

Russian policy interests sounded much like those of the Soviet era, a sharp contrast with the views of his predecessor, Kozyrev. Both as foreign minister and as prime minister, Primakov dominated Russian relations with the United States until the Putin era.[2]

A REVOLUTION IN RUSSIAN FOREIGN POLICY

In foreign as in domestic policy, Boris Yeltsin proved himself a revolutionary. The direction of change had been set by the sweeping policy changes of Gorbachev and former foreign minister Eduard Shevardnadze, but Yeltsin's early proposals went much farther, calling for full partnership with the United States and the other democratic states, for a cooperative program aimed at complete elimination of weapons of mass destruction, and for an expansion of the role of the United Nations in managing international conflicts.

Yeltsin lost no time in seeking common ground with the Western states on arms issues. On January 29, 1992, shortly after the creation of the new Russia, he issued a comprehensive statement, "On Russia's Policy in the Field of Arms Limitation and Reduction."[3] Beginning with the assertion that "nuclear weapons and other means of mass destruction in the world must be eliminated," he announced that the new Russian leadership would recognize all arms commitments of its predecessor and would also pursue a "radical reduction in nuclear arms." He proposed forming an "International Agency for the Reduction of Nuclear Arms," affirmed his commitment to the US-Soviet Strategic Arms Reduction Treaty (START II), submitted to the Russian Supreme Soviet, and announced a series of unilateral measures Russia had already taken to curtail its weapons arsenal.

The statement was comprehensive in its coverage: tactical and strategic nuclear weapons; antimissile defense and space; nuclear weapons testing and production of fissionable materials for weapons; and nonproliferation of weapons of mass destruction, including chemical and biological weapons. It also proposed dramatic reductions in the Russian defense budget and conversion of military industries to civilian production needs.

Yeltsin stressed Russia's reaffirmation of its commitments under the Treaty on the Non-Proliferation of Nuclear Weapons and announced that "we expect the earliest possible accession to the treaty, as non-nuclear-weapon states, of Belarus, Kazakhstan, and Ukraine, as well as of other CIS member-states." The three states specifically mentioned, which held huge arsenals of nuclear weapons, were expected to transfer them to Russian control.

He also announced preparations for Russian acceptance of the guarantees of the International Atomic Energy Agency on nuclear exports, and he endorsed the international system of nonproliferation of missiles and missile technology and the efforts of the "Australia Group" to monitor chemical exports. He noted the work in the Russian Federation on legislation to regulate exports of "dual-purpose materials, equipment, and technologies that could be used to create nuclear, chemical, or biological weapons, as well as combat missiles," and he talked of planning for a monitoring system and of accepting the "guiding principles for trade in weapons that were approved in London in October 1991."

Shortly after his remarkable statement, Yeltsin departed for New York (with a stop in London for a visit with Margaret Thatcher and prime minister John Major) to deliver a speech to the UN Security Council on January 31, 1992. The distinguished *Izvestiia* journalist Stanislav Kondrashov captured the drama of Yeltsin's UN appearance: "For the first time in modern history, Russia is acting on its own and independently of the Soviet Union, as the largest of the eleven new states of the still unfledged commonwealth with its unclear future. From the Western viewpoint, nothing poses a greater threat to that security today than the uncontrolled and, God forbid, nuclear breakup of the gigantic, demoralized armed forces of the former Soviet Union."[4] Recalling Khrushchev's speaking to the UN in 1960 of global class struggle, and Gorbachev in 1988 preaching "universal human values, the removal of ideology from international relations, total repudiation of the use of force, and the principle of freedom of choice," Kondrashov noted that Russia's new representative was "no longer a Communist, no longer a Socialist, but a reformer, populist, and pragmatist, who for the first time in Russian history was democratically elected to the office of president by popular vote." The difference was clearly evident in the radicalism of his proposals, and nowhere more so than in his plan for a global defense system.

In presenting his idea for a global defense system in his speech to the UN Security Council that January 31, Yeltsin said: "I believe that the time has come to pose the question of creating a global system for the protection of the world community. It could be based on a reorientation of the US Strategic Defense Initiative (SDI) using high technologies developed in Russia's defense complex."[5] In a press interview on the following day he amplified his proposal by suggesting that "this system could be manufactured and put into place through the joint efforts of the United States and Russia, and perhaps other nuclear powers as well."[6] Paul Gigot, of the *Wall Street Journal*, commented: "Mr. Yeltsin's words this week suggested that he wants to go beyond out-of-date arms control to cooperation."[7]

From the beginning of his leadership of independent Russia, Yeltsin presumed to speak for the other Soviet successor states as well as Russia on questions of nuclear weaponry. He arranged for transfer of the nuclear weapons in Ukraine, Belarus, and Kazakhstan to Russia, an action seen as a protection against nuclear proliferation. The presidents of these states did not instantly accept Yeltsin's proposal.

President Leonid Kravchuk of Ukraine challenged Yeltsin's authority to negotiate on behalf of the other three CIS nuclear states. In mid-March 1992 he suspended the transfer of tactical nuclear weapons to Russia, insisting on prior guarantees that the weapons would be destroyed under the supervision of an international commission.[8] The differences appeared to have been reconciled, however, by early April, when representatives of most of the Soviet successor states (excluding only Turkmenistan, Tajikistan, and Kyrgyzstan), met with the defense ministers of European states in Brussels. On the eve of the meeting, US secretary of defense Richard Cheney received assurances from the four nuclear republics of the CIS that all of them except Russia would be nuclear free by 1994.

But the issue was not settled. At a meeting of the "nuclear four" in Moscow shortly after the Brussels meeting, it was still impossible to gain agreement on who would accept the START II treaty signed by Gorbachev and Bush on July 31, 1991. The notion of dividing the Soviet Union into four nuclear powers was unacceptable to Washington. Secretary of state James Baker warned Ukraine of the need to remove nuclear weapons from its territory, noting that the United States would provide future aid "to those states that demonstrate commitment to freedom, democracy, and free markets, as well as nuclear security."[9] The inference was clear: nuclear security could best be guaranteed by having Russia alone the successor as nuclear power to the Soviet Union. The Ukraine defense minister, Konstantin Morozov, accepted this with his indication that Ukraine would comply with US wishes.

Even as efforts to control nuclear proliferation among the new states of the former Soviet Union were being threatened, a new challenge appeared with the news of an agreement between Russia's Glavkosmos space agency and the Indian Space Research Organization. Russia had agreed to provide equipment worth some $400 million for a rocket capable of launching satellites into near-earth orbit. The United States charged that the agreement conflicted with the Missile Technology Control Regime (MTCR) and threatened economic sanctions if it was not canceled. The Russian response was in every way conciliatory. While noting that Russia had not been a signatory of the MTCR, and describing the agreement with India as entirely peaceful, it agreed to enter consultations with India, meanwhile suspending the transfer of rocket and space equipment.

Both the Indian and the Russian press criticized the US intervention, but an *Izvestiia* correspondent noted the international concern about the Indian nuclear program and about the Indian government's "categorical refusal" to sign the Treaty on the Non-Proliferation of Nuclear Weapons. He also noted the charge by Russian diplomats in India that "the US has undertaken to eliminate the Russian defense and space industries."[10] The Indian issue would prove to be the first of many such disagreements with the United States during the Yeltsin years. As cooperation in larger security matters proved disappointing, so cooperation on proliferation diminished. Moreover, throughout the period the government was under enormous pressure from the arms industry and the military to allow exports of weapons that provided revenues for both that were desperately needed.

NEW AGREEMENTS ON ARMS CONTROL

Despite the conflict over the Indian deal, Presidents Yeltsin and Bush produced a surprisingly broad and speedy nuclear arms reduction agreement at their meeting in Washington in June 1992. It provided that the total stockpile of Russian and American strategic nuclear arms be reduced from 21,000 warheads to 6,000–7,000 by 2003, and possibly earlier. A reporter for *Izvestiia* quoted an unnamed member of the US National Security Council who commented, the month before the meeting, that "the chemistry of personal relations between Bush and Yeltsin is good, perhaps even better than it was between Bush and Gorbachev, since we now have a democrat in front of us."[11] And the discussions went beyond reduction of warheads, including the possibility of replacing the 1972 Anti-Ballistic Missile (ABM) Treaty with a joint project for defense against nuclear attack. Yeltsin's brilliant speech to a joint session of the Congress was interrupted eleven times by standing applause.

An *Izvestiia* reporter noted with black humor that the agreement would leave Russia "with a pitiful nuclear arsenal capable not of destroying the whole planet 1,000 times over but of destroying only half of it once," but that it could be the beginning of an authentic US-Russian partnership.[12]

The vision of the new relationship was expressed in the "Charter of Russian-American Partnership and Friendship" signed by the American and Russian presidents at their June meeting. It outlined an impressive agenda of Russian-US and "Euro-Atlantic" cooperation in matters of arms and political conflict. Noting "the indivisibility of the security of North America and Europe," it stressed the linkage between the North Atlantic Cooperation Council (NACC), NATO, the Western European Union (WEU), and the Conference on Security and Cooperation in Europe (CSCE) and proposed inclusion of the Commonwealth of Independent States in that company of organizations responsible for "maintaining security and peace in this region." The charter emphasized the importance of cooperation to prevent the proliferation of weapons of mass destruction: "The two sides will work toward strengthening and improving regulations governing the nonproliferation of weapons of mass destruction, including nuclear, biological and chemical weapons, missiles and missile technology, as well as destabilizing conventional weapons."[13] It was agreed that this effort would be pursued both bilaterally and in multilateral organizations such as the Coordinating Committee on Multilateral Export Controls.

A major feature of the Washington agreements—proposed by Yeltsin in January and closely linked to his proposals for protection against nuclear proliferation—was the agreement on a global defense system (GDS). Though immensely important and innovative, it was overshadowed by the agreements on reduction of nuclear arms. Writing about this agreement a few weeks later, two distinguished Russian arms specialists noted that "the proliferation of weapons of mass destruction has become a fait accompli. *Indeed, one can only guess how many countries will possess these weapons* within a few years and how prepared they will be to use them without much hesitation."[14]

The authors argued that conventional methods of preventing technology transfer could be effective only with the cooperation of all nations capable of facilitating proliferation of missiles and nuclear weapons, and that this was impossible to achieve. The Washington agreement, if followed by the creation of "an effective GDS [as Yeltsin had proposed], in conjunction with the maintenance of powerful Russian and US nuclear arsenals, would be an important new element both in strengthening the nonproliferation regime and in providing a real guarantee that such weapons will not be used by those countries that already have them or are very close to acquiring them."

To their critics, who argued that the whole scheme (which was not unlike an earlier proposal of President Reagan's) was naive about the possibilities of US-Russian cooperation, the two arms specialists responded that the United States and Russia were already making "a clear transition to partnership—and eventually to allied relations." There were also other potential advantages to both sides from cooperation on the GDS. Russia could offer very advanced research and development in the field, and the Russian defense industry, desperately in need of funding, would benefit from GDS-related projects. The writers also argued that to facilitate this effort, it would be necessary to take an entirely new view of the ABM Treaty: "The treaty was signed during the cold war and reflects realities of that time. In our view, the treaty in its present form has basically served its purpose. We propose that the treaty be amended in certain ways to make possible the elimination of a number of restrictions that are no longer in keeping with the demands of the times—especially with regard to the testing of individual components of a missile defense."[15]

Clearly these specialists' proposal, like Yeltsin's, was based on the assumption that the nations with the technological capacity to develop an effective missile defense no longer needed it to defend against one another. By undertaking joint development of an antiballistic missile system, they could protect both themselves and the world from the danger of proliferation of weapons of mass destruction, a process they were unlikely to be able to halt. From a later perspective, Russian acknowledgment of the possibility of revising the 1972 ABM Treaty seems surprising, but the United States did not follow up on Yeltsin's GDS proposal, and the question of missile defense became prominent again only in the late Yeltsin era when the United States began to discuss deployment of its own missile defense system, together with the termination of the ABM Treaty. Yeltsin had challenged the United States with a comprehensive new concept of bilateral ties—a full partnership—and with a highly original usage of the partnership to achieve global control over weapons of mass destruction through collaboration on missile defense. Issues of nuclear missile defense would continue to be a central element of the bilateral security agenda, but Yeltsin's daring vision of full US-Russian partnership in this crucial matter made no progress.

The issue of NATO expansion proved to be one of the most difficult and persistent problems of Russian relations with the United States and Western Europe in the postcommunist era. The possibility of the eastward expansion of NATO was delivered to Yeltsin at a poignant moment—on the eve of the parliamentary elections in December 1993, only a few months after the armed insurrection in the parliament and a time when the whole future of his reform program hung in the balance. Both he and foreign minister Andrey Kozyrev had repeatedly indicated their preference for a new European security system, preferably one based on a restructuring of the Conference on Security and Cooperation in Europe (CSCE), not on NATO, the organization that symbolized the history of East-West division and confrontation. The idea of regional security organizations being subordinate to a new and comprehensive security organization had already been incorporated into the earlier Charter of Russian-American Partnership and Friendship.

The head of the Foreign Intelligence Service, Yevgeny Primakov, presented one of the first extended Russian analyses of the question of NATO expansion—"Prospects for the Expansion of NATO and Russia's Interests"—in November 1993.[16] The report argued the need for "transformation of the alliance from a military-political grouping oriented toward repulsing external threats to an instrument for ensuring peace and stability on the basis of the principles of collective security." It expressed serious concern about the lack of clarity of aims and priorities on two aspects of the current process: "changing the alliance's general purpose and the parallel expansion of its political functions and its geographic scope." The hasty expansion of the alliance's geographic scope (moving up to the borders of the former Soviet Union) could draw it into "complicated processes fraught with the possibility of acute struggle in the East European states." Such developments could well delay "NATO's transformation into a universal peacekeeping and stabilizing force" and, by creating "danger for the Russian Federation's interests . . . reduce the chances for finally overcoming the split in the continent and lead to relapses into bloc politics . . . in which NATO's zone of responsibility would . . . [reach] the borders of the Russian Federation."

Primakov stressed that the developing changes in NATO could, in time, impose heavy new security requirements on Russia, endangering both its military reforms and its economy. He noted that his report was strongly supported by the Ministry of Defense and the General Staff, and he added: "I don't know a single organization that is in fundamental opposition to our report. And that includes the Foreign Ministry." Statements by Foreign Minister Kozyrev in the weeks that followed seemed to confirm his assertion.

Kozyrev appeared to be communicating the Russians' concerns effectively to NATO in early December at meetings of the NATO Council and the North Atlantic Cooperation Council (NACC). Russian press reportage viewed NATO's new Partnership for Peace plan as one that would provide for full cooperation between the countries of Eastern Europe and those of the CIS on specific issues without the latter's membership in the NATO bloc. One reporter quoted Kozyrev as saying of bloc expansion that "the idea has been buried" and that the decision by consensus included "not only NATO and Russia, but also the Central and East European countries."[17] He was confident that the idea of expanding the NATO bloc had been abandoned in favor of various forms of partnerships among all the states under the auspices of the NACC, an arrangement endorsed by consensus at the NACC meeting. He had presented to that body his plan for uniting as equal partners all the leading regional organizations in the Euro-Atlantic space within the CSCE, a plan that included NATO, the CIS, the Western European Union, the European Union, and other entities. He noted that the NATO leadership regarded the NACC and the partnership program as a sort of waiting room for NATO membership but indicated that Russia had no intention of joining the queue.

But neither Kozyrev's arguments nor an appeal from Yeltsin could halt NATO's action to expand its membership, announced just before the December 12 Russian elections. Both the German defense minister, Volker Rühe, and the US secretary of defense, Les Aspin, confirmed that NATO would extend its boundaries eastward and accept new members.

Russian discussion of NATO expansion became increasingly negative during 1994. Following Lithuania's request for NATO membership on January 5, Yeltsin spokesman Vyacheslav Kostikov announced that "granting membership to countries located in immediate proximity to Russia's borders . . . could ultimately lead to military and political destabilization."[18] The *Segodnia* reporter who quoted Kostikov's remark also noted, however, that Bill Clinton, by now the US president, favored giving Eastern and Central European countries associate rather than full NATO membership under the Partnership for Peace Program, which was scheduled for review by the NATO

Council a few days later. Clinton was quoted as favoring this plan to avoid a "division of Europe," while Lech Wałęsa called for nothing less than Poland's "immediate admission to NATO, with security guarantees." Mikhail Gorbachev commented that Clinton actually opposed NATO expansion as an action that would weaken American control of NATO, whereas the Partnership for Peace would facilitate extension of US power in Eastern Europe and was further evidence of American pursuit of "a unipolar world."[19] He argued that "on the grounds of the alleged possibility that Russia could turn toward an imperial policy, the US is itself creating grounds for suspecting its imperial intentions."

The political scientist Vladislav Chernov rejected Gorbachev's negative interpretation of Clinton's motives. He noted that the former Soviet-bloc countries' pressure for integration into NATO was not an American power conspiracy but a product of Russia's past relations with Central and Eastern Europe: "The regrettable fact that persistent anti-Russian sentiments have formed in the USSR's former sphere of influence is payment for our Soviet past. I am convinced that no matter what Russia is or what it does, we will not be able to change this situation quickly."[20]

He did, however, provide a formidable list of problems that would be created for Russia by the integration of Central and East European states into NATO. These included joint military exercises along Russia's border, a rearmament to fit NATO standards—which would foreclose opportunities for Russian arms industries—and, most important, a direct challenge to Russian efforts to form a collective security system for the nine CIS member countries. The latter was a central feature of the so-called Russian Foreign Policy Concept, developed just one year earlier, and it had been the basis of the CIS Collective Security Treaty. Chernov argued that introduction of the Partnership plan would replace CIS collective security with a series of bilateral agreements between NATO and individual CIS countries. His pessimistic conclusion was that "the effect of joining or not joining the Partnership will be roughly the same for us. In both cases Moscow . . . will be left in the position of the odd man out." The only solution acceptable to Russia would be a total reconfiguration of the NATO bloc that "provides full membership to every country that wants to join an all-European system of collective security, including Russia." This, he acknowledged, "would no longer be NATO but a military-force mechanism of the Conference on Security and Cooperation in Europe."

Interviewed in Naples, Italy, at the time of the G-7 meeting, Kozyrev spoke of his persistent problems with the Russian parliament, whose communist-agrarian majority portrayed him as a stooge of the West. They are, he noted, "hysterical about political rapprochement between the West and Russia. They understand that they are losing ground."[21] On the other hand, he also found Western leaders deficient in understanding the plight of the Russian democrats: "there is a real lack of sensitivity [toward Russia] that strikes me as too much self-assurance, even arrogance."

Among Kozyrev's irritations with Western leaders was their criticism of Russian security actions in the CIS, especially in the Caucasus and Central Asia, criticisms that occasionally made veiled references to renascent Russian imperialism and were offered as justification for offering the security guarantee of NATO membership to states of Central and Eastern Europe. His answer to such commentary was to note Russia's "success in avoiding . . . a repeat of the Yugoslav tragedy on the territory of a nuclear superpower . . . [by not taking] an imperial path . . . [or trying] by force to restore the Union state."[22] He made it clear that Russia did not think it necessary to have an external mandate for peacekeeping actions in the CIS; such actions were based on the mutually agreed needs of sovereign states. At the same time, he spoke positively of the latest WEU report, "Relations with Russia," and urged the eventual establishment of a Russia-WEU Consultative Council.

The essence of Kozyrev's argument was a return to the proposals Yeltsin had made in early 1992 for a full strategic partnership between the United States and Russia. A succinct and compelling statement of that position in an *Izvestiia* article in March 1994 was offered just at the time when, in both countries, a growing body of opinion was arguing that such a partnership was neither feasible nor desirable. US policy on NATO membership and the central role of NATO in European security, with Russia excluded, seemed to have foreclosed the possibility altogether.[23]

Kozyrev's argument was a plea for a better understanding by the Western democracies of the vital connection between the success of Russian democracy and the full incorporation of Russia into the Western security system:

There is no sensible alternative to partnership, unless, of course, one considers the possibility of missing a historic chance to form a democratic Russian state and transform the unstable post-Communist world into a stable and democratic world to be such an alternative. These two goals are directly connected. They are especially dear to Russia's democrats, who have already—more than once—encountered armed (not to mention vehement political) resistance from the opponents of reform. We will continue to struggle to attain these goals, even if we are not heard or correctly understood by our natural friends and allies, the democratic states and governments of the West.

He criticized both those in the West who argued that "Russia is doomed to totalitarianism and confrontation with the world around it" and domestic reactionaries who insisted that "East and West are incompatible." He also challenged those who argued that Russia's place as a great power had ended with the Soviet Union: "The Russian Federation is doomed to being a great power. Under Communists or nationalists, an aggressive and menacing power; under democrats, a peaceful and prosperous power. But a great power! This, naturally, leads to the conclusion that it can only be an equal partner, not a junior one." Kozyrev also cautioned the United States against impatience with US-Russian differences on policy issues ("partnership does not mean renouncing . . . a policy of defending one's national interests, or, at times, competition and disputes"). And anticipating a line that would be advanced more aggressively by his successor, he warned against the American temptation "to see only one leading power in today's world."

The core of Kozyrev's argument was that NATO was not the appropriate instrument for bringing the Euro-Atlantic democratic states together for contemporary needs:

There is a danger of an unwarranted emphasis on NATO and partnership with it to the detriment of the Conference on Security and Cooperation in Europe, a broader and more multipurpose structure. That would be a big mistake. Victory in the cold war was won not by NATO's military machine but by the CSCE's democratic principles. It is the CSCE that should play the central role in transforming the system of Euro-Atlantic cooperation into something truly stable and democratic.

In September 1994 Kozyrev had ample opportunity to make his arguments in Washington, where President Yeltsin accompanied him for extended discussions with President Clinton and deputy secretary of state Strobe Talbott. There is no indication in Kozyrev's later comments of the accommodating spirit of the American side in those discussions, particularly its willingness to seek inclusion of Russia in a restructured Euro-Atlantic security system and its sympathetic review of the Russian positions.[24] Clinton and Talbott made every effort to explain their concept of the new NATO as a comprehensive Euro-Atlantic security organization that would include Russia. Thinking that they had secured a favorable response to their proposal, they were deeply distressed when Yeltsin described it at a Budapest meeting in December as a plan for a "Cold Peace."

A central problem for Yeltsin in his relations with the United States was much like the one that confronted Gorbachev in the Reagan years. Gorbachev was under constant pressure from conservatives in the Politburo to limit his domestic reforms and arms reductions. Opposition to Yeltsin's foreign policy from both nationalists and communists was motivated by fear that after the collapse of Russian control both in Eastern Europe and in the former republics of the Soviet Union, the entry of those countries into NATO would create great danger for Russia. Fortunately, both Reagan and Clinton combined an impressive talent for constructive negotiation with superb diplomatic advisors. The dialogue between Reagan and Gorbachev played a key role in the successful completion of negotiations to end the Cold War. Similarly, Clinton established a linkage and dialogue with Yeltsin that began to move their two countries toward a settlement of the NATO issue by pursuing the effort to broaden the NATO security structure to include Russia.

Friction over NATO expansion subsequently reached a new stage with the introduction of discussion of entry of the Baltic states, which would be the first of the former Soviet republics to enter NATO. And despite early but unrealized promise of Russian entry into NATO in the early Putin period, Russian anxiety about NATO entry by other former Soviet republics remained a major concern.

RUSSIA AND EAST ASIA

With the end of the Cold War, Russia's new leaders also had to reexamine the security situation in Asia. Their hope was that the new era would provide an opportunity to partner with the United States and its allies in Asia as well as in Europe. That hope would be quickly dashed.

The East Asian counterpart of NATO during the Cold War had been the US-Japan Security Treaty, which the United States employed, together with its alliances with South Korea and Taiwan, to contain the Soviet Union, China, and North Korea. The improvement of US-China relations following the

Sino-Soviet conflict of the 1960s had left Soviet power the central focus of the US-Asian security system.

It was China and North Korea with which Russian relations were first strained following the communist collapse. Both countries charged Gorbachev and Yeltsin with betraying the communist legacy. They criticized with particular vehemence Yeltsin's radical democratic reforms, which the Chinese feared might encourage the recently suppressed democracy movement in China. The Russians, meanwhile, looked eagerly toward Japan, South Korea, and (to a lesser extent) Taiwan as dynamic and prosperous democracies with enormous wealth and technological capacity that could help in the economic revival of both European Russia and the Russian Far East. But Japan's Russian policy centered on the demand that Russia return the "Northern Territories" (the southern Kurile Islands), which Russia had taken from Japan at the end of World War II.[25] Yeltsin was prevented from meeting this precondition of expanded cooperation by powerful domestic political opposition to augmenting Russia's already enormous territorial concessions. Hopes of building a close and remunerative relationship with Japan were soon disappointed. Russia turned instead to South Korea, also a democracy and capable of playing a significant role in Russia's economic development. But by the end of 1992 it was clear that Russia was even less likely to play a central role in a post-Cold War US security system in northeast Asia than to become a full partner in a new European security system. In contrast to Europe, however, there was another possible "strategic partner" for Russia in East Asia—China.

RUSSIA AND CHINA: THE BACKGROUND

Despite China's public criticism of Gorbachev for betraying communism, a major transformation of Russian-Chinese relations began during the Gorbachev era, when the pragmatic domestic economic reforms and foreign policy of Deng Xiaoping meshed with the Gorbachev reforms to produce a settlement of many of the issues that had created a quarter-century of conflict between the two countries. Soviet concessions to China on Afghanistan, border delineation, and the deployment and size of Russian military forces near China's borders achieved a much-improved relationship and a restoration of state-to-state and Party-to-Party relations, celebrated by Gorbachev's Beijing visit in May 1989. In the longer term, however, these changes were far less important than those that followed the seismic shocks of the next thirty months—the collapse of communist power in Eastern Europe and the Soviet Union and the dismantling of the Soviet Union itself, which in the short run frightened and alienated the Chinese leaders with its challenge to their own communist system.

A key element of the longer-term transformation of the Russia-China relationship was the huge reduction of Russian territory and power following the Soviet collapse. Independent Russia held 18 percent less territory and 59 percent less population in Asia than had the Soviet Union. The economic output of the new Russian state was also greatly reduced during the first five years following the Soviet collapse. With a simultaneous reduction of Russian armed forces over the 1990s, from more than 5 million to 1.7 million, and with all components of the military system—land, sea, and air—in decline and disarray, the threat of Russian military power to Chinese security was greatly reduced.

The change was unprecedented in modern Russian history. Though backward by Western standards, the nineteenth-century Russian Empire had the military and economic power to conquer Central Asia and take enormous territories from the Chinese Empire in the Far East. Russian military and industrial expansion under the Soviets had provided an overwhelming economic and military advantage over communist China until the Soviet collapse. But the huge losses of territory, population, and economic output in Russia after the demise of the Soviet Union greatly reduced the size of the Russian economy in relation to those of China and Japan.

A comparison of Russian and Chinese GDP over the past century offers impressive evidence of Russia's losses. Russia's GDP was 58 percent of China's in 1897 (and fourth in the world, behind the United States, Britain, and China); it was about 20 percent of China's after the end of the Soviet Union. The changed relationship with Japan and the United States was equally striking. Russia's GDP was about 3.5 times larger than Japan's in 1897; Japan's is 5.3 times larger than that of the postcommunist Russian state. The United States' GDP was less than twice that of Russia's in 1897 but has recently been nearly ten times as large.[26] The enormous decline in Russia's relative economic power, combined with a much more rapid decline of its absolute and relative military power vis-à-vis its two most powerful Asian neighbors, has been an important factor in the transformed Russian position in Asia generally and relative to China in particular.

It is of course possible that Russia's mid- and long-term growth potential could shift the present unfavorable balance. Russia has a high level of education and technological development, a high level of urbanization, and the world's largest supply of natural resources, including vast energy resources. Moreover, its promising political changes (democratization and decentralization) and economic restructuring (price liberalization, privatization, and opening to the world economy) seem to support those who predict an economic boom in the next generation, which could substantially improve Russia's economic and political advantages vis-à-vis China.

These facts of Russia's economic power position in Asia are a vital background to understanding Russia's postcommunist relations with China. They oblige Russian leaders, whatever their politics, to recognize that Russia is very much weaker with respect to China than it was during the Soviet period or at any time during the previous century and a half. They must recognize that Chinese economic and military power is steadily expanding while Russia's economy is still weak and its military power greatly reduced. Additionally, the collapse of the Soviet Union greatly strengthened China's geopolitical position relative to Russia's. China's borders with Mongolia and Kazakhstan extend from eastern Siberia to near Astrakhan on the northern shore of the Caspian Sea. Russia now shares a border with only one of the former Soviet Central Asian republics, whereas China has a common border with three.

RUSSIA FINDS A CHINESE PARTNER

Given the changes in the Russian-Chinese power relationship after 1991 and foreign minister Andrey Kozyrev's assertion at the beginning of January 1992 that "the developed countries of the West are Russia's natural allies," it seems at first surprising that Russia and China were soon celebrating a strategic partnership. But the cause is not difficult to find. Failing to achieve inclusion in the US-led security system in either Europe or Asia, and deeply disappointed in the scale and quality of economic ties developed with the United States and its European and Asian allies, Russian leaders sought other partners, and in East Asia China proved to be the most important. After canceling a September 1992 trip to Japan out of frustration with the absolute priority of the Kurile Islands issue in Japanese negotiations, Yeltsin made his way to South Korea in September and then visited Beijing in December. The action contributed to a long stalemate in Russian-Japanese relations but to a rapid improvement and expansion of relations with China. It was the beginning of a fundamental reorientation of Russia's strategy in East Asia, turning away from the United States and its regional alliance structure and toward China.

Yeltsin had at home a broad group of centrist, communist, and nationalist political leaders favoring expanded cooperation with China. The pressure they exerted was greatly increased by the calls of the military-industrial bloc for sustaining Russia's arms industries by increasing military exports to China. The subsequent rapid growth of trade, the reconciliation of border issues (urged by the military to reduce border defense requirements), the bilateral renunciation of the use of force, and the commencement of large shipments of aircraft, missiles, tanks, and submarines to China gave evidence of a broad expansion of Sino-Russian cooperation.

One learns only a small part of the meaning of the much-mentioned strategic partnership between Russia and China from official statements. Its meaning is most easily found by noting the coincidence of Russian and Chinese foreign policy on key issues. In many of these the evidence of shared interests and cooperative policies—bilateral, regional, and global—is impressive.

In bilateral relations, a major objective was to achieve a maximum reduction of sources of tension over borders and border military deployments, and progress in these matters was substantial. Only the opposition of Russian regional leaders held back settlement of the few remaining border issues.

A second major objective, to maximize economic interaction, was evident in huge energy projects—oil, natural gas, and electricity—in which China offered much of the investment and a channel through which Russian energy could serve not only China but also other states of East Asia. It is instructive to contrast Russia's supportive policies toward Chinese interests with the delays, restrictions, and arbitrary contract changes imposed on American and other foreign companies trying to do business in Russia. This contrast was evident not just in Russia proper but also in CIS member Kazakhstan, where direct and indirect pressures from Russia imposed delays and losses on Chevron while China's vastly larger oil extraction and pipeline construction project gained speedy endorsement and support. The enormous importance of this policy is clear from the fact that the Asian market has by far the largest potential for growth in energy demand of any part of the world.

A third component of the partnership policy was cooperation in Central Asia, from which both governments recognized they had much to gain. Cooperation with the Russian and Kazakh governments helped China block efforts by Turkic people in Xinjiang to gain support or build bases among sympathizers in Kazakhstan for their resistance to Chinese rule. Both governments sought stability in the region, which meant, among other things, prevention of penetration by radical Islamic groups. Cooperation with Russia was an essential prerequisite for the enormous opportunities opening to China in Kazakh oil. In the broadest sense, Russian-Chinese cooperation enabled both countries to avoid the costs of regional competition for influence and provided, instead, a competitive advantage for both in developing the region's energy resources under a kind of double hegemony.

Finally, a fourth component of the cooperation was arms. Russia has been China's chief arms supplier, allowing the Chinese to circumvent US restrictions on important arms categories.

Looking beyond strictly bilateral issues, both China and Russia, in their official commentaries on broad foreign policy objectives, stressed the need to cooperate against US hegemony in the post-Cold War world—that is, against the domination of the single superpower—and to build instead a multipolar global system in which no single power could dictate policy to the others. Behind the rhetoric lay considerable opposition in both countries to major aspects of US policy. For China, the United States was the feared sponsor of human rights—for Uighurs, Tibetans, and Chinese dissidents, among others—and the defender of Taiwan against forcible incorporation into China. In brief, US policy challenged Chinese irredentist claims, Chinese rule over non-Chinese, and Chinese domestic human rights policies. The fight against "unipolarity" was in substantial part a preventive propaganda offensive against criticisms and policy initiatives that challenged Chinese policy. Russia's main grievance continued to be the eastward extension of NATO, an action seen as excluding Russia from a broader, cooperative, post-Cold War European security system and as isolating it. Significantly, Russia endorsed China's claim to Taiwan, and China reciprocated by denouncing the NATO extension and supporting Russian policy in Chechnya.

Until the late Yeltsin era, Russia's attack on US policy focused heavily on the US-Japanese Security Treaty and on discussions of broadening cooperation under the treaty. Subsequently, Russian policy emphasized expanding direct ties with Japan, catering there, as in Europe, to Japan's policy differences with the United States. One of the most important aspects of the policy of both countries—operating under the banner of resistance to

US hegemony—concerned the proliferation of nuclear and biological weaponry and missile delivery systems.

THE PRIMAKOV EFFECT

The Russian financial meltdown of August 1998 that brought government debt default, the collapse of the ruble, and the implosion of the banking system also brought important changes affecting Russia's partnership with China. The short-term reform prime minister, Yevgeny Primakov, replaced Sergey Kirienko under pressure from the powerful communist faction in the Duma. As foreign minister, Primakov had sought cooperation with China against what he described as the danger of American hegemony in a "unipolar" world power structure. As prime minister he was in a much more powerful position to pursue a new China policy. His purpose was favored by international events, most crucially NATO's attack on Yugoslavia in the spring of 1999. That action added greatly to Russia's negative evaluation of NATO, which had begun with its incorporation of Poland, Hungary, and the Czech Republic and had grown in response to discussions of membership for successor states of the former Soviet Union.

China eagerly endorsed the Russian position on these matters and was rewarded by Russian support for its claim to Taiwan and by shipments of Russian high-technology weapons. The two parties were drawn even closer by the United States' announcement of its intention to deploy a regional nuclear missile defense system in Alaska to protect itself against accidental or intentional launching of nuclear missiles in northeast Asia.

Other developments were much less favorable for the expansion of cooperation between Russia and China. Projections made in 1998 of substantial trade growth, along with hopes for large-scale Sino-Russian energy projects in Siberia and the Far East, went largely unrealized. Meanwhile, the Chinese program for dismantling the huge structure of state-owned industry in its northeast had foundered, creating social and economic dislocation for millions of Chinese workers just across the border from Russia's Far Eastern territories and, in the worst case, the possibility of heavy illegal Chinese immigration into those territories.

But economic issues were not the focus of Sino-Russian dialogue during the last two years of Yeltsin's presidency. Policy statements from both parties, increasingly critical of the foreign and security policies of the United

States and its European and Asian allies, dominated their main meetings. Three issues were prominent in Russian and Chinese attacks on the United States and its allies: NATO's action in Yugoslavia, renewed Russian military action in Chechnya, and the United States' proposed deployment of the missile defense system in Alaska. All three had important implications for Russian-Chinese and Russian-American relations.

In both Beijing and Moscow, official policy statements conveyed essentially the same message: the post–Cold War world contains several major powers but only one superpower. As the sole superpower, the United States was using its vast military-technological capacity to establish a global hegemony. It was steadily expanding its military capacity, pursuing strengthened alliances in Europe and Asia (with NATO and Japan), and applying a foreign policy doctrine of "humanitarian intervention" to justify violation of the sovereignty of other states—as in Yugoslavia.

The Chinese portrayed US policy as a strategy for containing China's power and its capacity to advance its regional and global interests. One part of that strategy was the expansion of both the membership and mission of NATO and its transformation from a defensive alliance into an offensive one. In the western Pacific, the main indicators of growing US power and ambitions were the US-supported expansion of Japan's regional military role and the planning of a missile defense system that would neutralize China's nuclear deterrent, giving the United States a more powerful position from which to limit Chinese policy initiatives.

NATO's commencement of bombing in Yugoslavia in March 1999 brought the Russians and Chinese together in condemnation of the United States and NATO. Chinese denunciation of the United States reached a hysterical crescendo following the accidental (intentional according to Chinese commentary) bombing of the Chinese embassy in Belgrade. Underlying the reaction was the view that US intervention in Yugoslav internal affairs indicated a policy that might be duplicated in actions against China, either over its domestic policies in Tibet and Xinjiang or in a situation in which China attempted to use coercion to unify Taiwan with the mainland.

The Russian reaction was equally strong, motivated both by rejection of NATO's right of intervention without UN approval and by fear of comparable action against Russia over Chechnya, a problem then returning rapidly to a boil. Both governments rejected the right of intervention on human rights grounds in the internal affairs of a sovereign state.

The outbreak of the Yugoslav conflict was soon followed by a visit to Moscow by Colonel General Zhang Wannian, vice chairman of the Central Military Commission of the People's Republic of China. The event included consultation with Sergey Stepashin, who had replaced Primakov as prime minister in May 1999, and it was described by Yeltsin as making "systematic progress toward strategic partnership."[27] Defense minister Igor Sergeev, following his meeting with Zhang, spoke of "an identical understanding of the emerging situation and . . . of prospects for the development of the world order." Among the agreements signed on this occasion was one providing for the admission of Chinese soldiers to Russian military educational institutions, to "study our approaches to tactics, operational skills, and strategic planning." Agreements were also signed for the purchase (through 2005) of Russian weapons systems, including SU-27 jets, radar stations, S-300PMU surface-to-air missiles, submarines, destroyers equipped with Miskit anti-ship missiles, and sea-launched operational-tactical and cruise missiles.

With the launching of the second Russian military action in Chechnya in August 1999, Russia's relationship with the European Community and the United States deteriorated, even as China strongly supported the Russian action. The mutual support of the two powers was emphasized by the fact that Yeltsin made what was, owing to his poor health, a difficult trip to Beijing in December. There, with the apparent approval of his host, Jiang Zemin, he bluntly rejected both European and American criticism and reminded President Clinton that Russia was a nuclear power. These developments prompted one Russian commentator to note that "the US and Western Europe . . . are, with their very own hands, molding the Russians and Chinese into a single enemy that is potentially no less powerful than their own Euroatlantic empire."[28]

Other Russian commentators were less convinced of the power and value of the Sino-Russian strategic partnership. Noting Yeltsin's repeated reference to multipolarity, the commentator Andrey Grachev asked what kind of Russian pole Yeltsin had in mind: "A pole of economic ruin, legal anarchy, political absurdity, and 'cleansings' in the Caucasus, or a pole of permafrost in relations between East and West?"[29]

A more substantial critique of Yeltsin's claims for the value of the partnership, by Yekaterina Kats, writing in *Segodnia,* probed the economic realities of the bilateral relationship. Kats reviewed the much-touted projects for Russian provision of electricity and oil to China, noting that both were on hold, with little promise for early resumption. She observed that Russia was only China's eighth largest trading partner, that China was Japan's largest partner in investments and trade, and that foreign investment in Russia was barely visible in comparison with the roughly $82 billion invested in China by Japan, Europe, and the United States. She argued that a "single signed contract [for a fighter plane] is certainly no basis for talking about serious strategic partnership."[30]

With Yeltsin's retirement at the end of December 1999, the important question was how his prime minister and soon-to-be acting president, Vladimir Putin, would react to Yeltsin's statements stressing Russia's nuclear weapons power. On one hand, he politely corrected Yeltsin's misunderstanding of the statement by President Clinton that had provoked Yeltsin's outburst in Beijing, but only four days later he ostentatiously visited the Plesetsk Range for the successful testing of Russia's most advanced nuclear delivery missile, the intercontinental ballistic missile Topol-M. In a speech there Putin asserted, "Certain countries and blocs . . . are attempting to interfere in our internal affairs. We will not permit this and will use every means at our disposal, both diplomatic and politico-military, to oppose it."[31] Clearly, the "Primakov doctrine" was alive and well, but trends in China challenged it powerfully.

THE CHINESE PARTNER SHIFTS THE BALANCE

The Russian-Chinese relationship in economic and military power was massively transformed during the Yeltsin era. On the eve of its demise, the Soviet Union had a larger GDP than China. A decade later, China's GDP was the world's third largest (following Japan and the United States) and had reached 35 percent of the US level. For many years second only to the United States, Russia now ranked sixteenth globally.

The shift in the two countries' relative military power was also impressive. China was spending $30–40 billion on defense, at least five times the Russian military budget. It was developing multiple independently targeted reentry vehicles for its nuclear warheads even as Russia phased out its own MIRVed missiles as required by START II, offering China the prospect of nuclear parity with Russia within ten to fifteen years. And as China moved toward superiority over Russia in regional economic and military strength, its ties with Russia had given it protection of its northern and Central Asian frontiers, assistance in maintaining stability on the Korean peninsula, and support in opposing Japanese and American regional security efforts. Meanwhile, China made no effort to bring Russia into its negotiations with the United States and Japan on Korean problems and no effort to facilitate serious military cooperation. It appeared that Russia had become, in effect, the junior partner in the "strategic alliance" with China.

Assuming that some Russian commentary of the time was correct—that Chinese strategy sought to achieve "a dominant role in the Asia-Pacific region and . . . global leadership"—it appeared that the premises of Russia's current China policy might be severely tested in later years.[32] The questioning of those premises, already begun by some Russian analysts, focused on both the expansion of China's economic and military power and the changes in foreign and security policy that were likely to accompany them.

In effect, Russian policy was supporting a trend toward Chinese domination of both East and Central Asia and possibly Mongolia, and Russia was getting virtually nothing in return. There was no evidence of an increase in Russian security from the effort, and much evidence of a decline. Meanwhile, the potential for social instability was growing in north China, which could bring a rush of Chinese immigrants into the Russian Far East, a territory still described in China as one of the losses from the "unequal treaties" imposed on China by the European powers and Japan in the nineteenth century. Even the expected economic benefits of cooperation with China were proving illusory. Russian trade with China was a mere one-tenth of China-US trade. Large-scale Russian-Chinese energy projects had failed to proceed as planned, China bypassed Russian passenger aircraft and other high-technology manufactures in favor of American or European models, and military imports from Russia were clearly short-term—a preparation for importing technology to facilitate China's manufacture of its own advanced arms.

In sum, it looked very much as if a future review of the "strategic alliance" by the Russian partner would reveal that the alliance had served China's interests far more effectively than Russia's. It had facilitated expansion of Chinese influence in former Soviet Central Asia; it had given China support in disputes with the United States and its Asian allies; it had endorsed China's policy on Taiwan; and it had facilitated Chinese access to the energy resources of Siberia, the Far East, and Central Asia. In general, it had made a major contribution to the expansion of Chinese military and political power in East Asia and to the increase of its influence in Central Asia. And despite offering such support, Russia was clearly viewed by China, and was treated, as a marginal power in the Asian system. The economic benefits for Russia were minimal, and it was experiencing a steady decline of its regional military power relative to China's.

The Russian-Chinese "strategic partnership" had gained strength from domestic and international events in the final Yeltsin years. Yet it was increasingly clear that the Russian side had miscalculated both the economic and security benefits of its partnership with China and the damage it might do to relations with the United States and its European and Asian allies.

Most long-range projections of the time predicted a China far more powerful than Russia, threatening both its influence and its territory in the Far East. A new development took place at the end of the Yeltsin era, however, that could be projected into the future: the restructuring of the Russian political and economic system that began with the appointment of Vladimir Putin as prime minister in August 1999.

When Putin, having been elected president, subsequently undertook his program for rebuilding the Russian state and economy, he emphasized the need for a stronger state, a more effective defense, and, above all, the rebuilding of the economy, on which success in all other areas ultimately depended. He recognized that the massive infusions of new capital and technology which the Russian economy desperately needed must come mainly from the United States, Europe, and Japan. Yet he inherited a sharply confrontational relationship with those powers, in which the Sino-Russian strategic partnership was an important element.

A contemporary issue of the *McKinsey Report*, which analyzes international economic affairs, reached an important conclusion: "On the economic side . . . we have found no fundamental constraints that would prevent Russia from quickly joining the ranks of the advanced economies."[33] Putin had a promising economic reform program and had already demonstrated his political talent by building the parliamentary majority required to implement it. Following the December 1999 parliamentary elections and his election to the presidency, he would launch a remarkable economic recovery and expansion in a very short time. He envisioned combining the favorable fundamentals on the Russian side—a highly educated and urbanized population, strong technological capacities, and the world's largest supply of natural resources—with an effective governmental structure and economic policy capable of realizing the country's enormous economic potential. He had repeatedly affirmed that once Russia had acquired these advantages, it would be able to attract and employ the foreign investment essential to full economic recovery and to realization of Russia's huge economic potential.

In this perspective it was clear that a successful domestic economic policy could bring Russia a much-expanded Asian economic role based on partnerships not just with China but also with Japan, South Korea, and the United States. Such economic partnerships might also help Russia achieve inclusion in the security systems of the United States and its Asian and European allies, the absence of which had been a central factor motivating the pursuit of strategic partnership with China.

RUSSIA AND KOREA

The collapse of the close relationship between Russia and North Korea (the Democratic People's Republic of Korea, or DPRK) began with the establishment of diplomatic relations between the Soviet Union and South Korea in September 1990. Described by Pyongyang as "a betrayal of socialism," this move was followed by a vigorous search for new relations with the United States, Japan, China, and South Korea, for which Russia was prepared to make major concessions. Responding to the new Soviet ties with South Korea, the North Korean Foreign Ministry announced in September 1990 that it would "take measures to provide for ourselves some weapons for which we have so far relied on the [Soviet] alliance."[34] The Soviet policy shift was thus used to justify North Korea's development of nuclear weapons. The alienation between the two states was greatly increased by the coming to power in Russia, after the failed coup of August 1991, of a Russian leadership that repudiated the communist system.

The simultaneous expansion of friendly relations between Russia and South Korea accelerated the deterioration of relations with the North. Failing in his efforts to secure cooperation with Japan, Yeltsin replaced a planned trip to Tokyo with one to Seoul in September 1992. There he worked for expansion of both economic and military cooperation and announced the end of the Soviet-North Korean Defense Treaty and a suspension of arms shipments. The rapid development of Russian-South Korean planning for defense cooperation that followed, including offers of Russian weapons and cooperation in US-South Korean military exercises, completed the alienation and prepared the way for North Korea's withdrawal from the Treaty on the Non-Proliferation of Nuclear Weapons in March 1993. Russia's demands that North Korea abandon plans for a nuclear bomb and its commitment to international sanctions merely encouraged further retaliatory measures from Pyongyang.

Foreign Minister Kozyrev was subjected to harsh attacks from domestic critics who charged that he had unnecessarily provoked North Korea into actions dangerous to Russian security. The attacks increased as it became clear that the United States, South Korea, and Japan were working out their own agreements with North Korea in which Russia was not a participant. These included an agreement in Geneva in October 1994 for suspension of the North Korean nuclear weapons program in exchange for less dangerous nuclear reactors and fuel oil and the creation in March 1995 of the Korean Peninsula Energy Development Organization. The latter provided financing and support for two light water reactors valued at $4.5 billion, along with 500,000 tons of heavy crude oil per year. Russia sought to participate by providing light water reactors (for which South Korea would pay) but was rebuffed, though other states were admitted and the program expanded.

Kozyrev's successor as foreign minister, Yevgeny Primakov, had contributed much to the criticism of his policies, and following his appointment in January 1996 Primakov initiated policies that aimed to reestablish ties with North Korea. Arguing that the main task was to create a coalition of powers opposed to US regional domination, he also sought a "strategic partnership" with China and closer relations with Japan and South Korea. The intention was to improve relations with both North and South Korea simultaneously, but the effort soon failed. A Russian deal to provide weapons to South Korea elicited the North Korean charge in October 1996 that Russia had joined "the camp of forces hostile to the Democratic People's Republic of Korea. If Russia continues . . . we will have to settle scores with it."[35] Clearly there was no improvement in the relationship, and even the tiny trade between the two countries continued to decline.

Russia's relations with South Korea also encountered serious roadblocks. Expansive economic cooperation plans were shattered by the East Asian economic crisis of 1997–98, and relations were severely disrupted by Russia's announcement of the arrest of the deputy station chief for South Korean intelligence in Moscow on charges of spying in the summer of 1998.[36] By early 1999, however, the spy scandal had been disposed of, and the two countries were discussing ambitious plans for trade and for major energy and transportation development projects.[37]

The main Russian concern continued to be uncertainty about North Korea's plans for nuclear weaponry. Russian initiative had concluded a Treaty of Friendship, Good Neighbor Relations, and Cooperation with North Korea in March 1999, an achievement that promised to improve relations with the DPRK and return Russia to the role of serious participant in discussions of North Korean issues. But Russian leaders continued to worry about the lack of a coherent security structure on the peninsula and the strains in US and Japanese relations with the DPRK.[38] Russian analysis contended that the improvement of US-Japanese relations with North Korea had been severely disrupted by the discussion of a plan for a joint theater missile defense system in response to the August 1998 North Korean missile launch. Russia and China jointly condemned the plan, because both powers were concerned not only over its effects on North Korean behavior but by the implications of such a deployment for their own security systems.

In sum, Russian policymakers sought to undo the perceived errors of their North Korean policy of the early nineties, develop good relations with both Koreas, and become a full participant not only in Korean affairs but also in rebuilding the entire regional security system. Their progress was not encouraging.

RUSSIA AND THE OTHER FORMER SOVIET REPUBLICS

Russia's relations with the other states that emerged from the dismantled Soviet Union were a major element, and a major challenge, in foreign and security policy throughout the Yeltsin years and afterward. Commonly described as the "near abroad," these states might also be called the "new abroad" to emphasize that they had previously been fellow members, with the Russian Republic, of a single federation whose dismantling gave the new Russian state a sudden and huge change of international boundaries and neighbors. A thoughtful Russian observer, Andrey Nuykin, assessed the action positively nearly five years later:

Believe me, the people who met at Belovezhskaya Pushcha in 1991 were political geniuses who saved their countries from an ocean of blood by their voluntaristic decision to turn administrative borders into borders between states at a single stroke. Understand: Giving us the opportunity to think things through would not have worked! The country and the world had to be confronted with a fait accompli that would be difficult to revise. Therein lay our salvation.[39]

Nuykin's tribute to the wisdom of Yeltsin and other national leaders in negotiating the voluntary and peaceful dismantling of the Soviet Union was offered in March 1996 in response to a majority vote mobilized by communists and nationalists in the Duma calling for a trial of Yeltsin and his Russian government colleagues on the charge of treason for destroying the union. In the discussion that followed the vote, Nuykin and others stressed the contrast of Yugoslavia's painful experience in handling competing national claims under Slobodan Milošević with the peaceful dismantling of the Soviet Union and the subsequent mainly peaceful relationships between Russia and fellow members of the Commonwealth of Independent States and the other Soviet republics that opted out of that body. They also observed that it was the coup organizers of 1991 who had destroyed the possibility of completing the plan for installing the democratic federal constitution of which Yeltsin was the chief designer and advocate.

Yeltsin had sought recognition of the sovereignty of the Soviet republics not as a means of destroying the union but as the foundational principle for constitutionally restructuring it. His vigorous advocacy of a democratic federation long before the 1991 August Coup, and his leadership of the resistance to the coup, made him a trusted partner and leader in the negotiations with the republics that followed the collapse of the central Soviet power. His attitude of acceptance and respect toward the national claims of the fifteen republics, including the right of secession and full independence, was the essential foundation both for the peaceful dismantling of the union and the subsequent viability of the CIS. On this basic issue, as on his economic reforms and his pursuit of a democratic constitution, Yeltsin faced tenacious opposition from Russian communists and nationalists who remained deeply opposed to the course he had taken in 1991 following the failed coup.

The Duma vote in the spring of 1996 was yet another instance of that opposition, which found broad support in the "red Duma" resulting from the December 1995 parliamentary elections. It was immensely fortunate, both for Russia and for the other CIS states, that such attitudes among the communists and nationalists did not control the policy of the Russian government. The power of the Duma majority was constrained by the very different composition and attitudes of the Council of the Federation, and the parliamentary power of both houses was limited by the president's constitutional controls over parliamentary action. The situation would have been radically altered by a Zyuganov victory in the 1996 presidential election, which would have given the communists both executive and legislative power and full control of Russian policy toward the former Soviet republics.

The underlying principle guiding Yeltsin and other republican leaders in the dismantling of the Soviet Union was that the boundaries of the newly independent republics should be precisely those established during the Soviet era. This decision "to turn administrative borders into borders between states at a single stroke" was bold indeed. But though the policy doubtless avoided much of the conflict that might otherwise have followed the collapse of the Soviet Union, it could not remove or resolve all the problems inherited from the structure of republic borders and many other features of the Soviet federal system, problems that would pose serious challenges in relations between Russia and the other former Soviet republics and between the Russian central government and the various national units of the Russian Federation itself, throughout the Yeltsin era and afterward.

Problems for relations between the new states were inevitably created by the arbitrariness of the Soviet-era republic borders, especially because they often made little allowance for the ethnicity of the included populations. The most striking example was that of the Russians, some 25 million of whom now found themselves living in non-Russian republics in which the fiat of Moscow no longer prevailed. The most important cases were Ukraine, where some 11 million Russians lived, and Kazakhstan, where nearly 40 percent of the population, concentrated in the north, was of Russian ethnicity. A similar situation in non-CIS former Soviet republics would also prove a problem for relations with Russia. Moscow's complaints about the treatment of Russians in former Soviet republics became a frequent cause of strain in intergovernmental relations.

The dismantling of the political and administrative structures and the economic relationships of a vast, centralized, unitary state created another set of problems. The complex interconnections of the Soviet socialist economy were abruptly severed, causing huge problems in virtually every area of the economic systems of the Soviet successor states. The problems were further complicated by the different approaches and experiences of the new states in their programs of political and economic transformation and by the abrupt loss of access for some to vital resources, especially energy and key raw materials, as well as the end of the centralized financial system and common currency.

Such sudden and extensive changes, rendered more painful by the rapid deterioration of economic and social conditions during the first period of economic reform, proved a powerful stimulus to communist and nationalist opposition to the Yeltsin government.

These opponents were greatly angered, first, by the dissolution of the Soviet state and by the fact that the post-Soviet Russian Federation contained, in 1993, only 50.8 percent of the 293.1 million inhabitants of the territories of the former Soviet Union. They also blamed the Yeltsin government for the economic disarray of the new era, ignoring the fact that Yeltsin had inherited an economy in an advanced stage of collapse. The widespread acceptance of this charge was demonstrated by the electoral support for nationalists and communists in the 1993 and 1995 parliamentary elections. That such views on national independence and state boundaries might come to dominate the policy of the Russian government was a source of great anxiety for Russia's neighbors in the near abroad, as was evident from their leaders' fearful reaction to the possibility of a presidential victory in 1996 by the communist leader Zyuganov, a man whose party had never accepted the legitimacy of dismantling the Soviet Union and sought power to reverse it.

Another complication following from the dismantling of the Soviet Union was the difficulty of Russian acceptance of the consequences of the independent international relationships forged by the non-Russian former Soviet republics. Throughout the Yeltsin years, Russian political leaders found it hard to establish economic, political, and security relationships with former Soviet republics as independent states, including those that joined the CIS. Accustomed to thinking of the borders of the former Soviet Union (and even those of the Warsaw Pact states) as defining their security zone, and still not fully liberated from the security perspectives of the Cold War, they were slow to accept the full foreign policy independence of former fellow Soviet republics. The presidential power provided by the 1993 constitution, however, together with Yeltsin's personal commitment to the republics' independence, offered protection against this danger and allowed the new states freedom to manage the challenges of independence and develop their own foreign and security policies, though not without some conflict with Russia.

The integrity of the new Russian state was also challenged by the demands of its significant non-Russian populations, who had their own national aspi-rations. The regional administrative units of the Russian Federation included twenty non-Russian national republics with a population of 21.7 million (14.6 percent of the total population), and in twelve of these Russians made up half or less of the population. The problem was uniquely difficult and dan-gerous in Chechnya, where a Chechen nationalist leadership organized an armed insurgency seeking an independent republic. But friction between Rus-sian and non-Russian peoples, even without separatist movements, would prove a complex problem in creating a satisfactory governmental structure for integrating the national republics within the Russian Federation.

Reviewing the charges of Russian nationalists and communists against the Yeltsin leadership, one is struck by their failure to distinguish between "state" and "empire" in Russian history. The critics had nothing to say about nationalist movements among the non-Russian peoples of the Russian Empire during the nineteenth and early twentieth centuries or about those peoples' efforts to obtain national independence following the collapse of the autocracy in 1917. Those efforts were crushed by Lenin in the aftermath of the Bolshevik Revolution, with the forcible reincorporation of most of the non-Russian peoples of the tsarist empire into the USSR. The repres-sion was brutally carried much farther by Stalin, who blocked even the lim-ited autonomy sought by communist leaders of the Soviet republics. Nor did the critics devote attention to the renascence of ideas of national inde-pendence in the underground political literature of non-Russian peoples during the Khrushchev and Brezhnev eras, though they condemned nation-alists' use of the new freedom of the Gorbachev years to form organizations demanding sovereignty for their nations.

But Yeltsin's liberal national policy was not without its defenders. Many informed Russian commentators, such as Nuykin, described the peaceful dismantling of the Soviet empire as both wise and irreversible and lauded Yeltsin's policy leadership. They also admired his subsequent efforts to build connections and cooperation among the nations of the former Soviet Union by mutual agreement, employing the positive elements of the legacy of the past, which included many economic, social, and cultural ties as well as the widely shared Russian language, to cooperate in the tasks of economic growth and protection of national security shared by all. The acceptance and imple-mentation of such a positive policy, however, met with formidable political, economic, and security challenges throughout the Yeltsin era.

DEVELOPING A CIS POLICY

The foreign policy of the early Yeltsin era gave Russian-CIS relations low priority. Emphasis was placed mainly on establishing Russia's credentials as the great-power successor of the Soviet Union by claiming the Soviet seat (and veto) on the UN Security Council and developing relations with the United States and Western Europe. This "Atlanticist" orientation elicited severe criticism from the "Eurasianist" critics of the Yeltsin foreign policy, who stressed the vital importance, especially for Russia's great-power status, of ties with Eurasia and particularly with the former Soviet republics, which Foreign Minister Kozyrev seemed to be ignoring.[40] A shift of policy appeared with Kozyrev's visits to some of these states in the spring of 1992. This change was followed in September by another indication of response to Eurasianist and nationalist pressure—Yeltsin's abrupt cancellation of a scheduled meeting with Japanese foreign minister Kiichi Miyazawa.[41] His explanation that the cancellation was motivated by "domestic reasons" was understood in Russia as a concession to nationalist concerns that he would yield to Japanese pressure for return of the four Kurile Islands taken from Japan at the end of World War II. Yeltsin understood that his opponents in the Russian parliament would block approval of cession of the islands, which they saw as yet another reduction of Russian state territory and of Russia's Eurasian mission.

Further evidence of concessions to parliamentary critics of his foreign policy came on Yeltsin's visit to the congress of the Civic Union political party in February 1993, where he not only promised to pursue integration of the CIS but also asserted "Russia's right to control conflict in the former Soviet Union."[42] Meanwhile, although Kozyrev continued to affirm his commitment to close ties with the West, he called for the lifting of UN sanctions against Serbia and Montenegro and affirmed Russia's intention to defend the interests of Russians in the non-Russian Soviet successor states as a high policy priority.

FOREIGN POLICY AND THE 1993 CONSTITUTION

Yeltsin clearly had presidential control of foreign policy in mind when he devised the new constitution approved in December 1993. His previous battles with the Congress of Peoples Deputies and the Supreme Soviet frequently concerned issues of foreign policy, and he sought to strengthen the hand of the presidential administration in this crucial area as in others. Hence the constitutional provision that "the President of the Russian Federation shall define the basic . . . foreign policy guidelines of the state" (Chapter IV, Article 80.3). The president was also specifically granted the right to "supervise the conduct of the foreign policy of the Russian Federation" (Chapter IV, Article 86.a). Equally important was the provision that "the President of the Russian Federation shall form and head the Security Council of the Russian Federation" (Chapter IV, Article 83.g), the main body responsible for formulating foreign and security policy.

Despite the presidential powers over foreign policy provided by the new constitution, the great strength of the communists and nationalists in the parliament elected in December 1993 guaranteed that the heavily Western-oriented policy of the first two years of Kozyrev's leadership in Russian foreign policy would continue to be vigorously challenged. Kozyrev made an extraordinary attempt (called "shock therapy" by some auditors) to convince Western statesmen of the policy danger these groups represented by the device of a surprising speech to the CSCE foreign ministers in Stockholm in December 1993. In it he voiced the opposition's views of the policy of NATO and the West European Union, and its proposals for Russian policy toward the CIS, as if they were those of the Russian government. Beginning with criticism of Western states' "plans to strengthen their military presence in the Baltics and other regions of the territory of the former Soviet Union and to interfere in Bosnia and the internal affairs of Yugoslavia," he went on to assert: "The space of the former Soviet Union cannot be regarded as a zone for the full application of CSCE norms. This is in essence post-imperial space, on which Russia will have to defend its interests using all available means, including military and economic means. We will firmly insist that all the former USSR republics immediately join in a new federation or confederation and will conduct a rigorous discussion on this matter."[43]

The shocked reaction of conference delegates to these policy concepts was replaced by very different responses when it became clear that Kozyrev's intention was to acquaint the delegates with views widely held in Russia (in this case taken from a foreign policy memorandum prepared for the Civic Union party) and strongly supported by the new parliamentary majority. Stunned by the possible consequences of such views guiding official policy, one delegate observed, "If what you said were to become Russia's official position, the European edifice would collapse." Kozyrev had thus done much to make European diplomats aware of the danger of a major current of Russian foreign policy opinion and to make Russians aware of the revulsion it inspired in Europe and the states of the former Soviet Union.

Despite Kozyrev's intentions, however, the political and economic problems of transition to effective independent statehood, both in Russia and in the other successor states, and the many related security problems would create formidable obstacles to controlling the negative views of the government's numerous political opponents on Russia's foreign policy generally and relations with the CIS in particular. The effects of their pressure would soon be apparent in both the processes and the substance of Russian policymaking. Institutionally, the pressure came not only from the parliament but also from the Defense Ministry and the intelligence agencies, both of which challenged the policy leadership of the Foreign Ministry. The influence of the Defense Ministry on Russian policy in the former Soviet republics became increasingly apparent from mid-1992, when its leadership announced a policy for those newly independent states stressing "the importance of defending the rights, freedoms, and legitimate interests of Russians living throughout the Near Abroad."[44]

The policy had been adopted by the Defense Ministry and endorsed by the Security Council independently of the Foreign Ministry. Following the military's crucial support for Yeltsin during the armed confrontation with the parliament in October 1993, evidence of Defense Ministry influence on policy was considerably increased, as in the reversal of the initial approval given to Lech Wałęsa for Poland's entry into NATO and the abandonment of the decision to limit Russian military forces to 1.5 million men (raised to 2.3 million).[45]

Kozyrev's foreign policy showed definite signs of the influence of nationalist groups during 1993 and 1994 as he took some of the positions he had scorned in his mock speech in Stockholm in December 1992. While rejecting the position of Zhirinovsky, the nationalist leader of the Liberal Democratic Party, that the former Soviet republics must be returned to "a union with Russia," he stressed that they lay within Russia's sphere of influence. Public opinion polls eliciting a two-thirds majority favoring a priority of relations with the former republics over relations with the West doubtless encouraged a change in Yeltsin's policy. Concern about the popular appeal of

Zhirinovsky's nationalist attack on the dissolution of the Soviet Union was also influential.

The governmental institutions involved in policy toward the CIS states included, in addition to the Foreign Ministry, the Security Council, the Ministry of Defense, and the Intelligence Service. Chaired by the president, the Security Council included as permanent members its secretary and the speakers of the Council of the Federation and the Duma. In theory the president could be outvoted in the Security Council, though the fact that he alone had the power to announce council decisions implied a power to prevent decisions he opposed from entering into force. Moreover, the 1993 constitution gave him ultimate responsibility for foreign policy, and the direction of foreign policy had already been assigned to the Security Council when it was created in December 1992. At that point the Foreign Ministry was left with the responsibility "to coordinate the endeavors to draft resolutions concerning the country's foreign policy."[46]

The influence of the military upon foreign policy, prominent during the Soviet era, was continued under Yeltsin, particularly in matters concerning the near abroad and NATO. For the military leaders the maintenance of Russian interests throughout the territory of the CIS was a primary concern. These interests were translated into policies that included direct intervention on behalf of local Russian populations in CIS states, efforts to thwart recruitment of CIS and former Warsaw Pact states into NATO, and military support of CIS states threatened by domestic insurgencies. Another dimension of the military influence was in matters affecting stability within the Russian Federation. The Ministry of Defense played the primary role in securing military intervention in Chechnya in December 1994, and it defied Yeltsin's orders to suspend the bombing of Groznyi late that month and in early January 1995.[47] The most dramatic example of military insubordination occurred during the Russian military intervention in the Trans-Dnestr region of Moldova, when the commander of the Russian Fourteenth Army, Aleksandr Lebed, who had been sent to the region in 1992 to end fighting involving Russian residents, refused to remove his forces once his task was completed. He rationalized his refusal on the grounds that it was his responsibility to protect the local Russian population, even though its secessionist effort had precipitated the conflict.[48]

Doubtless the most prominent and influential spokesman on the CIS in the Russian intelligence community was the head of the Foreign Intelligence Service, Yevgeny Primakov. His views are especially important because he became foreign minister in 1996 and prime minister in 1998.

In a September 1994 report to Russian and foreign journalists, Primakov began by noting fears abroad that "centripetal processes in the commonwealth could revive the union state in its previous capacity as an adversary of the West."[49] He dismissed such fears as groundless, asserting that "it is an indisputable fact that the new states' sovereignty has a high degree of stability. That achievement is virtually irreversible." But while denying the possibility of reviving the former union state, Primakov criticized the Russian "neo-isolationists," who held the view that "an agreement on economic union would be burdensome for Russia and might even complicate relations with the West." He was equally critical of "neo-isolationists" in other CIS states, who feared that economic integration "would weaken the sovereignty of the CIS states, strengthen the influence of Moscow, and impede development of relations with other states."

Primakov's argument for economic integration of the CIS stressed the legacy of a single economic space, the necessity of a shared pattern of economic reform to achieve reintegration, and the examples of successful economic integration provided by the European Union, the Association of Southeast Asian Nations, and the North American Free Trade Agreement. He acknowledged, however, that the pattern and pace of economic reform in other republics varied significantly from those of Russia and that "until they are fitted to the Russian model it will be altogether impossible to form a common economic space in the commonwealth." He saw economic integration as "the only way to lessen tensions in interstate relations" created by the large Russian populations in the other states of the commonwealth.

In describing the security challenges confronting the CIS states in his 1994 report, Primakov stressed the unstable situation in Afghanistan, which, with its population of Tajiks and Uzbeks in the north, had become a security threat for both Tajikistan and Uzbekistan. He stressed as well the expanding influence of Iran and Turkey. An additional complication was the effects of "Islamic extremism," which he defined as "a movement aimed at the forcible spread of Islam, the suppression of forces resisting this action, and a change in the secular nature of the state."

Primakov argued that Russia had a right to "active involvement in the settlement of conflict situations" along its borders, noting that these conflicts were dangerously destabilizing for some regions of the Russian Federation.

Some of them caused fatalities among the Russian population and sent "streams of refugees" fleeing into Russian territory, imposing economic costs and serious social instability. But he insisted that "no peacekeeping action in the CIS has been conducted without the agreement of the parties at conflict." He argued the necessity of Russian participation in protecting the external borders of all CIS states, because of the extraordinary porousness of the internal borders between those states.

Primakov concluded with alternative scenarios for the future development of the CIS. The first involved the formation of "a common economic space." State sovereignty would be retained, but with powers delegated to "suprarepublic structures" that would administer "uniform systems for credit and monetary circulation, customs and taxes, a court of arbitration, etc." He also envisaged the possibility of extensive economic integration and integration of military forces for meeting shared security needs, leading in turn to some form of political integration, possibly a confederation. Clearly favoring this outcome, he saw it as offering "expanded economic cooperation, including an influx of foreign capital investment." He noted with disdain that "a number of Western countries are interpreting the role that Russia might play in uniting the republics of the former Soviet Union as 'imperial,' while integration is perceived as a process of restoring the USSR."

Primakov's second scenario was one in which "isolated development" was chosen—"the rupture of economic ties and the abandonment of cooperation in the production sphere." The resulting economic decline would bring out all the negative potentials in many of the CIS states—nationalism, antidemocratic trends, criminalization, suppression of ethnic minorities and violation of human rights, increased Islamic extremism, and the breakup of some states.

A third alternative was for a CIS state other than Russia to form an increasingly integrated group and possibly move to "external centers of influence."

Primakov asserted that the Western powers favored a situation in which the Russian Federation was assigned "the role of a country with a very limited set of interests and tasks." He was certain that Russia would reject such a "unipolar world." At the time of the report's appearance there was much speculation about its possible connection with two other events: Yeltsin's trip to the United States and a request by Kiev for a postponement of the CIS summit meeting. Primakov insisted that the report had been prepared at the initiative of the Foreign Intelligence Service (FIS), but it would subsequently become clear that integration of the CIS under Russian leadership was the centerpiece of his policy as foreign minister.

Meetings of the Council of CIS Heads of State in the years following Primakov's report, including those when he served as foreign minister (1996–98), offered scant evidence of support from other CIS states for his favored scenario—expanded economic integration and defense cooperation followed by movement toward a political confederation. At a February 1995 Council meeting in Almaty—since 1994, the new name of Alma-Ata—attended by the presidents of eleven states and one speaker of parliament, Yeltsin, serving as chairman, noted that although previous sessions had reached many agreements, there was "no sign of their implementation," and he appealed for a breakthrough in the area of economics. But the focus of discussions was chiefly on security issues, resulting in a declaration of commitment by the partners to a collective security concept that took the form of the Collective Security Treaty of the CIS states.

Viktor Chernomyrdin, noting the number of agreements signed, predicted that "an economic union of the CIS states will be established sooner or later." A sharp conflict arose, however, over the main security issue raised by Yeltsin in a protocol on the joint defense of the borders of the CIS. The protocol provided for shared responsibility for the defense of the external (non-CIS) borders of all the republics. Although the group accepted a collective security concept and the Collective Security Treaty, Ukraine and Azerbaijan rejected Yeltsin's proposal for a joint protocol on the collective defense of the external borders of the CIS. Russia, Kazakhstan, Tajikistan, and Kyrgyzstan supported it, but the proposal was not adopted.[50] The majority of the republics rejected the Russian concept of dividing republic borders with the rest of the world from those between republics. The Ukrainian foreign minister, Gennady Udovenko, affirmed the general adequacy of Ukrainian troops for the defense of the republic's borders with non-CIS states but indicated a need for assistance in building defenses on its border with the Russian Federation![51]

At the May 1995 summit meeting of the CIS leaders in Minsk, Moldova and Azerbaijan joined the group of states rejecting the treaty on joint protection of CIS external borders. Meanwhile, Chernomyrdin's keynote speech "voiced a firm conviction that the union will be resurrected, but on the basis of normal, civilized, market principles . . . [adding that] no one has any thoughts of encroaching on anyone else's sovereignty."[52] His elaboration of the "elements of a common customs space" did, however, evoke serious concerns about protecting sovereignty. These elements included coordination of economic reforms, standardization of national laws, common rules for organizing currency markets, coordinated foreign economic policies, and open borders between member states as well as joint protection of external borders. The bitter rejection of the proposal by the Ukrainian deputy prime minister and minister of foreign economic affairs noted that such a system would oblige Ukraine to go to Moscow to resolve problems in trade relations with Minsk or Almaty. The new initiatives in economic policy appeared to be winning as little support as a treaty aiming at the collective defense of the shared international borders of the CIS, and for the same reason: fear of subordination to Russia.

The legacies of the Soviet empire and the Cold War remained powerful obstacles to the achievement of a Russian-led security system for the former Soviet states, frustrating initiatives to build new security arrangements both among the former Soviet republics and between those states and the states of the former Warsaw Pact. In the closing months of 1995 the question of Russian security ties with the commonwealth states was intensely debated as the NATO powers continued with their plans for eastward extension of their alliance. At a September Kremlin press conference Yeltsin asserted that "when NATO comes right up to Russia's borders, one can consider there to be two military blocs." He promised to establish constructive ties with the republics of the former union, to replace the Warsaw Pact.[53] He also warned that the NATO action in Bosnia was "only the first sign of what could happen if that organization were expanded." He expressed extreme dissatisfaction with Andrey Kozyrev's policy, implying that the foreign minister's style of dealing with the NATO powers was responsible for NATO's expansion policy, which he called "a major political mistake that is fraught with the potential for war throughout Europe."

Yeltsin's hard line on NATO's eastward expansion was confirmed by Defense Minister Grachev, who spoke of creating a Russian-led alliance of CIS states and possibly states of Central and Eastern Europe. Grachev also recommended threatening refusal to ratify the START II Treaty on the reduction of offensive weapons and regrouping of strategic nuclear forces.[54] An academic foreign policy specialist, Yakov Plyas, noted that the reaction of the CIS leaders to Yeltsin's speech had been negative and that many Russian generals felt "the creation of a defensive alliance within the CIS framework would be a step backward, a return to the cold war."[55] According to Plyas, this outcome could be avoided "if the sides were to show good judgment, prudence, and pragmatism and proceed from the principle of defensive sufficiency." He argued that "the new Russian politicians make a mistake in idealizing the West. The NATO countries, too, made a mistake in deciding to expand eastward. . . . [They] could not have done a greater disservice to nascent Russian democracy."

The end of 1995 saw Kozyrev's foreign policy, with its primary focus on relations with the West and close ties to the United States, facing widespread opposition. His tenure as foreign minister would soon end. His position was challenged not only by the expansion of NATO but also by the December 1995 Duma elections, which greatly increased the power of the communists and reaffirmed the strong position of Zhirinovsky's nationalist Liberal Democratic Party. Zhirinovsky's hostility to the West, and to the United States in particular, was expressed in his typically extreme style in a widely distributed pamphlet titled "Plevok na zapad" (Spit on the West).

Yeltsin's concern about these developments was reinforced by the growing criticism of Kozyrev's policy emanating from most Russian political groups and the certainty that it would influence the forthcoming presidential election. A prominent Russian policy analyst observed that NATO expansion "struck a powerful and perhaps fatal blow to the foundation of Kozyrev's diplomacy."[56] He added that "a Kremlin leadership that surrenders the theme of Russian greatness to the opposition runs the risk of changing places with that opposition very quickly." It appeared that NATO's expansion policy was having the dual effect of weakening Russia's commitment to US partnership and greatly increasing its commitment to firmer ties with the CIS. The problem was to secure the commitment of other CIS leaders to such ties, and this would require the removal of existing conflicts, the most pressing of which were those with Moldova and Ukraine, though success in these efforts was no guarantee of increased CIS integration.

Although Moscow had approved a treaty on the pullout of Russian forces from the predominantly Russian-populated trans-Dnestr region of Moldova in October 1994, the nationalists and communists in the Duma had blocked ratification of the agreement and suspended action on the reorganization of the Russian Fourteenth Army, which worked with the Russian population. At the end of 1995 the Duma demanded that Moldova declare the Dnestr region a "zone of special interests for the Russian Federation" and recognize the Dnestr Moldovan Republic, based in Tiraspol, whose leadership had been supported by General Aleksandr Lebed. Moscow's subsequent efforts to convince the Moldovan government that it should provide a special legal status for the Dnestr region compatible with Moldovan sovereignty was unsuccessful, but the Russian leader of the Dnestr Moldovan Republic, Igor Smirnov, went forward with a referendum proclaiming it a "sovereign independent state," surpassing the Moldovan government's formula of "an autonomous entity with broad powers." Passed by an 80 percent vote with a 60 percent voter turnout, the referendum provided for the Dnestr Moldovan Republic to be a sovereign state with membership in the CIS. The presence of a substantial delegation of communist and agrarian deputies from the Russian Duma in the Dnestr region during the referendum was evidence of their effect upon Moscow's CIS policy.[57]

A CHALLENGING YEAR FOR THE CIS

The year 1996 brought both problems and opportunities for Yeltsin's policy of strengthening the links and cooperation among the CIS states. Dealing with both was greatly complicated during the first half of the year by the great stress of the presidential campaign, following on the December parliamentary election that had produced the "red Duma." Yeltsin's communist rival Zyuganov spread fear among many CIS leaders and some former Warsaw Pact states that Yeltsin's election as Russian president would endanger their independence.

The year began promisingly with a January summit of CIS leaders at which Yeltsin was elected head of the CIS for the third time. The summit participants reached decisions on several important issues, such as collaborative peacekeeping operations in CIS states. It was agreed that all such operations would require a special mandate from the UN, that they would be collective, and that antiterrorism units from each state would participate in them. The main cases of cooperation in dealing with interethnic and regional conflicts in CIS states that were discussed at the meeting were those of Tajikistan and Georgia. It was decided to extend the mandate of the peacekeeping forces in Tajikistan for an additional five months and to adopt the essentials of Georgian president Eduard Shevardnadze's plan for settling the Abkhaz conflict, which involved cooperation of the CIS states in extending the peacekeeping action and in isolating the leadership of Abkhazia both politically and economically. Shevardnadze stressed that the challenge of "aggressive separatism" faced many CIS states.

Another issue was that of strengthening the so-called customs union and payments union. Yeltsin expressed the view that Russia, Belarus, and Kazakhstan, with open borders and the absence of customs duties between them, had already developed a legal and regulatory foundation and were "completely ready for economic integration."[58] He also noted that Uzbekistan, Tajikistan, and Kyrgyzstan had made somewhat less progress toward readiness for integration.

The promising trends of the January 1996 summit were soon threatened by Zyuganov's initiative in the Duma in March and April attacking the 1991 Belovezh agreements guaranteeing the independence of the republics. The Duma resolution reaffirming the validity of Lenin's 1922 union treaty caused panic about the probable change in Russian policy should Zyuganov become president. Zyuganov's initiative accelerated the movement of the former Soviet states toward affiliation with NATO that Yeltsin opposed, and it encouraged negotiations for future entry into the European Union in preference to Yeltsin's vision of CIS economic and political integration. A Russian journalist vividly described the effects of Zyuganov's actions: "Whereas up to now the movement of our former Soviet neighbors toward NATO and the European Union has been relatively unhurried, in a matter of days that movement has become frenetic and hence absolutely irreversible. Their Western partners, meanwhile, are now proposing new forms of military-strategic cooperation to the East Europeans."[59]

President Zhelyu Zhelev of Bulgaria advised the NATO Council that "the Duma's decision will increase the determination of Russia's neighbors to join NATO." Another significant response was apparent from the speeches delivered at a huge rally in Minsk, Belarus, on March 25 protesting both the Duma action and the "two-faced union" that President Lukashenko had recently negotiated with Russia.[60] Clearly Zyuganov's attack on the freeing of the nations of the Soviet Union was no help to Lukashenko's ongoing effort to reintegrate Russia and Belarus.

Across the spectrum of Russian political opinion, the most serious grievance about the disintegration of the union had been the separation of Belarus and Ukraine from Russia. The profound cultural, social, and economic ties among the three, their long history of joint nationhood, and the large ethnic Russian and Russian-speaking populations in both made complete separation difficult for Russians to understand and accept. Only Belarus, however, would prove amenable to seeking a new form of union with Russia. Negotiations reached fruition with the signing in Moscow on April 2, 1996, of a treaty creating a union state.[61]

The agreement followed a visit by Lukashenko in late March and included the creation of supranational bodies: a supreme council consisting of the presidents, the prime ministers, and the heads of the legislatures; an executive committee (government); and an interparliamentary congress (common parliament). Lukashenko compared the role and power of these bodies with those of their counterparts in the European Union. He also explained that the union would have a special joint budget for shared programs and its own emblem and flag, that the two states would guard their borders jointly, that the union would be open to new states, and that members of the union could withdraw unobstructed with six months' notice. Yeltsin's press secretary, Sergey Medvedev, reported that this was not a new state and that the union did not compromise its members' sovereignty and independence.

UKRAINE

No Russian relationship within the CIS was more important for Russia than that with Ukraine, but it had been troubled by many conflicts. Yeltsin took a bold initiative to remove the main elements of conflict between the two states in 1996–97, clearly feeling that Russian-Ukrainian differences could be resolved.

President Kuchma of Ukraine was very much in favor of good relations with Russia, but political attitudes in Ukraine were by no means favorable to the kind of initiative that Lukashenko was taking on behalf of Belarus. The essence of Kuchma's international policy was the pursuit of closer ties with Europe. In an April 1996 speech to deputies to the Council of Europe Parliamentary Assembly he spoke of Ukraine's determination to carry out the constitutional and other reforms required to meet European Union standards, emphasizing that "Ukraine's course aimed at the transformation of a formerly totalitarian society into a democratic and open one that is subject to the rule of law."[62] He stressed the importance of developing good economic relations within the CIS, but he also affirmed that Ukraine sought to become a member of the European Union. He observed that "a return to the USSR is impossible; reality has shown that the CIS hasn't worked, and it appears that all the other interstate associations aren't going to work either." On the question of forming a new European security system, however, he urged that Russia's interests be taken into account to avoid "confrontation between two camps or the building of a new Berlin Wall." His goal was "a Euro-Atlantic security structure for all the European countries." The Ukrainian president's views were favorable to Russian-Ukrainian cooperation, if not to a much expanded role for the CIS, but both presidents confronted much internal opposition to their efforts to reduce conflicts between their states.

Russian nationalists and communists had never ceased their denunciation of Yeltsin for his role in the separation of the two states, and Ukraine had active nationalist organizations sowing mistrust of Russia and seeking to minimize the power of the CIS, which many perceived simply as a cover for the restoration of Russian imperial power. Russian nationalists contributed to the tension either by denying the legitimacy of Ukraine's separate statehood or by demanding border revisions to bring predominantly Russian-inhabited territories into the Russian Federation. In this tense environment the most inflammatory issues were a protracted confrontation over control of the former Soviet Black Sea fleet and its bases in the Crimea and the possibility of Ukrainian entry into NATO. Despite these frictions, Russia had continued to provide essential supplies of natural gas to Ukraine, allowing enormous arrears in payments, though it had occasionally threatened to suspend vital deliveries as Ukraine's debt mounted. The conflict over ownership of the Black Sea fleet and its base facilities in the Crimea required five years to reach a final agreement, meanwhile eliciting Russian nationalists' claims that Sevastopol (the main base for the fleet) was a "Russian city" and that Khrushchev's cession of Crimea to Ukraine had been illegitimate.

Yeltsin's trip to Kiev in May 1997 for final negotiations on an agreement was a clear demonstration of his understanding of the importance of the Russian-Ukrainian relationship and his determination to reach a settlement. Prime Minister Chernomyrdin, Foreign Minister Primakov, and several other key members of his government accompanied him. Chernomyrdin and Ukrainian prime minister Pavel Lazarenko signed the agreement. The fleet had been divided (81.7 percent of the ships to Russia and 18.3 percent to Ukraine) in 1995. The new agreement allowed Russia to lease the main bays at Sevastopol together with infrastructure, airfields, and test ranges for twenty years for a total of $2.5 billion, which was to be paid from Ukraine's debt to Russia for gas deliveries. The agreement was combined with a Treaty of Friendship, Cooperation, and Partnership that included a commitment from Russia to accept Ukraine's borders and to renounce the threat or use of force or economic pressure (as in a previous case of suspending gas deliveries for nonpayment) in bilateral relations.[63]

Yeltsin's press secretary, Sergey Yastrzhembsky, called the agreement "the most important foreign policy action Russia will take in 1997." He noted that the great improvement in Russian-Ukrainian relations would diminish concern over NATO expansion, and he insisted that Russia had long ago recognized Crimea and Sevastopol as Ukrainian territory, though there was still "a narrow group of people who are making their political careers on the Sevastopol problem." One of these people was identified on a Ukrainian sign posted outside the Mariinskii Palace, where Yeltsin was received, advising, "Luzhkov, don't poke your pig's snout into Crimea!" Happily, the official Russian view was not that of Moscow mayor Yury Luzhkov but that of Yeltsin, as articulated by Foreign Minister Primakov: "Relations with Ukraine are perhaps our most important priority. We must establish not simply good neighbor but fraternal relations with Ukraine."

A complementary view from the Ukrainian side was offered by Volodimir Gorbulin, secretary of Ukraine's National Security and Defense Council, who said that "the treaty removes all of Russia's territorial claims against Ukraine. . . . for the fist time, a foundation has been laid for strategic partnership."[64] Yeltsin's crucial leadership in stabilizing Russia's relationship with Ukraine in this important agreement can be fully appreciated only against the background of the fierce opposition to it in both Ukraine and Russia. In Russia, vocal opponents ran the gamut from Mayor Luzhkov to Vladimir Lukin, chairman of the Duma Committee on International Affairs, and Georgy Tikhonov, chairman of the Duma Committee on Affairs of the CIS. Luzhkov insisted that Sevastopol was "a Russian city," Lukin described the agreement as "mere words," and Tikhonov warned that the agreement would prepare the way for Ukraine's entry into NATO. Yeltsin's unqualified respect for the sovereignty of fellow CIS states and his appreciation of the vital importance of the Russian-Ukrainian relationship helped once again to remove a dangerous problem of CIS interstate relations in the postcommunist transition.

Russian criticisms of Yeltsin's deal with Ukraine came from a broad cross-section of political opinion, from liberal to nationalist and communist. The critics expressed a wide range of interests and concerns—claims on Ukrainian territory and complaints about the position of Russians in Ukraine, about the drastic reduction of economic ties, and about security issues. Because of the size and importance of Ukraine, many feared the possibility of its joining NATO. Despite these challenges, Yeltsin, Primakov, and others continued their efforts to integrate the CIS, particularly in economic and security matters, to the end of the Yeltsin era. The guiding policy vision was essentially the first option in Primakov's earlier policy memorandum on Russia and the CIS, with particular emphasis on the advantages of pursuing economic integration and the dangers of Russian isolation by the eastward extension of NATO. In general, though, the results of Russian initiatives at subsequent meetings of representatives of the CIS were profoundly discouraging. Despite setbacks, the pursuit of integration continued, though more by the effort to create subgroups of cooperating CIS states than by efforts directed at the CIS as a whole.

One important example was the formation in March 1996 of the Union of Integrated States (UIS), a pact signed by Russia, Belarus, Kazakhstan, and Kyrgyzstan that promised to form a common market and coordinated financial and social policy.[65] Its administrative bodies consisted of the Interstate Council, chaired by Lukashenko, and the Integration Committee. Despite Yeltsin's enthusiastic announcement that the union was open to other states, presidents Aliev of Azerbaijan and Karimov of Uzbekistan expressed a complete lack of interest, and his encouragement of Bulgaria to consider membership caused a mass protest in Sofia.[66] Ukraine was meanwhile talking increasingly of joining the European Union.[67] And because the core of the UIS had been the Russia-Belarus Union, support for the UIS enterprise was diminished in Russia and elsewhere by Lukashenko's reactionary changes in the constitution of Belarus, which radically diminished the power of the parliament.[68]

Yeltsin's intention of using the UIS as a base for interstate integrative efforts that could be extended to the CIS as a whole was evident at the Kremlin meeting of the Interstate Council of the four states in the Kremlin in October 1997. He proclaimed proudly that the council, which was headed by Nursultan Nazarbaev, had "adopted a very bold decision on a customs union and customs duties," telling journalists that the UIS would provide the model for similar action in the CIS. Other commentary from participants and observers noted that no serious progress had been made on the plan for an integrated customs union and that "the process of bringing these countries' domestic laws and norms into closer alignment . . . is proceeding at a snail's pace."[69]

A meeting of CIS heads of state held in Chișinău, Moldova, on the day after the UIS meeting in the Kremlin gave scant encouragement to Yeltsin's notion that the UIS "four" would provide support for integration within the CIS as a whole. A reporter noted that "a smooth glide into comprehensive integration is not in the cards." She reported President Karimov of Uzbekistan's rejecting "integration at various speeds" and finding "the union of two (Russia and Belarus) and the union of four (Russia, Belarus, Kazakhstan, and Kyrgyzstan) to be a factor that undermines the commonwealth and gives rise to unequal relations."[70] Karimov's comment was typical of many bitter exchanges at the meeting, which Yeltsin found profoundly discouraging. A report in *Kommersant* gave a gloomy summary of the mood of the meetings: "The deep-rooted conflicts among the states, the mutual enmity among the presidents, and the dissension among members of the official delegations were plain to see, more blatantly obvious than ever before."[71]

The most conspicuous conflict at the meeting was that between Shevardnadze and Primakov over the separatist movement in Abkhazia, but sharp criticisms of Russian policy were forthcoming from Moldova and Azerbaijan as well. Russian efforts to establish a CIS committee for eliminating conflicts over commonwealth territory, a body Primakov sought "to carry out administrative measures and directly lead peacekeeping operations," was rejected by the foreign ministers assembled at the conference. Modest advances were achieved in plans for joint defense of air space, but these were greatly varied between states and in no sense a comprehensive agreement or plan.

In October 1997 both the UIS and the CIS—Russia most of all—were challenged by the creation of a rival foursome linking Georgia, Ukraine, Azerbaijan, and Moldova (GUAM).[72] The stress of the group's declaration on "promoting integration into European and Euro-Atlantic structures" offered a double challenge to Russia: a regional association of which it was not a member and the pursuit of closer ties with Europe and the United States. And the challenge went further. President Aliev of Azerbaijan stressed complaints by members of the group against Russia, such as Georgia's dissatisfaction with Russia's peacekeeping role in its struggle with separatists in Abkhazia and Russia's role in the Azerbaijani conflict with Armenia over Nagorno-Karabakh. Moldova's president, Petru Lucinschi, spoke of his country's interest in access to the fuel resources of the Transcaucasus, and Aliev indicated Azerbaijan's willingness to transport its oil to the West via Ukraine and Moldova.[73] It now appeared that efforts to use the new UIS to create the broad cooperation among the CIS states that had eluded the existing CIS apparatus was a failure.

THE LAST PHASE: YELTSIN'S LEGACY TO THE CIS

The final years of Yeltsin's presidency found the Russian government and the leadership of the major political parties greatly preoccupied with problems and conflicts within the CIS. Repeated Russian efforts to develop integrating structures and policies achieved little or no success, and the latest regional initiative, GUAM, did not even include Russia.

Konstantin Zatulin, director of the Institute of CIS Countries, was a joint author with Andranik Migranyan of an important analysis of the status of the CIS in March 1997.[74] Expressing deep concern about developments before and during the recent Chişinău CIS meeting, it carried the ominous title "The Beginning of the End of History." Zatulin's strongly nationalist views made him a bitter critic of Yeltsin's CIS policies, as can be inferred from the authors' summary of the CIS "problem": "Disintegrative processes are becoming prevalent in the CIS . . . and a real threat has arisen of the realization, with the participation of the West and states neighboring the CIS, of Zbigniew Brzezinski's concept of the creation of geopolitical pluralism and multicentrism in the post-Soviet space."

Zatulin and Migranyan's concept of proper arrangements in the "post-Soviet space" assumed acceptance of Russian dominance in the territory of the former Soviet Union, combined with a minimum tolerance of separate national interests and aspirations on the part of the other republics. Zatulin vociferously criticized Yeltsin's recent concessions to Ukraine, and he became the leader of the nationalist Great Power Social-Patriotic Movement in November 1998. He had already served for some time as an assistant to Mayor Luzhkov of Moscow.[75] Migranyan continued to hold the views, similar to Zatulin's, that he had offered in the scholarly debates on Russian CIS policy several years earlier. Their article offers a good example of the views of Russian nationalists about Russian relations with the CIS states in the final phase of the Yeltsin presidency and after.

The authors made a wholly negative assessment of the current state of Russian relations with the states of the CIS, giving roughly equal responsibility for the situation to the Russian government and the leaders of the CIS states. The Russian leadership received the major blame (for its "failure to follow through") for the doubtful future of the Russian-Belarusian union, which was described as "the only real hope of statists in Russia and pro-Russian forces in the former Soviet Union republics . . . for the role of catalyst of the integration process in the CIS."[76]

With Ukraine the problem was its "systematic evasion of productive participation in the CIS." Although Russia "had done everything it could for Ukraine and then some," Ukraine used Russian concessions "to do many things—from discussing membership in NATO to assimilating the Russian and Russian-speaking population [of Ukraine] as quickly as possible and finally closing the books on the question of Crimea and Sevastopol." In addition, there was the deal with Kazakhstan to push Russia out of Baikonur, the attempt to create a trans-Caucasus oil transport corridor bypassing Russia, and the intention to use the GUAM agreement as a step in building "an anti-Russian cordon" from the Black Sea to the Baltic, even as Russia offered generous bilateral terms on trade and tariffs—and much more. But although the authors recommended against ratification of the Russian-Ukrainian treaty of May 31, 1997, it would be ratified by an overwhelming majority of the Duma in December 1998. Foreign minister Igor Ivanov's warning that refusal of ratification would push Ukraine toward NATO appeared to have considerable effect.[77]

The scene in Central Asia was also profoundly worrisome when viewed through Russian nationalist spectacles, because the CIS states of this vital region continued to distance themselves from Russia. On the plus side for the nationalists, Russia retained a peacekeeping force in Tajikistan, nuclear weapons facilities in Kazakhstan, and border troops in Kyrgyzstan. Moreover, an agreement between warring Tajik groups had removed concern about Tashkent's pursuit of a greater Uzbekistan. But there was much concern about Russia's loss of control of the mineral resources of the region, particularly in the Caspian basin, and the increased role of Western transnational corporations.

As with Ukraine, the nationalists were concerned about the fate of the substantial Russian population in Central Asia, notably the very large group in northern Kazakhstan. The decision by President Nazarbaev to shift Kazakhstan's capital from Almaty to Akmola in the north was perceived as an effort to strengthen the ethnic Kazakh position in the region. Another concern was the political trend in Kazakhstan following the removal of the progressive prime minister Akezhan Kazhegeldin, which was understood to mean, according to Zatulin and Migranyan, that "Nazarbaev's comparatively Europeanized regime is gradually turning into a kind of 'Middle Eastern family despotism.'"

The worst-case scenario envisaged by Zatulin and Migranyan was an anti-Russian axis of Ukraine, Georgia, Azerbaijan, Kazakhstan, and Uzbekistan, "drawing a median line across the Eurasian mainland, trying to consign 'democratic Russia' to the continental backwoods." Their only consolation was that the internal volatility of these states meant that "given a concentration of Russian Federation efforts in certain areas, they could very quickly face the choice of being friends with Russia or not existing at all."

Zatulin and Migranyan's treatment of the situation in the trans-Caucasus was highly critical of Russian policy, particularly its failure to provide consistent support for Armenia and its ambivalence on the issue of Abkhazian separatism. As with Central Asia, they focused much concern on energy issues, particularly the appearance of a pipeline project to take Central Asian oil through Azerbaijan and Georgia to the Turkish port of Ceyhan, "furthering an increase in Western and Turkish influence in Azerbaijan and Georgia." To these concerns they added the fear that "Russia's presence in its own North Caucasus republics is becoming increasingly dim."

The ideological core of Zatulin and Migranyan's harsh critique of Yeltsin's CIS policy through the end of 1997 was contained in its opening warning that the "participation of the West and the states neighboring the CIS" would bring "geopolitical pluralism and multicentrism in the post-Soviet space." Surely it was a credit to Yeltsin that he accepted these trends as an inevitable and positive product of the dismantling of the overwhelming centralism of the Soviet state and its replacement by fifteen independent states. It was to his credit that he sought to build collaborative administrative structures and policies that would contribute to the security and prosperity of all, meanwhile constraining the considerable political forces in Russia that favored coercive reintegration of a Russian-dominated federation as a means of rebuilding Russia's status as a great power.

His efforts to build a voluntary and effective commonwealth of independent states encountered many obstacles and frequent disappointments, but the accomplishments were nonetheless impressive. They included his strong personal leadership of the CIS, in which he was repeatedly elected to head the presidents' group, his effective personal relationships with fellow presidents, including his active pursuit of organizational structures and policies crucial to interstate political, economic, and security cooperation and settlement of serious bilateral disputes, and the example of his reform achievements in Russia.

Certainly Yeltsin shared many of the concerns detailed by Zatulin and Migranyan. He had been an early and harsh critic of the eastward extension of NATO, as had such liberal reformers as Kozyrev and Gaidar, but not because former Soviet states did not have the right to control their own security policy. It was rather that the eastward expansion of NATO seemed to replicate the Cold War division of Europe between NATO and the Warsaw Pact, and it implied that Russian foreign policy aims duplicated those of the Soviet Union. It seemed unnecessary as a security measure and an obstacle to his efforts to build effective security and other forms of cooperation within the CIS. At the same time, both Yeltsin and his colleagues were aware of the legitimate concern in other countries about the revival of Russian imperialist policies that might follow a political victory by his nationalist and communist opponents, a danger that inspired both the offering of NATO expansion and its acceptance by former Warsaw Pact and other CIS states.

The final two years of Yeltsin's leadership of policy toward the CIS displayed both the continuity of his efforts to build effective cooperation within that organization and his concern about developments that challenged Russian interests and security. At the April 1998 Moscow CIS conference Yeltsin concentrated on the economic issues that blocked the building of a common economic space.[78] Issues connected with energy, transportation, taxation, and the operation of transnational companies across state borders caused much conflict in the relations among the member states. The effort to build a more effective administrative structure and leadership for economic cooperation motivated one of Yeltsin's first actions in his new term as chairman of the Council of Heads of State of the CIS: the selection of Boris Berezovsky as CIS executive secretary and Ivan Rybkin as a new Russian deputy premier for CIS Affairs. The appointment of Berezovsky had been preceded a few days earlier by Yeltsin's threat to remove him from the country. He now expected him "to build a real commonwealth," proceeding from the conviction that "private capital is the only force capable of consolidating the CIS."[79] The appointment had been sponsored by Leonid Kuchma of Ukraine and strongly endorsed by President Karimov of Uzbekistan. Berezovsky started promisingly with an interstate forum in July, headed by the two countries' prime ministers, Sergey Kirienko and Utkir Sultanov, respectively, that focused on building an effective customs union.

Yeltsin's collaboration with Karimov was becoming increasingly close and productive. A central issue that brought them together was that of Islamic extremism. During the Moscow summit Yeltsin agreed to form an alliance, also joined by President Emomali Rakhmonov of Tajikistan, to combat the spread of what they called either "aggressive fundamentalism" or "Wahhabism" in Central Asia.[80] A public trial in Uzbekistan of militants belonging to Wahhabi Islamic extremist groups had revealed the existence of Wahhabi camps in Afghanistan and Pakistan as well as Tajikistan, the training of Uzbek militants for the struggles in Afghanistan and Tajikistan, and the development of a plan to rebuild the eighteenth- and nineteenth-century Khanate of Kokand on a fundamentalist basis in Uzbekistan's Fergana Valley. The Uzbek government had undertaken measures to control the growing number of unregistered mosques and the penetration of local government structures by imams.

Relations with other key CIS states, meanwhile, were moving much less smoothly. Relations with Kazakhstan showed serious signs of deterioration. Pleading the pressure of the financial crisis developing worryingly during the summer of 1998, Yeltsin canceled his first state visit to Kazakhstan and the chance for joint signature of an impressive group of agreements fundamental to the future relationship of the two countries, covering customs, citizenship laws, nuclear fuel enterprises, the use of the Baikonur space complex, and much else. It was generally understood that the real reason for canceling the visit was Russia's continuing resistance to division of the northern Caspian seabed, despite an earlier indication that Yeltsin would sign such a treaty. Yeltsin also chose not to attend a meeting with Kazakhstan, Kyrgyzstan, Tajikistan, and China that was scheduled to approve results of meetings of the five nations' leaders in Shanghai (1996) and Moscow (1997) on measures to build confidence and reduce arms along their shared borders. It was apparent that China was steadily increasing its influence in Central Asia with its active investment efforts and vigorous foreign policy.[81]

The issue of national rights in the Caspian Sea was proving extremely difficult to resolve. Russia and Kazakhstan were agreed on the idea of a seabed division, but Azerbaijan sought a division allowing the littoral states to control not only the seabed but also the water mass and the sea surface, in order to exercise sovereign rights to the use of its sector. Turkmenistan added further complexity with its proposal to establish control for littoral states of a forty-five-mile coastal zone, leaving other waters of the Caspian for joint exploitation.

AN OVERVIEW OF RUSSIAN
FOREIGN POLICY UNDER YELTSIN

Russian reform leaders began the postcommunist era with ambitious hopes of full partnership with the democratic states in building a new world order. After a promising beginning, it began to seem to them that the security policies and structures being built by the democratic states in Europe and East Asia minimized Russia's role and could pose a threat to Russian security. In Europe Russia faced a security system based on a restructured NATO, a legacy of the Cold War, the primary mission of which had been containment of Soviet power and which was now expanding eastward. Russian frustration with this arrangement persisted despite the concessions made later that provided for Russian consultation and crisis participation with NATO.

A parallel problem persisted in East Asia, where the American-led alliances and security system continued to be based on the legacy of the Cold War era—the US-Japan Security Treaty and the US alliance with South Korea. From the Russian perspective the management of the successive crises in Yugoslavia and on the Korean peninsula, with Russia's influence and participation either minimized or excluded, epitomized its post-Cold War predicament and failure. Russia's response was the development of a foreign policy concept that defined the United States as an ambitious, monopolistic superpower that must be countered by a variety of Russian regional agreements and alliances. With that concept operating, it is no surprise that the Russians opposed US development of a nuclear missile defense that threatened to diminish or negate their own nuclear defense along with that of the states toward whose new or growing nuclear armories it was ostensibly directed. Yeltsin's proposal in 1992 for a cooperative global missile defense system had sought to avoid this quandary, but it was ignored by the American side.

American reluctance to embrace the new Russia as a partner had its own rationale, shared by fellow NATO powers and by states previously subject to Russian power, both former Warsaw Pact partners and several of the CIS states. The protracted and painful political and economic transition of postcommunist Russia was fraught with potential for dangerous—even disastrous—collapse of the democratic enterprise. The still-powerful communist and ultranationalist leaders suggested the potential for restoring authoritarian and imperialist policies, encouraging US security policies that allowed for the possibility of major reversals of Russian leadership and policy and a threat to the independence of former subject states. Russia's brutal war in Chechnya and its export of nuclear technology were taken by many as evidence that its transformation of outlook and policy was incomplete.

The huge reductions of Russian military and economic power after the Soviet collapse led some observers to conclude that Russia was less important than the Soviet Union in the power calculations of the new age. Yet the great and continuing geopolitical importance of Russia was inescapable, because of the size and quality of its population, the vastness of its territory and resources, and its crucial place in the difficult and potentially dangerous processes of change in the many states along its long border from Europe to the Far East. These factors had combined with the high level of its economic, scientific, and technological development to make it a formidable threat in the years of the Cold War. But that threat had derived from the political and ideological apparatus and the policy objectives of the controlling communist power.

The destruction of communist rule was accompanied by a great reduction of Russia's territory and of its economic and military power. But Russia continued to control the strategic heartland of Eurasia, and its full economic and political recovery within a new democratic political system and modern market economy would certainly guarantee it great influence in Eurasia and the rest of the world. It was unwise to take seriously assertions that Russia had ceased to be a great power on the evidence of temporary setbacks. The fundamental challenge remained: how to complete and maximize the integration of a new Russia, both politically and economically, into the community of democracies. This was the aim of Yeltsin and the Russian democrats from the moment they acquired power, and they saw the support of that mission by the democratic states as an essential supplement to their efforts in a protracted and dangerous struggle for the success of their domestic reforms and foreign policy, and even the survival of their power in Russia.

The development of an effective policy by Russia's former Cold War opponents was dependent on their estimation of the direction and scope of the Russian transformation following the collapse of communist rule and of the ways in which their own foreign policy could contribute to a positive outcome in that complex and difficult historic change. The first major act of the Russian democratic leaders was the peaceful dismantling of the Soviet Union. In comparison with many of the protracted and costly struggles in the territories of some European colonial states after World War II, or in contemporary Yugoslavia, this was indeed a "velvet revolution." Yet many Western critics, including government policymakers, journalists, and academics, continued to talk of the irrepressibility of Russian imperialism. They appeared to underestimate the great power shift following the emancipation of the Warsaw Pact states and the reunification of Germany. They ignored the mammoth act of liberation and focused on the problems that followed—failing to appreciate that most of the ensuing problems were a complex legacy of the Soviet past rather than products of the attitudes and policies of the new leadership.

The most difficult and intractable problems were those that appeared from the struggles of minority nationalities, such as the Chechens in the Russian Federation, the Armenians in Azerbaijan, and the Abkhaz in Georgia, to achieve their independence. The decision to affirm the territorial boundaries of Soviet republics at the dissolution of the Soviet Union would not be easy to guarantee and would produce many conflicts, including a major disaster in Chechnya.

The dominant figures in Russian policymaking circles continued to stress the "irreversibility" of the dissolution of the Soviet internal empire that followed the 1991 revolution, whatever their communist and nationalist critics were saying. This commitment continued throughout the Yeltsin years, reflecting the firm position of Yeltsin himself. Although he aspired to economic and political reintegration of the former republics that had joined the CIS, he insisted that this be a voluntary and democratic process, on the model of the European Union. There was, however, a crucial limitation on this view, evident in the Yeltsin leadership's opposition to CIS states joining NATO, an action fully consistent with their national independence. Not until the Putin era did efforts to achieve full integration of Russia into NATO seem to hold promise of reducing Russian concern about the eastward extension of that organization, though limits on Russia's full partnership in NATO still proved difficult to reduce.

The scope of the political and economic transformation during the Yeltsin era was too often underestimated and undervalued by Western observers.[82] The vision and determination of the Yeltsin leadership produced a democratic constitutional system from the wreckage of totalitarian power. The successful introduction of a functional constitution in 1993 and the three subsequent parliamentary and two presidential elections established the foundations of a Russian democracy—imperfect and incomplete, but undeniably a major achievement. A dramatic step in the process was the voluntary resignation of the twice-elected leader of Russia's democratic revolution. What the foreign critics of the economic and social changes of his era had too often failed to recognize was that Yeltsin's reform efforts had been distorted or blocked in myriad crucial ways by a persistent majority of communist and other political groups opposed to their basic purpose. Though the 1993 constitution had created the needed executive power for the president, it was not until the victory of pro-government forces in the December 1999 parliamentary elections that the president could count on the legislative support required for the completion of his program.

The need for a full integration of Russia into the security structures of the Western democracies was undeniable. The argument that its current political structure and leadership and its incapacity for building a democracy rendered it unfit for that role was surely wrong. What was needed was a fair-minded evaluation of past efforts—Russian *and* Western—to achieve that goal, and a vigorous and imaginative approach to renewing and strengthening those efforts.

Russian democrats had repeatedly stressed the damage that NATO's eastward expansion imposed on their efforts. A widespread Russian reaction to the news that most of the East European states sought to join NATO was described by Russia's ambassador to the United States, Vladimir Lukin: "In thousands of Russian cities and villages, the reaction of Russia's people . . . will be the same: 'We have been betrayed.'"[83] A close observer of the Russian scene, deputy secretary of state Strobe Talbott, noted that opponents of a Western orientation of Russian policy used NATO enlargement as "proof that the West is bent on humiliating Russia, keeping it weak, plotting its demise."[84] The basis of these fears was the perception that NATO expansion was a hostile military action directed against Russia; there was little or no understanding of NATO's postcommunist political role. Hence, NATO's expansion policy contributed much to the declining popularity of pro-Western political figures such as Foreign Minister Kozyrev.

Some American and other Western leaders tried to stress NATO's political role in stabilizing postcommunist Eastern Europe rather than building an alliance against Russia. Hence the effort to give Russia formal participation in NATO affairs by the introduction of the Founding Act on Mutual Relations, Cooperation and Security in May 1997, an act that was soon followed by invitations to Poland, Hungary, and the Czech Republic to join NATO. But though the intention of the Founding Act was to allay Russian fears about NATO's intentions, serious differences soon arose over the purposes of the new agreement. It was clear that the Founding Act, without a full-time support apparatus and with operations centered in ad hoc committees and monthly meetings of permanent representatives, did not provide what the Russians sought. Further negotiations between Foreign Minister Primakov, Secretary of State Madeleine Albright, and NATO Secretary General Javier Solana produced the Permanent Joint Council (PJC), intended to provide regular dialogue between Russia and NATO.

This effort to provide an institutional structure for dialogue between NATO and the Russians was also a disappointment to the Russian side. There was no clear agreement on the agenda and objectives of the PJC, and the organization was given neither a permanent headquarters nor a secretariat. Most disappointing was the inability of the Russians to participate in NATO deliberations before bloc positions were formed, an arrangement obviously designed to avoid Russian influence during decision making. The PJC came to be regarded as a talking shop while Russian policymakers concentrated on direct approaches to member countries.

The crisis in Kosovo proved a disaster for the progress of Russian-NATO cooperation and the PJC. Although the PJC discussed the Kosovo situation in 1998 and agreed that Russia would participate in conflict resolution, it was clear by October that the gap between Russia and the NATO powers had not been closed. When NATO's ultimatum to Yugoslavia was rejected and bombing was undertaken in March 1999, the Russians left the PJC in protest. Their objection was not only to the action itself but also to the fact that it was not validated by a UN mandate. The Russians charged that NATO had both diminished Russia's Security Council vote and rejected the central role of the UN in global peacekeeping.[85] Both Russian governmental statements and public opinion polls expressed a hostile reaction to the NATO action against Yugoslavia. The hostility was doubtless greatly magnified by the parallel between their problems in Chechnya and those of the Yugoslav government in Kosovo.

The years since the end of the Yeltsin presidency have demonstrated an impressive continuity of many of the problems and concerns in foreign and security policy that dominated the Yeltsin years, especially in relations with the United States. Extensive exchanges between the American and Russian presidents and their aides have focused on the familiar issues of the ABM Treaty and US plans for deploying a missile defense system. An evaluation of these discussions by the distinguished political analyst Andrey Piontkovsky, written a week before the September 11, 2001, terrorist attack on the United States, noted that the Russian side was prepared to settle the antiballistic missile question by agreeing to restrictions on their use, but the US leadership appeared to have adopted a "fundamentalist" position "that rejects all arms control treaties in principle [in order to] secure for itself the broadest possible choices of unilateral strategic decisions."[86] Piontkovsky's prediction that the United States was likely soon to abandon the ABM Treaty unilaterally was followed three months later—on December 13, 2001—by precisely that action.

Meanwhile, the September 11 attack had brought vigorous US participation, with extensive Russian support, cooperation, and appreciation, in preparations for an antiterrorist campaign. The campaign included NATO support, US agreements with the CIS Central Asian states, the support of Pakistan against the Taliban, and US preparation for a campaign in Afghanistan. The US response brought much praise from prominent Russian diplomats and journalists. One commentator expressed the widely held view that Vladimir Putin had achieved a major shift of Russian policy toward Europe and the United States, recognizing that ties with the West were crucial: "Putin's strategic objective is to restore Russia's power through liberal market reforms and integration into Western political institutions. His tactical goals are to join with the Europeans in forcing the United States to 'play by the common rules' and, as he said in an interview with American reporters, to make Washington a more reliable partner."[87]

A Russian diplomat linked the September 11 attack to Chechnya: "The latest events confirm the importance of seeing the situation in Chechnya in the context of struggle against international terrorism. Also, the September events showed that the real threat comes not from ballistic missiles that are going to be countered with a national missile defense system, but from organized international terrorism that is emerging as a formidable force."[88]

Putin, meanwhile, described the new relationship with the United States as "a program of long-term partnership." He stressed President George W. Bush's endorsement of a closer Russian relationship with NATO that brought Russia into the new "Group of Twenty" (nineteen current NATO members plus Russia) for the adoption and implementation of policy decisions. He also spoke of "a serious and positive transformation of our relations," including expanded economic cooperation and eventual recognition of Russia as a market economy and its inclusion in the World Trade Organization (WTO).[89]

However, as Putin left Russia for meetings in Washington, DC, and Texas, another commentator, noting America's casual approach to the treaty system controlling nuclear missiles and the ABM Treaty, as well as Bush's expanding list of Russian critics, warned of the need for other partners (Europe, China, and India) "when America's pretensions to hegemony become too absolute."[90] Other commentators expressed concern that Bush's unilateral actions on major security issues would weaken Putin's position vis-à-vis ultraleftists and nationalists and could also encourage China to expand its strategic nuclear power.[91]

But this view was countered by a leading policy specialist, Sergey Karaganov, who stressed the need for both Russia and the United States to take a new view of their relationship: "Since the early 1990s, Russia and America have frozen themselves in a position of being half enemies, half partners. This indeterminate status casts a shadow on their entire relationship. Putin has proposed that we get out of this in-between situation."[92]

An important indicator of positive change came with the improvement of Russian relations with NATO following Russia's close cooperation with the NATO powers in Afghanistan. British prime minister Tony Blair offered a plan to replace the Permanent Joint Council with a new structure called the Russia-North Atlantic Council (called "NATO at Twenty" by some NATO representatives). Lord Robertson, the secretary general of NATO, affirmed that "Russia and NATO are both essential security players in Europe."[93] Despite reservations on the part of some who questioned Russia's suitability for full voting membership, a new perception of Russia was developing that promised full membership in NATO and full participation in the European security system.

The NATO partnership itself was soon severely tested in the run-up to the Iraq war, which imposed major strains on Russian-US relations in 2002–3. The Russians opposed the US invasion of Iraq on the grounds that the UN weapons search had not been completed and that the invasion, without authorization by the UN Security Council, violated international law. Russian opposition was accompanied by the reminder that the population of the Russian Federation included 20 million Muslims. Fortunately for President Putin, France and Germany shared his view on the war. During a February 2003 visit to Paris, where the shared opposition of the three countries to the war was confirmed, Putin stated his position: "Russia, France, and Germany, like the majority of the international community, feel that the problem of Iraq can and must be solved by diplomatic means. Our position is . . . aimed at minimizing damage stemming from the possible existence of weapons of mass destruction in Iraq, avoiding harm to the civilian population and not violating international law."[94]

Commentary in the Russian press following Putin's policy statement in Paris was generally strongly supportive. Noting the quandary that the US policy presented, one commentator observed that Putin's statement would be unwelcome in Washington, "but in the final analysis, Putin has other audiences to play to—in Russia, Europe, and Asia—that are no less important."[95]

> *What struck me was that Mr. Yeltsin, unlike President Gorbachev, had escaped from the communist mindset and language.*
>
> —MARGARET THATCHER[1]

THE YELTSIN LEGACY

> *What any of us, including myself, might have done [in Yeltsin's position] is anyone's guess. You can characterize that period however you like, and you can judge the actions of the first president of the Russian Federation however you like, but one thing is certain: precisely when Boris Nikolaevich Yeltsin was leading Russia, the people of our country, the citizens of Russia, got the main thing that all those reforms were intended to give them—freedom. That is Boris Nikolaevich Yeltsin's huge historical contribution.*
>
> —VLADIMIR PUTIN[2]

THE RESIGNATION OF BORIS YELTSIN AS RUSSIAN PRESIDENT marked the end of one of the most important and successful political careers of the twentieth century. Upon his departure from office, much remained to be done to complete Russia's transformation from a vast communist-ruled empire and socialist economy to a new and greatly diminished Russian state with a fully effective democracy and market economy. Yet Yeltsin could claim a major part of the credit for organizing and leading the democratic movement before the collapse of Soviet power, for building its power base in the Russian Republic and the Russian presidency, for overcoming the effort to destroy it in August 1991, and for providing the program and leadership that carried it forward decisively against formidable obstacles and powerful political resistance during the ensuing years of his presidency. His firm commitment to the democratic cause and his keen strategic and tactical sense as a political leader were decisive factors in Russia's transformation.

In comparison with that of most of his fellow presidents of former Soviet republics, Yeltsin's commitment to democratic policy and institutions and a market economy was outstanding. Until near the end of his presidency he faced communist and nationalist legislative majorities who resisted essential elements of his political and economic reform program. And though he received much domestic and foreign criticism for the extensive powers granted to the president in his December 1993 constitution, without such powers the composition of subsequent parliaments might simply have reproduced the dangerous stalemate of the preceding era—or produced a major counterrevolution. Moreover, Yeltsin confirmed his commitment to the new constitutional system by retaining parliamentary and presidential elections even when their actual or potential outcomes threatened all that he had achieved.

The most dangerous problem Yeltsin confronted in the new parliament—the strong communist representation elected in 1995—was a reflection of the character of leadership within that party. The Russian communist leader Zyuganov dominated a movement that had resolutely rejected the conversion of communism into social democracy that was evident in the former communist states of Eastern Europe. The traditional communist outlook of his party foreclosed the possibility of effective cooperation with Yeltsin in his economic and political reforms and even supported reversal of the brilliant reform of the beginning of his leadership that granted independence to the national republics of the Soviet Union. The communists employed instead a policy of constant resistance and harassment toward the Yeltsin government, seeking to block the implementation of its current policies, dispose of its accomplished reforms, and remove Yeltsin from power.

Unfortunately, Russian liberals were so fragmented that both their political organizations and their political influence were greatly reduced by the inability of most of their parties to secure the required minimum percentage in the party list competition for legislative elections. Yegor Gaidar and others tried repeatedly to form an electoral alliance of reform parties, but in vain. Yeltsin's last prime minister and presidential successor, Vladimir Putin, would soon build effective legislative support for the government's program by creating a strong pro-government party (United Russia) that first built a legislative majority by cooperating with other parties and individuals and then acquired its own majority parliamentary representation. Thereafter, the combination of extraordinary presidential powers provided by the constitution and a parliamentary majority led by a presidential party gave new impetus to important reforms, though there were, as with Yeltsin in 1993, some concerns that the policies and power of the new president might pose risks for Russian democracy.

One of the most important legacies of Yeltsin's era was his commitment to the sovereignty and independence of the republics of the former Soviet Union. He faced continuing political attacks for this policy throughout his presidency from both communists and nationalists, and both groups feared and condemned the eastward extension of NATO, especially when it incorporated former Soviet Baltic republics. They would later become still more vociferous when confronted by evidence of the wish of some former Soviet republics, including members of the Commonwealth of Independent States, to cooperate with and possibly enter the European Union. Yeltsin continued to the end of his presidency his effort to build an effective CIS organization capable of coordinated economic and security policies, but in vain. His efforts were greatly weakened by the policy and actions of Russian communist and nationalist leaders, which inspired fear of renascent Russian imperialism among leaders of other CIS states and discouraged their acceptance of closer economic and political ties with Russia.

Another problem inherited by Yeltsin's successor was that of the relationships between Moscow and the regional governments of the Russian Federation. The most troublesome were those in the Muslim national republics, and the outcome in Chechnya—an armed insurrection inspired by Moscow's rejection of a demand for national independence—was followed by a brutal war with Russia (1994–96), a test period of Chechen independence (1996–99), and then a renewed Chechen military action seeking extension of the separatist action to neighboring Dagestan, which renewed and expanded the tragic conflict. The severity of the problems in Chechnya were much intensified by the legacy of Stalin's brutal persecution of that small nation during World War II and by his successors' denial of the return of deportees for many years afterward.

Yeltsin achieved a successful settlement of another potentially dangerous nationalist challenge in Tatarstan by offering a generous autonomy (rather than the independence demanded by the Chechen leader Dudaev).

But in the Russian regions of the Federation, too, the central government faced a continuing challenge from governors whose exercise of power frequently violated their constitutional obligations and whose management of tax revenues often gave the central government a pathetically inadequate share of public revenues, contributing much to the ongoing fiscal crisis of the Yeltsin years.

As Yeltsin departed, Russia still faced major challenges in the conversion of its economy. The financial collapse of August 1998 had been an alarming demonstration of the economy's weaknesses, and the list of reform challenges was still formidable sixteen months later, at the time of Yeltsin's resignation. Prime Minister Putin's success in building a pro-government majority in the December 1999 elections was probably the key factor convincing Yeltsin of his capacity to carry forward stalled economic and other reforms, as he would indeed do as president, securing crucial legislation on private property in land and tax reform and soon achieving impressive levels of economic growth. Like Yeltsin, Putin would soon face conflict with the "oligarchs" who had acquired enormous wealth from ill-regulated privatization, but his expansion of the government's political power in both the parliamentary (1999) and presidential (2000) elections would give him a strong position for meeting the challenge. The solid parliamentary majority supporting Putin gave him power in such matters that Yeltsin lacked throughout his presidency, although in this matter, as in his constitutional changes, his policy evoked some concern about his commitment to democratic procedures.

In the last phase of his presidency and after his retirement, Yeltsin continued to offer thoughtful observations on events current and past that expressed the key values and purposes that had guided his remarkable political career. One example is his response to questions addressed to him on the tenth anniversary of his famous speech at the Central Committee of the Soviet Communist Party in October 1987, which brought his expulsion from the Politburo and from his position of Moscow Party secretary. Noting that his critical remarks in that speech where not harsh, as charged, but "mild, sparing, and even gentle," he suggested that the severity of the treatment he had received was because "I had dared to express criticism and voice my own opinion . . . at a plenary session closed to journalists." He continued by noting the immense contrast with the current situation in Russia: "I'm criticized a great deal in the State Duma and the newspapers and from various other platforms. And that's as it should be . . . we have done away with the *diktat* of the Communist Party and escaped from the bonds of ideological conformity."[3]

In late 1997 Yeltsin was caught up in a major controversy concerning his planned veto of a Duma-approved law titled "On Freedom of Conscience and Religious Associations." His reason for a proposed veto was that "many provisions in the law infringe on human and civil rights and freedoms as spelled out in the Constitution, establish inequality among different faiths, and are at odds with international commitments that Russia has assumed."[4] A barrage of criticism of Yeltsin's veto plan came from the Duma, from Patriarch Aleksy II of the Russian Orthodox Church, and from the Communist Party of the Russian Federation. But his position had considerable support in Russia and abroad, most notably from Pope John Paul II, who saw the law as a dangerous threat to Catholics in Russia. The Duma opponents of the planned veto detailed their concerns about the recent spread of the activities of foreign religious groups such as the Church of Scientology, Jehovah's Witnesses, and the Korean Unification Church of the Reverend Sun Myung Moon.[5]

Yeltsin has been interviewed on occasion since his retirement about his reactions to the performance of his successor, and his comments have been generally positive. But he has also occasionally indicated his policy preferences, as in his comment on the appropriate government response to the Beslan tragedy of September 2004, a terrorist attack on a school in the North Ossetia region of the Russian Federation that killed hundreds of children: "I firmly believe that the measures the country's leadership will embark upon after Beslan will be in keeping with the democratic freedoms that are Russia's most valuable achievement of the past decade. We will not allow ourselves to depart from the letter and, most importantly, the spirit of the Constitution that the country adopted in a nationwide referendum in 1993."[6]

The Beslan event was quickly followed by Putin's proposals for modifying the Russian political system, which represented significant changes in the constitution. He proposed that the executive heads of the regions be chosen by regional legislatures from a list of candidates presented by the president. He offered this revised arrangement as a measure needed to strengthen executive leadership, explaining: "The basic point here is that with respect to matters under the jurisdiction of the Russian Federation and matters under joint jurisdiction, the bodies of executive power at the center and in the Federation members form a single system of authority—one that should operate, accordingly, as a single, unified, and co-subordinated organism."[7]

To achieve this goal he proposed presidential control of the selection of gubernatorial candidates, combined with the president's right of dissolution of provincial legislative assemblies and making his own gubernatorial appointment if the regional legislature failed to follow the process. The simultaneous abolition of the constitutional arrangement providing for half of the Duma membership to be elected from constituencies rather than party lists and its replacement by an arrangement providing a membership chosen entirely from party lists was clearly intended to bring an even larger majority of the Duma under the control of his United Russia Party.[8]

The ensuing vigorous debates in the regional legislatures suggested that Yeltsin's 1990 invitation to the Russian regions to "take as much sovereignty as you can swallow" had been taken seriously. In Tatarstan, President Mintimer Shaymiev noted that "seventy percent of the people who have come to power in the regions have displayed incompetence, and more than half of them came to power by unknown means," but he was still unwilling to grant the president powers that would "establish total control over regional legislative bodies, which would deny even the theoretical possibility of ignoring the president's will . . . and depart from the letter and, most importantly, the spirit of the Constitution that the country adopted in a nationwide referendum in 1993."[9] Resistance and even rejection of the changes was also encountered in other administrative regions. The main resistance came from Yabloko and the Union of Rightist Forces, although there were signs of resistance even from some members of Putin's party, United Russia.

The resistance to the new procedure for choosing regional governors provided good evidence that the practice of regional self-government had taken firm root during the Yeltsin years. The vigorous debate about proposed changes and the active political opposition, both in the regional governments and in the regional and national press, offered evidence of confident commitment to the constitutional rights and freedoms inherited from the Yeltsin years. Unfortunately, it sometimes also obscured the element of illegal and corrupt activity, which was a major concern for Putin. Another impressive example of the Yeltsin legacy was the powerful Ukrainian resistance to the Putin government's intervention in the Ukrainian presidential election in 2004. It was accompanied by the commitment of the Ukrainian democratic leadership to the national independence that Yeltsin had supported and to a domestic reform program resembling Yeltsin's.

Russia and the other former Soviet republics had every reason to be deeply grateful to the main leader of one of the most ambitious, progressive, and successful political transformations in modern history. He had brought them much closer to reaching the reform goals that had been brilliantly and courageously articulated by intellectual dissidents of the post-Stalin era but only partially implemented by the reforms of the Gorbachev years. Yeltsin's words and deeds amply justify calling him "Russian liberator."

Young Boris with his family, mid 1960s. Back row, from left: Yeltsin; brother, Mikhail; mother, Klavdiya; father, Nikolay; front row: sister, Valentina; wife, Naiha; and daughters, Tatyana and Yelena. © SYGMA/CORBIS

NOTES

INTRODUCTION

1. Chubais's statement was made in an interview presented in Public Broadcasting Service, *Boris Yeltsin: A Legacy of Change,* Films for the Humanities and Sciences, August 2000, directed by Daniel Wolf. I served as chief consultant for this production.

2. One study that suggests that Gorbachev was inclined from the beginning of his tenure in 1985 to accept the collapse of communist rule in Eastern Europe is Matthew J. Ouimet's *The Rise and Fall of the Brezhnev Doctrine in Soviet Foreign Policy* (Chapel Hill: University of North Carolina Press, 2003). The "Brezhnev Doctrine," instituted after the Soviet invasion of Czechoslovakia in 1968, held that socialist political transformation was an irreversible historical phenomenon and that the members of the socialist community had the right and obligation to preserve established Marxist regimes by any means necessary, including military force. Nevertheless, after

events in Poland in 1980–81 Moscow found this position untenable and secretly abandoned it in 1981 while continuing to proclaim it publicly. As Ouimet persuasively argues, the Soviet leadership recognized that an invasion of Poland would not only be difficult militarily but also cost the Kremlin desperately needed Western economic support. During the rest of the 1980s, Ouimet holds, the Soviet leadership found it prudent to follow this precedent, and the same reasoning was applied to Moscow's relations with the rest of Eastern Europe. Ouimet's research offers a good explanation for the Kremlin's seeming indifference in the face of the declining fortunes of these governments during the 1980s.

1 REFORM OR REVOLUTION

1. Yeltsin's hope has been realized more fully than he apparently thought possible in 1990. Like Gorbachev, he was taken by surprise by the Soviet collapse. In the early twenty-first century only China, Cuba, North Korea, and Vietnam still adhere to that "obsolete ideology from the nineteenth" century. In any case, Yeltsin's remark reveals his awareness of the philosophical bankruptcy of Marxism-Leninism and the pervasive influence of ideology on Soviet life, quite apart from his practical criticisms of Soviet institutions. With few exceptions, Western historiography after the 1950s has tended to marginalize ideological questions and focus on the institutional shortcomings of the Soviet system, arguing the merits of noncommunist theories of economic growth and social development as demonstrated by their practical success. This is unfortunate, because Soviet leaders from Lenin to Gorbachev took purely philosophical issues very seriously. Gorbachev's declaration about his communist convictions suggests that perestroika, despite its institutional innovations, was anything but a repudiation of the foundations of socialism. As Yeltsin implies here, problems of Marxism-Leninism, rooted in philosophical currents of the nineteenth century, contributed heavily to the country's difficulties even late in the Gorbachev era. In the end, they played a key role in the Soviet collapse. See Oscar J. Bandelin, *Return to the NEP: The False Promise of Leninism and the Failure of Perestroika* (Westport, CT: Praeger, 2002).

2. Philip Taubman, "Russia's Blood Feud: An Enmity That Shaped History," *New York Times,* June 24, 1996, A14.

3. Boris N. Yeltsin, *Against the Grain* (New York: Simon and Schuster, 1994), 182–83.

4. Ibid., 188–92.

5. Aleksandr Yakovlev, interviewed in Public Broadcasting Service, *Boris Yeltsin: A Legacy of Change,* Films for the Humanities and Sciences, August 2000, directed by Daniel Wolf. Yakovlev was sharply critical of Yeltsin's remarks, even though he endorsed Yeltsin's claim that there had been a worrisome slowdown in Gorbachev's reform program.

6. Yeltsin, *Against the Grain,* 199.

7. "Conduct Restructuring Energetically," *Pravda,* Nov. 13, 1987, 1–3 (*CDSP* 39, no. 45, Dec. 9, 1987).

8. Nina Andreeva, "I Can't Forgo Principles," *Sovetskaia Rossiia,* March 13, 1988 (*CDSP* 40, no. 15, Apr. 27, 1988).

9. "The Party Is in the Forefront of Restructuring," *Sovetskaia Rossiia,* April 15, 1988, 3 (*CDSP* 40, no. 15, May 11, 1988).

10. "The CPSU Central Committee's Theses for the Nineteenth All-Union Party Conference," *Pravda,* May 27, 1988, 1–3 (*CDSP* 40, no. 21, June 22, 1988).

11. Yeltsin, *Against the Grain,* 220, 222–24.

12. "Speech by Comrade B. N. Yeltsin, First Vice Chairman of the USSR State Construction Committee and USSR Minister," *Pravda,* July 2, 1988, 10 (*CDSP* 40, no. 35, Sept. 28, 1988).

13. "Speech by Comrade M. S. Gorbachev at the Conclusion of the All-Union CPSU Conference," *Pravda,* July 2, 1988, 1 (*CDSP* 40, no. 35, Sept. 28, 1988).

14. "Verbatim Report of the Congress of People's Deputies, Fourth Day," *Izvestiia,* May 28, 1989, 1–7 (*CDSP* 41, no. 23, July 5, 1989). Kazannik, an assistant professor from Omsk State University, gave up his seat precisely in order to assure Yeltsin's membership in the Council of Nationalities of the Supreme Soviet. He made the choice of Yeltsin a condition of his resignation, and though Gorbachev, as presiding officer, on legal advice rejected the appropriateness of a conditional resignation, he invited the members to vote on the issue and secured an overwhelming majority in favor of acceptance of the resignation in tandem with acceptance of Yeltsin as a deputy.

15. "M. S. Gorbachev's Speech at the Conclusion of the Work of the First Session of the Supreme Soviet," *Pravda* and *Izvestiia,* Aug. 5, 1989, 1–2 (*CDSP* 41, no. 31, Aug. 30, 1989).

16. Yeltsin, *Against the Grain,* 255.

17. Ibid., 262.

18. Ibid., 250–51.

19. Daniil Granin, "Reading Yeltsin," *Literaturnaia gazeta,* Sept. 5, 1990, 10 (*CDSP* 42, no. 35, Oct. 3, 1990).

20. The speeches of Gorbachev and Yeltsin were presented in *Pravda* and *Izvestiia* on February 6, 1990, 1–2 (*CDSP* 42, no. 6, March 3, 1990).

21. The vote on Russian sovereignty on June 12, 1990, was 907 in favor, 13 against, and 9 abstaining.

22. A. Davydov and V. Kurasov, "Two Contenders, Two Programs," *Izvestiia,* May 26, 1990, 1–2 (*CDSP* 42, no. 21, June 27, 1990).

23. "Speech by M. S. Gorbachev," *Izvestiia,* May 23, 1990, 1, 5 (*CDSP* 42, no. 21, June 27, 1990).

24. Andrey Nuykin, "A Tragedy? No, a Farce," *Komsomol'skaia pravda,* June 30, 1990, 3 (*CDSP* 42, no. 26, August 1, 1990). One estimate held that twenty thousand people had resigned from the Moscow Party organization as a protest against the leadership and policy decisions at the congress. Pavel Gutentov, "A Reputation Must Be Fought For," *Izvestiia,* June 28, 1990, 1 (*CDSP* 42, no. 26, August 1, 1990).

25. N. Musenko and O. Stepanko, "Who Will Defend the Peasant?" *Pravda,* June 12, 1990, 4 (*CDSP* 42, no. 24, July 18, 1990).

26. M. Berger, "The Russian Version of Reform," *Izvestiia,* July 1, 1990, 1 (*CDSP* 42, no. 25, July 25, 1990).

27. "Speech by B. N. Yeltsin, Chairman of the Russian SFSR Supreme Soviet," *Pravda,* July 8, 1990, 4 (*CDSP* 42, no. 32, Sept. 12, 1990).

28. Ibid.

29. The main elements of the program were summarized by the editors of *Izvestiia* in the article "Man, Freedom and the Market," Sept. 4, 1990, 1, 3 (*CDSP* 42, no. 35, Oct. 3, 1990).

30. M. Berger, "Sosenki without the Pines," *Izvestiia,* Aug. 27, 1990, 3 (*CDSP* 42, no. 35, Oct. 3, 1990).

31. A. Davydov and V. Kurasov, "Russian Deputies Vote 'Yes,'" *Izvestiia,* Sept. 12, 1990, 1 (*CDSP* 42, no. 37, Oct. 17, 1990).

32. "A Choice Has Been Made," *Sovetskaia Rossiia,* Sept. 18, 1990, 2 (*CDSP* 42, no. 37, Nov. 17, 1990).

33. "M. S. Gorbachev's Concluding Remarks at the Plenary Session of the CPSU Central Committee," *Pravda,* Oct. 11, 1990, 1 (*CDSP* 42, no. 42, Nov. 21, 1990).

34. "The Union Treaty and Russian Sovereignty," *Izvestiia,* Nov. 14, 1990, 2 (*CDSP* 42, no. 46, Dec. 19, 1990).

35. Soviet authorities had sponsored the formation of a Committee of National Salvation in Lithuania as a counter to the democratic nationalist leadership, with an organization and ideology supporting traditional Soviet state authority and policy.

36. A. Stepovoy and S. Chugaev, "What the Referendum Showed," *Izvestiia,* March 21, 1991, 3 (*CDSP* 43, no. 11, April 17, 1991).

37. "Resolution of the USSR Supreme Soviet: On the Results of the USSR Referendum on March 17, 1991," *Pravda,* March 22, 1991, 1 (*CDSP* 41, no. 11, April 17, 1991).

38. "On Temporarily Suspending the Holding of Rallies, Street Processions and Demonstrations in Moscow [Decree of March 21]," *Izvestiia,* March 26, 1991, 2 (*CDSP* 42, no. 12, April 24, 1991).

39. "On Urgent Measures to Stabilize the Situation in the Country and Overcome the Crisis," *Pravda,* April 24, 1991, 1 (*CDSP* 42, no. 17, April 29, 1991).

40. N. Andreev, "A Constructive Document," *Izvestiia,* April 30, 1991, 1 (*CDSP* 43, no. 17, April 29, 1991).

41. Vasily Selyunin, "Will Yeltsin Be One of the Ten?" *Komsomol'skaia pravda*, April 30, 1991, 2 (*CDSP* 43, no. 17, April 29, 1991).

42. "Concluding Remarks of M. S. Gorbachev . . . at the Plenary Session of the Central Committee," *Pravda*, April 27, 1991, 1–2 (*CDSP* 43, no. 17, April 29, 1991).

43. Vladimir Kuznechevsky, "A Coup Attempt? No, Just an Intrigue," *Rossiiskaia gazeta*, June 26, 1991, 1 (*CDSP* 43, no. 25, July 14, 1991).

44. Jack F. Matlock Jr., *Autopsy on an Empire* (New York: Random House, 1995), 540–44.

45. Ibid., 551.

46. "Treaty of the Union of Sovereign States," *Izvestiia*, Aug. 15, 1991, 1–2 (*CDSP* 43, no. 31, Sept. 4, 1991).

47. "Communique on the Plenary Session of the Central Committee of the Communist Party of the Soviet Union," *Pravda*, July 26, 1991, 1 (*CDSP* 43, no. 30, August 28, 1991).

48. A. N. Yakovlev, "I Have Decided to Reject Marxism," *Sovetskaia Rossiia*, Aug. 3, 1991, 1 (*CDSP* 43, no. 31, Sept. 4, 1991).

49. "A naughty schoolboy" was a descriptive title used by an *Izvestiia* reporter on August 24, 1991.

50. Eduard Shevardnadze, *The Future Belongs to Freedom* (New York: Free Press, 1991), 220.

51. Vladimir Bukovsky, *Moskovskii protsess* (Moscow: Russkaia Mysl'-Izdatel'stvo MIK, 1996), 480.

52. Stenogramma zasedaniia Komissii po rassledovaniiu prichin i obstoiatel'stv gosudarsvennogo perevorota na temu: "O roli repressirovannykh organov v gosudarstvennoi perevorote 19–21 avgusta 1991 g.," Feb. 4, 1992, 115–16.

53. The members of the SCSE were O. D. Baklanov, first vice chairman of the USSR Defense Council; V. A. Kryuchkov, chairman of the USSR State Security Committee (KGB), V. S. Pavlov, prime minister of the USSR; B. K. Pugo, USSR minister of internal affairs; V. A. Starodubtsev, chairman of the USSR Peasants' Union; A. I. Tizyakov, president of the Association of State Enterprises and Industrial, Construction, Transportation, and Communications Facilities; D. T. Yazov, USSR minister of defense; and G. I. Yanaev, acting president of the USSR. The appellation "Gang of Eight" is an apparent allusion to the "Gang of Four" in China who, after the death of Mao Zedong in 1976, were blamed for the Cultural Revolution (1966–76) and its horrible abuses.

54. The original lists of people whose arrest on August 19 had been authorized by Kryuchkov were destroyed on August 21 by KGB officers. The state commission investigating the KGB later retrieved a substantial number of the names with the help of KGB operatives. Among the many names included were most of the leaders (including Yeltsin) of the RSFSR government. *Argumenty i fakty* 38, September 1991, 8 (*CDSP* 43, no. 40, Nov. 6, 1991).

55. *Pravda* and *Izvestiia*, August 20, 1991, 1 (*CDSP* 43, no. 33, Sept. 10, 1991).

56. Ibid.

57. *Megalopolis-Ekspress,* Aug. 19, 1991, 1.

58. *Kuranty,* August 19, 1991, 1.

59. I. Ovchinnikov, "In the Light of Conscience," *Izvestiia*, Aug. 22, 1991, 6 (*CDSP* 43, no. 34, Sept. 25, 1991).

60. *Komsomol'skaia pravda,* Aug. 27, 1991, 3 (*CDSP* 43, no. 34, Sept. 25, 1991).

61. "Statement by the Secretariat of the CPSU Central Committee," *Pravda*, Aug. 22, 1991, 2 (*CDSP* 43, no. 34, Sept. 25, 1991).

62. "Gorbachev Forced to Answer for Coup," *Izvestiia*, Aug. 24, 1991, 2 (*CDSP* 43, no. 34, Sept. 25, 1991).

63. The words are those of the *Izvestiia* reporters S. Chugaev and V. Shchepotkin, "As Deputies Squabble, the Union Breaks Up," *Izvestiia*, Aug. 28, 1991 1–2 (*CDSP* 43, no. 35, Oct. 2, 1991).

64. Igor Sinyakevich, "An Ordinary Miracle in the Belarusian Supreme Soviet," *Nezavisimaia gazeta,* Aug. 27, 1991, 3 (*CDSP* 43, no. 35, Oct. 2, 1991).

65. Svetlana Gamova, "Moving toward a New Life," *Soiuz*, Aug. 27–Sept. 4, 1991, 19 (*CDSP* 43, no. 35, Oct. 2, 1991).

66. Gagit Karapetyan, "Armenia Prepared for Guerrilla Warfare and Is Now Prepared to Say Good-Bye to the USSR," *Nezavisimaia gazeta*, Aug. 24, 1991, 3 (*CDSP* 43, no. 34, Sept. 25, 1991).

67. Boris Yeltsin, *The Struggle for Russia* (New York: Times Books, 1994), 105–6.

68. *Izvestiia,* Sept. 4, 1991, 4–7 (*CDSP* 43, no. 37, Oct. 16, 1991).

69. Vitaly Portnikov, "Ukraine Votes for Independence," *Nezavisimaia gazeta*, Dec. 3, 1991, 1, 3 (*CDSP* 43, no. 48, Jan. 1, 1992).

70. "Agreement on the Creating of a Commonwealth of Independent States," *Rossiiskaia gazeta,* Dec. 10, 1991, 1–2 (*CDSP* 43, no. 49, Jan. 8, 1992).

71. Vladimir Skachko, "Rukh and Ukraine Favor Doing Away with Soviet Power Once and For All," *Nezavisimaia gazeta,* Dec. 28, 1992, 3 (*CDPSP* 44, no. 52, Jan. 27, 1993).

72. "Statement by the President of the USSR," *Izvestiia*, Dec. 10, 1991, 2 (*CDSP* 43, no. 49, Jan. 8, 1992).

73. G. Alimov, "Kazakhstan Interprets the New Realities," *Izvestiia*, Dec. 10, 1991, 2 (*CDSP* 43, no. 49, Jan. 8, 1992).

74. N. Matukovsky, "The Creation of a New Commonwealth Should Avert Tragedy," *Izvestiia*, Dec. 10, 1991, 2 (*CDSP* 43, no. 49, Jan. 8, 1992).

75. I. Demchenko, "Prices Will Be Freed in the Three Republics at the Same Time," *Izvestiia*, Dec. 10, 1991, 2 (*CDSP* 43, no. 49, Jan. 8, 1992).

76. Otto Latsis, "There Is Still a Chance," *Izvestiia*, Dec. 10, 1991, 3 (*CDSP* 43, no. 48, Jan. 1, 1992).

77. S. Chugaev, "Ryzhkov and Chebrikov Want to Convene a Congress," *Izvestiia,* Dec. 11, 1991, 1 (*CDSP* 43, no. 50, Jan. 15, 1992).

78. S. Chugaev, "The Union Parliament Didn't Enter into a Confrontation," *Izvestiia,* Dec. 13, 1991, 2 (*CDSP* 43, no. 50, Jan. 15, 1992).

79. V. Vinogradova, "Another Version of the Agreement on the CIS Has Appeared," *Rossiiskaia gazeta,* Dec. 14, 1991, 1 (*CDSP* 43, no. 50, Jan. 15, 1992).

80. B. Matukovsky, "The Agreement on a Commonwealth of Independent States Is Ratified," *Izvestiia,* Dec. 11, 1991, 1 (*CDSP* 43, no. 50, Jan. 15, 1992).

81. Uzbekistan was a special case: its final approval had to wait for the republic's presidential election and referendum on independence, scheduled for December 29.

82. V. Ardaev, "The Results of the Ashkhabad Meeting Bring a Sigh of Relief from the Country and the World," *Izvestiia,* Dec. 14, 1991 (*CDSP* 43, 50, Jan. 15, 1992).

83. The Alma-Ata declaration and supplemental agreements were published in *Pravda* and *Izvestiia* on December 23, 1991, 1–2 (*CDSP* 43, no. 51, Jan. 22, 1992).

84. "The President of the USSR Resigns," *Rossiiskaia gazeta,* Dec. 26, 1991, 1–2 (*CDSP* 43, no. 52, Jan. 29, 1992).

85. See, for example, Inna Muraveva, "It Was, It Was," *Rossiiskaia gazeta,* Dec. 27, 1991, 1 (*CDSP* 43, no. 52, Jan. 29, 1992).

2 THE POLITICS OF REFORM, 1991–99

1. "Decree of the President of the RSFSR on the Activity of the CPSU and the RSFSR Communist Party," *Rossiiskaia gazeta,* Nov. 9, 1991, 2 (*CDSP* 43, no. 45, Dec. 11, 1991).

2. Yegor Gaidar, *Days of Defeat and Victory* (Seattle: University of Washington Press, 1999), 144–45.

3. Dmitry Oreshkin, "Regional Solitaire on the Eve of Constitution Day," *Segodnia,* June 8, 1993, 3 (*CDPSP* 45, no. 23, July 7, 1993).

4. Boris Yeltsin, *The Struggle for Russia* (Times Books, 1994), 188–89.

5. Richard Sakwa, "Introduction," in *The Struggle for Russia: Power and Change in the Democratic Revolution,* by Ruslan Khasbulatov (London: Routledge, 1993), xvi–xvii.

6. "The Union Treaty and Russian Sovereignty," *Izvestiia,* Nov. 14, 1990, 2 (*CDSP* 42, no. 46, Dec. 12, 1990).

7. I. Elistratov, V. Kurasov, and G. Shipitko, "Law on President of Russia Adopted," *Izvestiia,* May 22, 1991, 2 (*CDSP* 43, no. 21, May 22, 1991).

8. Ibid.

9. Ruslan Khasbulatov, *The Struggle for Russia: Power and Change in the Democratic Revolution* (London: Routledge, 1993), 244–46.

10. Aleksandra Lugovskaya, "Preparations for Constitutional Conference Near Completion," *Izvestiia,* June 2, 1993, 2 (*CDPSP* 45, no. 22, June 30, 1993).

11. Vladimir Todres, "The Right to Secede: The Last Trump Card in a Big Game," *Segodnia,* June 4, 1993, 2 (*CDPSP* 45, no. 22, June 30, 1993).

12. Ibid.

13. Calling itself the "All-Russia Constitutional Conference," the opposition meeting was convened by the Public Committee for Defending the Constitution and the Constitutional System, the Russian Unity parliamentary bloc, and a number of political parties and movements. It is described in Aleksandr Frolov, "United Only in Negation," *Sovetskaia Rossiia,* June 5, 1993, 2 (*CDPSP* 45, no. 22, June 30, 1993).

14. Ibid.

15. The condensed text of the speech is provided in "On a Democratic Russian State System and the Draft of a New Constitution," *Rossiiskie vesti,* June 8, 1993, 2 (*CDPSP* 45, no. 23, July 7, 1993).

16. Georgy Ivanov-Smolensky, "The Coming and Going of Khasbulatov," *Izvestiia,* June 8, 1993, 1–2 (*CDPSP* 45, no. 23, July 7, 1993).

17. Nikolay Troytsky, "Once Again They Ended Up Fighting in the Kremlin," *Megapolis-Ekspress,* June 9, 1993, 3 (*CDPSP* 45, no. 23, July 7, 1993).

18. Speech by Ruslan Khasbulatov at the Supreme Soviet on June 9, *Rossiiskaia gazeta,* June 10, 1993, 3 (*CDPSP* 45, no. 22, June 30, 1993).

19. Vasily Kononenko, "The Constitutional Conference Moves toward a Compromise," *Izvestiia,* June 10, 1993, 1 (*CDPSP* 45, no. 23, July 7, 1993).

20. Ibid.

21. Vasily Kononenko and Georgy Ivanov-Smolensky, "One Can Be in Opposition to the Government, but One Must Not Be in Opposition to the Fatherland," *Izvestiia,* June 11, 1993, 1 (*CDPSP* 45, no. 22, July 7, 1993).

22. Sergey Stankevich, "The Constitution Will Inevitably Be Provisional," *Nezavisimaia gazeta,* June 15, 1993, 2 (*CDPSP* 46, no. 23, July 7, 1993).

23. "Statement by Russian Federation People's Deputies," *Rossiiskie vesti,* June 15, 1993, 1 (*CDPSP* 45, no. 23, June 15, 1993).

24. Lyubov Tsukanova, "Today the Initiative Is in the Hands of the President," *Rossiiskie vesti,* June 15, 1993, 1 (*CDPSP* 45, no. 23, July 14, 1993).

25. Vasily Kononenko, "The Constitutional Conference Approves the Draft of a New Constitution for Russia," *Izvestiia,* July 13, 1–2 (*CDPSP* 45, no. 28, Aug. 11, 1993).

26. Ibid.

27. Vera Kuznetsova, "Soviet Authorities at the Local Level Will Begin the Process of Approving the New Basic Law," *Nezavisimaia gazeta,* July 13, 1993, 1, 3 (*CDPSP* 45, no. 28, Aug. 11, 1993).

28. Vladimir Todres, "The Local Soviets Want to Ratify the Constitution . . . ," *Segodnia,* July 13, 1993, 2 (*CDPSP* 45, no. 28, Aug. 11, 1993).

29. Georgy Melikyants, "The Constitution's Adoption Should Not Be Postponed until Autumn," *Izvestiia.* July 14, 1993, 4 (*CDPSP* 45, no. 28, Aug. 11, 1993).

30. Vera Kuznetsova, "The Parliament Is Getting Ahead of the President," *Nezavisimaia gazeta,* July 17, 1993, 1 (*CDPSP* 45, no. 28, Aug. 11, 1993).

31. Sergey Parkhomenko, "Shock Constitutional Reform Has Bogged Down," *Segodnia,* July 23, 1993, 2 (*CDPSP* 45, no. 28, Aug. 11, 1993).

32. Ibid.

33. "Ryabov Accuses Khasbulatov of Shifting Once and For All to a Dictatorship of Personal Power," *Izvestiia,* June 26, 1993, 2 (*CDPSP* 45, no. 26, July 28, 1993).

34. *Rossiiskie vesti,* Aug. 13, 1993, 1 (*CDPSP* 45, no. 32, Sept. 8, 1993).

35. Ibid.

36. Petr Akopov, "A Council of the Federation Will Be Created: Will It Become An Instrument of Renewal?" *Rossiiskie vesti,* Aug. 14, 1993, 1 (*CDPSP* 45, no. 33, Sept. 15, 1993).

37. Ibid.

38. Anatoly Kostyukov, "The Council of the Federation—'Boyars versus Nobles,'" *Megapolis-Ekspress* 33, Aug. 25, 1993, 16 (*CDPSP* 45, no. 33, Sept. 15, 1993).

39. Ibid.

40. Speech to the Supreme Soviet, reported in *Nezavisimaia gazeta,* Aug. 21, 1993, 1.

41. Ibid.

42. Ivan Rodin, "The Russian Federation Supreme Soviet Will Override the Veto on Friday," *Nezavisimaia gazeta,* Aug. 26, 1993, 2 (*CDPSP* 45, no. 34, Sept. 22, 1993).

43. Aleksandr Bekker, "Boris Fedorov: The Next Two Weeks Will Be a Time of Political Choice," *Segodnia,* Aug. 24, 1993, 11 (*CDPSP* 45, no. 34, Sept. 22, 1993).

44. Ibid.

45. Ryabov had charged that under Khasbulatov the Supreme Soviet had become a "political monolith, since the deputies left in it have common political views," but Khasbulatov's efforts to have him removed were unsuccessful. Khasbulatov warned him about "next time." Petr Zhuravlev, "The Draft Constitution Will Be Assembled Piece by Piece," *Segodnia,* Sept. 16, 1993, 1 (*CDPSP* 45, no. 37, Oct. 10, 1993).

46. Ibid.

47. Vasily Kononenko, "The Presidential Council Recommends that Elections Not Be Delayed and that a Constitutional Law Be Prepared," *Izvestiia,* Sept. 15, 1993, 1 (*CDPSP* 45, no. 37, Oct. 10, 1993).

48. Irina Rishina, "The President Listens to Writers," *Literaturnaia gazeta,* Sept. 22, 1993, 3 (*CDPSP* 45, no. 37, Oct. 10, 1993).

49. "Will the Congress Not Deal with the Constitution but Instead Replace the Government?" *Segodnia,* Sept. 18, 1993, 1 (*CDPSP* 45, no. 37, October 10, 1993).

50. Elena Tregubova, "Soviet Power Will Take Root in This Land," *Segodnia,* Sept. 21, 1993, 3 (*CDPSP* 45, no. 37, Oct. 13, 1993).

51. Vitaly Tretyakov, "Yeltsin and Khasbulatov: A Fight to the Death?" *Nezavisimaia gazeta,* Sept. 21, 1993, 1 (*CDPSP* 45, no. 37, Oct. 10, 1993).

52. President's speech to the nation, September 21, 1993.

53. "On Stage-by-Stage Constitutional Reform in the Russian Federation," *Rossiiskie vesti,* Sept. 22, 1993, 1 (*CDPSP* 45, no. 38, Oct. 20, 1993).

54. Ibid.

55. The justification for this description, and for announcing that Yeltsin had ceased to be president, was Article 121.6 of the constitution: "The powers of the president of the Russian Federation may not be used to change the national-state structure of the Russian Federation or to dissolve or suspend any legitimately elected body of state power; if this is done, these powers are terminated immediately."

56. Petr Zhuravlev, "What the Russian Supreme Soviet Did on Sept. 21–22," *Segodnia,* Sept. 23, 1993, 1 (*CDPSP* 45, no. 38, Oct. 20, 1993).

57. Pavel Felgengauer, "President Yeltsin Has Done Nothing Unconstitutional," *Segodnia,* Sept. 23, 1993, 1 (*CDPSP* 45, no. 38, Oct. 20, 1993).

58. Yeltsin, *Struggle for Russia,* 259–60.

59. "The Constitutional Crisis and Possible Measures to Overcome It," *Rossiiskaia gazeta,* Sept. 23, 1993, 1 (*CDPSP* 45, no. 38, Oct. 20, 1993).

60. Indira Dunaeva et al., "Most Parties and Trade Unions Assess the President's Actions as Unconstitutional," *Nezavisimaia gazeta,* Sept. 23, 1993, 2 (*CDPSP* 45, no. 38, Oct. 20, 1993). Gorbachev first gave his views from abroad to an Italian reporter, but he made them more explicit in an article that appeared in Moscow in *Moskovskie novosti* 40, Oct. 3, 1993, 2 (*CDPSP* 45, no. 38, Oct. 20, 1993), titled "Victory Will Be the Beginning of Defeat."

61. Grigory Yavlinsky, "The President's Decree is Illegal and the Supreme Soviet's Actions are Illegitimate," *Segodnia,* Sept. 23, 1993, 1 (*CDPSP* 45, no. 38, Oct. 20, 1993).

62. Vladimir Emelianenko, "The Provinces' Offensive against the Kremlin," *Moskovskie novosti* 40, Oct. 3, 1993, 17 (*CDPSP* 45, no. 38, Oct. 20, 1993).

63. Yeltsin, *Struggle for Russia,* 262–63; "Who Thinks What about the President's Decree," *Nezavisimaia gazeta,* Sept. 23, 1993, 3 (*CDPSP* 45, no. 38, Oct. 20, 1993).

64. Yeltsin, *Struggle for Russia,* 266.

65. "Lessons of Impeachment," *Slovo,* May 19–20, 1999, 1 (*CDPSP* 51, no. 20, June 16, 1999).

66. *Argumenty i fakty* 41, 1993, 1 (*CDPSP* 45, no. 42, Nov. 17, 1993).

67. "Decree of the President of the Russian Federation: On Holding a Nation-

wide Vote on the Draft Constitution of the Russian Federation," *Rossiiskie vesti,* Oct. 19, 1993, 1 (*CDPSP* 45, no. 42, Nov. 17, 1993).

68. *Izvestiia,* Nov. 10, 1993, 1.

69. Vladimir Lysenko, "At a Fork in the Road," *Nezavisimaia gazeta,* Nov. 11, 1993, 1 (*CDPSP* 45, no. 45, Dec. 8, 1993).

70. Dmitry Kuznets, "The Communists Intend to Repeal the Constitution—The LDPR Could Help Russia's Choice Protect It," *Segodnia,* Dec. 29, 1993, 2 (*CDPSP* 45, no. 52, Jan. 26, 1994).

71. Vera Kuznetsova, "Yeltsin Closes Down the Parade of Sovereignties," *Nezavisimaia gazeta,* Nov. 4, 1993, 1 (*CDPSP* 45, no. 44, Nov. 24, 1993).

72. Dmitry Volsky, *Segodnia,* Nov. 6, 1993, 1 (*CDPSP* 45, no. 44, Nov. 25, 1993).

73. Marina Kalashnikova, "Spontaneous Redistribution of Power by Regions Is Ending," *Nezavisimaia gazeta,* Nov. 2, 1993, 2 (*CDPSP* 45, no. 44, Nov. 24, 1993).

74. Dmitry Obolensky, "Boris Yeltsin Is Staying," *Segodnia,* Nov. 9, 1993, 1 (*CDPSP* 45, no. 45, Dec. 8, 1993).

75. Mikhail Leontev, "A Guarantee against Communism," *Segodnia,* Sept. 30, 1993, 1 (*CDPSP* 45, no. 39, Oct. 27, 1993).

76. The decree was published in *Rossiiskaia gazeta,* Oct. 21, 1993, 1 (*CDPSP* 45, no. 42, Nov. 17, 1993).

77. Vladimir Todres, "Free Elections: Boris Yeltsin Issues Tickets of Admission for Elections," *Segodnia,* Oct. 21, 1993, 2 (*CDPSP* 45, no. 42, Nov. 17, 1993).

78. Nikolay Troytsky, "Politics: 'Senators' and Duma Members Don't Promise a Quiet Life," *Megapolis-Ekspress* 1, Jan. 5, 1994, 16 (*CDPSP* 46, no. 1, Feb. 2, 1994).

79. "The President of Russia's Speech to the Federal Assembly," *Rossiiskaia gazeta,* Feb. 25, 1994, 1, 3–7 (*CDPSP* 46, no. 8, Feb. 25, 1994).

80. Petr Zhuravlev, "The Central Electoral Commission Recognizes the Duma Elections as Valid," *Segodnia,* Dec. 30, 1995, 1 (*CDPSP* 47, no. 52, Jan. 24, 1996).

81. Gleb Cherkasov, "The Duma Denounces the Belovezhskaya Agreements," *Segodnia,* March 16, 1996, 1 (*CDPSP* 48, no. 11, April 10, 1996).

82. "Back to the USSR," *Kommersant,* March 16, 1996, 1, 3 (*CDPSP* 48, no. 11, April 10, 1996).

83. Boris Yeltsin, *Midnight Diaries* (New York: Public Affairs, 2000), 24.

84. The details of the campaign change and its effects are superbly analyzed in Michael McFaul, *Russia's 1996 Presidential Election: The End of Polarized Politics* (Stanford, CA: Hoover Institution Press, 1997).

85. Zyuganov's experience in the 1996 election is carefully analyzed in two important books on the CPRF: Joan Barth Urban and Valery D. Solovei, *Russia's Communists at the Crossroads* (Boulder, CO: Westview Press, 1997), and Luke March, *The Communist Party in Post-Soviet Russia* (Manchester: Manchester University Press, 2002).

86. Daniel Williams, "Honeymoon Ends for Yeltsin Deputy," *Washington Post Foreign Service,* August 3, 1997, A22.

87. In preparing this commentary, I have found *Russian Economic Trends, Monthly Update,* published by the Russian European Centre for Economic Policy, a convenient and informative source of information on trends in the Russian economy.

88. On Black Tuesday, October 11, 1994, the ruble's value plunged 27 percent in a single day after the Russian Central Bank failed to intervene to support it.

89. *New York Times,* July 14, 1998, A1.

90. Ibid.

91. Amy Knight, *Spies without Cloaks: The KGB's Successes* (Princeton, NJ: Princeton University Press, 1996), 131.

92. *New York Times,* March 4, 1999, A4.

93. Ibid., quoting Yevgeny K. Svanidze, host of the *Zerkalo* news interview program on the government channel.

94. *Russian Economic Trends,* 10 February 1999, 6–12.

95. Interview, 1999, for Public Broadcasting Service, *Boris Yeltsin: A Legacy of Change.*

96. Putin's interesting career receives well-informed treatment in a book by Alexander Rahr, published in Russian as Aleksandr Rar, *Vladimir Putin: Nemets v Kremle* (Moscow: Olma-Press, 2002).

97. Sergey Sergievsky, "The Presidential Campaign as a Motivating Force for Regional Political Elites," *Nezavisimaia gazeta,* March 17, 2000, 1, 4 (*CDPSP,* 52, 11, Apr. 12, 2000).

98. Yevgeny Yevdokimov, "Central Electoral Commission Confirms Putin Victory," *Vremia MN,* April 6, 2000, 2 (*CDPSP* 52, no. 14, May 3, 2000).

3 BUILDING A NEW ECONOMY

1. "Boris Yeltsin Calls on the Congress to Strengthen Executive Power," *Izvestiia,* Oct. 30, 1991, 2 (*CDPSP* 43, no. 44, Dec. 4, 1991).

2. An excellent analysis of the condition of the Russian economy at the end of the Gorbachev period is provided in Anders Åslund, *How Russia Became a Market Economy* (Washington, DC: Brookings Institution Press, 1995), 41–50.

3. Joseph R. Blasi, Maya Krumova, and Douglas Kruse, *Kremlin Capitalism: The Privatization of the Russian Economy* (Ithaca, NY: Cornell University Press, 1997), 29.

4. Vladimir Tikhomirov, *The Political Economy of Post-Soviet Russia* (New York: St. Martin's, 2000), 237.

5. Ibid., 241.

6. The "loans for shares" privatization that followed from this calculation is brilliantly described and analyzed in Chrystia Freeland, *Sale of the Century: Russia's Wild*

Ride from Communism to Capitalism (New York: Crown, 2000), the main source for the present commentary.

7. Maksim Filimonov, "Privatization in Russia Hangs by a Hair," *Nezavisimaia gazeta*, Jan. 25, 1996, 4 (*CDPSP* 48, no. 6, March 6, 1996).

8. Aleksandr Bekker, "Chubais Isn't Just a Name," *Segodnia*, Jan. 18, 1996, 2 (*CDPSP* 48, no. 3, Feb. 14, 1996).

9. Mikhail Berger, "Candidates for the Russian Presidency Hold a Debate in Davos, Switzerland, 'Polling Place,'" *Izvestiia*, Feb. 6, 1996, 1–2 (*CDPSP* 48, no. 5, Feb. 28, 1996).

10. Boris Boyko, "The State Duma on Privatization: The Government Is Under Investigation," *Kommersant*, Feb. 10, 1996, 2 (*CDPSP* 48, no. 6, March 6, 1996).

11. Tikhomirov, *Political Economy*, 249.

12. Paul Klebnikov, "The Khodorkovsky Affair," *Wall Street Journal*, Nov. 17, 2003, A-20. Mr. Klebnikov's book *Godfather of the Kremlin: Boris Berezovsky and the Looting of Russia* (New York: Harcourt, 2000) is, like Chrystia Freeland's *Sale of the Century*, an excellent source of information on the "loans for shares" privatization.

13. Tikhomirov, *Political Economy*, 254–56.

14. *Russian Economic Trends*, February 10, 1999.

15. Yeltsin, *Midnight Diaries*, 269.

16. Ibid. 270–71.

17. Ibid., 276.

18. Mikhail Leontev, "A Free Market Is Not Afraid of Any *Zaveriukha*," *Segodnia*, Oct. 28, 1993, 1 (*CDPSP* 45, no. 44, Nov. 24, 1993).

19. "Principles of USSR and Union-Republic Legislation on Land," *Izvestiia*, March 6, 1990, 1–2 (*CDSP* 42, no. 13, May 2, 1990).

20. G. Bystrov, "Give the Peasant Land and Freedom—Only in This Way Can the Lack of Rights Be Ended and Agriculture Extricated from Its Impasse," *Izvestiia*, Aug. 26, 1990, 2 (*CDSP* 42, no. 34, Sept. 26, 1990).

21. Leontev, "A Free Market Is Not Afraid," 1.

22. Andrey Sizov, "Russian Law on Grain Intensifies Inflation," *Izvestiia*, June 18, 1993, 4 (*CDPSP* 45, no. 24, July 14, 1993).

23. Aleksandr Bekker (interviewer), "Boris Fedorov: The Next Two Weeks Will Be a Time of Political Choice," *Segodnia*, August 24, 1993, 11 (*CDPSP* 45, no. 34, Sept. 22, 1993). Lobov's analysis—that budget cutting would cause dangerous social tension—was presented in a report prepared by the Russian Ministry of Economics and reported in *Rossiiskie vesti*, Aug. 17, 1993, 3 (*CDPSP* 45, no. 34, Sept. 22, 1993).

24. Valery Konovalov, "Another Battle for the Harvest Is Under Way, but Not for Grain—for Grain Prices," *Izvestiia*, July 14, 1994, 1 (*CDPSP* 46, no. 28, Aug. 10, 1994).

25. Petr Zhuravlev, "The Duma: Federal Budget for 1995 Adopted on Third Reading," *Segodnia*, Feb. 25, 1995, 1 (*CDPSP* 47, no. 8, March 22, 1995).

26. Yulia Latynina, "Breadwinners: The Ministry of Economics Warns that the Russian Countryside Has Become Addicted to the 'Budget Narcotic,'" *Segodnia*, July 31, 1996, 3 (*CDPSP* 48, no. 31, Aug. 8, 1996).

27. Ibid.

28. Valery Konovalov, "Ministry of Agriculture Greets Spring: This Time without Panic," *Izvestiia*, Feb. 17, 1992, 2 (*CDPSP* 44, no. 7, March 18, 1992).

29. Yury Chernichenko, "The Land Awaits a Plowman and the Treasury Awaits Revenues," *Kuranty*, Jan. 18, 1992, 5 (*CDPSP* 44, no. 5, March 4, 1992).

30. Valery Konovalov, "As Long as the Peasant Is Not an Owner, He Can Be Ordered Around," *Izvestiia*, April 17, 1992, 1 (*CDPSP* 44, no. 16, May 20, 1992).

31. Valery Konovalov, "Why Rutskoi's Agrarian Program Frightened the Agrarian Deputies," *Izvestiia*, April 20, 1992, 2 (*CDPSP* 44, no. 16, May 20, 1992).

32. Valery Konovalov, "Collective Farm Chairmen Form a Party while Private Farms Conclude an Agreement with the Government," *Izvestiia*, Feb. 14, 1992, 2 (*CDPSP* 44, no. 7, March 18, 1992).

33. Yelena Tokareva, "A California Worm's Struggle against Socialism," *Rossiiskaia gazeta*, April 27, 1993 (*CDPSP* 44, no. 16, May 20, 1993).

34. "Decree of the President of the Russian Federation: On the Regulation of Land Relations and the Development of Agrarian Reform in Russia" (Decree no. 1767), *Izvestiia*, Oct. 29, 1993, 1–2.

35. The plan for the conversion of the system of property and the creation of independent peasant farms was similar to a model developed by the International Finance Corporation (IFC) and also contained ideas from the land reform sponsored by Boris Nemtsov in Nizhnii Novgorod.

36. Leontev, "A Free Market Is Not Afraid," 1.

37. Gaidar speech, *Komsomol'skaia pravda*, June 16, 1994, 1.

38. Laura Belin and Robert W. Orttung, *The Russian Parliamentary Elections of 1995: The Battle for the Duma* (Armonk, NY: M. E. Sharpe, 1996), 114–15.

39. Yelena Tregubova, "Senate Refuses to Pass Civil Code," *Segodnia*, Nov. 17, 1994, 2 (*CDPSP* 46, no. 46, Dec. 14, 1994).

40. *Rossiiskie vesti*, Feb. 17, 1995, 1.

41. Vasily Shchurov, "Has the Muzhik Gotten Land?" *Trud*, March 13, 1995, 1.

42. Aleksandr Dzyublo, "A New Framework for Private Farming Is Being Prepared," *Izvestiia*, Jan. 14, 1998, 2 (*CDPSP* 50, no. 2, Feb. 2, 1998).

43. Production figures through 1995 are available in Stephen Wegren, *Agriculture and the State in Soviet and Post-Soviet Russia* (Pittsburgh: University of Pittsburgh Press, 1998), 128. Figures on these and other production issues have appeared regularly in the Russian press. See Yelena Yakovleva, "Russia Has Succeeded in Putting an End

to Grain Imports, but Not for Long," *Izvestiia*, Jan. 12, 1995, 2 (*CDPSP* 47, no. 2, Feb. 2, 1995); and Aleksandr Nazarchuk (minister of agriculture and food), *Izvestiia*, Oct. 24, 1995, 1 (*CDPSP* 47, no. 43, Nov. 22, 1995) (complete text). For the later 1990s see Mikhail Vasilevich Sharov, "Hobbles for Putin: The Looming Agricultural Crisis," *Nezavisimaia gazeta*, Feb. 8, 2000, 4 (*CDPSP* 52, no. 6, March 8, 2000).

44. Otto Latsis, "Russia's Economy Is Tired of Falling," *Izvestiia*, Feb. 22, 1995, 2 (*CDPSP* 47, no. 8, March 22, 1995).

45. Yelena Yakovleva, "Our Countryside Still Lives by the Laws of 70 Years Ago," *Izvestiia*, March 15, 2000, 2 (*CDPSP* 52, no. 12, April 19, 2000).

46. Ibid.

47. Aleksandr Andyukhin, "Governors Raise Grain Prices," *Kommersant*, Oct. 15, 1999, 7 (*CDPSP* 51, no. 41, Nov. 10, 1999).

48. Almira Kozhakhmetova, "Governors Revert to Primitive Behavior in Closing Province Borders," *Novye izvestiia*, Oct. 14, 1999, 1–2 (*CDPSP* 51, no. 40, Nov. 3, 1999).

49. Pavel Gres, "Aleksandr Rutskoi Allows Police to Earn Some Extra Money on the Harvest," *Novye izvestiia*, Sept. 1, 1999, 1 (*CDPSP* 51, no. 35, Sept. 29, 1999).

50. Sergey Zhdakaev, "Seize Everything: Vasily Starodubtsev Returns to Grain Requisitioning," *Izvestiia*, Sept. 2, 1999, 2 (*CDPSP* 51, no. 35, Sept. 29, 1999).

51. *Izvestiia*, Jan. 13, 1998, 4 (*CDPSP* 15, no. 1, Feb. 3, 1999).

52. Guy Chazan, "Companies Turn Collectives into Profitable Businesses," *Wall Street Journal*, Feb. 15, 2001.

53. Sergey Sergievsky, "Ayatskov Is Prepared to Take on the President in Court," *Nezavisimaia gazeta*, July 30, 1998, 2 (*CDPSP* 50, no. 30, Aug. 26, 1998).

54. Andrey Gavryushenko, "Land Law Adopted in Samara Province," *Izvestiia*, June 27, 1998, 2 (*CDPSP* 50, no. 26, July 29, 1998).

55. *Moscow News*, October 22–28, 2003.

4 THE NEW RUSSIA AND THE WORLD

1. A superb presentation of Gorbachev's analysis and calculations in the making of his policy, which contributed so much to the end of the Cold War, can be found in Jack F. Matlock's *Autopsy on an Empire*, 667–72. Matlock's remarkable insider's view of Gorbachev's relationship with the West during the last phase of the Cold War is further explained in his *Reagan and Gorbachev: How the Cold War Ended* (New York: Random House, 2004). Presidents Reagan and Bush, as well as Mikhail Gorbachev, were extremely fortunate to have in Matlock, then the US ambassador to the Soviet Union, an advisor and intermediary with an extraordinary background and understanding of the people and events with which they were dealing during the last phase of the Cold War and afterward.

2. Primakov's perception of his aims and accomplishments during this time are interestingly described in his memoir, *Gody v bol'shoi politike* (Moscow, 1999), beginning on page 201.

3. B. N. Yeltsin, "On Russia's Policy in the Field of Arms Limitation and Reduction," *Rossiiskaia gazeta*, Jan. 30, 1992, 1–2 (*CDPSP* 44, no. 5, March 4, 1992).

4. Stanislav Kondrashov, "Yeltsin's Western Itinerary," *Izvestiia*, Jan. 28, 1992, 1, 5 (*CDPSP* 44, no. 5, March 4, 1992).

5. *Rossiiskaia gazeta*, Feb. 3, 1992, 1, 3.

6. Ibid.

7. Paul Gigot, "Yeltsin to Bush: New Thinking on Nuke Defenses," *Wall Street Journal*, Jan. 31, 1992, A14.

8. Kravchuk's protest concerning Yeltsin's failure to consult with the other CIS nuclear states was reported under the title "Yeltsin Didn't Consult Me" in *Izvestiia*, Feb. 3, 1992, 2 (*CDPSP* 5, no. 44, March 5, 1992).

9. Nikolay Paklin, "Russian Rockets for India," *Izvestiia*, April 17, 1992, 5 (*CDPSP* 45, no. 16, May 20, 1992).

10. Sergey Mushkaterov, "Minister A. Zlenko," *Izvestiia*, April 15, 1992, 4 (*CDPSP* 44, no. 15, May 13, 1992).

11. Paklin, "Russian Rockets for India," 5.

12. "Charter of Russian-American Partnership and Friendship," *Rossiiskaia gazeta*, June 19, 1992, 1, 5 (*CDPSP* 44, no. 24, July 15, 1992).

13. *Rossiiskaia gazeta*, June 19, 1992, 1–2 (*CDPSP* 44, no. 24, July 15, 1992).

14. Sergey Blagovolin and Ilia Surkov, "Do We Need a Global Defense System?" *Krasnaia zvezda*, Aug. 7, 1992, 3 (*CDPSP* 44, no. 32, Sept. 9, 1992), emphasis in original. Sergey Blagovolin was president of the Institute for National Security and Strategic Studies (INSSS), and Ilia Surkov was its vice president.

15. The subject of the level of development of Russian research on missile defense technology has received little attention in the West, though in fact it was highly developed and probably competitive with US development of related technology.

16. A condensed version of the document was published in Andrey Poleschchuk, "Is an Expansion of NATO Justified?" *Nezavisimaia gazeta*, Nov. 26, 1993, 1, 6 (*CDPSP* 45, no. 47, Dec. 22, 1993).

17. Dmitry Gornostaev, "Russia Won't Be Taking Exams," *Nezavisimaia gazeta*, Dec. 8, 1994, 4 (*CDPSP* 46, no. 46, Dec. 14, 1994).

18. Valery Zhdannikov, "Russia Concerned about NATO Expansion," *Segodnia*, Jan. 6, 1994, 1 (*CDPSP* 46, no. 1, Feb. 2, 1994).

19. Mikhail Gorbachev, "Carte Blanche: NATO Summit in Brussels—Time of Missed Opportunities," *Nezavisimaia gazeta*, Jan. 13, 1994, 2 (*CDPSP* 46, no. 2, Feb. 2, 1994). Gorbachev's use of the term *unipolar world* to describe the essence of the new US global policy is the first I have found in the documentation of the period,

though it later became a core concept in the analysis of Yevgeny Primakov, both as foreign minister and as prime minister.

20. Vladislav Chernov, "Moscow Should Think Carefully before Replying to NATO's Proposal," *Nezavisimaia gazeta*, Feb. 23, 1994, 4 (*CDPSP* 46, no. 2, Feb. 9, 1994).

21. *Time Magazine Archive*, July 11, 1994, vol. 144, no. 2.

22. Leonid Velekhov, "Diplomacy: Kozyrev Demands Material Support for Russian Peacekeeping Efforts," *Segodnia*, Dec. 2, 1994, 1 (*CDPSP* 46, no. 48, Dec. 28, 1994).

23. The article was titled "Russia and the US: Partnership Is Not Premature, It Is Overdue," *Izvestiia*, March 11, 1994, 3 (*CDPSP* 46, no. 10, April 6, 1994).

24. This subject is covered thoroughly and informatively by Strobe Talbott in his diplomatic memoir, *The Russia Hand* (New York: Random House, 2002), especially 137–46 and 151–69. It is clear from the summary of the discussions with Yeltsin and Kozyrev in Washington that the Americans were open to eventual Russian inclusion in the new security system.

25. For an excellent study of the protracted Russo-Japanese conflict over the islands issue, see Gilbert Rozman, ed., *Japan and Russia: The Tortuous Path to Normalization* (New York: St. Martin's, 2000).

26. *Economist*, Dec. 20, 1997, 67. GDP in the American comparison is calculated at 1990 purchasing power parity (ppp).

27. "Moscow and Beijing Strive for Deep Integration in Military Realm," *Nezavisimaia gazeta*, June 16, 1999, 2 (*CDSP* 51, no. 24, July 14, 1999).

28. Dimitry Gornostaev, "Yeltsin Reminds Clinton and the World that Russia Is Still a Nuclear Power," *Nezavisimaia gazeta*, Dec. 10, 1999, 1, 6 (*CDPSP* 51, no. 50, Jan. 12, 2000).

29. Ivan Safranchuk, "Friend Boris, You're Wrong!" *Moskovskie novosti* 48, Dec. 14–20, 5 (*CDSP* 51, no. 50, Jan. 12, 2000).

30. Yekaterina Kats, "Simulation of Cooperation," *Segodnia*, Dec. 10, 1999, p. 5 (*CDPSP* 51, no. 50, Jan. 12, 2000).

31. "What We Make Missiles For," *Kommersant*, Dec. 15, 1999, 1 (*CDPSP* 51, no. 50, Jan. 12, 2000).

32. "Rossiia mezhdu tsentrami sily," *Nezavisimoe voennoe obozrenie* 112, Oct. 9–15, 1998, 4.

33. "Reflections on Russia," *McKinsey Quarterly* 1, 2000, 41.

34. Andrew Mack, "The Nuclear Crisis on the Korean Peninsula," *Asian Survey* 33, no. 4, April 1993, 342.

35. "North Korea's Final Warning to Moscow," *Kommersant*, Oct. 1, 1996, 4 (*CDPSP* 48, no. 39, Oct. 23, 1996).

36. "Relations between Moscow and Seoul Enter 'Off Season,'" *Segodnia*, July

9, 1998, 3 (*CDPSP* 50, no. 28, Aug. 12, 1998). See also Igor' Korotchenko, "Five South Korean Intelligence Agents to Be Expelled from Russia," *Nezavisimaia gazeta,* July 21, 1998, 2 (*CDPSP* 50, no. 29, Aug. 19, 1998).

37. Deputy foreign minister Grigory Karasin, "Our Concept Is Security through Economics," *Nezavisimaia gazeta,* March 26, 1999, 6 (*CDPSP* 51, no. 12, Apr. 21, 1999).

38. G. Toloraya and P. Iakovlev, "How to Undo the Korean Knot," *International Affairs* 45, no. 3, 1999, 91–92.

39. Andrey Nuykin, "The Opposition Has Already Laid in a Supply of Handcuffs," *Rossiiskie vesti,* March 19, 1996, 1–2 (*CDPSP* 48, no. 11, April 10, 1996).

40. Bruce D. Porter and Carol R. Saivetz, "The Once and Future Empire: Russia and the Near Abroad," *Washington Quarterly,* Summer 1994, 75–77.

41. Alexei G. Arbatov, "Russia's Foreign Policy Alternatives," *International Security,* Fall 1993, 24.

42. Ibid., 45.

43. Maksim Yusin, "Ministers of Foreign Affairs of the Conference on Security and Cooperation in Europe Were Convinced that a Coup Had Occurred in Russia," *Izvestiia,* Dec. 15, 1993, 6 (*CDPSP* 45, no. 49, Dec. 23, 1993).

44. Quoted in Porter and Saivetz, "Once and Future Empire," 87.

45. Neil Malcolm, "The New Russian Foreign Policy," *The World Today,* February 1994, 31.

46. Suzanne Crow, "Processes and Politics," *RFE/RL, Research Report,* 14 May 1993, 48.

47. "After Chechnya," *Economist,* Jan. 14, 1995, 44.

48. Charles King, "Eurasia Letter: Moldova with a Russian Face," *Foreign Policy,* Winter 1994–95, 42.

49. "Russia and the CIS: Does the West's Position Need Adjustment?" *Rossiiskaia gazeta,* Sept. 22, 1994, 1, 6 (*CDPSP* 46, no. 38, Oct. 19, 1994).

50. Sergey Parkhomenko and Natalya Gorodetskaya, "Proposal on Joint External CIS Border Fails to Pass," *Segodnia,* Feb. 11, 1995, 1 (*CDPSP* 47, no. 6, March 8, 1995).

51. Vitaly Portnikov, "Not Everyone Cared for Russia's Border Concept," *Nezavisimaia gazeta,* Feb. 11, 1995, 1 (*CDPSP* 47, no. 6, March 8, 1995).

52. Vladimir Abarimov, "A Nonaligned Movement Emerges in the CIS," *Segodnia,* May 30, 1995, 3 (*CDPSP* 47, no. 22, June 28, 1995).

53. Aleksey Zuychenko, "Boris Yeltsin Warns of Possibility of Reviving Warsaw Treaty Organization," *Segodnia,* Sept. 9, 1995, 1 (*CDPSP* 47, no. 41, Nov. 8, 1995).

54. Leonid Velekhov, "Grachev Proposes that 'Everyone' Help Russia Meet Its Commitments," *Segodnia,* Nov. 16, 1995, 2 (*CDPSP* 47, no. 46, Dec. 12, 1995).

55. Yakov Plyas, "The New Russia and Parity of Forces," *Nezavisimaia gazeta,* Oct. 13, 1995, 2 (*CDPSP* 47, no. 41, Nov. 8, 1995).

56. Aleksey Pushkov, "Russia's Foreign Policy," *Nezavisimaia gazeta*, Nov. 16, 1995, 1, 5 (*CDPSP* 47, no. 47, Dec. 20, 1995).

57. Svetlana Gamova, "Unrecognized Republic Votes for Independence and Separate Membership in CIS," *Izvestiia*, Dec. 26, 1995, 2 (*CDPSP* 47, no. 52, Jan. 14, 1996).

58. Yulia Ulyanova, Natalya Konstantinova, and Nodar Broladze, "CIS Leaders Reach Agreement on All Issues," *Nezavisimaia gazeta*, Jan. 20, 1996, 1 (*CDPSP* 48, no. 3, Feb. 14, 1996).

59. Natalya Kalashnikova, "Eastern Europe in the Dust of Belovezhskaya," *Kommersant*, March 28, 1996, 1, 4 (*CDPSP* 48, no. 13, April 13, 1996).

60. Sergey Anisko, "In Minsk a Rally of Thousands of People Protests 'Two-Faced' Union," *Segodnia*, March 26, 1996, 1 (*CDPSP* 48, no. 12, April 17, 1996).

61. Georgy Bolt, "The Russian-Belarusian Talks on a Union," *Kommersant*, March 26, 1996, 4 (*CDPSP* 48, no. 12, April 17, 1996).

62. Vladimir Skachko, "Republic Prepared to Become Model European State," *Segodnia*, April 24, 1996, 8 (*CDPSP* 48, no. 17, May 22, 1996).

63. Vladimir Golubev, "It Took Five Years of Negotiations to Decide the Fate of the Black Sea Fleet," *Rossiiskie vesti*, May 30, 1997, 1, 3 (*CDPSP* 49, no. 22, July 2, 1997).

64. Viktor Timoshenko, "The Accords between Boris Yeltsin and Leonid Kuchma Come under Critical Fire—Nevertheless, Their Ratification in the Supreme Council in Kiev and Approval by the Federation Council in Moscow Are Virtually Assured," *Nezavisimaia gazeta*, June 3, 1997, 1 (*CDPSP* 49, no. 22, July 2, 1997).

65. Natalya Kalashnikova, "Lukashenko Is Named the Integrator of Four Republics," *Kommersant*, March 30, 1996, 1, 3 (*CDPSP* 48, no. 13, Apr. 24, 1996).

66. Andrey Apostolov, "Bulgarian Foreign Ministry Plans to Deliver Note," *Segodnia*, Apr. 6, 1996, 6 (*CDPSP* 48, no. 14, May 1, 1996); Elmira Akhundova, "Aliyev and Karimov Don't Miss the USSR and the Treaty of Four Doesn't Inspire Them," *Literaturnaia gazeta* 23, June 5, 1996, 2 (*CDPSP* 48, no. 23, June 5, 1996).

67. Skachko, "Republic Prepared to Become Model European State."

68. Report by the Council on Foreign and Defense Policy, "Bringing Russia and Belarus Closer Together," *Nezavisimaia gazeta* 5, April 29, 1997, 1–2 (*CDPSP* 49, no. 17, May 28, 1997).

69. Yury Popov, "The Four's Decisions—They Could Affect the Fate of Integration in the Post-Soviet Space," *Rossiiskie vesti*, Oct. 23, 1997, 1–2 (*CDPSP* 49, no. 43, Nov. 26, 1997).

70. Lyudmila Feliksova, "Time to Tackle Fundamental Questions," *Rossiiskaia gazeta*, Oct. 24, 1997, 2 (*CDPSP* 49, no. 43, Nov. 26, 1997).

71. Ivan Budakov, "We Must Break through the Wall," *Kommersant*, Oct. 25, 1997, 1 (*CDPSP* 49, no. 43, Nov. 26, 1997).

72. Lyudmila Feliksova, "GUAM—Another Foursome," *Rossiiskaia gazeta*, Dec. 2, 1997, 7 (*CDPSP* 49, no. 48, Dec. 31, 1997). In April 1999, GUAM would become known as GUUAM with the addition of Uzbekistan.

73. Ibid.

74. Konstantin Zatulin and Andranik Migranyan, "The Beginning of the End of History," *Sodruzhestvo NG, Nezavisimaia gazeta* 1, Dec. 1997, 1–2 (*CDPSP* 49, no. 50, Jan. 14, 1998).

75. Polina Kanevskaya and Vyacheslav Lebedev, "Great Power Gets a Leader—Movement of Former Rutskoi Supporters Integrates into Moscow Mayor's Bloc," Nov. 20, 1998, 3 (*CDPSP* 50, no. 47, Dec. 23, 1998).

76. Zatulin and Migranyan, "Beginning of the End of History."

77. "State Duma Ratifies Russian-Ukrainian Treaty. . . ," *Rossiiskaia gazeta*, Dec. 26, 1998, 2 (*CDPSP* 50, no. 52, Jan. 27, 1999).

78. Olga Bogoslovskaya, "From Chișinău to Moscow," *Trud*, April 30, 1998, 2 (*CDPSP* 50, no. 17, May 27, 1998).

79. Yury Chubchenko and Nikolay Babichev, "Berezovsky Takes to the CIS's Expanses," *Kommersant*, April 30, 1998, 1 (*CDPSP* 50, no. 17, May 27, 1998).

80. Ilias Tashmatov, "To Keep Uzbekistan from Becoming Tajikistan," *Kommersant*, May 7, 1998 5 (*CDPSP* 50, no. 18, June 3, 1998).

81. Mekhman Gafarly, "For the First Time a Trend toward Deteriorating Relations between Kazakhstan and Russia Is Developing," *Nezavisimaia gazeta*, June 27, 1998, 1 (*CDPSP* 50, no. 26, July 29, 1998).

82. For a brilliant critical review of three examples of this approach, see Daniel Treisman, "Blaming Russia First," *Foreign Affairs* 79, no. 6, Nov.–Dec. 2000, 146–55. Treisman makes telling comparisons between the generally negative presentation of Russia's performance and that of other states.

83. Susan Eisenhower, "Russian Perspectives on the Expansion of NATO," in *NATO and the Quest for Post-Cold War Security*, edited by Clay Clemens (New York: St. Martin's, 1997), 141.

84. Quoted by John Feffer in "US-Russian Relations: Avoiding a Cold Peace," *Foreign Policy*, Nov. 15, 1996.

85. The failure of the PJC is presented in Peter Trenin-Straussov, "The NATO-Russia Permanent Joint Council in 1997–99: Anatomy of a Failure," Berlin Information Center for Transatlantic Security, July 1999.

86. Andrey Piontkovsky, "Moment for Truth—How to Alter the Course and Content of Russian-American Strategic Stability Consultations," *Nezavisimaia gazeta*, Sept. 4, 2001, 6 (*CDPSP* 53, no. 36, 2001).

87. Vladimir Frolov, "From Self-Isolation to Interaction," *Vremia MN*, Nov. 23, 2001, 5 (*CDPSP* 53, no. 47, Dec. 19, 2001).

88. Boris Piadyshev, "After the Terrorist Attack in the US," *International Affairs* 47, no. 5, 2001.

89. Nikolay Golygin, "To Their Mutual Satisfaction," *Trud*, Nov. 24, 2001, 4 (*CDPSP* 53, no. 47, Dec. 19, 2001).

90. Stanislav Kondrashov, "Shish Kebab, Texas Style," *Vremia MN*, Nov. 17, 2000, 3 (*CDPSP* 53, no. 46, Nov. 12, 2001).

91. Boris Volkhonsky, "Moving toward a New Arms Race," *Kommersant,* Dec. 15, 2001, 8 (*CDPSP* 53, no. 50, 2001).

92. Maxim Gilkin, "There Is No 'Third Way'—Will the President Be Able to Convince the Elite and the Public of That?" *Obshchaia gazeta* 47, Nov. 22–29, 2001 (*CDPSP* 53, no. 46, 2001).

93. Speech given at Volgograd Technical University, November 22, 2001.

94. Elmar Gusenov, "Vladimir Putin and Jacques Chirac Find a Common Language on Almost All Issues," *Izvestiia*, Feb. 12, 2003, 2 (*CDPSP* 55, no. 6, March 12, 2002).

95. Quoted in Aleksey Pushkov, "Putin the Tightrope Walker and the Antiwar Entente" (*CDPSP* 55, no. 6, March 12, 2002).

THE YELTSIN LEGACY

1. Margaret Thatcher, *The Downing Street Years* (New York: HarperCollins, 1993), 804. Thatcher made this remark about her first encounter with Yeltsin in April 1990. She lamented that the Americans did not agree with her assessment of Yeltsin's potential: "When I reported later in Bermuda to President [George H. W.] Bush on my favourable impressions of Mr. Yeltsin he made it clear that the Americans did not share them. This was a serious mistake."

2. Vladimir Putin speaking at a press conference for Russian and foreign journalists at the Kremlin, January 31, 2006; posted at www.kremlin.ru/appears/2006/01/31/1310_type63380type63381type82634_100848.shtml.

2. "Ten Years Ago and Today," *Segodnia*, October 28, 1997, 1 (*CDPSP* 49, no. 42, Nov. 26, 1997).

3. "Presidential Veto: The Law Must Not Provide Grounds for Religious Conflicts," *Rossiiskie vesti*, July 24, 1997, 1 (*CDPSP* 49, no. 30, Aug. 7, 1997).

4. "It's Time to Bring Religious Missionaries to Their Senses," *Rossiiskaia gazeta*, Dec. 28, 1996, 4 (*CDPSP* 49, no. 30, Aug. 7, 1997).

5. Boris Yeltsin, "We Will Not Depart from the Spirit and Letter of the Constitution," *Moskovskie novosti* 35, Sept. 17–23, 2004, 10 (*CDPSP* 56, no. 37, Oct. 13, 2004).

6. "Vladimir Putin Speaks on Matters of Governance and on Strengthening the Country's Security System," *Rossiiskaia gazeta*, Sept. 14, 2004, 1, 3 (*CDPSP* 56, no. 37, Oct. 13, 2004).

7. These changes were submitted as a package of amendments to the federal laws on General Principles for the Organization of Legislative and Executive Governmental Bodies in the Members of the Russian Federation and on Basic Guarantees of Russian Federation Citizens' Electoral Rights and Their Right to Participate in Referendums.

8. Yekaterina Vorobeva and Alla Barakhova, "Mintimer Shaymiev Puts Limits on Vladimir Putin's Rights," *Kommersant,* Oct. 26, 2004, 1, 3 (*CDPSP* 56, no. 43, Nov. 24, 2004).

SELECTED BIBLIOGRAPHY

COLLAPSE OF COMMUNISM

Bandelin, Oscar J. *Return to the NEP: The False Promise of Leninism and the Failure of Perestroika*. Westport, CT: Praeger, 2002.

Billington, James H. *Russia Transformed: Breakthrough to Hope: Moscow, August 1991*. New York: Free Press, 1992.

Brzezinski, Zbigniew. *The Grand Failure: The Birth and Death of Communism in the Twentieth Century*. New York: Charles Scribner's Sons, 1989.

Carrère d'Encausse, Hélène. *The End of the Soviet Empire: The Triumph of the Nations*. New York: Basic Books, 1993.

Coleman, Fred. *The Decline and Fall of the Soviet Empire: Forty Years that Shook the World, from Stalin to Yeltsin*. New York: St. Martin's, 1996.

Dobbs, Michael. *Down with Big Brother: The Fall of the Soviet Empire*. New York: Alfred A. Knopf, 1997.

Felshman, Neil. *Gorbachev, Yeltsin and the Last Days of the Soviet Empire*. New York: St. Martin's, 1992.

Fowkes, Ben. *The Disintegration of the Soviet Union: A Study in the Rise and Triumph of Nationalism*. New York: St. Martin's, 1997.

Gaidar, Ye. T. *Gosudarstvo i evoliutsiia*. Moskva: Izdatel'svo Evraziia, 1995. Translated by Jane Ann Miller as *State and Evolution: Russia's Search for a Free Market*. Seattle: University of Washington Press, 2003.

Grachev, Andrei S. *Final Days: The Inside Story of the Collapse of the Soviet Union*. Boulder, CO: Westview Press, 1995.

Hahn, Gordon M. *Russia's Revolution from Above, 1985–2000: Reform, Transition, and Revolution in the Fall of the Soviet Communist Regime*. New Brunswick, NJ: Transaction, 2002.

Herspring, Dale R. *The Soviet High Command, 1967–1989: Personalities and Politics*. Princeton, NJ: Princeton University Press, 1990.

Hough, Jerry F. *Democratization and Revolution in the USSR, 1985–1991*. Washington, DC: Brookings Institution Press, 1997.

Khasbulatov, Ruslan. *The Struggle for Russia: Power and Change in the Democratic Revolution*. London: Routledge, 1993.

Kotkin, Stephen. *Armageddon Averted: The Soviet Collapse 1970–2000*. New York: Oxford University Press, 2001.

Lane, David, and Cameron Ross. *The Transition from Communism to Capitalism: Ruling Elites from Gorbachev to Yeltsin*. New York: St. Martin's, 1999.

Matlock, Jack F., Jr. *Autopsy on an Empire: The American Ambassador's Account of the Collapse of the Soviet Union*. New York: Random House, 1995.

Ouimet, Matthew J. *The Rise and Fall of the Brezhnev Doctrine in Soviet Foreign Policy*. Chapel Hill: University of North Carolina Press, 2003.

Pilkington, Hilary, and Galina Yemelianova. *Islam in Post-Soviet Russia: Public and Private Faces*. London: RoutledgeCurzon, 2003.

Putsch: The Diary. Three Days that Collapsed the Empire. Introduction by Boris Yeltsin. Oakville, Ontario: Mosaic Press, 1992.

Shevardnadze, Eduard. *The Future Belongs to Freedom*. New York: Free Press, 1991.

Steele, Jonathan. *Eternal Russia: Yeltsin, Gorbachev and the Mirage of Democracy*. London: Faber and Faber, 1994.

Tikhomirov, Vladimir. *Anatomy of the 1998 Russian Crisis*. Melbourne: Contemporary Europe Research Centre, 1999.

BUILDING A NEW GOVERNMENT

Ahdieh, Robert B. *Russia's Cultural Revolution: Legal Consciousness and the Transition to Democracy, 1985–1996*. University Park: Pennsylvania State University Press, 1997.

Brown, Archie. *Contemporary Russian Politics: A Reader*. Oxford: Oxford University Press, 2001.

Colton, Timothy J., and Jerry F. Hough. *Growing Pains: Russian Democracy and the Election of 1993*. Washington, DC: Brookings Institution Press, 1998.

Colton, Timothy J., and Robert C. Tucker. *Patterns in Post-Soviet Leadership*. Boulder, CO: Westview Press, 1995.

Ebon, Martin. *KGB: Death and Rebirth*. Westport, CT: Praeger, 1994.

Eckstein, Harry, Frederic J. Fleron Jr., Erik P. Hoffmann, and William M. Reisinger. *Can Democracy Take Root in Post-Soviet Russia? Explorations in State-Society Relations*. Lanham, MD: Rowman and Littlefield, 1998.

Gill, Graeme, and Roger D. Markwick. *Russia's Stillborn Democracy? From Gorbachev to Yeltsin*. Oxford: Oxford University Press, 2000.

Hosking, Geoffrey A., Jonathan Aves, and Peter J. S. Duncan. *The Road to Post-Communism: Independent Political Movements in the Soviet Union, 1985–1991*. London: Pinter Publishers, 1992.

Hough, Jerry F., Evelyn Davidheiser, and Susan Goodrich Lehmann. *The 1996 Russian Presidential Election*. Washinton, DC: Brookings Institution Press, 1996.

Journal of Post-Soviet Democratization, vol. 7, no. 2. Washington, DC: Heldref Publications, 1999.

March, Luke. *The Communist Party in Post-Soviet Russia*. Manchester: Manchester University, 2002.

McFaul, Michael. *Russia's 1996 Presidential Election: The End of Polarized Politics*. Stanford, CA: Hoover Institute Press, 1997.

Nelson, Lynn D., and Irina Y. Kuzes. *Radical Reform in Yeltsin's Russia: Political, Economic, and Social Dimensions*. Armonk, NY: M. E. Sharpe, 1995.

Remnick, David. *Resurrection: The Struggle for a New Russia*. New York: Random House, 1997.

Simes, Dimitri K. *After the Collapse: Russia Seeks Its Place as a Great Power*. New York: Simon and Schuster, 1999.

Smith, Gordon B., ed. *State-Building in Russia: The Yeltsin Legacy and the Challenge of the Future*. Armonk, NY: M. E. Sharpe, 1999.

Smith, Kathleen E. *Mythmaking in the New Russia: Politics and Memory in the Yeltsin Era*. Ithaca, NY: Cornell University Press, 2002.

Sperling, Valerie. *Building the Russian State: Institutional Crisis and the Quest for Democratic Governance*. Boulder, CO: Westview Press, 2000.

Treisman, Daniel S. *After the Deluge: Regional Crisis and Political Consolidation in Russia*. Ann Arbor: University of Michigan Press, 2002.

Urban, Michael. *The Rebirth of Politics in Russia*. Cambridge: Cambridge University Press, 1997.

Weigle, Marcia A. *Russia's Liberal Project: State-Society Relations in the Transition from Communism.* University Park: Pennsylvania State University Press, 2000.

BUILDING A NEW ECONOMY

Åslund, Anders. *Building Capitalism: The Transformation of the Former Soviet Bloc.* Cambridge: Cambridge University Press, 2002.

———. *How Russia Became a Market Economy.* Washington, DC: Brookings Institution Press, 1995.

Barylski, Robert V. *The Soldier in Russian Politics: Duty, Dictatorship, and Democracy under Gorbachev and Yeltsin.* New Brunswick, NJ: Transaction, 1998.

Blasi, Joseph, Maya Kroumova, and Douglas Kruse. *Kremlin Capitalism: Privatizing the Russian Economy.* Ithaca, NY: Cornell University Press, 1997.

Christensen, Paul T. *Russia's Workers in Transition: Labor, Management, and the State under Gorbachev and Yeltsin.* DeKalb: Northern Illinois University Press, 2001.

Freeland, Chrystia. *Sale of the Century: Russia's Wild Ride from Communism to Capitalism.* New York: Crown, 2000.

Gustafson, Thane. *Capitalism Russian-Style.* Cambridge: Cambridge University Press, 1997.

Lane, David, ed. *Russia in Transition: Politics, Privatisation and Inequality.* New York: Longman, 1995.

Lavrov, Alexei M., and Alexei G. Makushkin. *The Fiscal Structure of the Russian Federation: Financial Flows between the Center and the Regions.* Moscow: East-West Institute, 2001.

Ledeneva, Alena V. *Russia's Economy of Favours: Blat, Networking and Informal Exchange.* Cambridge: Cambridge University Press, 1998.

McFaul, Michael. *Russia's Unfinished Revolution: Political Change from Gorbachev to Putin.* Ithaca, NY: Cornell University Press, 2001.

Medvedev, Roy. *Post-Soviet Russia: A Journey through the Yeltsin Era.* New York: Columbia University Press, 2000.

Nazarenko, V. I. *Problems of the Agricultural Economy in Russia following the Disintegration of the USSR.* Tokyo: Food and Agricultural Policy Research Center, 1995.

Nichols, Thomas M. *The Russian Presidency: Society and Politics in the Second Russian Republic.* New York: St. Martin's, 1999.

Nordenstreng, Kaarle, Elena Vartanova, and Yassen Zassoursky. *Russian Media Challenge.* Helsinki: Gummerus Publishing, 2001.

O'Brien, David J., and Stephen K. Wegren. *Rural Reform in Post-Soviet Russia.* Washington, DC: Woodrow Wilson Center Press, 2002.

Russia's Uncertain Economic Future: Compendium of Papers Submitted to the Joint Economic Committee, Congress of the United States. Washington, DC: US Government Printing Office, 2002.

Shevtsova, Lilia. *Yeltsin's Russia: Myths and Reality.* Washington, DC: Carnegie Endowment for International Peace, 1999.

Smith, Gordon B. *State-Building in Russia: The Yeltsin Legacy and the Challenges of the Future.* Armonk, NY: M. E. Sharpe, 1999.

Tikhomirov, Vladimir. *Anatomy of the 1998 Russian Crisis.* Melbourne: Contemporary Europe Research Centre, 1999.

White, Stephen. *Russia's New Politics: The Management of a Postcommunist Society.* Cambridge: Cambridge University Press, 2000.

BUILDING A NEW FOREIGN POLICY

Aron, Leon, and Kenneth M. Jensen. *The Emergence of Russian Foreign Policy.* Washington, DC: United States Institute of Peace Press, 1994.

Beschloss, Michael R., and Strobe Talbott. *The Inside Story of the End of the Cold War.* New York: Little, Brown, 1993.

Cohen, Ariel. *Russian Imperialism: Development and Crisis.* Westport, CT: Praeger, 1996.

Colton, Timothy J., and Robert Legvold. *After the Soviet Union: From Empire to Nations.* New York: W. W. Norton, 1992.

Coppieters, Bruno, Alexei Zverev, and Dmitri Trenin. *Commonwealth and Independence in Post-Soviet Eurasia.* London: Frank Cass Publishers, 1998.

Garnett, Sherman W. *Rapprochment or Rivalry? Russia-China Relations in a Changing Asia.* Washington, DC: Carnegie Endowment for International Peace, 2000.

Garnett, Sherman W., Alexander Rahr, and Koji Watanabe. *The New Central Asia: In Search of Stability.* New York: Trilateral Commission, 2000.

Kraus, Michael, and Ronald D. Liebowitz. *Russia and Eastern Europe after Communism: The Search for New Political, Economic, and Security Systems.* Boulder, CO: Westview Press, 1996.

Mandelbaum, Michael. *The New Russian Foreign Policy.* New York: Council on Foreign Relations, 1998.

Olcott, Martha Brill, Anders Åslund, and Sherman W. Garnett. *Getting It Wrong: Regional Cooperation and the Commonwealth of Independent States.* Washington, DC: Carnegie Endowment for International Peace, 1999.

Ross, Robert S. *China, the United States, and the Soviet Union: Tripolarity and Policy Making in the Cold War.* Armonk, NY: M. E. Sharpe, 1993.

———. *East Asia in Transition: Toward a New Regional Order.* Armonk, NY: M. E. Sharpe, 1995.

Rozman, Gilbert. *Japan and Russia: The Tortuous Path to Normalization, 1949–1999*. New York: St. Martin's, 2000.

Talbott, Strobe. *The Russia Hand: A Memoir of Presidential Diplomacy*. New York: Random House, 2002.

Trofimenko, Henry. *Russian National Interests and the Current Crisis in Russia*. Brookfield, VT: Ashgate Publishing, 1999.

Wishnick, Elizabeth. *Mending Fences: The Evolution of Moscow's China Policy from Brezhnev to Yeltsin*. Seattle: University of Washington Press, 2001.

BIOGRAPHIES AND MEMOIRS

Aron, Leon. *Yeltsin: A Revolutionary Life*. New York: Thomas Dunne, 2000.

Brown, Archie. *The Gorbachev Factor*. Oxford: Oxford University Press, 1996.

Gaidar, Yegor. *Dni porazhenii i pobed*. Moskva: Vagrius, 1996. Published in English translation as *Days of Defeat and Victory*. Seattle: University of Washington Press, 1999.

Gorbachev, Mikhail. *Memoirs*. New York: Doubleday, 1995.

Khasbulatov, Ruslan. *The Struggle for Russia: Power and Change in the Democratic Revolution*. London: Routledge, 1993.

———. *Velikaia rossiiskaia tragediia*. 2 vols. Moskva: TOO SIMS, 1994.

Lourie, Richard. *Sakharov: A Biography*. Hanover, NH: University Press of New England, 2002.

Medvedev, Zhores A. *Gorbachev*. New York: W. W. Norton, 1986.

Primakov, Yevgeny. *Gody v bol'shoi politike*. Moskva: Kollektsiia Sovershenno sekretno, 1999.

Solovyov, Vladimir, and Elena Klepikova. *Boris Yeltsin: A Political Biography*. New York: G. P. Putnam's Sons, 1992.

Thatcher, Margaret. *The Downing Street Years*. New York: HarperCollins, 1993.

Yakovlev, Aleksandr. *Omut pamiati*. 2 vols. Moskva: Vagrius, 2001.

Yeltsin, Boris. *Against the Grain*. New York: Simon and Schuster, 1990.

———. *Midnight Diaries*. New York: Public Affairs, 2000.

———. *The Struggle for Russia*. New York: Times Books, 1994.

———. *Prezidentskii marafon: Razmyshleniia, vospominaniia, vpechatleniia* [The presidential marathon: Thoughts, recollections, impressions]. Moskva: AST, 2000.

INDEX

energy and, 244, 246; GUAM and, 243; Nagorno-Karabakh and, 56, 244; Russian CIS policy and, 243, 246; Union of Integrated States and, 242, 244; union treaty (USSR) and, 38

Baburin, Sergey Nikolaevich, 78
Baikonur Cosmodrome, 245, 248
Bakatin, Vadim Viktorovich, 41
Baker, James Addison III, 200
Baklanov, Oleg Dmitrievich, 46, 269n53
Baltic Military District, 55
Baltic states: impact of perestroika on, 37; independence movements of, 7, 29, 55–56; NATO and, 209, 229, 259. *See also* Estonia; Latvia; Lithuania
banking system. *See* banks, private; banks and banking system
banks, private: Bank Menatep, 159, 161; benefits from Soviet collapse, 159; and bonds, 129; Central Bank subsidy of, 157; collapse of, 170; deficit and, 137, 170; first appearance of, 155. *See also* banks and banking system; Central Bank
banks and banking system: agriculture and, 172, 177, 188; budget deficit and, 166; collapse of, 132, 135, 170, 215; debt and, 141, 161, 167, 169; Duma and, 138, 172; financial crisis of 1997–98 and, 125; financing of, 135–37; Gorbachev reforms and, 153; inflation and, 156, 276n88; investment in, 128–31, 134, 170, 172; market economy and, 115–16; media and, 124; oligarchs and, 124, 159–61, 167; price controls and, 151;

reform of, 31, 34, 140, 145, 151, 155, 159. *See also* banks, private; Central Bank
Barannikov, Viktor Pavlovich, 97
Barsukov, Mikhail Ivanovich, 120
Bashkortostan, 80
Belarus: Belovezh agreements and, 61–64, 116; CIS policy and, 61, 116, 198, 200, 243; collapse of communist power, 54; government of, 242; independence, 29, 54; nuclear weapons and, 198, 200; Union of Integrated States and, 242; Union of Sovereign States and, 60; union with Russia, 238, 239, 242, 245; UN membership, 65; USSR union treaty (1922) and, 64; USSR union treaty (1991) and, 38
Belovezh Agreements: approval of, 61; significance of, 223–24; USSR union treaty (1991) and, 63; Zyuganov's attempt to repeal, 116, 121, 238
Berezovsky, Boris Abramovich: CIS executive secretary, 247–48; conflict with Yeltsin, 247–48; oligarch, 154, 165, 168; opposes privatization, 126; opposes Yeltsin reforms, 168, 169; supports Yeltsin candidacy, 168
Berger, Mikhail Lvovich, 163
Beslan terrorist attack (2004), 261
biological weapons. *See* arms control: biological weapons
Birlik popular front (Uzbekistan), 57
Black Sea fleet, 240
Black Tuesday (October 11, 1994), 128, 158, 276n88
Blair, Tony, 255
Boldin, Valery Ivanovich, 46

Bolsheviks: agrarian socialism and, 174; model for October 1993, 100; October (Bolshevik) Revolution and, 3, 227; politics of, 25–26; Starodubtsev compared to, 187; Yeltsin compared to, 91; Yeltsin compares Khasbulatov and Rutskoy to, 99

bond market, 125, 129, 131–32, 138, 156, 159, 167–70

Bosnia, 229, 235

Brazil, 125

Brezhnev, Leonid Ilich, 4, 227

Brezhnev Doctrine, 265n2

Britain, 145, 211

Brzezinski, Zbigniew, 244

budget administration: benefits of financial crisis, 171; Chubais and, 162; deficits, 136, 151, 152, 154–59, 166, 168–70; and first republic (1991–93), 73, 89, 91, 198; foreign aid and, 138; IMF and, 135–36, 166–67, 172; military budget compared with that of China, 218; political difficulties with, 115, 123, 140–41, 164–65, 168; preliminary CIS, 162; Putin and, 11, 145; reform of, 128, 130; and second republic (1993–present), 177–78; union with Belarus and, 239

Bulgaria: and NATO, 238; and UIS, 242

Bulletin of the Central Committee of the CPSU, 17

Burbulis, Gennady Eduardovich, 63

Bush, George Herbert Walker: August Coup and, 41; Gorbachev and, 196, 201; Matlock and, 279n1; START II and, 200; Yeltsin and, 201, 285n1

Bush, George Walker, 255

business. *See* enterprise

Butenko, Anatoly Pavlovich, 49

Camdessus, Michel, 136

Caspian Sea, 212, 245, 248–49

Catholics, 261

Caucasus, 56, 139, 207, 217, 246; energy and, 244, 245. *See also* Adygeia; Armenia; Azerbaijan: Nagorno-Karabakh; Chechnya; Dagestan

Central Asia: Achalov and, 97; August Coup and, 57; China and, 212–14, 218–20, 248; CIS and, 64, 207, 245, 246; Islam and, 248; national movements relatively weak, 56–57; oil and, 246; Russian budget and, 177; Russian Empire and, 211; Russian population of, 246; September 11 and, 254. *See also* Kazakhstan; Kyrgyzstan; Tajikistan; Turkmenistan; Uzbekistan

Central Bank, 96; currency issue and, 128, 151, 156; debt and, 129, 131, 136; and private banks, 129; reform process and, 173–74, 156–57, 158; resists Supreme Soviet control, 97; ruble and, 129, 276n88; and subsidy of banks and industry, 157, 172. *See also* banks, private; banks and banking system

Charter of Russian-American Partnership and Friendship, 202, 204

Chechnya, 9, 90, 251, 254, 255; first Chechen war, 116, 117, 119, 138–39, 141, 173, 214, 227, 231, 250, 259; second Chechen war, 143, 146, 216, 217, 259

chemical weapons. *See* arms control: chemical weapons

Cheney, Richard Bruce (Dick), 200

Chernomyrdin, Viktor Stepanovich:
administration of, 126, 127, 133,
140; appointed prime minister,
74, 77; CIS policy and, 234, 240;
defends Chubais, 162; dismissed
as prime minister, 168; gas industry and, 74, 149, 154, 158; Gerashchenko and, 98; IMF and, 137; Our
Home Is Russia and, 143; 1996
election and, 118; Putin and, 140;
reappoints Gaidar to government,
156; supports higher deficits, 168

Chernov, Vladislav, 206

China: Central Asia and, 212–14, 218–
20, 248; communism and, 210–12,
266n1; economic considerations
and, 152, 211–13, 215, 217–21; "Gang
of Four," 269n53; immigrants to
Russia, 219; Primakov's courting
of, 197, 215; Russian Empire and,
211; Russian Federation and, 197,
210–20; strategic considerations,
197, 210, 212–16, 218–21, 255; US
and, 209, 214, 215–16, 218, 219;
USSR and, 210–12; value of relationship for Russia questioned,
217–18; Xinjiang and, 214

Chubais, Anatoly Borisovich: assesses
Yeltsin's historical role, 5, 6, 139;
debates Zyuganov at World Economic Forum, 163, 164; democratic
reform and, 133, 141, 162, 164; economic policies of, 124, 127, 158–63,
166–67, 182, 190; IMF and, 131–32;
Korzhakov and, 120; 1996 election
and, 118–20, 162–63; Putin and,
140; removed from cabinet, 117, 127

Church of Scientology, 261

Civic Union Party, 110, 228, 229

civil code, 112, 182, 189–90, 261

civil society, 86; constitution and, 92,
261; Putin and, 145

Clinton, William Jefferson (Bill): builds
rapprochement with Yeltsin, 209;
NATO and, 205–6, 208–9; and
Russian policy in Chechnya, 217,
218

cobalt, 162

"Cold Peace," 209

Cold War, 52, 60, 197, 235, 236, 247,
249, 250; ABM Treaty and, 203;
CSCE and, 208; end of, effects,
195–96, 209–10, 214, 216, 226,
251; Gorbachev and, 10, 196, 209,
279n1; Reagan and, 209

collective farms (USSR), 30, 175, 176,
177, 179; transformation of, 10, 152,
180–83, 185, 186

Collective Security Treaty (CIS), 206,
234

collectivization (USSR), 16, 21, 174

Commission to Analyze the Results
of Privatization in 1992–96 and to
Establish the Responsibility of Officials for Its Negative Results, 164

Committee of National Salvation,
268n35

Committee on Property and Privatization, 164

Commonwealth of Independent States
(CIS), 58–65, 237–49, 259; formation of, 61, 68, 224; Gorbachev and,
64, 65; membership of, 65; opposition to, 11, 116; policy of, 64–65,
199, 202, 228–49; Russian foreign policy and, 99, 113, 197–200,
205–7, 213, 225, 226, 228–49 passim; Yeltsin and, 66, 77, 99, 224,
244–49

debt. *See* budget administration: deficits; currency; economy; gross domestic product

Dementey, Nikolay Ivanovich, 54

democracy. *See* constitutional reform; democratization; Yeltsin, Boris Nikolaevich: ideological transformation of

Democratic Party of Russia, 39, 111

Democratic Press Front, 50

Democratic Russia movement, 29, 32, 38, 43, 45, 98

democratization (USSR), 14, 15, 21, 25; promotion of 7, 8, 21–23, 27–29, 32–34, 42, 50, 51, 58, 59, 66; resistance to, 18, 21, 23, 27, 28, 34, 42, 50, 51, 58, 66

Deng Xiaoping, 210

Destroyers, 217

Dnestr Moldovan Republic, 237

Dnestr region (Moldova), 231, 236–37

Drach, Ivan Fedorovich, 54

Draft Law on Peasant Farming, 185

drought, 185, 187

dual power (in 1917), 72; concept applied to Yeltsin era, 90, 99, 105

Dudaev, Gen. Dzhokhar Mussaevich, 259

Duma. *See* Federal Assembly

Dunaev, Andrey Fedorovich, 97

Dyachenko, Tatyana Borisovna, 118

East Germany (German Democratic Republic), 140

economy: general issues of, 148–49, 190–92; Gorbachev legacy and, 150–54; politics and, 122–38, 164–66, 171–74; reform program and, 5, 10, 74, 89, 124, 126, 140–41, 150–64, 166–71, 178–190. *See also* banks and banking system; budget admin-

istration; currency; enterprise; financial crisis of 1998; gross domestic product; land reform; natural resources; "oligarchs"

education: funding for, 42, 138, 146, 178; military, 217; state of, 190, 212

Eksportkhleb, 177

elections (USSR), post-Soviet: *of 1991* (Uzbekistan) 271n81; *of 1993*, 9, 95, 96, 103–5, 109, 110–13, 114, 115, 117, 140, 157–58, 182, 194, 204, 205, 226; *of 1995*, 9, 71, 113–16, 117, 119–20, 121, 122, 123, 140, 142, 162, 164–66, 183, 197, 224, 226, 236, 237; *of 1996*, 70, 71, 116–20, 122–23, 124, 139, 141, 147, 161, 162, 164–66, 168, 225, 236, 237, 275n85; *of 1999*, 11, 71, 115, 123, 126, 139, 140, 141–42, 143, 145, 171–74, 191, 192, 194, 220, 252, 260; *of 2000*, 126, 139, 140, 146, 171–74, 220, 260; *of 2003*, 191; *of 2004* (Ukraine), 262; 19th Party Conference, 23; 28th Party Congress, 31; Congress of People's Deputies, 7, 23, 24, 27; Kyrgyzstan presidency, 58; RSFSR presidency, 8, 40, 45, 46, 51; Supreme Soviet, 7, 29; Tajikistan presidency, 58. *See also* democratization

electricity, 126, 166, 213, 217

electronics, 144

energy industry, 74, 124, 125, 145, 152, 161, 165, 166, 212; Chernomyrdin and, 74, 149; foreign policy and, 212–15, 219, 222–23, 225–26, 244, 246, 247; Kirienko and, 127; lobby of, 154, 157, 158; Nemtsov and, 127, 167. *See also* electricity; gas; nuclear energy; oil enterprise, Russian Federation: agricultural, 10, 165, 177–78, 183, 185, 186, 189; bonds and, 168; cooperative, 179; financial support of, 74, 125, 156–57, 59, 165; Five-Hundred-Day Program and, 35–36; foreign, 115, 121, 140, 162–64, 213; free, 145, 156; loans for shares and, 160–62; 1996 presidential campaign and, 118; nuclear, 248; oligarchs and, 160, 168; private, 10, 115, 148, 186, 189, 191; privatization of, 74, 140, 152, 153, 158–59; red directors and, 159; reforms and, 126, 128, 130, 151, 154, 155, 159, 167, 173, 191; revenue and, 126, 156; state, 73, 126, 151, 152, 158, 168; subsidies of, 158

enterprise, USSR: cooperatives and, 15, 153; foreign, 15; industrial, 54; lease and, 150; private, 150; privatization of, 15, 34–35, 54; reforms and, 36, 153, 154; state, 15, 34–35, 43, 150, 153, 154, 156

Estonia, 7, 35, 38, 55, 65

Europe, Eastern: Brezhnev Doctrine and, 265–66n2; CIS and, 205; communist rule ends, 5, 10, 14, 29, 51–52, 196, 209, 211; CPRF and, 70, 258; Gorbachev and, 265–66n2; NATO and, 194, 205, 207, 209, 235, 253; reform in, 5, 23, 26; Russian Federation politics and, 194, 235; Shevardnadze and, 5; Soviet legacy and, 206; US and, 206, 253; Yeltsin and, 23, 26, 235

Europe, Western, 191, 204, 217, 228. *See also* European Community/ European Union (WEU)

European Commission for Democracy through Law, 85

European Community/European Union (WEU), 202, 205, 217, 229; Belarusian-Russian union and, 239; CIS integration policy and, 232, 238, 251; CIS membership in, 239, 242, 259; Ukrainian institutions and, 54, 239; Ukrainian membership aspired to, 239, 242

exports: chemicals, 199; IMF and, 158; military, 201, 213; natural resources, 125, 153, 157; nuclear 199; technology, 199

Far East, 210, 211, 215, 219, 220, 250

farming. *See* agrarian reform

fascists (Nazi Germany), 9

Fatherland/All Russia (OVR), 142

February Revolution (1917), 3; contrasted with August Coup, 51

Federal Assembly, 9, 95–96, 106, 109, 111, 112

—Council of the Federation (upper house): CIS Security Council and, 231; counterweight to Duma, 224–25; founded, 9, 90–91, 93; landownership and, 182; *1993* election and, 104, 110–12, 182; *1995* election and, 113–16, 120–21, 123, 158, 197, 224, 236; powers, 107–8, 111, 173; Primakov and, 173; protocol of, 95, 96, 109

—lower house: Belovezh Agreements and, 238; Committee on Affairs of the CIS, 241; Committee on International Affairs, 241; Council of the Federation and, 224–25, 231; Dnestr region and, 236–37; Federal Assembly and, 95, 96, 109; opposition calls for trial of Yeltsin, 224; opposition hindrance of reform, 116–18,

GUAM/GUUAM (Georgia, Ukraine, Armenia, and Moldova; later Uzbekistan), 243, 244, 245, 284*n*72
gubernii, 81
Gusinsky, Vladimir Aleksandrovich, 124, 154, 165, 168

Harvest: *of 1998*, 135, 171; *of 1999*, 187
health care, 42, 138, 146, 178, 190
Higher Court of Arbitration, 108
Hitler, Adolf, 9
human rights, 60, 64, 145, 214, 216, 233
humanitarian aid, 136
"humanitarian intervention," 216
Hungary, 191, 215, 253

Imports: agricultural, 175, 176, 177, 185; financial crisis of August 1998 and, 135, 171; military, 219
India, 201, 255
Indian Space Research Organization, 201
Indonesia, 125, 128, 169
industrialization (Soviet), 21
information science, 144
Institute for National Security and Strategic Studies (INSSS), 280*n*14
Institute of CIS Countries, 244
Institute of Oriental Studies, 134
Institute of World Economy and International Relations (IMEMO), 134
International Agency for the Reduction of Nuclear Arms, 198
International Atomic Energy Agency, 199
International Finance Corporation (IFC). *See* World Bank
International Monetary Fund (IMF), 123, 132, 134, 135–38 157–59, 163, 167, 169, 170, 172

Inter-Regional Group (IRG), 7, 24, 25
Interros, 160
Interstate Council (UIS), 242
Interstate Economic Committee (USSR), 62
investment: debt and, 126, 127; domestic, 125, 128, 145, 161, 191; foreign, 121, 125, 140, 144, 145, 163, 167–68, 172, 181, 190, 191, 213, 218, 221, 223, 248; government, 34, 174, 175; private, 115, 163; shortage of, 125, 139, 144
Iran, 232
Iraq, 256
Isakov, Vladimir Borisovich, 88
Islam, 58, 214, 232, 233, 248; Muslims, 256, 259
Islamic Renaissance Party (USSR), 58
Italy, 98, 207
Izvestiia newspaper, 23, 49, 63, 74, 78, 83, 188, 199, 201, 202, 207

Japan: financial support from, 131, 170, 220, 221; foreign investment of, 218; Kurile Islands and, 228, 281*n*25; North Korea and, 222, 223; and Russia, 209–14, 216, 218–19, 221, 249
Jefferson, Thomas, 93
Jehovah's Witnesses, 261
Jiang Zemin, 217
judicial reform (Russian Empire), 81

Karaganov, Sergey Aleksandrovich, 255
Karelia, 22, 106
Karimov, Islam Abduganievich, 57, 242, 243, 248
Kats, Yekaterina, 217–18
Kaunas television and radio center (Latvia), 55

Miyazawa Kiichi, 228

Moldova, 37–39, 55, 231; CIS and, 234, 236–37, 243–44; GUAM and, 243

monarchy (pre-1917), 3. *See also* autocracy; *individual monarchs*

Mongolia, 212, 219

Montenegro, 228

Moon Sun Myung, 261

Morozov, Col. Gen. Konstantin Petrovich, 200

Moshanu, Aleksandru Konstantin, 55

Muslims. *See* Islam

multipolarity, 217. *See also* "unipolar world"

Nagorno-Karabakh, 56, 244

Narodnyi deputat newspaper, 25

Nationalism: CPRF and, 120; CIS and, 233; USSR and, 65

Nationalists. *See* Liberal Democratic Party of Russia

National Salvation Front, 81, 88, 89, 98, 109

National Sports Foundation, 158

NATO, and Russian Federation foreign policy, 11, 194, 196, 197, 202, 204–9, 214–16, 229–59 passim

NATO at Twenty, 256

natural resources, 144, 145, 152–54, 161, 212, 214, 219, 220, 226, 244–45, 250. *See also specific resources*

Nazarbaev, Nursultan Abishevich, 57, 61, 64, 242, 246

Nazarchuk, Aleksandr, 279n43

Nazism, 9

"near abroad," 10, 99, 116, 197, 223, 226, 231. *See also* Commonwealth of Independent States

Nemtsov, Boris Yefimovich, 123–24, 126, 127, 133, 141, 166–68, 278n35

nickel, 162. *See also* Norilsk Nickel

Niyazov, Saparmurad Ataevich, 64

nomenklatura, 57, 76, 153

Norilsk Nickel, 160, 161, 166

Norsi oil refinery, 127

North America, 4, 202

North Atlantic Cooperation Council (NACC), 202, 205

North Korea. *See* foreign policy: North and South Korea

North Ossetia (Russian Federation), 261

NTV Television, 124

nuclear armaments. *See* arms control: nuclear weapons

nuclear energy, 248

Nuykin Andrey Aleksandrovich, 93, 223–24, 227

October 1993, insurrection of, 70, 71, 95–99, 101–3, 105, 109, 156, 230

October (Bolshevik) Revolution (1917) 3, 72, 100

Ogonek magazine, 22, 23

oil, 125, 153–55, 160, 165, 167, 169; Central Asia and, 214, 244–46; China and, 213, 217; North Korea and, 222

"oligarchs," 121, 124, 153, 159, 160–61, 165, 167, 168, 260

Omsk State University, 267n14

Oneksimbank 160, 161

"On Russia's Policy in the Field of Arms Limitation and Reduction" (Yeltsin), 198

"On the Coordination of Economic Policy," 62

opinion polls: foreign policy and, 230, 254; Nemtsov and, 123; 1996 election and, 116, 117, 119, 165; 1999

election and, 142, 143; October 1993
and, 102, 103; Putin and, 146
Oslon, Aleksandr Anatolevich, 118
Ostankino Television Center, 100, 101
Otechestvo, 139, 142
Ouimet, Matthew J., 265–66n2
Our Home Is Russia (NDR), 113, 114,
115, 143, 183

Pakistan, 248, 254
Palm, Viktor Alekseevich, 25
Parliament. *See* Congress of Peoples'
Deputies; Federal Assembly;
Supreme Soviet, USSR
Parliamentary Center, 93
Partnership for Peace, 205, 206
Party of Economic Freedom, 98
Party of Russian Unity and Accord,
107, 110
Patrikheev, Col. Gen. Valery Anisimo-
vich, 56
Pavlov, Valentin Sergeevich, 40–41, 45,
46, 269n53
"Pavlov Coup," 40–41
payments union, 238
peasantry: private agriculture of, 175,
179, 180–81, 184–90; Russian
Empire and, 175, 188. *See also* land
reform
Peasants' Land Bank, 188
Peasants' Union (USSR), 30, 269n53
pensions, 121, 123, 126–27, 130, 168, 185
perestroika, 17, 18, 20, 27, 30, 37, 39,
41, 44, 73, 266n1. *See also* Gorbachev, Mikhail Sergeevich: reform
program of
Permanent Joint Council (PJC), 253,
255, 284n85
Peter I (Peter the Great), Emperor, 5,
81, 139

Philippines, 125
Piontkovsky, Andrey Andreevich, 254
platinum, 162
"Plot of the Doomed." *See* August
Coup
plots, private farming. *See* peasantry
Plyas, Yakov, 235, 236
Poland, 191, 206, 215, 230, 253,
265–66n2
Politburo (USSR) members: Gorbachev,
19, 28–29, 196, 209; Karimov, 57;
Maslyukov, 171; Nazarbaev, 57;
Shenin, 46; Shevardnadze, 44;
Yakovlev, 44; and Yeltsin, 5–6,
15–18, 22–24, 31, 44, 260
Polozkov, Ivan Kuzmich, 29, 30
Pope John Paul II (Karol Józef
Wojtyła), 261
Popov, Gavril Kharitonovich, 25, 41
Popular Democratic Party, 57
Potanin, Vladimir Olegovich, 154,
159–61, 165
poverty, 5, 112, 123, 127, 135, 166,
170–71
Pravda newspaper, 18, 21, 23
presidential constitution, 71, 79–81,
85; significance of, 105, 107–10,
112, 115, 121, 173–74
Primakov, Yevgeny Maksimovich:
authoritarianism and, 173; and
China, 197, 215; CPRF and, 101, 133,
134–37, 171, 173; dismissed, 138, 142,
172–73; FIS and, 204, 232; foreign
aid and, 134, 138–39, 172; as foreign
minister, 117, 133–34, 197–98, 232;
foreign policy and, 197, 198, 215–18,
232–33, 240–43, 253; as prime minister, 133, 170, 171, 232, 240; "unipolar world" and, 280–81n19; US and,
197, 222; Yavlinsky and, 134

Udovenko, Gennady Iosifovich, 234
Ugra Agrofirm, 189
Uighurs, 214
Ukraine: Belovezh Agreements and,
    61, 116; CIS and, 62, 65, 198, 234–
    36, 244–48; departification, 54;
    Gorbachev vacation during August
    Coup, 44; independence, 29, 54,
    60–61; nuclear weapons and, 200;
    Russian population of, 225; Russian
    ties to, 238–44; union treaty and,
    38, 60
unemployment, 5, 135, 170
Union of Integrated States (UIS),
    242–44
Union of Rightist Forces (URF), 142–
    43, 262
Union of Sovereign States (USS): as
    basis of new union treaty, 41–42;
    as prelude to Commonwealth of
    Independent States, 60
Union of Soviet Socialist Republics
    (USSR). *See* August Coup; Com-
    monwealth of Independent States
union treaty (1922, USSR), 29, 31, 40,
    42, 55, 64, 116, 194, 238; attempt
    to recast, 36–43, 45, 59, 60, 63, 67
"unipolar world," 134, 197, 206,
    215, 233, 280–81n19. *See also* multi-
    polarity
United Energy Systems, 126, 127, 160
United Nations, 196, 198, 216, 228,
    237, 254, 256; CIS membership of,
    65; Security Council, 65, 199, 228,
    254, 256; Universal Declaration of
    Human Rights, 42; Yeltsin and, 199
United Russia Party, 258, 262
United States: economic policy and,
    145; economic support of, 131, 170,
    200; GDP of compared to Russian

Empire, 211; missile defense and,
    199–200; Russian Federation and,
    11, 134, 144, 197–201, 203, 204,
    207–21 passim, 228, 233, 236, 243,
    249–50, 252, 254–55; "unipolar,"
    134, 197–98; USSR and, 195, 218;
    Yeltsin tour of, 26
Unity (Edinstvo), 142
Uzbekistan: CIS and, 64, 232, 238,
    243, 245, 248, 271n81; conflict with
    Russian Federation, 242, 245, 246;
    independence, 57; Islamic extrem-
    ism and, 248; UIS, 38, 242

Valeev, Damir Zhavatovich, 80
Varennikov, Army Gen. Valentin
    Ivanovich, 46
"velvet revolution," 251
Vietnam, 266n1
Voronin, Yury Mikhailovich, 96
voucher privatization, 155, 158

Wages: average, 135, 138; decreases in,
    170, 185, 186; unpaid, 119, 121, 123,
    126–27, 165, 166, 168, 186, 189
Wahhabism, 248
Wałęsa, Lech, 206, 230
Wall Street Journal, 200
Warsaw Pact (1955), 247; former mem-
    bers of, 11, 193, 194, 197, 226, 231,
    235, 237, 247, 250, 251
weapons (biological, chemical, nuclear).
    See arms control
weapons of mass destruction, prolifer-
    ation of, 197, 198, 199, 200, 201,
    202–3, 215
Weimar Republic (Germany), 9
Western European Union (WEU). *See*
    European Community/European
    Union